Holland Drop Zone

Mark van den Dries

Translated by Major Robert A. Hebert, USAF (Retired)

HOLLAND DROP ZONE

The Crash of an American Bomber in a Dutch Polder

Uitgeverij Aspekt

Holland Drop Zone

© 2014 Uitgeverij ASPEKT
© Mark van den Dries

Amersfoortsestraat 27, 3769 AD Soesterberg, Nederland
info@uitgeverijaspekt.nl - http://www.uitgeverijaspekt.nl

Original title: Noodsein boven Zeeland
Translation: Major Robert A. Hebert, USAF (Retired)
Cover design: Mark van den Dries
Cover painting: Bram de Jong
Interior: Maarten Bakker

ISBN: 9789461536068
NUR: 680

All rights reserved. No part of this book may be reproduced or translated in any form, by print, photo print, microfilm, microfiche or any other means without written permission from the publisher.

Contents

Preface	7
The Netherlands, Holland and the Dutch	17
Chapter 1 War in Zeeland	23
Chapter 2 Resistance in the Polders	35
Chapter 3 The Eagle leaves its nest	57
Chapter 4 Gerow's crew	71
Chapter 5 The Bridge	87
Chapter 6 Factories and traitors	105
Chapter 7 From Hope to Despair	119
Chapter 8 Holland Supply Drop Zone	129
Chapter 9 Parachutes in the sky	151
Chapter 10 Hay Barns and Interrogations	171
Chapter 11 Separate Ways	183
Chapter 12 A Time for Reflection	191
Chapter 13 Some Kind of Disease	205
Chapter 14 Life and Death	221
Chapter 15 Freedom and Captivity	235
Chapter 16 The Russians are coming!	259
Chapter 17 Fire and Snow	271
Chapter 18 The Forest	281
Chapter 19 Behind the Lines	289
Chapter 20 The Aftermath of the War	299
Chapter 21 Traces of The Past	341
Chapter 22 So, what's next?	363
The crew and The helpers of Joe and Ely	365
Acknowledgement	371
Sources	375
Names Register	389

Preface

I was born in 1966 in the Netherlands and I still live there. That is why the story of this book was first published in Dutch, my native language. The main part of this story is about the German occupation of my country during World War II and about a small team of townspeople who were part of the Dutch resistance movement and stood up to this oppression. It is also about a B-24 crew of American airmen who risked their lives to liberate our country. I decided to pursue an English translation so the families of the crew could read this story.

Dad, I need to interview someone about the Second World War. It's for a school paper." If you have teenage children, this may sound familiar. In 2006 my oldest daughter, Daphne, asked me whom she could interview for this. Although my father, Peter van den Dries, was still a toddler during the war, I knew he had quite a lot to say about this subject. I advised her to have a talk with him about it. Peter van den Dries was the last of three generations of schoolteachers. He also was my teacher in elementary school so I expected him to relate some fascinating stories about the past. I also knew he possessed two interesting files (collected by my grandfather, Piet van den Dries) filled with original documents, newspaper clippings and photographs from World War II. After he retired, my father remained a schoolteacher at heart and wrote a complete story for his granddaughter. He included everything my grandfather told him about the war as it happened in the Netherlands and especially in the province of Zeeland, where my father grew up. Daphne used his story for her paper and took the files to school to show them to the class. She received a good grade for her project.

My grandfather's files remained in our home and on a lazy Sunday afternoon I started to browse through them. I come from a family of teachers. Although I have not continued in this tradition, I must have inherited an interest in history from my parents. I am grateful to them for this. Because my father was a teacher, he had the same days off as his children. That's why we went on vacation more than once a year. During our summer holiday, we traveled to distant places like Denmark or France, and during the shorter holidays to neighboring countries like Germany or Belgium. My brother, sister, and I visited numerous European museums, castles and churches during these trips. Although these trips weren't always voluntary on our part, the diverse cultures helped me develop a lifelong interest in history.

My grandfather's files were about World War II, while my imagination had always been more focused on the pre-historic, classic or medieval times and not so much on that gritty period in recent history. As I grew older, I began to develop an interest in the history of my ancestors. While researching my family tree I could not avoid the deep wounds that World War II had slashed not only into my father's family, but in my mother, Ineke's, family as well.

During the war, my mother's parents, Leendert and Mina Beuns, lived in Flushing (*Vlissingen*), a harbor city on the former island Walcheren, in the province of Zeeland. They lived near the well-known shipyard De Schelde where Leendert was a ground worker and later metalworker. He was involved in the construction of the famous ship *M.S. Willem Ruys* (it was later renamed the *M.S. Achille Lauro* and became famous because of a 1985 hijacking by the Palestine Liberation Organization (PLO), in which a Jewish American in a wheelchair was murdered and thrown overboard.) The German invaders used the De Schelde shipyard during World War II to control the strategically important Western Scheldt River in Flushing.

The shipyard was an important target for Allied bombers. Of all the Dutch cities, Flushing had to cope with the most bombings. Because of this continuing threat, my pregnant grandmother had to evacuate to a country house in the fisherman's village, Yerseke, on the neighboring peninsula South Beveland. This is where my mother was born on January 24, 1943. Exactly five months later, twelve Lockheed Ventura bombers from the 464 Squadron, Royal Australian Air Force (RAAF) took off from their base at RAF Methwold in Norfolk, England. Their target was the shipyard.

As soon as the sirens wailed, my grandfather ran across the square, but he never made it to the bomb shelter. After the bombing ceased, 23 bodies were covered with sheets and placed in rows on the square to be identified. My 22-year old grandmother, who had just became a widow, had to search for her husband's corpse and had to step over the other dead bodies to find him. When my grandmother was about eighty, she told me that she still suffered from nightmares in which dead hands from under the sheets touched her ankles.

My grandfather's funeral was equally sad. Because of all the commotion, my grandmother could make only one phone call to inform her family of the tragedy. Only Willem Harthoorn, her sister's husband, who lived in the village 's Heer Arendskerke on South Beveland, dared to travel to Flushing.

More bombings were expected, so all the victims of the Flushing air strikes were buried in great haste. The funerals were chaotic, forcing my grandmother and her brother-in-law to walk behind an unidentified coffin, and never knowing in which grave her husband was buried. When they returned to my grandmother's home, they discovered her house was completely destroyed by another bomb raid. She had lost everything. Willem took her and her baby to 's Heer Arendskerke and gave them shelter. Willem was a butcher by trade and also did some illegal butchery to provide meat for people who were hiding from the Germans. One day he was arrested and was sent to the North German Neuengamme concentration camp. He never returned.

Although my mother was only 6 months old when her father died, the consequences of these events shaped a large part of her childhood.

But let's return to my father's family. While I searched through the story that my father wrote for his granddaughter, I read about the citizens of Zeeland and the difficulties the head of a Catholic school in a small village had to encounter. And my father wrote about the crash...

The crash... Yes, I had heard of it since my early childhood. It was a piece of family history that was brought up on birthdays or other family gatherings. As I leafed through my grandfather's files and looked at the pictures, my thoughts returned to my own memories. Like my grandparents, our family lived in the city of Goes. It was a quiet city on the former island of South Beveland in the province of Zeeland. Because I was asthmatic from birth and had a strange allergic reaction once the salty sea winds blew in from the west, our family was more or less forced to live further inland, in the center province of Utrecht. When I was five, my father found a job as a headmaster in the town of Maarssen, along the beautiful Vecht River. Instead of having an accent from Zeeland, I grew up with a Utrecht accent. Because of the two-hour driving distance to Goes, we saw my grandparents only a few times a year, usually on a Sunday. Sunday was a day when most shops in the Netherlands were closed. You could shoot a cannon in the main streets of Goes without hitting anyone.

Although my brother, my sister and I were often bored by these visits, I also have warm memories of them. My grandmother, Katrien, was a real mother hen, short and robust in stature, very caring, a good cook, very keen on cleanliness and strict in her beliefs. Grandpa Piet was a stately, well-read gentleman who quietly accepted his wife's will, but at times could also be quite stubborn. He was also a remarkably tall man and I am told I must have inherited his tall stature. Grandfather was keen on traveling: especially to Anglo-Saxon countries. He was an avid lover of history and art and visited many museums and landmarks. My grandparents were of the Catholic faith. This played an important part in their lives. They believed in going to mass every Sunday. Because he played the organ quite well, Grandfather was often asked to play during masses in the St. Mary Magdalena Church in Goes. But he also played in Protestant services. That difference didn't mean much to him. Even after retirement, he always remained a real teacher like his son. While on vacation, I sent him a card in my children's handwriting. When I visited him, he would thank me kindly for the wonderful card, and give it back with all the misspellings underlined in red ink. I still have a number of art and history books on my shelf where he had underlined spelling and printing errors and written improvements in the margins.

As I grew older our relationship deepened. Somehow, we understood each other. I think it was because we shared a common interest in history and art. I took a four-year course in commercial art at the School of Graphics in Utrecht, something that interested him. He bought some of my early work and proudly showed it to everyone who came to visit him. The last time I saw him was just before his death in the summer of 1992. My grandmother had preceded him in 1985. When Grandfather became seriously ill, my father and I visited him in the hospital. I hung a picture of his newborn great-granddaughter, Daphne, above his hospital bed. We did not speak much, his illness hit him hard, but when I said goodbye, he embraced me and kissed me. I knew he meant it to be a goodbye, and it was.

Now, back to my childhood. There was something exciting about my grandfather from Goes. There were stories about him. I never knew the exact details. I only knew Grandfather had helped two American airmen during World War II after their bomber crashed. For this act of assistance to the Allied forces, he received an English and an American award. For some reason, he sent the American award back. I also remember that in old photographs of my grandparent's garden there was an unusual foreign object. In my own scrapbook I have one photo of me as a toddler, wearing a pretty blazer, a pair of shorts and sandals. I'm looking a bit pensive on the lawn before a large house where a strange object was placed in a flowerbed. According to my father, this was a propeller of the American bomber that crashed near the town where he was born. I seem to remember this object myself, but that photo in my scrapbook could have influenced my memory.

There was something exciting about my grandfather, something I could brag about at school when the war was mentioned. However, to me, the most amazing thing about my grandfather was the fact that he could take out his teeth (that was a miracle only the world's best magicians could match), but in second place was the fact he had done something special during the war. When my brother and I were still in primary school, Grandfather gave us two American uniform emblems. He received them from one of the crewmembers he helped. Against the strict orders of my father, we took them to school to brag about them in the schoolyard. One of the emblems was lost, perhaps exchanged for a handful of marbles. Who knows? I still have the other one.

Grandfather rarely talked about the war. When my brother and I were about 14 years old we took a car trip through the region on one of those quiet Sunday afternoons. I remember the weather was nice. We stopped at a farmhouse. My grandfather told us he wanted us to meet his cousin, Pier van 't Westeinde. They were together in the resistance during the war. His cousin was a nice old gentleman. I do not remember exactly what they talked about, but I noticed a certain camaraderie between them as they spoke about earlier times.

"Come along with me, boys, I've got something interesting," said Pier with twinkling eyes. We followed him and grandfather to a barn and he pulled something forth. *"Look, boys! This is a machine gun from the bomber that crashed here. Here is another one."* Our eyes were as big as saucers. *"Can you really shoot it?"* I asked, expecting a demonstration. *"Well, they are disabled, you know,"* said Grandfather, laughing. They also showed us a propeller from the bomber, placed in Pier's garden. I could not have imagined that thirty years later, I would design an information panel for these same two guns and propeller that are on display at a museum right now.

After I read my father's story, I looked at all *his* father's photographs, clippings and documents. They were collected in a red plastic ring binder with transparent sleeves. Among Grandfather's photos, I found a picture of the bomber crew, ten men, and all young by the looks of them. I wondered who they were and what they had experienced. I saw they looked into the sun, somewhere to the left. There was only one who smiled. The others did their best to look tough in their cool flight jackets with fur collars. Behind them, I saw part of a bomber airplane.

I began to read the clippings, some from Dutch newspapers, but also a number from U.S. newspapers. I read the police report with detailed eyewitness reports from Heinkenszand, the village where the crash had occurred and where my grandparents had lived at that time. The story fascinated me. I realized my grandfather, as a teacher and avid lover of history, knew that this story should not be forgotten. Although he didn't talk about it to other people, perhaps this was the reason why he decided to tell my father all that he knew. It is possible he considered writing down this story, or hoped someone else would do this for him.

As a child of the modern age, I searched Google to find out more about this bomber and crew. After searching American web sites, I discovered the aircraft's name, the names of the crewmembers and their last mission. The genie was out of the bottle. It was the beginning of a quest that would consume much of my free time in the next few years. The story intrigued me, not only because it is my grandfather's but also because it is an unknown story. It turned out to be a jigsaw puzzle with pieces of information scattered over two ring binders, a few American and Dutch web sites, some dusty archives, and the vivid memories of a handful of elderly eyewitnesses. As in an ordinary jigsaw puzzle, separate pieces have no use and are doomed to be lost over time. However, if someone puts the pieces together, they create a recognizable image.

My quest to complete the puzzle has taken me through countless web sites, dozens of books and records, to museums, former battlefields, foreign military cemeteries and many places in Zeeland. I researched various organizations at home and abroad. I contacted families of those involved with the Dutch Resistance, as well as the American airmen. I was able to meet many of them in person, in Zeeland, and later, some in the U.S. One of the eleven American families was untraceable and another family did not respond to my letters. However, I learned a member of the ten-man crew, the pilot, was still alive. In Willem Visser, who overhauled one of the bomber's propeller discovered in an orchard, I found an enthusiastic comrade who managed to establish important contacts in Heinkenszand. He interviewed eyewitnesses who were children at the time but are now in their 80s or 90s. We even organized a digging at the crash site, where we searched for remains of the bomber.

All these different sources gave me valuable pieces of the puzzle. Some of them were small details, other were complete and detailed reports. I found funny anecdotes, heroic stories, but also gruesome scenes that revealed the cruel spirit of Nazism.

I was particularly affected by two of these reports. I received the first one from Sjaak van Biezen, son of the blacksmith and resistance leader, Nico van Biezen. Nico wrote a detailed report about his service as a soldier during the Dutch Mobilization, during the German invasion and his resistance work in Heinkenszand. For most of his life, Nico never spoke much about it, but decided to write down his memories when his health began to deteriorate. He died just before he wrote about the crash, but his notes revealed enough information to tell an interesting and emotional tale.

The second came from Darlene Southwell, widow of the radio operator Elton Southwell. Her husband also never talked much about the war. His experience on that historic September day in 1944, his miserable journey through Germany and Poland, and the even more hideous march back, were too painful to tell. He decided to put his memories on paper to ensure his memories survived. Not long after he finished the story he died. Darlene and other members of her family read my letter, in which I talked about my research. They collectively decided I could include Elton's memoirs in my book. I think you can understand that I was very impressed and honored.

These two reports broadened my perspective of the crash. It was no longer just a Zeelandic or an American story. It expanded to include the beginning of the war; the mobilization of the Dutch troops, all the way to the last, fatal convulsions of the German Empire. These memoirs confirmed my conviction that this little story in a great war is worth telling. My efforts resulted in the Dutch book called *Noodsein Boven Zeeland* (Distress Call over Zeeland), published in December 2012. Because it's not only a Dutch story, but also an American story, many people from the U.S. have inquired when there will be an English translation. Well, here it is… and more. After the Dutch version was published, more pieces of the puzzle were given to me, and are included in this translation. Although I realize many other pieces have been lost to time and will probably never be found, I think this puzzle is a good illustration of my grandfather's story.

I would like to dedicate this book to that team of brave young men from different parts of the United States who put their lives on the line on *the other side of the pond*, who lost their lives, or were scarred for life. I also dedicate this book to that group of brave men and their wives from Zeeland, brought together by friendship, family ties, accidental circumstances and a deep resentment against the Nazi power that tried to suffocate their sense of freedom.

Mark van den Dries

Our Paths Crossed

In 2008, I began an exhaustive genealogical search for family members to complete my family tree. My Uncle Normand was quite elusive. I met him in my youth but knew little about him. In 2006, across the Atlantic, Mark van den Dries began his expanded research concerning an American B-24 that crashed near the village of Heinkenzand in the Netherlands. My Uncle was the tail gunner on that aircraft.

I knew Normand was a POW during WWII. This knowledge led me to Annette Tison at the 392nd Bomb Group Memorial Association web page (www.b24.net) in 2010. In March 2011, I received an e-mail from Mark who also was in contact with Annette. She gave Mark my e-mail address. I was the only relative of Normand B. (Frenchy) Hebert known to exist in the 392nd community. Coincidently, via my genealogy research, I also connected with my cousin, Michele, Normand's daughter, and discovered she had a brother, Brian.

Mark sent me a synopsis of his original book *Noodsein Boven Zeeland*, loosely translated *Distress Call over Zeeland*. I was immediately captivated. As Mark and I exchanged e-mails, I expressed my desire to read the book. Then, like the dreaded flak he often refers to, Mark sent me a good news bad news e-mail. The good news: his book was going to be published in December 2012. The bad news: it was going to be published in Dutch and I would not be able to read it.

Undaunted, I replied that even if I had to translate it one word at a time, I would. He sent me the Foreword and Chapter 1 and said, "*Go for it.*" Several weeks later, I sent him my translation. Mark was quite surprised at how accurate it was. With the exception of Dutch slang and adverbs that do not translate very well, I had captured the gist of his story.

Mark sent contributing family members of the crew a copy of his book. None of them could read Dutch. As I began translating the rest of the book, Mark shared the work with them. It was still very rough but they understood where he was going with the story.

In July 2013, Mark and his family visited the United States for the first time and met with me and my wife, Paula, in Colorado. By then, I had translated the entire book and knew there was much more to do if it were going to be published in English. Mark and I had a serious talk about publishing an English version. By then, he had added new information to the story. This meant more translation and some serious editing.

Mark's father, Peter, sealed the deal. He commented how pleased he was that Mark and I were going to pursue an English translation. "*Now all the Americans will be able to read how thankful we Dutch are for what your boys did. If it was not for them, we would not have our freedom today,*" he said. We needed to move ahead with this work.

This year, Paula and I will travel to the Netherlands to participate in a 70th anniversary memorial service for two of the crewmembers, Gene Kieras and Ed Yensho, who sacrificed their lives for freedom. It was an honor to work on this translation for the crew family members. The Dutch have never forgotten their liberators.

Major Robert A Hebert, USAF (Retired)

Mark van den Dries and Robert Hebert with a model of a B-24 Liberator at the Air Force Academy in Colorado Springs, Colorado. (002a)

The author is at his grandparent's home in Goes.
In the flowerbed, you can see the propeller from the bomber. (002)

High Flight

Oh! I have slipped the surly bonds of earth
And danced the skies on laughter-silvered wings;
Sunward I've climbed, and joined the tumbling mirth
Of sun-split clouds - and done a hundred things
You have not dreamed of - wheeled and soared and swung
High in the sunlit silence. Hov'ring there
I've chased the shouting wind along, and flung
My eager craft through footless halls of air.
Up, up the long delirious, burning blue,
I've topped the windswept heights with easy grace
Where never lark, or even eagle flew -
And, while with silent lifting mind I've trod
The high untresspassed sanctity of space,
Put out my hand and touched the face of God.

Written by Pilot Officer John Gillespie Magee, No 412 Squadron, RCAF (Royal Canadian Air Force). Gillespie was killed in his Spitfire on December 11, 1941.

The Netherlands, Holland, and the Dutch

The official name of my country is *Nederland*. In English, it is called the Netherlands. It is part of the Kingdom of the Netherlands, which consists of the Netherland's twelve provinces and some Caribbean islands. The Netherlands had many official names in the past, but Holland was never one of them. Holland refers to two provinces, North Holland and South Holland. Because the principal cities and seaports are located in this area, Holland became the unofficial name. Even though Zeeland and the bomber's drop zone were not part of the two Holland provinces, I have chosen to name this book *Holland Drop Zone*. The name is based on the mission's official name, *Holland Supply Drop Zone*. Because most foreigners use the name Holland and the name sounds catchier than the Netherlands, often we also use it. We wonder why people call us Dutch. It is not a name we invented. A few centuries ago, the common name for our language was *Diets*, which has a link to *Deutsch* (German). Nobody, except the English uses the name Dutch anymore.

The Province of Zeeland

I currently live in the province Utrecht while most of the story takes place in the province of Zeeland, where I was born. To understand this story, I shall tell you something about Zeeland, the place of the crash and the birthplace of my family.

Zeeland means *Sea-Land*. Zeeland is located in the southwest of the Netherlands. In the west, the North Sea pounds at Zeeland's many dikes. In the north it is bordered by the province of South Holland and in the east, by the province North Brabant. The only part of Zeeland that is part of the mainland is Zeelandic Flanders, a strip bordered by Belgium in the south.

Long ago, Zeeland was nothing more than a muddy delta, consisting of a number of islands that often flooded during high tide and reappeared at low tide. Even before the Romans invaded the Low Countries, Celto-Germanic tribes inhabited these islands. The ocean provided plenty of food, including fish, mussels, and oysters, but the sea was also a constant threat. Living on the islands meant accepting the many floods that changed the shape of the islands and killed hundreds of people. The sea gave and the sea took away.

Zeelanders expanded the islands by building dikes around shallow parts of the sea. After draining the water, new land, called *polders* was created. The marine clay at the surface was very fertile. The polders were clustered to increase the size of Zeeland and also of many other Dutch provinces. Like its neighbor Holland, Zeeland became a thriving international, seafaring power during the 16th and 17th centuries. Harbor cities like Flushing and Veere flourished. Many ships set sail to explore and colonize new worlds or to wage war. The Dutch explorer, Abel Tasman, discovered the islands of New Zealand, later named after the province Zeeland.

Foreign powers, like the Romans, the Spanish and the French, invaded and left Zeeland, but the sea was always there, providing food and creating wealth, while assailing the dikes, eroding and creating land. Twenty percent of the Netherlands is below sea level, but Zeeland is located almost entirely below sea level, except for some dune areas. The province has endured several deadly floods. During the North Sea Flood of 1953, a combination of heavy wind, high tide, and low barometric pressure, created a storm tide, killing more than 1,800 Dutch people in Zeeland, South Holland, and North Brabant. The same North Sea Flood also caused fatalities in Belgium, England and Scotland.

During the flood, my parents and grandparents slept in the attic with their suitcases packed. It was a close call, but luckily the only dike that protected their area withstood the destructive power of the storm tide. If not, the deadly seawater would also have engulfed the city of Goes and the whole surrounding area. My family did what they could to support the victims of the storm. They gave shelter to the refugees and helped fill sandbags to strengthen the dikes that were in danger. The North Sea Flood led to the creation of the Delta Works, a series of construction projects in the southwest Netherlands designed to protect a large area of land around the Rhine-Meuse-Scheldt delta from the sea. The Works consists of dams, sluices, locks, dikes, levies and storm surge barriers. The Delta Works is one of the largest man-made structures on earth. Some have called it one of the seven wonders of the modern world.

South Beveland

The first known ancestor that bears my surname was Adam van den Dries. We don't have his birthdate, but we do know he married Maria Verachterd in 1668. With their children they lived on a farm in Hoboken[1], a village near the Belgium harbor city of Antwerp. Traditionally, the first-born son inherited the farm, so his second son, Adriaan, had to seek his fortune elsewhere. Adriaan did not remain in Hoboken. He and his wife heard of the fertile polders on the other side of the Western Scheldt River and in 1690, they crossed the river and bought a small farm on the former Zeelandic island of South Beveland (*Zuid-Beveland*). His farm was near the village 's-Heer-Arendskerke and the city Goes, where most of his offspring would remain for the coming centuries. South Beveland is the largest peninsula in Zeeland. It is located north of the Western Scheldt River and south of the Eastern Scheldt River. The peninsula is connected with the main land of North Brabant by what I would like to call the *tail* of South Beveland. Since 1871, it was also connected by a railway embankment with Walcheren, the large island in the west. The main city of South Beveland is Goes, the city where I was born.

Most people on the peninsula were either farmers or fishermen. My ancestors from Adriaan's branch were farmers, millers, and tree nurserymen; hard workers, with their wooden clogs firmly in the thick clay. The family soon adapted to the islands customs. Every island in Zeeland had its own traditional dresses, with Catholic and Protestant variations. Looking at old photographs I see most of my ancestors wearing the traditional Catholic dress from South Beveland. The men wore black three-piece suits with two large, silver discs decorating the belt around their waists and two smaller ones on their collar. Their hair was trimmed straight on their foreheads. They wore round black hats. The women dressed in layered garments. Around their necks they wore necklaces with precious red coral or black jet. They covered their hair with wide lace caps decorated with copper ornaments.

My male ancestors played a leading role in the local archery guilds. At first, like in other parts of Europe, these guilds were a civilian army, founded for the protection of the region, but in peaceful times they were archery clubs. During tournaments they placed a feathered plume called a *parrot* on a high pole, which the contesters, dressed in traditional costume, tried to remove with their arrows. In Adriaan's line, the first ancestor who did not earn a living in agriculture was my great grandfather Pieter. Instead of following in his father's footsteps as a tree nurseryman, he became a headmaster, as did his son Piet and his grandson Peter.

1: The American city Hoboken, New Jersey near Manhattan, New York was once a Dutch harbor. New York was once called New Amsterdam until the British took over the city. That is why many names in that area remind you of Dutch cities and villages like Harlem (*Haarlem*), Brooklyn (*Breukelen*), Flushing (*Vlissingen*) and New Utrecht (*Utrecht*). In Adriaan's days the Belgium city Hoboken near Antwerp was Dutch because Belgium was part of the Netherlands until 1830.

(003)

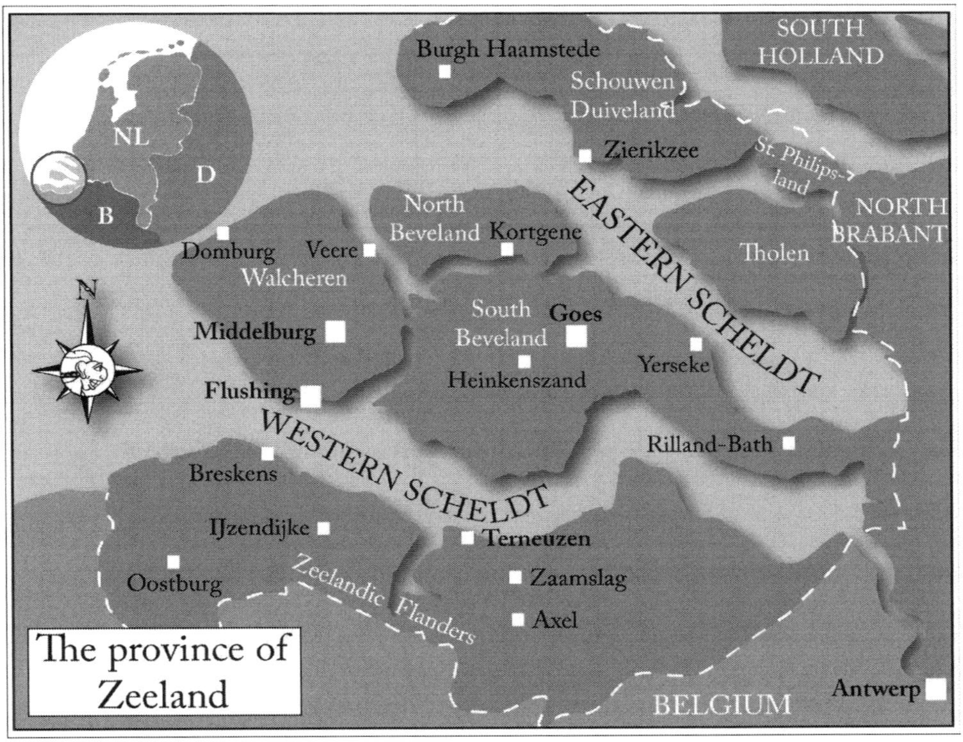
The province of Zeeland
SOUTH HOLLAND
Burgh Haamstede
Schouwen Duiveland
Zierikzee
St. Philipsland
NL
D
B
North Beveland
Kortgene
EASTERN SCHELDT
NORTH BRABANT
Tholen
Domburg
Veere
Walcheren
South Beveland
Goes
Middelburg
Yerseke
Heinkenszand
Flushing
WESTERN SCHELDT
Rilland-Bath
Breskens
IJzendijke
Terneuzen
Oostburg
Zaamslag
Zeelandic Flanders
Axel
BELGIUM
Antwerp
N

(004)

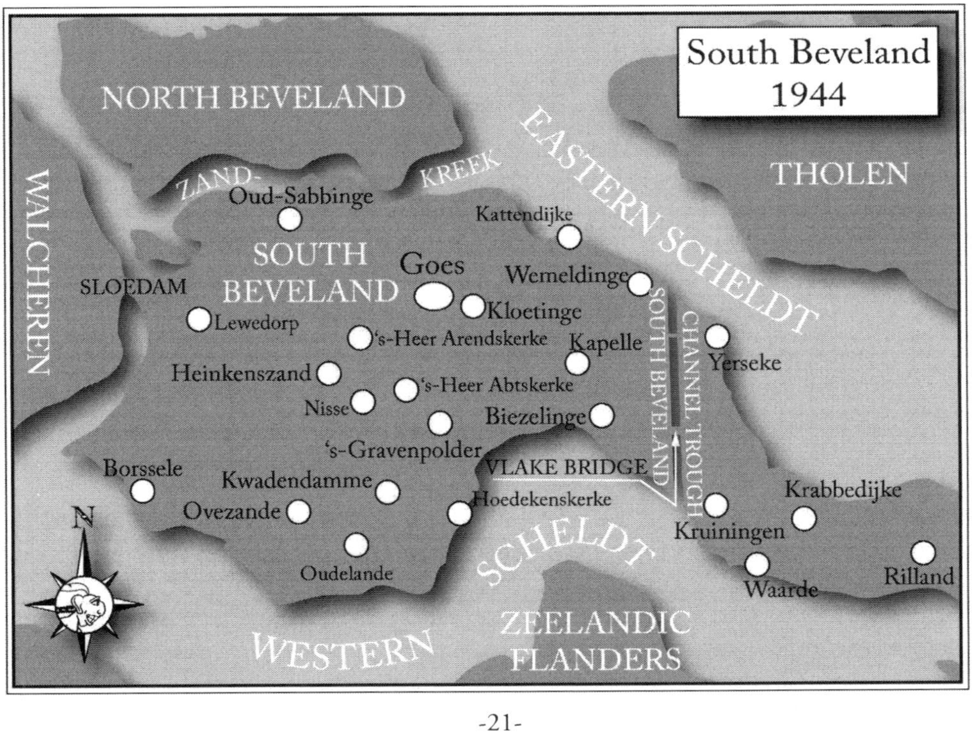
South Beveland 1944
NORTH BEVELAND
EASTERN SCHELDT
THOLEN
WALCHEREN
ZAND-
KREEK
Oud-Sabbinge
Kattendijke
SOUTH BEVELAND
Goes
SLOEDAM
Wemeldinge
Kloetinge
Lewedorp
's-Heer Arendskerke
Kapelle
SOUTH BEVELAND
CHANNEL TROUGH
Yerseke
Heinkenszand
's-Heer Abtskerke
Nisse
Biezelinge
's-Gravenpolder
VLAKE BRIDGE
Borssele
Kwadendamme
Hoedekenskerke
Krabbedijke
Ovezande
Kruiningen
SCHELDT
Oudelande
Waarde
Rilland
N
WESTERN
ZEELANDIC FLANDERS

This photo from the 1890s shows two of my 2nd great grandparents: Jacobus van den Dries, a tree nurseryman, and his wife Tannetje Remijn, both in traditional costumes. (005 and 006)

Chapter 1

War in Zeeland

In 1933, the *Nationalsozialistische Deutsche Arbeiterpartei* (National Socialist Laborers Party, NSDAP), also known as the NAZI Party, seized power in Germany. Opinion in the Netherlands was divided. During the Great War - WWI - the country remained neutral. Its only part came later, when it provided a safe home for Kaiser Wilhelm III after he fled from Germany to the Dutch village, Doorn.

In the thirties, the Great Depression also hit the Netherlands hard, causing much poverty and discontent. Many Dutchmen hoped for better times with good economic prospects. Some embraced the ideas and the aspirations of our eastern neighbors, while others looked with suspicion at the expanding arms industry and the fierce anti-Jewish, bellicose rhetoric proclaimed by the Nazi party in Nuremberg.

After Austria and Czechoslovakia joined the Third Reich in March 1938, the Dutch government realized that Hitler might not limit his control to these two countries. By the end of September, the Netherlands government announced a military mobilization was at hand. Conscripts were drafted from different regions of the country to man strategic positions. A few days later, the order was withdrawn. This attitude was typical of the Netherlands in the years between the wars.

As in the Great War, the government tried to remain neutral, but war cries echoed from the east, and the Dutch began to feel uneasy. The Dutch government hoped their country was of no significance to the Germans since they were focused on France. However, the Dutch soon became aware their country was strategically important. In the thirties, the French and German border was protected by the Maginot Line, a line of fortifications to shield France against a surprise attack from Germany. Because the Belgian and German borders were also well guarded, the Dutch provinces of North Brabant and Zeeland became a strategically important German route to France.

In August 1939, a call for general mobilization sounded once again. All Dutch conscripts between 1924-1939, had to resign their jobs and rejoin their units immediately. Under the command of General Winkelman, they formed defense lines to protect the Netherlands against the German threat from the East. Once the call for arms sounded, 250,000 men obeyed. Because the Dutch army had few military bases, many soldiers were billeted in private homes, schools, or whatever buildings were available. Wherever they were stationed, an extraordinary law was forced upon the citizens. The Government granted the military access to private homes and property. For example, under this law, the citizen's best horses were seized to transport war equipment.

One of the conscripts was a young blacksmith from the village of Zaamslag in Zeelandic Flanders. This blacksmith, Nico van Biezen, would play an important role in this story. Nico's father died when Nico was just one and a half years old. He was also blacksmith and had his own forge in Zaamslag. After Nico's father died the forge was sold. As a child Nico always wanted to follow his father's footsteps. In September 1936, Nico moved to South Beveland to the town Heinkenszand, not far from the city of Goes. He bought an old forge and a house on the Stationsweg, at the junction of Dorpsstraat and Clara's Pad, the three main roads in Heinkenszand. Immediately after he moved in, he set up his blacksmith shop. The following year he married his fiancée, Suus Geensen, from the city of Axel, also in Zeelandic Flanders.

Nico wrote: *"On April 22, 1937, we first got married in the town hall of Axel and after that in the Dutch Reformed Church at Zaamslag. The wedding text was from Psalm 121:2, 'My help cometh from the Lord, who made heaven and earth.' On April 23, we traveled to our new home, and on that same day we went to work. In our case, it went like clockwork and we lived a happy life. However, it was a bad time economically, but with diligence and good skills it was possible to earn a living. Our happiness grew in a short time. On April 21, 1938 our daughter was born, a beautiful child called Rietje. We were all healthy, the blacksmith shop went well and it seemed we could have a joyful future. But then this villain emerged in Germany, a scoundrel that became a murderer of millions of people. He completely shattered our happiness. Before the war, I was an army sergeant at the Horse Artillery Corps, also known as the Yellow Riders. I had to report to headquarters again. The General Mobilization became a fact. I had to close my forge while my wife had to stay alone with our child. Good-bye to good luck, good-bye to happiness and prosperity. As being a quartermaster I was instructed to receive horses and to deliver them to Bergen op Zoom, a city located in North Brabant. The last day in Bergen op Zoom my wife and child visited me. I received an enlarged photograph of them as a gift. I was very pleased with their visit, but bringing them back to the train station was difficult. She was a brave woman and of good spirit. We both held on to our wedding text. It gave me a lot of pain that I would not be able to continue to help or support these two treasures. How on earth should they manage?"*

The concerns of the Dutch government proved to be justified. On September 1, 1939, a week after the Dutch army began the General Mobilization, *Fall Weiss*[1], the German attack on Poland began. Despite fierce opposition from the Polish armed forces, a treaty between their German neighbors from the west and the Russian neighbors from the east mangled this country. Two days after the invasion of Poland, the United Kingdom and France declared war on Germany. What everyone feared became true. Europe again began the battleground for a war that spread all over the world, like an ink stain. As in the Great War, the Dutch government hoped to remain neutral, yet maintained close contact with the British and French governments and continued to mobilize troops.

Nico: *"Our destination was the Peel, a region in the south east of the Netherlands, close to Dutch and German borders. Every day we spent our time with the horses. We tried anything to make our days more useful. The Netherlands wanted to remain neutral as it had during 1914-1918, but in the meantime the Germans overran Europe. The German people crawled like slaves for this sadist Hitler. With a Sieg Heil, the German army plunged the world into a fire of destruction. In the Peel, there were many soldiers who worked on tank traps and made barbed wire barriers. We, the mounted soldiers, helped them with this and also had to take care of the horses. I had my own horse and I have ridden it whenever I could. Sometimes, we had to do a parade ride when some bigwig came to visit. Fortunately, because I had my own business, I eventually was given a leave. While I was home, we started to work as early as possible. I needed to do as much work as I could before I had to return to the military.*

The following incident occurred one morning. We were at work early when about half past six there was a man from the Work Inspection at the door. It turned into a roaring argument. I didn't want to answer his questions and asked him if he was not ashamed of himself harassing me while I had so many problems. I had the feeling I was dragged down in a swamp and that this man was giving me the last push on the head. I was so angry I chased the man out the door with an iron rod in my hand. He was lucky that he could close the door in my face. By the time I caught up with him, he was in his car and sat there with the door locked. I was white hot and smashed a few dents in his car roof. But when I calmed down I asked myself: What have I done? My wife was upset and my old servant confused. I had attacked an official and damaged government property. My immediate boss in the army was 1st Lt. Van Aken, a lawyer in civilian life. He wrote a letter to the Labor Department and we heard of it no more."

The Dutch mobilized conscripts waited during the harsh winter. In January 1940, an *Elfstedentocht* was planned. It is a skating race in the northern province of Frisia that can only be organized when the whole track of ditches, canals and lakes between eleven cities is frozen solid. It occurred that year for the first time since 1933.

During the spring Dutch fears were realized. Germany attacked Norway and Denmark on May 9, 1940. Now it was our turn. The invasion began on May 10th when German troops simultaneously invaded the Netherlands, Belgium, and Luxembourg during an operation called *Fall Gelb*.

Nico: *"The Germans attacked us with a great number of planes. However, our march and the positioning of our guns proceeded orderly. After one day, we got the message to withdraw behind the Waterlinie, an important line of defense. We had two bridges; so-called boat pontoon bridges laid by the Engineers. German planes bombarded these bridges despite of our anti aircraft fire. However, all our people made it across the bridges. A horse was hit and the animal died screaming in pain. We threw the animal into the Meuse River because it obstructed the bridge. Our main task was clear: kill as many paratroopers as possible from behind our positions. Each five men got a machine gun and a car. We hunted and killed these paratroopers with an overwhelming hatred. When things settled down, our thoughts went back home. I had a woman with child, unprotected, and abandoned. I was praying and cursing. The hate and I do mean hate, the terrible thoughts that I had for the enemy. They made people miserable, destroyed young families and caused death and destruction. Perhaps it would threaten my family too... That beautiful woman and that dear child... dead? Damn! Damn, damn them! Shoot them down! How can a man be so full of hate? Of course our comrades were also hit. I saw them lie in the church in the village of Zoelen. Amongst them there was no one that I knew. The fleeing of our government and the Queen to safe England, on May 13, was a blow to the morale for us Dutchmen. But it was better this way!"*

That morning, Nico's wife, Suus, and daughter were in Heinkenszand. The people awoke to the sound of German bombers, bombing the airports of Zeeland. Now it was impossible to deny the dreaded war had broken out. Zeeland would not be spared. The Dutch soldiers with their outdated weapons were no match for the highly trained and superior equipped German forces. They had no choice but to retreat or surrender.

Vital points such as bridges and airports were mercilessly bombed. East of the province of Zeeland, the Dutch armed forces tried valiantly to stop the advancing German troops, who had begun inundating the tail of the former island of South Beveland that separated Zeeland from North Brabant. From the villages that were flooded by the water a somber procession of cars, horse carts, bicycles, and walking refugees, began. The refugees were in search of a safe haven in South Beveland and the next peninsula, Walcheren. The Dutch soldiers received help from Zeelandic Flanders: French troops crossed the Western Scheldt River and swarmed through Walcheren and South Beveland to protect their homeland from the Germans who intended to attack France through Zeeland and Belgium. During German bombing, the French entrenched themselves behind hastily raised lines.

While French and Dutch troops tried to take down German planes and paratroopers, Dutch soldiers, along with local police forces, hunted for German spies living in Zeeland, members of the Dutch *Nationaal Socialistische Beweging* (National Socialist Movement, NSB), and other suspicious individuals. On May 14, a radio news bulletin reported Rotterdam had been bombed, despite the fact the city had previously surrendered. This was a great blow. The attack was retaliation against the Dutch resistance who tried to delay the German invasion. The bombardment killed 800 people with 80,000 people left homeless.

Nico: *"What a mean crime! Rotterdam bombed. So many civilians killed. 'Surrender or more cities will be flattened.' More civilians killed! Murderers! Bastards! We were taken prisoner of war and were rounded up in the meadows around Hei en Boeicop, a land of pastures and water. I filed the number of my horse from its hoof and traded the horse with a farmer who I had just met before, for a farmer's overall. I had thrown my saber, rifle and other equipment into the water, but I kept my revolver. I really wanted to go home. I was possessed by that thought. It was too far to walk and occasionally I got a ride. I reached home and thanked God. My woman and child were safe and waited for me, though with much fear and trembling. I have to thank our neighbors, doctor Griep and pastor Renting for the help and assistance they gave my family."*

The Germans demanded the Dutch government's surrender. They promised other Dutch cities would suffer Rotterdam's fate if they didn't. The country was forced to its knees. The government of the Netherlands surrendered a day later, except for Zeeland, where the army refused to put down their weapons. Although it was obvious Zeeland would also eventually surrender, the Dutch government wanted to stall for time to support the retreating French.

On May 14, the same day they accepted the military surrender, German troops overran opposition in Bath and the Zanddijk. They conquered South Beveland on May16. To their horror, the people from Zeeland saw heavily armed German troops marching through the polders, wiping out the last resistance in South Beveland and Walcheren.

Although Dutch soldiers who escaped arrest were demoralized and surrendered, the French troops fought fiercely and suffered heavy losses at the Sloedam[2], the railway dam that connected South Beveland and Walcheren. Middelburg, the main city of Walcheren, was hit and largely destroyed. Initially, it was assumed that German bombs caused this destruction. There were indeed Heinkel 111 aircraft seen above the city, but subsequent studies showed that the city was destroyed mainly by artillery fire. It is even possible that French shells may have hit the city.

The Germans were in a hurry because the Zeeland coast was important to them. They saw Zeeland as a springboard to England, which was on their list to become part of the Third Reich. While the Germans were advancing to the coast, the battle-weary French retreated over the Western Scheldt River to Zeelandic Flanders. There, on May 30, the last piece of the Netherlands fell to the Germans.

On May 30, Germany appointed the Austrian jurist and politician, Arthur Seyss-Inquart, to be in command of the Netherlands. This State Commissioner of the occupied Dutch territories was ordered to prepare the Dutch population to join the Nazi dream. Under him were four General Commissioners: one for security, one for justice, one for finances and one for spreading the national socialist ideas among the population. In Zeeland, the highest German authority was State Commissioner Willi Münzer, who reigned from the village Koudekerke on Walcheren. His main task was to promote National Socialism to the Zeelanders. By doing so, he would make Zeeland glad to be part of the Nazi empire. The main Dutch authority in Zeeland was a man from Axel, Province Commissioner Petrus Dieleman.

Thousands of French and Dutch soldiers on Walcheren were imprisoned and then marched off to the east, through South Beveland. They spent the night out in the open, without food or water. They were transported by trucks and trains to the city of Breda in North Brabant. Dutch National Socialist Party (NSB) and other pro-German people were released from the camps.

The German occupation began. The *Wehrmacht* took their positions and filled the streets. Initially, life was calm. Many Dutch citizens were angered by the destruction of Rotterdam and Middelburg, but the German soldiers they met in the streets and in the shops seemed decent, friendly men. Although they gradually began to display all the worst characteristics of an occupying army, those German soldiers were not the most hated. They were often ordinary men who spent good money in the Dutch shops and restaurants. After all, the pragmatic Dutch middle class knew the Germans were the only ones with money. Rather, the Dutch reserved their greatest hatred for the countrymen who belonged to the NSB or offered assistance to the occupiers. The leader of the NSB in Zeeland, Jan Dekker, from the city of Goes, opened a district office in his hometown. Before the war, members of the *Weerbaarheidsafdeling* (Defensibility Department, WA, the department within the NSB that guarded the meetings and demonstrations from being disrupted by protesters) were forbidden to wear uniforms. With the Germans now firmly in power, the WA members could now proudly wear their black uniforms in public.

Nico: *"There were also NSB marching exercises in our village. They wore black uniforms with large hats adorned with gold braid and of course their fine shiny boots. These were dangerous people, those traitors!"*

Although the Germans were initially trying to impress the Zeeland people with their uniforms and ostentatious parades, the pressure of hostile occupation was soon felt. NSB men largely replaced the top Dutch police officers. Both the Dutch police forces and the *Royal Marechaussee* (a Dutch police force that performs both military and civil duties) merged to become an extension of the *Sicherheitsdienst* (the intelligence agency of the SS) and the *Grüne Polizei* (the green uniformed regular police force of Germany). Applicants, who aspired to a position in the new police force, had to endure a militaristic training based on the Nazi ideology. Because the local police had to enforce orders of the occupying forces, many were seen as collaborators. Of course, there were policemen who chose to cooperate with the new regime. These men worked their way to the top in a short time. But many other agents used their position to assist the public during these confusing times. Many risked their lives to warn the resistance movement of an impending raid or hide people on the run from the German occupation. They tried but could not prevent total German control.

Nico: *"We were overwhelmed by all those new measures, many related to the supply of iron and steel. We also had to register our belongings at various agencies. But it came down to this; the Germans took as much as possible from our rich country. What the Germans had left, we had to divide as economically as possible."*

Zeelanders who openly rejected National Socialism were soon identified and arrested, or publically beaten by collaborating fellow Dutchmen of the WA or later by the newly installed *Landwacht* (Land Guard), a paramilitary branch consisting mainly of NSB men. There was strict censorship in newspapers. The entire country had to obey a 2000 hours[3] curfew and cover all windows to deceive the Allied bombers. Almost everything - food, clothing, footwear, and tobacco - were obtained with coupons provided by the German authorities. By May 1941, every Dutch citizen aged 14 and older had to carry an identity card at all times. The Germans built countless roadblocks and checked the identity card of every person. People of Jewish descent had a *J* stamped on their identity card. The cards made it possible to identify and persecute Jews, resistance fighters and other people who were in hiding. It didn't take long for pro-German public servants to replace Jewish public servants.

A year later the Germans, assisted by Dutch collaborators, began picking up Jewish people and transporting them. They were dragged from Amsterdam to the transit camp Westerbork, in the province of Drenthe, and then further to the east, where the Nazis tried to exterminate the European Jewry. Not only Jews, but everyone with an important job who was known as anti-German was relieved from office and replaced by members of the NSB and other sympathizers of Nazi Germany. Clergy, preaching against the harsh and neo-pagan doctrine, were sometimes betrayed by their own church members, arrested and imprisoned. In response to the Dutch resistance, the General Commissioner for the Safety and SS police leader, Hanns Rauter, commissioned the arrest of one thousand leading Dutch citizens. They were interned in two camps: St. Michielsgestel and Haaren, both in North Brabant. In the event of an attack on a German occupier or his henchmen, these hostages would be shot in retaliation.

In May 1943, civilians had to surrender all radios. Buildings transport, and goods were confiscated. Strategically located Zeeland was soon declared a *Sperrgebiet* (Prohibited Area) where a special permit was required to enter or leave. The German plan to conquer England was abandoned, but the Reich had to defend itself against British and - later on - American attacks from the sea. As a result, the whole coast of the Netherlands became part of Hitlers Atlantic Wall, defenses that ran from northern Norway to the French and Spanish border. Over 17,500 bunkers were built along this line, including numerous concrete bunkers and beach barriers on Walcheren.

After the capitulation of the Dutch army in May 1940 all Dutch prisoners of war were sent home, although the generals were interned in Germany. When the Germans noticed that former Dutch soldiers tried to set up resistance groups, all Dutch officers and non-commissioned officers were required to register in May 1941. They were made prisoners of war again and interned. In April 1943 also the 300.000 drafted soldiers had to register in Amersfoort (province of Utrecht) or Assen (province of Drenthe). This resulted in the April-May Strike after which nearly two hundred people were killed in reprisals. Radio Oranje tried to persuade the listeners not to obey and many men went into hiding. Eventually 11.000 Dutchmen were transported to work camps in Germany, where they had to work for the heavy industry.

Nico: *"One day all former prisoners of war had to register at a Nazi transit camp in the city of Amersfoort. I made it to Amersfoort, but never reported to the camp. When we left in the morning, I kissed my wife and my treasure of a child. With a 'see you tomorrow' I stepped out the door with a small suitcase in my hand, filled with food. But my neighbors had a different idea, because they came dragging with large suitcases. My neighbor Jaantje was so filled with tears that she could hardly speak. She was convinced that the separation with her husband Jan would last for years. My other neighbor Piet had a good heart: he promised her husband that he would help Jaantje as best he could. That gave Jan some relief. Once we were on the train, he showed a bit more willpower. We shared great laughter when Jan wanted to take his tobacco out of his suitcase. When he opened it, he saw that instead of tobacco he had everything else: tins with shoeshine, brushes, rolled up warm vests, long johns and socks for a year! The soldier sitting next to my neighbor unrolled the long johns that were the suitcase. It was a very hot day so we had many laughs because of that. My poor neighbor had to drag his heavy suitcases all the way through Amersfoort."*

Nico probably could avoid going to Germany because he had a statement of indispensability.

1: *Fall Blau* (Plan Blue) = the military preparatory studies of the German army.
Fall Weiß (Plan White) = the conquest of Poland.
Fall Grün (Plan Green) = the conquest of Czechoslovakia.
Fall Gelb (Plan Yellow) = the conquest of the Low Countries.
Fall Rot (Plan Red) = the conquest of France.
2: The old dam (called the Causeway in English) formed the connection between the peninsulas South Beveland and Walcheren. The causeway itself no longer exists as such; land on both sides of the former railway embankment has been reclaimed and has become farmland. Five monuments were erected to commemorate the French losses in 1940 and the Canadian losses in 1944.
3: All times, except in some quotes, will be given using the 24-hour clock. Eight in the morning thus appears as *0800 hours* and eight at night as *2000 hours*.

Nico van Biezen during the Mobilization. (007)

The forge of Nico and Suus. (008)

The photo of Rietje and Suus, given to Nico by his wife. (009)

Suus and her husband Sergeant Nico van Biezen in his uniform. (010)

Chapter 2

Resistance in the Polders

The region known as the *Bag* of South Beveland hangs like a sack under the peninsula. It is a beautiful area characterized by miles of winding dikes whose sides are planted with rows of poplar trees. Many farms in the polders have black painted barns. The frames of the windows and doors of these barns are painted white, so the farmer can find his way in the dark. The soil is fertile and the climate is mild and favorable for growing vegetables and fruit. The area is well known for its apple and pear orchards.

Most villages in the Bag are part of the municipality Borsele. This administrative center is not the similar sounding village of Borssele, but in the village of Heinkenszand. It is the largest populated village in the municipality. Heinkenszand was a small island off the coast of South Beveland until the beginning of the 14th century when monks drained the shallow water around it by building dikes, joining it to the main island. From the air, you would see that Heinkenszand consists of a cluster of 18 polders. The village itself was created by building houses on either side of a dike, now called the Dorpsstraat, the main street of Heinkenszand. In the past, there were two large villas in Heinkenszand, giving the town some elegance. Villa *Huize Watervliet* was later demolished and replaced by the estate *Landlust*. Around the turn of the last century the villa estate *Barbestein* made way for the Roman Catholic Church of St. Blasius and its rectory.

In August 1944, the month this story begins, Heinkenszand was an independent municipality. It consisted of three main streets that met in a T-junction: Dorpsstraat, the main street where most of the shops and the main buildings were located, Stationsweg, and perpendicular to these two: Clara's Pad that began where the other two came together. Other roads were unpaved paths. Most roads surrounding the village were created on top of the polder dikes.

Like everywhere in the Netherlands, life changed in Heinkenszand during the German occupation.

Heinkenszand during the war

Evacuees from the tail of South Beveland fled to the village due the movements of the Dutch and French armies. They punctured the dikes to prevent the German army from invading the former island. The families took all they could carry to the west, fleeing the rising sea that turned their fields into salty, mud plains, too deep to drive a car and too shallow to sail a boat. Many citizens of Heinkenszand sheltered these refugees.

Heinkenszand was a rather quiet village, but in the files of the municipality I did find some interesting facts. Like the one about May 15, 1940, one day before the German army conquered the Vlake Bridge that crossed the Canal through South Beveland. On this day Jean Marie Dormic, a 33-year-old French soldier, died from his injuries in the emergency hospital in Heinkenszand. He was a 1st Class Gunner assigned to the 307th Artillery Regiment and came from the village of Edern in the northwestern part of France. In the neighboring village Lewedorp a machine gun bullet, probably from a German fighter, hit him. After he was found, he was taken to the Public Elementary School in Heinkenszand, which had been converted to a hospital during the mobilization. After his death, Jean was entombed at the general cemetery in Heinkenszand, where a masonry headstone marked his grave.

The next day, German forces conquered the Vlake Bridge and swarmed all over South Beveland. Don't think the conquest of Heinkenszand went very heroic: while riding their stolen bikes, two German soldiers stopped at the emergency hospital located in the school. One of them climbed on the back of the other to look inside and exclaimed: *"Ah, das ist ein Krankenhaus!"* (*"Ah, that's a hospital!"*) Then they walked back to their bikes and left the village. That is how Heinkenszand was incorporated into the Third Reich.

Zeeland was strategically important and the inhabitants of Heinkenszand not only had to share their buildings with evacuees but also with a large number of German soldiers. For example, the Roman Catholic St. Joseph School served as a military barracks. Homes and barns were used in the same way. The 45-year-old mayor of Heinkenszand Aloys (Lou) Mes[1], was not replaced by a NSB mayor like many of his colleagues, but he had to report to Petrus Dieleman, the German appointed Commissioner of the Province of Zeeland.

The citizens of Heinkenszand soon understood they had to watch their steps, not only because of the German soldiers who were settling everywhere, but because the individuals they knew posed the gravest danger. It might be a neighbor, classmate or colleague. These were citizens who ignored their countrymen's feelings and welcomed the Germans with open arms. One of the most fanatical National Socialists of Heinkenszand was the painter, Kees Klap, who lived on the Dorpsstraat. Kees was a member of the NSB and later became head of the local Landwacht. This organization founded in March 1944, was a fanatical paramilitary NSB group. The members carried shotguns. Initially, they wore the black NSB uniform, but later they were equipped with a gray field jacket with a grenade insignia on the collar, a gray cap, black pants, and black leather boots. These uniforms meant these guards didn't operate under the command of Anton Mussert, leader of the NSB, but under the command of the SS General Hanns Rauter, leader of the German intelligence service and the police. A member of the Landwacht earned between fifty and sixty guilders a week, a high salary in times of shortages and unemployment.

Because the men from the Landwacht were natives, the Germans used them to monitor important buildings and to verify identities at roadblocks. Their main task was to track down and arrest people labeled by the Germans as undesirable or dangerous. Like everywhere else in the Netherlands, these undesirable elements soon disappeared from society in Heinkenszand. The pastor of St. Blasius Church was arrested after preaching anti-German sermons from the pulpit. More arrests followed.

Clarisse Cohen, the wife of notary Dirk van Werkum was the only Heinkenszand resident of Jewish descent. Investigation proved she had four Jewish grandparents. When Clarisse registered at the town hall, Mayor Mes refused to put the letter *J* (for Jew) on her identity pass. On March 24, 1942, the mayor received a letter from the German authorities ordering Clarisse and her half Jewish children to leave the province and report in Amsterdam. The mayor pretended he never received the order and subtly counteracted the mandate. He also tried to cancel the order that required the woman and her children to wear the Star of David by sending the authorities their proof of membership in the Dutch Reformed Church. The Germans were not impressed and ordered her to report in Amsterdam. The family survived the war. They left Zeeland in 1950 to live in North Holland. At an age of 78, Clarisse died in 1970 in Heemstede.

German forces overran large territories in Europe, resulting in an ongoing shortage of metal for the Third Reich's war industry. On December 4, 1942, Mayor Mes, like all mayors in Zeeland, received a letter from Province Commissioner Dieleman ordering confiscation of all the bells from all the churches in Zeeland. Only clocks with a special historical value *might* be spared. Dieleman ordered the mayor to inventory the bells in his village and send the results to him. The few clocks in Zeeland that were spared had previously been inventoried by an inspector and labeled with a whitewashed letter *M* (*Monument*.)

On December 5, Mayor Mes responded there were three church bells in town, one in the tower of the Dutch Reformed Church and two in the tower of the Roman Catholic Church. None of these bells were marked by the letter M. The Dutch Reformed Church clock was cast in 1649 and Mayor Mes argued that it had great historical value. He requested this clock be spared because it was also used to alarm the population in case of an emergency. Dieleman responded that all clocks without the letter M would be confiscated. On behalf of the *Rüstingsinspektor*[2] (equipment inspector), Dieleman ordered the mayor to ensure that the removal of the bells would happen in an orderly manner. On March 3, the dreaded letter landed on Mes' desk, announcing a NSB contractor from the province of Limburg would remove the three bells. The mayor was ordered to paint a white letter *P* (*Prüfung* = Approved) ten inches high on each of the bells.

With sorrow the citizens watched as their bells were removed from the towers. They were taken to a warehouse in Goes and then transported to Hamburg Germany, where 200 bells from Zeeland were smelted in the Norddeutsche Affenerie or the Zinnewerke Wilhelmsburg to make bullets and other war equipment. There was one small consolation. The German government compensated the owners of these treasures with 75 cents per kilogram. When the bells from other villages were removed, sometimes this warning was written on the wall of the towers: *"He who shoots with church bells, shall never win the war!"*

The Wehrmacht commanded the *Arbeitseinsatz*, a labor program that forced citizens to work for the German authorities. In protest, Mayor Mes and his colleagues subsequently resigned. Dieleman tried to persuade them to change their decision. Their refusal was considered an act of protest. Many mayors were arrested and imprisoned, but Mes went into hiding. Deputy Mayor G.P. Beaufort temporarily succeeded him, followed by the NSB Mayor, Christiaan Kole. In retaliation for Mes' disappearance, his wife Caroline was interned in the infamous SS concentration camp, Vught. While she was locked up, the Germans tried to claim the family furniture, but evacuees from the village of Walcheren who lived with the family had already removed the furniture to a safe place.

It was common to force Dutch citizens to work for German industry, and in the countryside. On beaches and in fields, they planted *Rommel Asparagus*[3], stakes of wood or metal to prevent the landing of amphibious vehicles and aircraft. These poles were sometimes connected with iron and barbed wire. On April 18, 1944, G.P. Beaufort, the acting mayor of Heinkenszand, wrote to the farmers of the village: *"The Province Commissioner has informed me that the fencing of lands (including the fences on dikes) are only allowed with one wire. Consequently, you must remove all other wire and wind it to reels and deliver them to the town hall before May 1. Additionally, you must submit a declaration of the number of kilograms and the appraised value. Barbed wire and normal wire should be wound on separate reels."*

Because he was a blacksmith, Nico van Biezen received a letter ordering him to give his heavy hammer, saw and pliers for the production and planting of the Rommel Asparagus. Nico did not want to hand over his tools to the occupier, so he simply hid them under a hedge. It was obvious that a blacksmith must have heavy tools in his possession, and the tools were soon found. It was a close call. Although he could have been jailed for this, Nico got away with a warning. To frustrate the Germans, forced laborers worked as slowly as possible while planting the Asparagus. Moreover, the doctors gave the men time off for the slightest pain and falsified their health reports. They did everything they could to slow down the work.

Immediately after the occupation, other opposition arose in and around Heinkenszand. Initially, overt protests were curtailed by threats of imprisonment. Other less ostentatious form of protest was refusing to cooperate with the Germans, cutting of family ties with people who helped them, and wearing Dutch national symbols on former national holidays.

The Group Griep

There was also organized resistance. In Heinkenszand, there was an active resistance group of fourteen members. These men, many with young families, saw the life they built threatened by the power that came marching into their village. Together they decided they could not wait for the Germans to leave and decided to resist. Several months after the German invasion, core members of the local group gradually joined the Zeelandic branch of the *Orde Dienst* (Order Agency), better known as the OD. Initially, ex-soldiers formed this group, organized to maintain order in the Netherlands once the occupiers left. When it became clear the Germans were not going to leave any time soon, the OD grew into a resistance movement joined by many civilians.

Ex-military man, Piet Kloosterman was from Nisse. He was and investigator of Inspection Price Control, a government institution to counteract black market prices. He was one of the first from Zeeland to join the OD. In 1940, he was asked by the national staff to organize several resistance groups in South Beveland. Kloosterman was appointed District Commander of the peninsula and gathered reliable men around him, especially ex-soldiers. One of them was Ko van 't Westeinde, ex-military and tree nurseryman from Baarsdorp, a small hamlet near Heinkenszand. Ko was appointed Section Head. We will read more about him later.

Men like Ko formed local groups. Gradually every city, village and hamlet had its own resistance group with its own commander. In 1944, there were 1200 South Beveland members of the OD. Membership varied by location. A hamlet like Baarsdorp had only 10 members, while the city of Goes had around 200. The OD was engaged in all kinds of resistance work, like sabotage, falsification of identity cards, and stealing ration coupons. When the Germans tried to deport men from Zeeland for forced labor elsewhere, the OD established an extensive network of hiding places for these people.

Using secret radios, the OD gathered messages from England, aired by the BBC and Radio Oranje, and passed this information to various clandestine newspapers. Members of the OD distributed illegal newspapers among the local population. By the end of 1943, the Allies requested the OD deliver information on the military situation in Zeeland. Gathering military data became an important task for the resistance fighters. They formed an intelligence agency named ID. Members of the ID drove through the area making notes and sketches of important German military equipment and the locations of NSB buildings. In Nisse, the policeman Vroombout collected the information and transferred it to OD leader, Piet Kloosterman. Eventually, the data was transmitted via a secret transmitter in Goes to Middelburg and on across the North Sea, or smuggled to England through Belgium, France, and Spain. Once it reached England, the Allied forces incorporated this information into military topographic maps fore use in impending invasion.

There was also a resistance group in Heinkenszand. This loosely organized group was simultaneously active in, or worked with, other resistance groups. The group was known unofficially as the *Group Griep*.

Nico van Biezen

Because he was a former soldier, blacksmith Nico was asked to become a member of the OD by Section Head Ko van't Westeinde. This was an offer Nico did not have to think about for long. As soon as he was appointed Local Commander, he gathered reliable comrades around him. Nico, his 30-year-old wife, Suus, and his 3-year-old daughter, Rietje lived in the house that was also their forge at the Stationsstraat. This building is still there and is a Chinese restaurant today. Nico was a skilled farrier who visited the farmers with his mobile shoeing stock. [4]

Nico: *"Our resistance group started by handing out pamphlets. One evening in 1941, Mr. Ko van't Westeinde, Section Head of the OD, brought 1st Lieutenant Scheffers to us. Coincidentally, I knew this man; he was the paymaster of the 7th Field Artillery Regiment and friend of my commander during mobilization. He stayed with us in hiding for just about 14 days. I found my first hiding place at the home of the widow Mol. Mr. Scheffers was in good hands and brought some joy in the life of the widow Mol and Maaike her daughter. They were good people. The Germans had just shot his best friend Ko Massee from Goes. Scheffers was a vital man, but the boredom was almost devastating for him. I organized a lot of hiding places for people, also hid them myself in my forge, making them servants in the house and in the workshop. Our house was always open as a shelter for refugees. I could take care of everything for these people: food, ration coupons, false papers, and if necessary clothing. Also, for a long time, I have been billeting German soldiers in my house and had up to four German blacksmiths in the workshop. At first I was not amused, but on the other hand, it was a good cover for our anti-German behavior."*

Kees Griep

Nico asked Dr. Kees Griep to join the local underground. *Griep* means Influenza, so you can imagine that the name Dr. Griep was often a source of amusement. The 49-year-old Kees, the man for whom the group was named, was from Rilland-Bath, in the *tail* of South Beveland. He and his wife, Corry Duinker, moved to Heinkenszand in 1922. Kees opened a medical practice in a house on Clara's Pad that still serves as a doctor's home. The family had three daughters, Iet, Attie, Nannie, and a son, Pim. Not long after his arrival, Kees was appointed the Municipal Doctor of Heinkenszand and received his wages from the municipality.

Kees was a good friend of Lou Mes, the mayor of Heinkenszand. During the holidays they and their families traveled to foreign countries together.

Kees was known as an active and socially conscious man. In addition to his practice, he was involved in all kinds of medical and social initiatives. He and his wife, Corry, participated in the local mother and nurse course and he was one of the first doctors to open a consultancy for infants in Zeeland. Kees was also involved in several clubs. He was the chairman of the local band, Euterpe, and president and director of the local art theater. Kees was also a member of the local *Vrijwillige Burgerwacht* (Voluntary Vigilante), a conservative and royalist paramilitary organization formed in 1935 for the protection of the Netherlands against undemocratic influences. The Germans disbanded this organization in 1940. As mentioned earlier, the Public Elementary School in Heinkenszand also functioned as an emergency hospital, so Kees, being the Municipal Doctor, also became the Hospital Director.

After the German invasion, Kees joined *Medisch Contact* (Medical Contact), an illegal organization of Dutch doctors who opposed the German medical organization *de Artsenkamer* (the Chamber of Doctors). Through contact relay letters, Medisch Contact advised the doctors how to handle the measures de Artsenkamer imposed. In an organized way they tried to influence food distribution, loyalty statements, medical examinations of forced laborers and mitigate German oppression of Jewish people. They also opposed forced sterilization. Because Kees was asked to work for *Centraal Beheer* (Central Control) a Dutch office that monitored ill workers, he became a Controlling Physician, responsible for home visits to patients. Because of this, he transferred his practice to Dr. Piet Staverman in 1942. Initially, Kees drove a Ford V8 to his home visits, but during the war, the wheels were removed and the car was put on blocks, so it could not be confiscated. Instead of the Ford, he drove an Italian Fiat with a gas generator that ran on firewood. During the occupation, Kees Griep and his wife hid several evacuees. With his organizational skills, his knowledge of the population, the respect he enjoyed in the area and most of all, his permit to travel without restrictions, he was a valuable addition to the underground movement.

Piet van den Dries

Kees Griep suggested to Nico van Biezen that headmaster Piet van den Dries would be a valuable member of the group. Piet and Kees were good friends. Piet was born in Houten, in the province Utrecht, but later returned to Zeeland where the family originated. He and his wife, Katrien Schipper, whom he married in 1936, had two daughters, Paula and Corrie, and a son, Peter. Piet's father was a head teacher and in 1938, Piet continued the tradition by becoming the headmaster of the St. Joseph School, a Catholic boys' school in Heinkenszand. Piet's exceptionally long and lean figure gave him a striking appearance. He was known for his extraordinary intelligence, but he was also notorious for his clumsiness. My grandfather's neighbor remembers that my grandfather failed his driver's test countless times. Piet very much had to watch his words during school lessons. It was known that NSB members gave their children instructions to report unwanted comments from their teachers. An internal letter[5] from the NSB on February 7, 1942, classified Piet as *"... outside school: very anti-National Socialist. Within school: neutral."* So he was being watched.

It was usual for a headmaster to live next to the school. Piet's house was on the Kerkdreef, a path that runs from the Dorpsstraat to the St. Blasius church. Further down the path there is the Lourdes Grotto, a small replica of the famous 1912 French shrine. In the first decade of the twentieth century, the veneration of Mary was very popular in Catholic Netherlands. After the cave's opening, hundreds of pilgrims walked along the path, past the teacher's house on the Kerkdreef. The school was located behind Piet's house. The house is still there, but the school has been demolished.

Once the German troops invaded the village, Piet was forced to vacate the premises so the school could serve as a German barracks. He had to deal with the German soldiers in his school, and with an officer who confiscated little Peter's room. This created a risky situation for Piet. His cousin, Ko van't Westeinde, the Section Head, had asked him to join the OD and to organize a local group, with his friend, Kees Griep, and village blacksmith, Nico van Biezen. Although there was a German officer in his house and a German company in his school, he agreed to join the group. But he had to watch his step.

Because he studied English at the University of Oxford, Piet was employed as an interpreter between the resistance groups and the Allied airmen that had crashed with their bomber or fighter in South Beveland. Besides his job as head of the school, Piet also gave private English lessons to the village people, especially to members of the resistance, so they could communicate with the allies through secret transmitters, with aviators that crashed in the area and, later, with the liberators. Like most resistance fighters, Piet owned a radio, a small crystal receiver, hidden inside a large matchbox in his office. Piet dared listen only when his wife, Katrien, stood guard in the corridor and gave the signal that the coast was clear. Then he waited for the first four notes of Beethoven's fifth symphony - the Morse Code V for Victory – before the announcement: *"Here is Radio Oranje, the voice of the fighting Netherlands!"*

Despite all the tension, the German billeting had its advantages. The German soldiers in the school behind Piet's house became acquainted with the family of the kind *Herr Haupt Meister* who spoke their native language so fluently. Because of this, Piet was sometimes able to get important information from them. The German units in Zeeland were replaced frequently during the occupation. All soldiers who were able to fight were sent to the front. In July 1944, the 165th Reserve Infantry Division was replaced by a weaker division, the 70th Infantry Division, formed only a month earlier. This unit consisted of three infantry regiments and the supporting units. The 70th Infantry Division, led by the 60-year Great War Veteran Lieutenant General Wilhelm Daser, was called the *Magen Division* (Stomach Division), because it consisted of soldiers who had stomach problems. While they were in Zeeland, they ate white bread, which gave them the name *Weissbrot Division* (White Bread Division). The soldiers of this division, who were stationed in Heinkenszand, were billeted in the school behind Piet's house, so the headmaster learned to know many of these men. He even got along with some of the officers, ordinary homesick men who cried when Allied bombers roared overhead, on their way to bomb cities where their families lived. But other officers were committed National Socialists, firmly convinced they would win the war. One such Hitler supporter was the officer billeted in Piet's house. Whenever Katrien cleaned this man's room, she turned around a stern portrait of Hitler. She dared not do this anymore after the officer caught her and gave her a scolding.

The children, expelled from their schools, took their lessons in the church, in the rectory, in a pub or in any other available room. During four and a half years of occupation, classes were moved a total of 19 times. Each time, the teachers, the students, and a large number of benevolent parents had to lug the books, tables, and chairs through the streets to another location. Schools had to comply with German rules. The occupier ordered the schools to provide German language lessons. Though Piet spoke the language fluently, he reluctantly shared this knowledge. He taught his class only a few words and spent most of the time parsing them. When the school inspector of the NSB expressed his displeasure, Piet argued that his students could not learn good German without learning to parse the words. His argument was noted, but no further reprisals followed. German textbooks replaced Dutch education materials.

Anything that hinted of Dutch patriotism and the Dutch Royal House was banned. Although the St. Joseph School gymnasium served as a stable and no other rooms were available, the Germans ordered compulsory gymnastics. Most children did not have good shoes, let alone sneakers.

On May 1, 1944, Kole, the NSB Mayor from Heinkenszand, asked Piet to make a list of school children who would like to go to Germany on vacation. In the mountains, they would enjoy healthy German care and with good nutrition. The mayor ordered Piet to ask some teachers whether they wanted to accompany them. No one in the village was interested and it is quite possible the request never left Piet's desk. Why the Germans wanted to move Dutch children to Germany is not clear. Perhaps it was to indoctrinate them with the National Socialism dream. They may even have planned to keep the children as collateral, in the event the bombings on German cities increased.

As time went by, only a few children attended Piet's classes. In fertile Zeeland, the population did not go hungry, but there were shortages. There was lack of clothing, footwear, and soap, so the parents preferred the children stay at home instead of sending them to school in rags and dirty faces. Moreover, many fathers were in hiding because of the forced labor laws, so their children had to work on the farms to ensure the food supplies.

On the weekend, when he was not busy with school matters and the pesky demands of the occupier, Piet like to ride his bicycle. Although Zeeland was *Sperrgebiet* (Prohibited Area), he regularly managed to get a *Sonderausweiss* (Special Permit) for traveling to Middelburg and Antwerp. He already spoke fluent German, but he told the authorities he had to go to Middelburg to study German and research his family history in Antwerp. With the permit in his pocket, Piet recorded as much data as he could concerning German positions in South Beveland, Walcheren and Zeelandic Flanders. He passed this information along to his nephew, Ko van 't Westeinde, who gave it to the district commander, Piet Kloosterman. Eventually, it reached the Allies overseas for use in preparation of the invasion.

Where danger, oppression, and fear of war prevailed, funny events helped to mitigate despair. Piet often had to deal with his naughty son, Peter. The German company billeted in his school was replaced by another and little Peter welcomed the new soldiers with a handshake, saying: "*Dag rotmof!*" ("*Hi, dirty kraut!*"). Piet understood he had better watch his language. Another time, little Peter was with a friend playing in the bike shed on the schoolyard. The Germans stabled their horses there. For the moment, there were no Germans or horses in sight. His friend was known as an incorrigible pyromaniac. He found a box of matches and urged Peter to light one. Peter was nervous and the match was too short. As a result the entire shed went up in flames. The Germans learned the names of the arsonists and they threw Peter's friend in jail. Peter was having a bath when the police came to arrest him. He held fast to the rim of the bathtub and cried they could not take him because he was naked. He did not go to prison, but had to go to bed with sore, red buttocks. One afternoon Peter came home with two bullets he had found somewhere. Startled, his mother ordered him to give them to the German cook, a reasonable man who worked in the barn next to the house, which served as a kitchen for the troops. The cook took the bullets from Peter and went on with his work. A moment later, the boy appeared in the kitchen with more bullets. *"Where did you find those bullets?"* asked the worried cook. Peter shrugged: *"In the schoolyard of course. There are boxes full of them!"*

The Van 't Westeinde -family

Ko van 't Westeinde and his brother, Pier, were sons in a family of seven children. They owned a fruit tree nursery called Westhof, inherited from their father, Piertje in 1935. *Pier* is an abbreviation of *Peter* or *Pieter* and *-tje* means little. Old Piertje was named that way because he was small in stature. Westhof was in the hamlet Baarsdorp, in the municipality of 's-Heer Arendskerke, within a large ring-shaped dike. The brothers were cousins of Piet van den Dries. The nursery was founded in 1870 by their grandfather, Jacobus van den Dries, also the grandfather of Piet van den Dries. This first nursery was located on the Westdijk in Heinkenszand. Because a son and daughter of Jacobus married a daughter and son of farmer Cornelis van 't Westeinde, these two families became closely related. Maria, the mother of Ko and Pier van 't Westeinde, was a *Van den Dries* and Cornelia, the mother of Piet van den Dries, was a *Van 't Westeinde*.

Both Jacobus' sons were not interested in inheriting the tree nursery. His son Jacobus became a priest and Pieter became a teacher. That is why his daughter Maria and his son-in-law Piertje, the parents of Ko and Pier, acquired the nursery at the Westdijk. This is where the seven children of Piertje and Maria were born. Piertje had a successful business growing yew trees. They flourished in the fertile Zeeland climate. The company attracted many foreign customers and from the profits, Piertje expanded the nursery and bought Westhof (also known as *'t* Westhof), a large polder within a ring dike. There were two farmhouses on Westhof. In 1944, Piertje lived in the largest house (his wife Maria died in 1938) and shared it with his unmarried children, 36-year old son, Pier, and his 29-year old daughter, Kee. His eldest son, Ko, and his family lived in the smaller house nearby. The old farmhouse at the Westdijk was rented out to farm hand, Kees Bek, and his family. Ko's tree nursery is still managed by members of his family. They grow walnuts now. When Piet, Ko's eldest son was a boy, he lived with his grandfather, uncle, and aunt because it was too crowded in Ko's house. Therefore, Piet had to walk back and forth between the two farms of the nursery. While walking he occasionally heard cursing from the German soldiers quartered in the company barns. When he shared his new German vocabulary with his grandfather, including *scheisse* and *donner wetter*, Piertje gave him a smack on the ears for cursing. The Van 't Westeinde family gave shelter to many refugees and hiders. Kee, the unmarried daughter of Piertje, played a mayor role in caring for them.

Riet, daughter of Kee: *"Being the unmarried daughter, she was responsible for the entire household because her mother died in 1938. The men had to work in the nursery and her sisters-in-law had to take care of their own families. So, during the war, while my mother tried to relieve her father's mourning, she also took care of all the hiders on the nursery."*

The 40-year-old Ko, a surly man of few words, was married to Nele Rijk who always dressed in the traditional style of the Catholic women of South Beveland. Ko and Nele had six sons, Piet, Martien, Kees, Bas, Wim, Jan, and a girl, Marietje. As the eldest son of Piertje, he was the main authority on the tree nursery. Because the nursery had foreign customers, Ko spoke English quite well. When the mobilization began, Ko had to register for military service. Before the war, he worked as a military motorcycle messenger in Meerkerk in South Holland. After the German invasion, a platoon of German soldiers was billeted in some barns on his property. District Commander Piet Kloosterman appointed him Section Head of the OD because of his military experience and the advantages his farm offered. His section consisted of the villages Nisse, 's-Heer Arendskerke, 's-Heer Abtskerke and part of Goes. In early 1944, the former deputy mayor of Goes, A. de Roo, one of the closest associates of Piet Kloosterman, became his successor, so Ko worked with him as well. Ko was also a Local Commander of the hamlet Baarsdorp and led a group of ten men. When forced labor was underway, Ko started hiding people by making them servants in his nursery. Ko was not Section Head of Heinkenszand. Initially, he was only indirectly involved in the Group Griep in Heinkenszand, but later he would work closely with his cousins' group. During the summer of 1944, the Allies asked the underground to create paramilitary groups. Ko organized the dropping of firearms and ammunition on his property by an Allied plane. At night, he and his staff placed burning barrels on the edges of the pasture to designate the drop zone. The plan was canceled at the last moment, because it was feared the quartered Germans would notice it. The shortage of weapons remained a problem for the newly created partisan groups.

Ko's 36-year-old brother Pier van 't Westeinde who's actual name was Pieter or Piet, was not married. He lived with his father Piertje, his sister, Kee, and his nephew Piet on the other farm of the nursery. During the occupation, he helped his older brother create false identity cards and food stamps and found hiding places for refugees.

Kees Franse

24-year-old Kees Franse was born in Heinkenszand. He was a member of the local gymnastics club and loved to ride his motorbike. He lived with his parents in the Dorpsstraat, where his father owned a shop where he sold and repaired clocks, watches and also red coral necklaces and metal ornaments that were both part of traditional dress of Zeeland. During the war, Kees often helped his father in the shop and also worked as a rope maker. On his motorbike, he visited the farmers in the area to sell ropes and products from the shop. Kees also worked as a public servant at the town hall. Here he handled the mayor's mail and performed all sorts of other tasks for the municipality. Kees also worked for LBD[6], the Dutch version of the ARP (Air Raid Precautions). He was an important source of information for the Group Griep because of his job at the town hall. He was also able to steal the necessary forms and stamps that the group then used to make fake identity passes and other documents. His daughter Elly recalls that her father spoke about a sabotaged German train that derailed from the track that ran through South Beveland. He told her he was involved with this attack. Whether other members of the Group Griep were involved is unknown.

There were other men affiliated with the resistance from Heinkenszand. Accountant Cees Paauwe, a man with a remarkably loud voice, was a good friend and neighbor of Nico Biezen. Cees could speak German well and often negotiated many affairs with the Germans while trying to pry information from them. Milkman Gilles Geschiere, with his knowledge of the villagers and the area was also an important source of information. Outside the core group was a group of young men. When ration coupons were transported in bags to the distribution office, the boys attacked the courier and stole the coupons. They often went to the village of Wolphaartsdijk to fight a large group of pro-German boys there.

Initially, the Group Griep did nightly sabotage actions. They burned down the combines used to supply the Germans. In response, the German authorities forced two random Dutch citizens to guard the combines each night. If a machine was sabotaged those two people would be shot. Because the group did not want the death of their fellow villagers on their conscience, the members decided on alternative acts.

1: Mayor, Dr., Mr., A.J.J.M. Mes, from Middelburg, was mayor of Heinkenszand from July 1926 to January 1944. From July 1935 to September 1941 he was a member of the Provincial Council of Zeeland and from June 1937 to June 1946 member of the House of Representatives. From July 1936 to September 1939 he also was mayor of Ovezande.
2: The task of these equipment inspectors was to insure that the national industry would meet the needs of the Wehrmacht.
3: The Rommel Asparagus were named after the German General-Field Marshal Erwin Rommel, also called the *Desert Fox*, for his campaigns in North Africa. From November 1943, Rommel was responsible for the defense of the Atlantic Wall. When he began, he noticed the organization of the Wall was very inefficient. From the moment he took command, he sped up the pace and decreed the beaches had to be armed with various barriers, including the Asparagus. Rommel was suspected of involvement in the failed assassination attempt on Hitler. On October 14, 1944 he was forced to commit suicide by taking a poison pill.
4: A wooden construction in which a farmer's horse can be restrained, so the blacksmith can work on its hoofs.
5: A response from the Circle Leader Circle 48 on the Group Leader of Goes.
6: The ARP helped the population to protect themselves against air attacks.

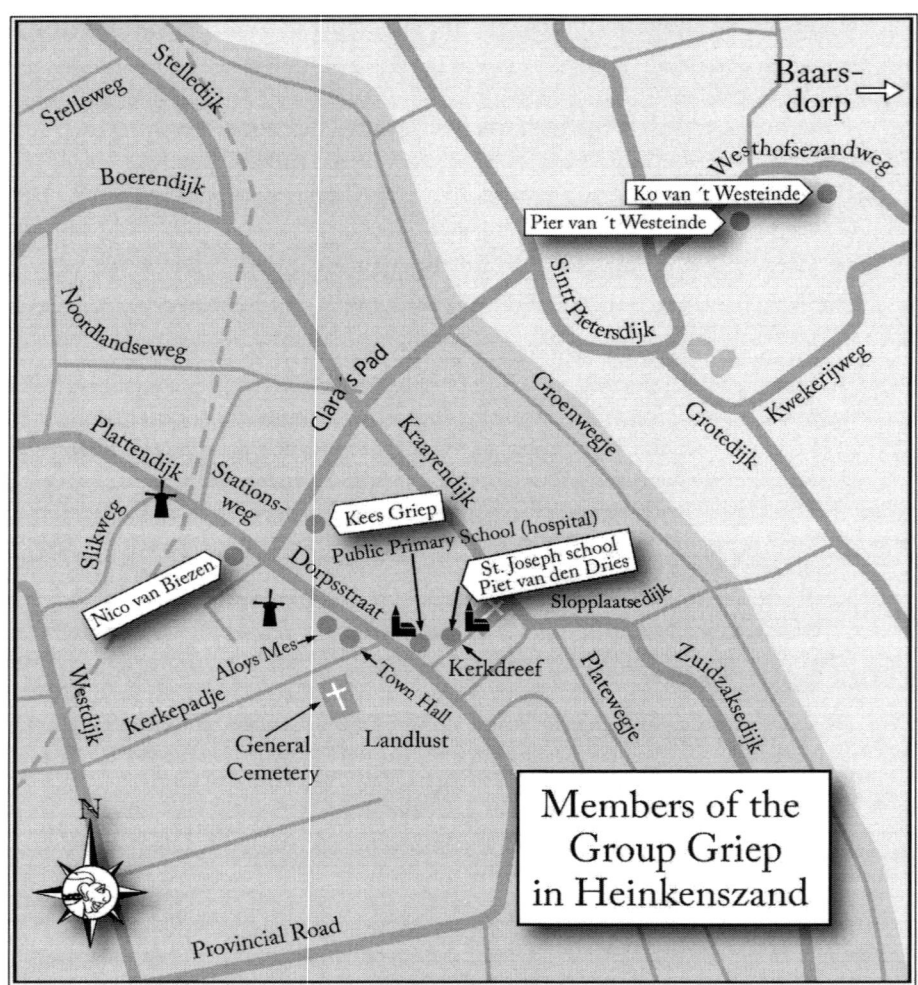

The large building on the left is the Public Elementary School that was turned into a hospital during the mobilization. On the right is the town hall of Heinkenszand. (012 - Mrs. Leu of Swaluw-Faes)

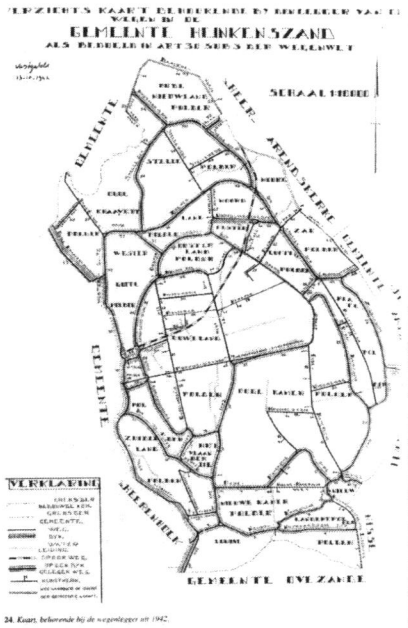

This 1942 map of Heinkenszand clearly shows that the village was formed by the clustering of polders. (011)

The mayor of Heinkenszand, Dr. Mr. Aloys (Lou) Mes. (014 - Catholic Documentation Centre)

A stolen bell from Kortgene, on which a white P is painted. (015 - Zeeland Library / Image Database Zeeland)

Lou Mes and Kees Griep on holiday on September 9, 1931 in Füssen, Germany, near the Austrian border. (015a)

The family of Kees Griep, jus after the war. L-R: Geert (boyfriend of Iet), Iet, Nanny, Corry, Kees, Attie and Pim. (016)

L-R: Nico van Biezen, Kees Griep and Piet van den Dries. (017, 018, 019)

L-R: Ko, Pier and their father Piertje van't Westeinde. (020, 021, 022)

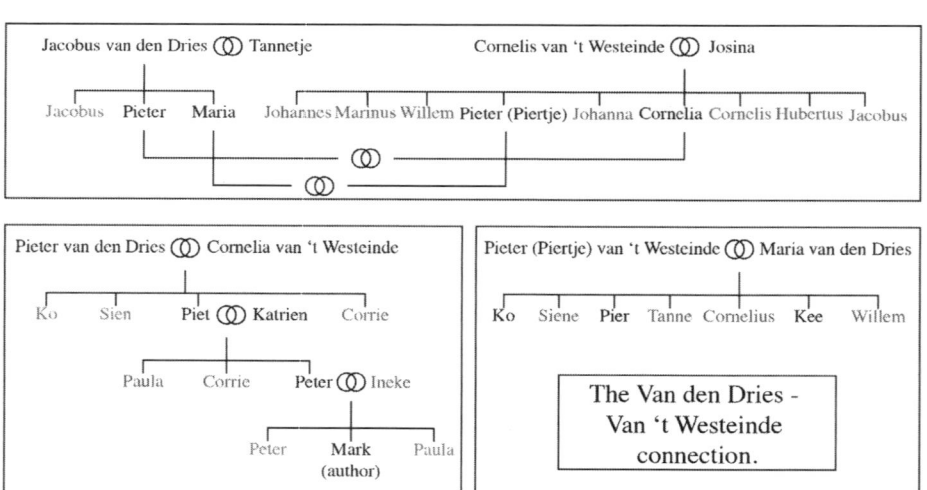

(022a)

The family of Ko van't Westeinde in 1943. L-R: Bas, Willem, Nele (in black mourning dress), Piet, Ko (father), Kees and Martien. (023)

On the left is the home of head master Piet van den Dries and on the right is the school. (024)

This is the gate of the former castle that marks the beginning of the Kerkdreef. On the end of this path is the St. Blasius Church. Piet lived in a house on the left side of this path. (025)

Kees Franse (025a and 025b)

Chapter 3

The Eagle leaves its nest

The 8th Air Force

When the Second World War began, the United States remained neutral although they gave the British material and financial support. American neutrality would not last for long. Because of the German aggression in Europe and the Japanese attack on Pearl Harbor, the US entered the war on two fronts. The main number of men and material went to Europe another large number went to the Pacific.

The United States Army Air Forces (USAAF), a component of the U.S. Army, was under the command of General Carl A. Spaatz. The 8th Air Force was one of sixteen Numbered Air Forces making up the Army Air Forces. It was later called the "The Mighty 8th." In January 1942, the 8th Air Force was organized to send bombers and fighters from the British Isles to conduct air attacks on the European continent.

Before the USAAF intervened, the British "Bomber Command" of the Royal Air Force (RAF) frequently targeted the mayor German industrial cities. Their aim was to break the German morale, to destroy the essential cogs of the German war machine and slow it down dramatically. Under the leadership of Air Chief Marshal Arthur Harris, Bomber Command employed the strategy of carpet-bombing, designed to systematically destroy 100% of the target. These missions were flown at night because the less agile British bombers were vulnerable to attacks from the German fighters.

The Americans saw no benefit to the strategy of carpet-bombing on German cities, which caused many civilian casualties. To be more effective the Americans wanted to destroy the German war industry by using precision bombing on factories. Their primary goals were factories making parts for submarines, aircraft, tanks, and other military equipment, and also oil refineries, marshaling yards, harbors and airports. They flew these missions in large formations, to minimize the large losses from enemy fighters. Several turrets, with edge machine guns protected the bombers. The B-17 Flying Fortress and its successor, the B-24 Liberator bombers flew these missions during daytime, so the crews could rely on line of sight to hit their targets.

Lieutenant General Ira C. Eaker commanded 8th Air Force and endorsed bomb missions without escort fighters despite heavy casualties and lost bombers. The many lost aircraft were unsustainable for the 8th Air Force. In January, 1944, Eaker was succeeded by Lieutenant General Jimmie H. Doolittle, who introduced a different strategy. To protect themselves from attacks by German fighters in the sky and anti aircraft artillery on the ground, the bombers were escorted by P-51 Mustangs, P-38 Lightnings and P-47 Thunderbolts, fast and agile fighters.

Although Bomber Command and the 8th Air Force did not have much confidence in each other's strategies, they complemented each other in an unparalleled air offensive against the German Reich. The Germans felt that they were in constant danger, day and night. Occasionally critical mistakes were made. On February 22, 1944, Nijmegen and Enschede, two cities in the east Netherlands near the German border, were mistakenly identified as German cities and bombed by U.S. aircraft. Despite these painful incidents, the combined strategy played a major role in the liberation of Europe.

392nd Bombardment Group

The 8th Air Force had three divisions that flew long-distance bombers. The 1st Bombardment Division flew the B-17 Flying Fortresses while the 2nd BD flew with B-24 Liberators. The 3rd BD initially flew both Flying Fortresses and Liberators, but because of the different flying speeds, which made a joined attack more difficult, all Liberators were transferred to the 2nd BD. From late 1943 on P-51 Mustangs usually escorted the bombers of the 2nd Bombardment Division because they had a longer range than the other fighters.

The 2nd Bombardment Division was divided into several Combat Bombardment Wings, which, in turn, were divided into Bombardment Groups. One of these groups was the 392nd Bombardment Group (Heavy). The term Heavy indicated the bombers were either Flying Fortresses or Liberators. Until June 1944 the 392nd was led by Colonel Irvine A. Rendle, followed by Col. Lorin L. Johnson until April 1945 and Col. Lawrence G. Gilbert for the rest of the war. These airmen wore a logo on their jackets, depicting a crusader riding a falling bomb. After the war, the bomb group was given the name *The Crusaders* by Colonel Robert E. Vickers in his book, *The Liberators from Wendling*. I will use this nickname from now on.

The Crusaders flew B-24H Liberators and were active from September 1943 to April 1945. They were part of the 14th Combat Bombardment Wing, stationed at Wendling Air Base, Station 118, in the eastern English county of Norfolk. In addition, the ground staff, the Crusaders consisted of four Bombardment Squadrons (BS); 576th BS, 577th BS, 578th BS and 579th BS. Each squadron supported an average of 12 Liberators. This number varied because many aircraft were lost and had to be replaced.

USAAF
(Numbered Air Forces)

1st Air Force Northeast United States	5th Air Force Philippines Australia Southwest Pacific	9th Air Force Middle East North Africa Europe	13th Air Force South Pacific
2nd Air Force Northwest United States	6th Air Force Caribbean Islands Panama South America	10th Air Force India Burma	14th Air Force China
3rd Air Force Southeast United States	7th Air Force Hawaii Central Pacific	11th Air Force Alaska	15th Air Force Mediterranean
4th Air force Southwest United States	**8th Air Force Europe**	12th Air Force North Africa Mediterranean	20th Air Force India/China Mariana Islands

8th Air Force
(Divisions)

1st Bombardment Division B-17 Flying Fortress Brampton Grange HQ Huntingdonshire	**2nd Bombardment Division B-24 Liberator Kettingham Hall HQ Norfolk**	3rd Bombardment Division B-17 Flying Fortress Elveden Hall HQ Suffolk

2nd Bombardment Division
(Combat Bombardment Wings)

2nd Combat Bombardment Wing	20th Combat Bombardment Wing	96th Combat Bombardment Wing
14th Combat Bombardment Wing	95th Combat Bombardment Wing	65th Fighter Wing

14th Combat Bombardment Wing
(Bombardment Groups)

44th Bombardment Group Shipdham Air Base	491st Bombardment Group North Pickenham Air Base
392nd Bombardment Group **Wendling Air Base**	492nd Bombardment Group Harrington Air Base

392nd Bombardment Group
(Bombardment Squadrons)

576th Bombardment Squadron	578th Bombardment Squadron
577th Bombardment Squadron	**579th Bombardment Squadron**

The B-24 Liberator

Militairy Aircraft of the USAAF had letter symbols, which indicated their purpose:

Attack	A	Photographic	F
Bombardment	B	Patrol Bomber	PB
Cargo (Transport)	C	Training, Primary	PT
Pursuit (Fighter)	P	Training, Basic	BT
Observation	O	Training, Advance	AT

In 1939, the American Consolidated Aircraft Corporation, commissioned by the U.S. Army, developed the four-engine B-24 Liberator, also called the Lib. The *B* in the name indicates Bombardment, *24* indicates it's the 24th bomber model built for the USAAF. A letter was added to indicate an improved version of the bomber. B-24D indicates the fourth version and B-24H the eight. The Liberator exceeded the Flying Fortress with a longer range of 1700 miles, a higher top speed of 300 miles per hour, and a higher maximum takeoff weight of 70,547 pounds (although trough safety and other modifications these statistics were somewhat reduced). Consolidated Aircraft Corporation incorporated many innovations into the design. The 64-foot aircraft included a three-point landing system, four 1,000 horsepower Pratt & Whitney R-1830 turbo supercharged radial engines, and a wingspan of 110 feet. It was equipped with a revolutionary fuel efficient wing shape, called the Davis Wing, a narrow-chord wing with low drag, a stable center of pressure, and lift at relatively small angles of attack. The new design was a success and other plants, such as Douglas and Ford, replicated the model in production. Although the fame of the Flying Fortress overshadowed the fame of the Liberator during the war, more Liberators rolled off the production line than any other aircraft. Consolidated Aircraft Company produced 18,482 Liberators.

The first Liberator had seven guns on board. When the first mass-produced Liberator, the B-24D, made its appearance in early 1943, three more guns were added bringing the number of the M2 Browning .50 caliber machine guns on board to ten. The B-24D did not have a maneuverable nose turret, but the B-24H version did. The 392nd BG was the first group to fly with these movable nose turrets, surprising the German fighters the first time they tried a head-on attack against the 392nd. Ford developed the B-24H at the Willow Run Assembly Plant in Michigan. This aircraft was 10 inches longer than its predecessor. It also had Plexiglas windows with a rotary mechanism on both sides. Other improvements were the bombardier's sight, an autopilot system, and a better fuel flow system.

To defend themselves against the German fighters, the B-24H was equipped with four turrets, each with two machine guns. The nose turret defended the front, the tail turret defended the back, and the top turret defended the aircraft against attacks from above. Protecting the underside was a rotatable turret, called the Sperry Ball Turret, named after the company that built it. Each turret was armed with two Browning .50 caliber machine guns that fired 750 to 850 bullets a minute, about 14 bullets a second.

To access the ball turret, the gunner would manually crank the guns straight down after takeoff. He could then open the hatch and climb in. Once inside, he turned on the turrets electrical and hydraulic power. Lying inside the turret in a fetal position, the gunner would sight between his legs, through the circular glass. The turret was powered by an electric motor, driven by two hydraulic units. One was for azimuth (sideways) and the other for elevation (up and down). Two handles controlled the turret. The firing buttons were placed on the upper surface of the handles. Liberator crews eventually removed the ball turrets because enemy fighters rarely attacked them from underneath the aircraft. Removal of the ball turret reduced drag and weight, increased the payload, and made it more fuel-efficient. For missions when heavy gun battles were expected they were reassembled and manned by a tenth man, the ball turret gunner.

Although the ball turret provided important protection for the underside of the bomber, it had many disadvantages. The turret was also the most vulnerable position in the bomber. The bulging turret was an easy target for German fighters or the dreaded anti-aircraft called *flak,* a German abbreviation for *FlugabwehrKanone.* When the bomber was hit and every second counted, it required enormous effort and time to climb out of the dome, grab and put on a parachute, and connect the harness hooks. If the landing gear was defective, requiring a belly landing, you would not want to be in the ball turret. Because enemy fighters rarely attacked the bombers from underneath, in 1944 the 8th Air Force decided to remove the 1,000 pounds weighing ball turrets in most Liberators. By doing this and welding a steel patch over the hole, they reduced drag and weight, increased the payload, and made it more fuel-efficient.

In spite of many improvements made to the B24H, the crew could not expect luxury or even safety. Most pilots had a love-hate relationship with this crude-looking bomber. The crews of the Flying Fortresses called the Liberator the *Flying Boxcar* or *Flying Coffin* and although that was to make fun of their B-24 colleagues, these nicknames were not far from the truth. Only the pilot and co-pilot had a safety belt and the interior was designed solely to provide space for all the necessary equipment. The crew thought it was a cantankerous, heavy, and unwieldy aircraft that was difficult to control. It required much muscle power to fly a Liberator for there was no power steering. The pathway to and from the back, called the *catwalk*, was so narrow a man could only cross by turning sideways. It was impossible to cross it wearing a parachute.

The only official entrance was a hatch in the back of the aircraft. The two doors that slid up along the fuselage when it opened and gave access to the bomb bay were a faster way to enter and exit. Members positioned in the front often climbed aboard through the narrow hole of the front wheel. This required agility, but got them right to the right position. To exit the bomber in flight there were more possibilities. The tail hatch and the bomb bay doors were the safest, but in case of emergency they could also bail out of a hatch in front of the top turret, the front wheel or even the waist window, but there was a great risk of hitting the stabilizers by doing that.

As mentioned, a Liberator flight was not for the faint of heart. The freezing wind blew through the wheel openings, the gaps on either side of the nose turret, and the bomb bay doors, which did not have weather stripping. Newer Liberators had rotatable Plexiglas windows protecting the waist gunner positions, but in earlier versions of the aircraft, gunners fired through two open bay windows, exposed to hurricane strength winds. At a high altitude temperatures ranged from 23 to -76°F. Only the cockpit was equipped with heaters, but they were defective most of the time or were removed, due to their dangerous proximity to the fuel lines. To stay warm, the crew wore electrically heated suits, gloves, and shoes, which frequently stopped functioning. They also wore heavy-duty flying suits, boots, and heavy gloves to prevent their hands from freezing to metal parts.

Not only was it very cold, the B-24 was not pressurized. At 10,000 feet most crews began to use the oxygen that was delivered through their masks, connected to oxygen tanks. Everything was carefully checked before takeoff, but in case of an emergency, caused by flak or fighter damage or a frozen oxygen supply line, they were forced to decrease the altitude. There were portable oxygen bottles on board, but they lasted only ten to fifteen minutes.

In the Liberator there was also no noise isolation and the crew had to endure the constant loud roar of the propellers. Even headphones and helmet flaps could not reduce the intensity of the noise. However, there was one advantage: the crew could not hear distant enemy shelling. They could only hear them when they were in the middle of the flak range.

Sometimes, after takeoff, gas leaks occurred, resulting in noxious fuel odors and accidents. The crew could not smoke until the gas fumes completely disappeared.

Initially the crewmembers had to fly 25 missions before they could return back home, but sometime in in the late spring/summer 1944 it was raised to 30. When the 8th Air Force achieved air superiority and casualties were reduced, it was raised to 35. The chance of surviving a combat tour was smallest at the beginning of the war but increased by the end. The crewmembers only had about 30% chance of succeeding all missions.

In the Pacific theater, the Liberator was employed both as bomber and cargo aircraft. It was equipped with radar, used to locate enemy submarines. In the European theater, Liberator crews bombed strategic targets, deep in enemy territory. Although heavily armed bombers flew in close formation supported by fighters, it was a hazardous job. The dreaded Messerschmitt Bf 109 (ME 109) and the Focke-Wulf (FW 190) both single-seat, single-engine fighters, were agile and could easily hit the slower, less agile bombers. A greater danger was the effective German ground fire. Because American bombers flew mostly in daylight, German flak could easily target American formations.

Despite these dangers, Air Force crews were all volunteers. Everyone had his own reasons. At that time, American men aged 18 to 46 were drafted, which almost always resulted in placement within the Army. To avoid the front line, many men opted to voluntarily register with the more appealing Air Force. Others volunteered to escape poverty and unemployment. Many second-generation immigrants, Poles, Czechs, Frenchmen, Italians, etc. signed up to fight for their old homeland and free it from fascist occupation. There were also men who were looking for adventure or just wanted to fly an aircraft.

1: The Consolidated Aircraft Company was founded in 1923 and was known for the development of flying boats like the PBY Catalina and the B-24 bomber in which many elements of the Catalina were applied.

The emblems of some of the units: L-R: USAAF, 8th Air Force, and the 392nd Bomb Group. (026, 027, 028)

A mural painting on the wall of the officer's mess at Wendling Air Base. (029 - www.b24.net)

The B-17 Flying Fortress. (030 - U.S. Air Force)

The B-24 H Liberator. (031 - U.S. Air Force)

Liberators at the Willow Run Assembly Plant in Michigan. (032 - U.S. Air Force)

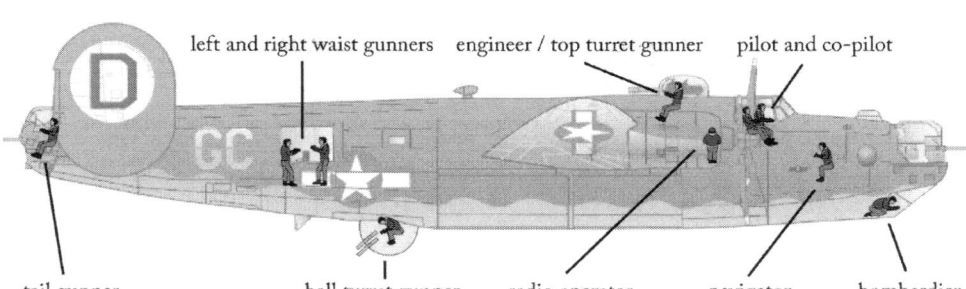

The positions of the crew in a B-24 Liberator. (033)

The B-24 Liberator *Poop Deck Pappy* of the Crusaders, recognized by the circle of the 2nd Bombardment Division and the letter D of the 392nd Bombardment Group. Under the aircraft you can see the retractable ball turret. (034 - www.b24.net)

The ball turret of a B-17. (035 - U.S. Air Force)

Left waist gunner S/Sgt. Loyce Ely in his flight suit. (036)

Two Liberators of the Crusaders on a mission. (037 - U.S. Air Force)

A Liberator on a mission to Germany. (038 - U.S. Air Force)

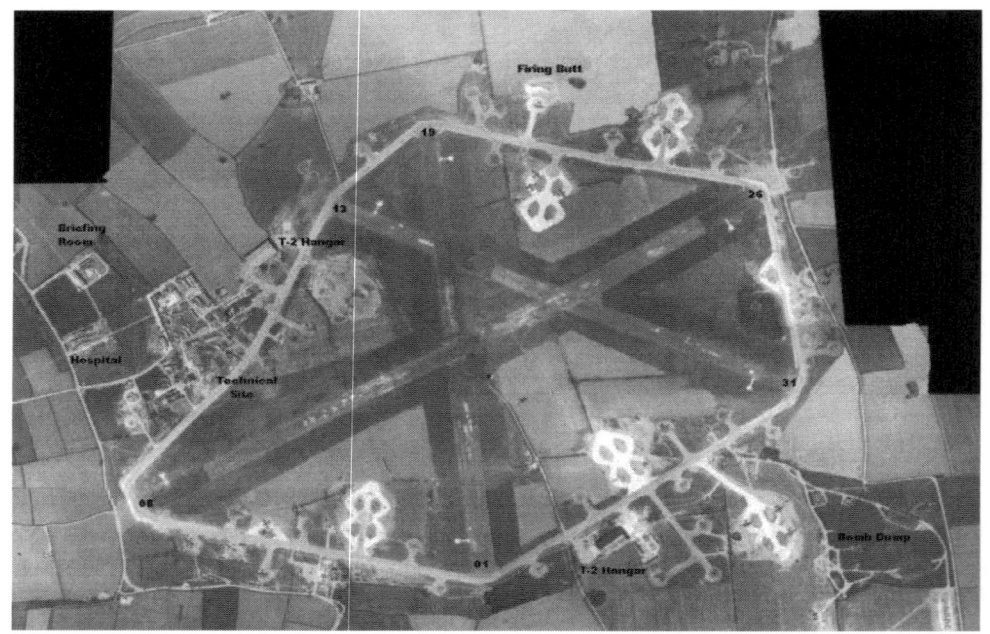

An aerial photo of Wendling Air Base. (038a – www.b24.net)

The control tower of Wendling Air Base. (038b – www.b24.net)

Chapter 4

Gerow's crew

In April 1944, ten young men gathered at the Pueblo Army Air Base (PAAB) in Colorado. On this base most crews were trained in the B-24 Liberator and some in the B-17 Flying Fortress. Later that year airmen on the base would also learn to fly the advanced B-29 Superfortress. At this training camp east of Pueblo, in the dry, dusty desert, the men were assigned to a crew. Before Pueblo the men were all trained for their assigned position at various schools. In the two and a half months of this final training, called Phase Training, they learned to work as a group, to rely on each other. Here they were forged into a cohesive team, a brotherhood of specialists learning how to tame this *Flying Boxcar* together. With this team they would soon face the horrors of war.

Information on this crew came from crewmember families, various databases and newspaper clippings with the exception of what Jim Gerow told me in his letter. In this book I use the air crewmembers' nicknames I found on the back of a group photo. According to family members these nicknames were also used at home. On Wendling crew lists, aircrews were usually named after their pilot.

Jim Gerow

23-year old Second Lieutenant (2/Lt) James A. Gerow was from Buffalo, New York. He was the pilot and crew commander. Jim, as he was usually called, enlisted on July 29, 1942, in Buffalo. Jim trained in five phases:

The first nine weeks of the Preflight Training at Maxwell Air Force Base in Alabama consisted of numerous tests, both physical and mental. Cadets were taught mathematics, theory of flight, ground operations, meteorology, navigation, aircraft recognition, physics, and Morse code. They also received physical training, running, marching, and weapon use. Those who successfully completed training became pilots. Those *washed out* were transferred to other training schools to become navigators, bombardiers, engineers, radio operators and gunners.

Jim's pilot training began during Primary Training at Hicks Field in Texas. Next to the theory lessons and the physical training, here he also received his first flying lessons in a PT-19 Cornell, a single-engine training aircraft. This training lasted nine weeks, containing 60-65 hours of flying time. It was followed by nine weeks (70 hours flying time) of Basic Training in a BT-13 Valliant, a single-engine training aircraft.

Jim received his next nine weeks (80 hours flying time) Advanced Training at Columbus Air Force Base in Mississippi. He flew the AT-17 Bobcat and the later version of the Bobcat, the UC-78 Bamboo Bomber, both twin-engine training aircraft. In December 1943, Jim received his Wings and was promoted to second lieutenant. In the same month, Jim married his fiancée, Delphine. At Hill Air Force Base in Salt Lake City, Utah, he trained on the B-24 Liberator, the four-engine bomber he would fly in Europe.

His final training, before leaving for Europe, was Phase Training at Pueblo Army Air Base (PAAB) in Colorado with his crew. This training lasted two and half months.

Fred Vallarelli

Jim's co-pilot was 25-year-old 2/Lt Frederick J. Vallarelli from Rye, New York. Fred came from a family of Italian immigrants. He enlisted on December 14, 1942 in New York City. Like Jim, he successfully completed all the above phases of pilot training.

Dave Grandon

21-year-old 2/Lt David P. Grandon was from La Salle, Illinois, and had three sisters. Dave got his high school degree at La Salle-Peru High School, and then studied at LaSalle-Peru-Oglesby (LPO) Junior College. He came from a family of newspaper publishers. Preston Grandon, Dave's father, was the editor of a local newspaper, *La Salle Daily Post-Tribune*, where Dave worked as an apprentice printer. On February 28, 1943, he enlisted in Chicago, then had to wait until November 28th to take the oath at Soldier's Field in Chicago. On January 30, 1944, his military service began. He was sent to Miami Beach, Florida for his training. In March, Dave moved to Western Reserve University in Cleveland, Ohio, for an aviator course he completed in May. After two months at the air base in Nashville, Tennessee, he went to Selman Field in Monroe, Louisiana, where he trained as a navigator-bombardier. In September 1943, he transferred to

Buckingham Field in Fort Myers, Florida, for a course in gunner training, completed by the end of November. On March 18, he returned to Monroe, LA where he received his Wings and was promoted to Second Lieutenant. Finally, he was sent to Pueblo, Colorado, assigned to Gerow's crew.

Joe Sulkowski

The bombardier of the crew was 23-year-old 2/Lt Joseph T. Sulkowski from Everson, Pennsylvania. Joe's parents were Polish immigrants. He was the oldest of eight children. In 1937, during the Great Depression, Joe attended high school in Scottdale, PA, close to Everson. He found no employment after graduation, so he joined the Civilian Conservation Corps (CCC), a government program for unemployed youth. The CCC was a semi-military organization, in which the men wore uniforms, slept in barracks, and worked six days a week. They were paid $30 a month, with $25 sent to their families. This helped to ease the poverty caused by the Great Depression.

Leaving the CCC in 1939, Joe worked in the R. E. Uptegraff Manufacturing Company transformer factory in Scottdale, with his father and his brother, Vincent. Although he was trained as a welder, he was hired to wind transformer coils and, later, as a mechanic. The German invasion of Poland in September 1939 had an enormous impact on his family, who had relatives and friends living there. From the Blitzkrieg to the attack on Pearl Harbor, there was very little reported in the news about the situation in Europe. The family was very worried. Joe and his brother were exempt from military service because the Uptegraff Company was a major supplier for the U.S. Army.

On December 3, 1942, Joe joined the Air Force, sister, Cecilia, became a nurse in the Army Nurse Corps in February 1943, 17 year old brother, Vincent, was allowed to take his High School exam early, and in March 1944, he joined the Navy where he worked as an electrician on a minesweeper. At the end of the war, Joe's brother, Walt, enlisted as a cadet in in the Air Force and was trained to be a navigator, but the war ended before he completed the training.

Joe's enlistment took place in Pittsburgh. He later wrote: "*One day I had a double date, together with a friend. We went to a movie in town with our girls. When we came back from the cinema, my friend asked me, 'Hey, Joe, the girls went shopping, what are we going to do?' I said: 'No idea, do you know of something to do?' He said: 'I thought some tests were going on in town, you coming?'*"

The Air Force administered the forty minute Army General Classification Test (AGCT) to measure intelligence and talent on the basis of 150 multiple-choice questions. On a whim Joe took the test and scored well above average, while his friend failed. The Air Force recruitment officer was impressed and offered Joe an opportunity to go to an Officer Training School (OTS), an offer that Joe took seriously. He wanted to become a bombardier. Being in the Air Force gave Joe the opportunity to avenge the invasion of his family's country. A bombardier had command of the entire aircraft while dropping his bombs. Bombardier training was intense and lasted longer than pilot training. The USAAF was experiencing a shortage of pilots due to the many aircraft losses in Europe, and encouraged Joe to become a pilot. But his mind was made up and he successfully completed bombardier training.

Morton Baker

The radio operator, the 23-year-old Staff Sergeant (S/Sgt) Morton Baker was born to a Jewish family in Manhattan, New York. When he was drafted, his mother, Rose, and a married sister, Jeanette were listed as next of kin. Morton was married to Mildred P. Hyman, in Brooklyn, New York. After graduating from high school, Morton worked in the damp room of the Cascade Laundry for a year. On December 24th 1942, he received his U.S. Army ID card. From February 1943 until July 1943 he trained at the Classification Centre (N.A.A.C.) in Nashville, Tennessee. Then in Dec 1943 he trained to become a radio mechanic in Sioux Falls, South Dakota, followed by training at Salt Lake City, Utah and Camp Kearns, Utah. On June 8th, he was transferred to Pueblo, Colorado. While a member of the crew, he was promoted to Technical Sergeant.

Eugene Kieras

Sergeant (Sgt) Eugene (Gene) J. Kieras was 20 years old and the youngest member of the crew. Like Dave Grandon, he came from La Salle, Illinois. He was both the flight engineer and a top turret gunner of the crew. In the event of a crewmember's death or injury, the engineer was required to take over any position, from gunner to pilot. Gene's father, John, was a veteran of the First World War. Gene had four brothers, Stanley, Edward, Ernest, and Raymond, who all served during the war. Gene was drafted in Peoria, Illinois, on April 9, 1943. In June, he was sent to the Aviation Mechanics School at Keesler Field in Mississippi and promoted to Private First Class.

On October 31, he received his diploma from the B-24 Liberator Bomber Mechanics School. Because he was also a top turret gunner, he trained as a gunner at the Flexible Gunnery School at Tyndall Field, Florida. On January 18, 1944, after completing gunnery training, he received his Wings and was promoted to the rank of corporal. After a few days of leave, he departed for Pueblo, Colorado, where he was assigned to Jim Gerow's crew. While a member of the crew, he was promoted to Staff Sergeant and later to Technical Sergeant.

Loyce Ely

26-year-old S/Sgt Loyce E. Ely was from Corcoran, California, and was the left waist gunner on Gerow's crew. He was the only crewmember from the West Coast. Everyone (including himself) called him by his surname, Ely (pronounced E-lee). Ely grew up in Quanah, Texas, 192 miles northwest of Fort Worth, and a few miles from the Oklahoma-Texas state line. He lived on a farm with his parents and had four brothers and four sisters. One of Ely's sisters died of diphtheria at age six. During the depression, Ely worked on the farm, and any other available jobs. In 1935, when he was 20 years old, the family moved to Corcoran where he and his father joined the Works Project Administration (WPA), an initiative established in 1935 by President Roosevelt to create jobs. Ely got a permanent job at the J.G. Bosswell Company, a large cotton construction company, where he worked as a truck driver and mechanic. On October 19, 1942, Ely was drafted in Fresno, California. He was sent to Laredo Air Base in Texas and Tyndall Field in Florida for gunner training. His brother, Gene, ended up in the Army, where he worked as a military policeman in Europe.

Ben Brink

S/Sgt Benjamin (Ben) E. Brink, the 24-year-old right waist gunner, came from the mountainous region of Irvona, Pennsylvania. He was the son of Samuel and Edith Brink. Ben's father worked in a clay mine and then as a fireman for the railroad. Ben's younger brother, Robert, was in the Army. He had three younger sisters, Grace, Norma and Evelyn. A few months after he graduated high school, Ben was enlisted in December 8, 1939 in Clearfield, Pennsylvania. At first Ben was trained to become a medic in the Army, but in 1943 he began his gunner training in the Air Force.

Normand Hebert

S/Sgt Norman B. Hebert was the 25-year-old tail gunner who manned the rear turret. He was from Woonsocket, Rhode Island, and the son of J. Arthur Hebert and Laura Duval Hebert. Because of his French-Canadian ancestry, the crew called him *Frenchy*. He had six brothers and two sisters. Two of his brothers served during WWII, and two more during Korea. Edgar was a flight instructor in the Air Force and saw action in North Africa. Paul was in the Navy and served on board the destroyer *USS Gherardi* (*DD-637*). On D-Day, the Gherardi was part of Admiral Don P. Moon's Assault Force *U*, for Utah Beach. Normand enlisted in the Army in 1935, when he was seventeen. He was anxious to join the fight and on December 10, 1941, three days after the attack on Pearl Harbor, he enrolled in the Air Force at Fort Benning, Georgia. He received his training at Tyndall Field, Florida. After transferring to Pueblo, Colorado, he joined Gerow's crew. He met and married Juanita J. Dudley in Pueblo.

Stan Davidoski

Ball turret gunner Staff Sergeant S/Sgt Stanley E. Davidoski came from Douglas County, in the north of Wisconsin. Stan was 34 years old and the oldest of the team. According to his files he only got his education on Grammar School. He enlisted on March 31, 1942 in Wausau, Wisconsin.

After completing training in Pueblo, the ten crewmen were transferred to Topeka Army Air Field in Kansas for medical and fitness testing. From Topeka they traveled by train to Camp Shanks, 30 miles up the Hudson River from New York City. This camp was called *Last Stop USA* for in the harbor the troop ship *RMS Queen Mary*, one of the largest passenger ships of her day, was waiting. On June 7th, the men, with their heavy duffel bags on one shoulder, embarked and the ship that took them to the distant European war arena.

The journey on the crowded ship lasted five days and twelve hours. It passed through the Firth of Clyde and entered the port of Gourock, on the south bank of the River Clyde in Scotland. From there they went to the former RAF airfield Cluntoe Air Base in Northern Ireland, one mile from the village Ardboe near the western shore of Lough Neagh, the largest lake in Northern Ireland. USAAF Station 238, as it was officially called, housed the No. 2 Combat Crew Replacement Center (2nd CCRC), which was opened in November 1943. The crews came to Cluntoe to brush up their tactics and practice formation flying. But basically they waited until a bomb group in England had casualties that needed to be replaced. That would become the bomb group where they were assigned. On July 20th the crew was sent to AAF Station Greencastle, also in Northern Ireland, for some further training. Ball turret gunner Stan Davidoski left the crew to be assigned to another bomb group. He flew twenty missions for both the 8th AF and 15th AF (Italy).

The rest of the Liberator crew traveled southeast to Wendling Air Base. This American base, near the village of Beeston, was the most northern base of the 8th Air Force. It was home to the 392nd Bomb Group. The men were assigned to the 579th Bombardment Squadron led by Squadron Commander, Major Myron H. Keilman.

Initially, Wendling Air Base was designed for the RAF Bomber Command, but in 1942, was assigned to the 8th Air Force. The American flag was raised for the first time on September 14, 1943. Once in American hands, residents were visited by hundreds of American military men on their rickety bicycles, who roamed the local shops, especially the nearby pubs like the *Ploughshare Pub* in Beeston. The base population grew to 2800 men. Over the course of the war, more than 3,400 men served in the ground crew and more than 2,300 combat airmen served at Wendling. Noted historian Roger Freeman said: *"For every combatant in 8th Air Force there were 20 personnel in a supporting ground role."*

While settling into designated *Nissen* huts (a variant of the *Quonset* hut) the crewmen might have wondered what happened to the men that had slept in their beds before them. The simple, semi-circular huts of corrugated steel were cheap and easy to assemble. They were also cold and windy, heated by a single coal stove in the middle of the hut. Several huts shared a latrine, showers, and sinks. The officers and NCO's slept in separate huts. The officers' huts had four beds, while the NCOs' huts had six beds. The base also included three runways, a perimeter taxiway, two large maintenance hangars, a bomb dump, fuel dumps with a capacity of 144,000 Imperial gallons, several offices, ammunition warehouses, various shelters, a hospital, a water tower, a swimming pool, officer/enlisted clubs, lots of maintenance facilities, and much more.

The new crews did not immediately participate in the missions. In the beginning of the war, American losses were so high that new crews could not be deployed quickly enough, but now, there were fewer aircraft losses and less need for fresh crews. So the new crews continued their theory training and flight training. They also received classroom training on survival in hostile territory after a crash. Experts were often present for the lessons. They were ordinary airmen lucky enough to have escaped captivity with assistance from local resistance groups. These men willingly shared their experiences with the new arrivals. After class the trainees reported to a makeshift photography studio. Because military men were forbidden to own civilian clothes, perhaps to make desertion more difficult, the studio was filled with shirts, jackets and ties that the men could borrow for this occasion. A photo of them in civilian clothes was taken, a picture they had to carry at all times. If the need arose, any resistance group could use the photo to fabricate a fake ID for them. Since all the airmen on the base wore the same clothes on the photos, German intelligence could soon identify which bomb group an American prisoner of war flew with, because of the clothes he was wearing in his photos.

After the lectures, flight training followed in which the crew sharpened their skills flying over the rural English countryside with its farmland and small village hamlets. They practiced shooting, dropping blue painted concrete practice bombs, and especially flying close together in large formations.

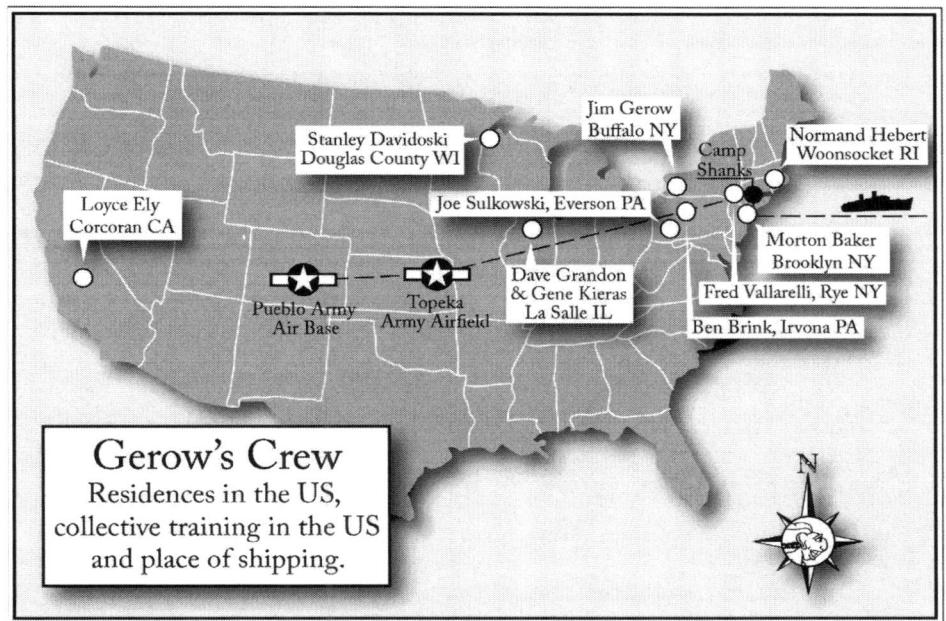

(039)

A group photo from April 1944, taken at the Pueblo Army Air Base in Colorado. Standing L-R: S/Sgt Benjamin E. Brink, S/Sgt Normand B. Hebert, S/Sgt Morton Baker, S/Sgt Stanley E. Davidoski, Sgt Eugene J. Kieras, S/Sgt Loyce E. Ely. Kneeling L-R: 2/Lt David P. Grandon, 2/Lt Joseph T. Sulkowski, 2/Lt James A. Gerow and 2/Lt Frederick J. Vallarelli. (040)

Standard sleeping quarters on Wendling Air Base. (041, 042 - www.b24.net)

A camouflaged bomb depot in a forest near Wendling Air Base. (043 - www.b24.net)

The cockpit of a B-24 Liberator. (044)

  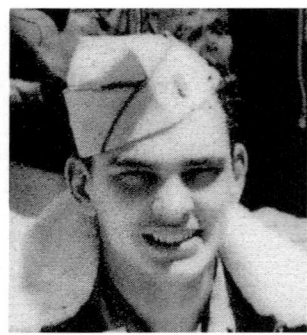

L-R: Jim Gerow, Fred Vallarelli and Dave Grandon. (045, 046, 047)

L-R: Joe Sulkowski, Morton baker and Gene Kieras. (048, 049, 50)

L-R; Loyce Ely, Ben Brink and Normand Hebert. (051, 052, 053)
Left: Stan Davidoski. (053a)

A lesson in reading maps. (054 - U.S. Air Force)

Gun training in a top turret. (055 - U.S. Air Force)

The position of a navigator. (056 - www.b24.net)

The positions of the two waist gunners. (057 - U.S. Air Force)

STUDENT PASS — LAREDO, TEXAS

DATE 12/28/42 LAAF — No. 5/46

ELY, LOYCE E. — Pvt.

NAME — GRADE

GOOD ONLY ON SATURDAY AND SUNDAY

PASS EXPIRES Jan. 31, 1943

DATE

PRIVILEGE TO VISIT NUEVO LAREDO, MEXICO

ONLY ON Jan. 9 & 10, 1943

DATE

COMMANDING

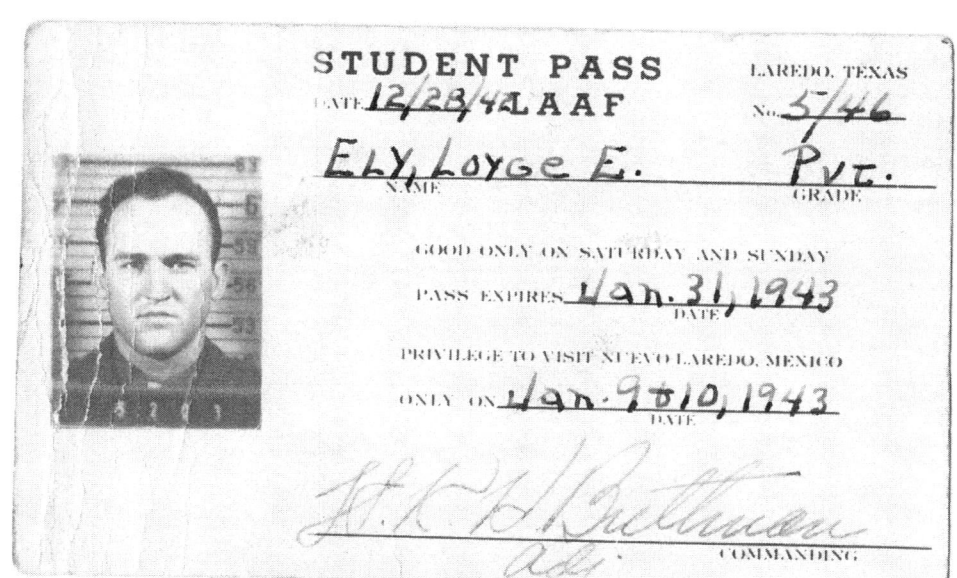

A pass for recruits from the Laredo Air Base in Texas. Ely was trained as a gunner on this air base. The pass was used during the weekends to cross the border to the Mexican city Nuevo Laredo. (060)

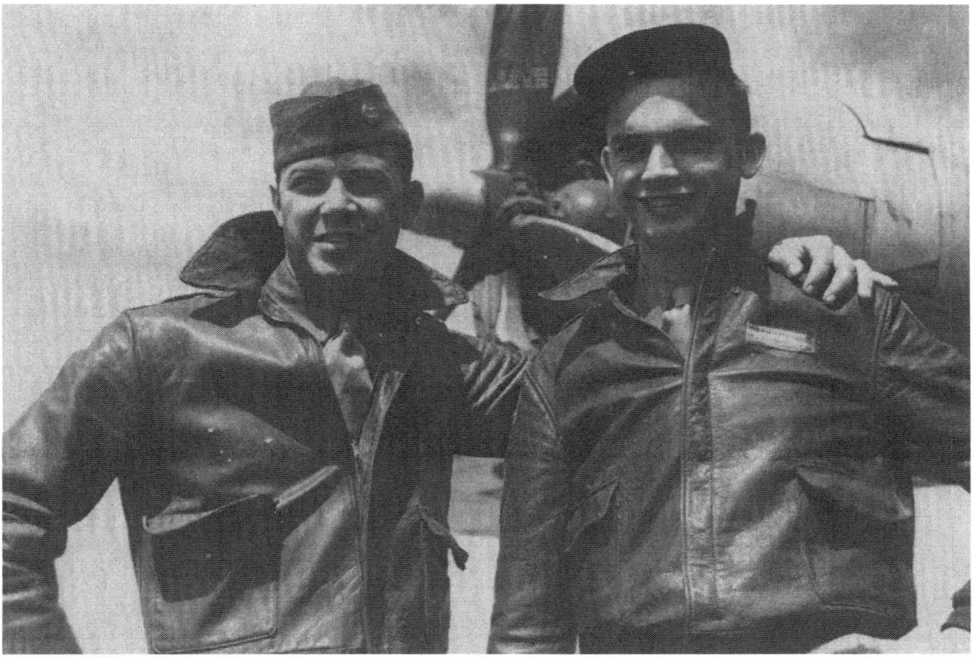

Dave Grandon and Joe Sulkowski at the Pueblo Army Air Base. (059)

Dave Grandon in Pueblo, Colorado. (058)

Chapter 5

The Bridge

In June 1944, the members of the Group Griep listened with great interest to their secret radios. They heard the voice of BBC newsreader, John Snagge, in his program *War Report* describing the June 6th allied invasion on the beaches of Normandy. The U.S. Commanding General Dwight D. Eisenhower led the joint operation. The American troops were under command of General George S. Patton while Field Marshal Bernard L. Montgomery led the British troops. The members of the resistance group in Heinkenszand also heard reports of the devastating effects of V1 rockets fired on England and were disappointed when they learned of the failed assassination attempt on Adolf Hitler, committed by *Oberst* (Colonel) Claus von Stauffenberg on July 20th.

On June 6, 1944, *Operation Overlord*, better known as *D-Day*, began. The German troops in the province of Zeeland were in turmoil. The residents witnessed long columns of soldiers heading south towards Belgium to crush the Allied advance in France. Hitler's Germany had every reason to worry. In September 1943, when Italy surrendered to the Americans, the Germans lost an important ally. For the first time the RAF and US-AAF can bomb targets in eastern Germany from air bases in Italy. In addition, Russian troops began to gain ground in Eastern Europe. Now there were even allied forces on French soil. The German Empire began to crumble, but it was far from defeated.

Progress was made on the European battlefield with *Operation Cobra*, an operation in which the allied troops fought to expand their position in Normandy. Allied bombers tried to weaken German positions in the area. Despite allied losses caused by friendly fire air strikes, Operation Cobra was a success, and the Allied advance through France began. The 392nd Bomb Group from Wendling also participated in the operation. In July, they successfully bombed targets along a strategically important road in the French town of Saint Lô. On August 2nd, they flew a second mission to France to bomb a bridge over the Somme River near the village of Corbie. A thick mist prevented the attack, so they choose to hit secondary targets. They observed no enemy fighters that day, but the accurate German flak caused considerable damage that day. The 579th bomb squadron was hit hard. Three of their bombers crashed on English territory, killing a co-pilot and a flight engineer on different planes.

On the morning of August 3rd, pilot Jim Gerow awoke his non-commissioned officers in their hut on Site 8, located in the heart of the English hamlet of Beeston. Next to site 8 was a farm where the soldiers of the squadrons sometimes performed chores in exchange for fresh milk and eggs. But many eggs were *liberated* during the night as well as the cow being milked when the farmer arrived in the morning. The men of the crew probably did not sleep well that night. The day before, they saw their captain's name on the flight manifest. They read the name with mixed feelings. They did not yet know whether it would be another training flight over the rustic English countryside, or an actual mission. The atmosphere was tense. They had about five hours between reveille and taking off for a mission. After they washed, shaved (to ensure a tight fit for their oxygen masks) and dressed, they walked together to the mess hall where they could spend an hour on their breakfast. Waist gunner Ely and flight engineer Gene had become good friends. They walked with waist gunner Ben, radio operator Morton, and tail gunner Frenchy to the mess for the enlisted personnel, while pilot Jim, co-pilot Fred, bombardier Joe and navigator Dave went to the officers' mess. Instead of scrambled eggs made from dried egg powder, they all were served fresh eggs for breakfast. Only mission crews got fresh eggs, so this had to be the day! In the rear of he mess awaited the Catholic and Protestant chaplains for spiritual aid. During breakfast, the squadron commanders handed out the Daily Bulletins to the men with new and stricter regulations[1]. It is doubtful the men were receptive to the information while they were eating their breakfast, because they also heard news about two fallen colleagues in their squadron. Most of the time the fate of men who did not return was uncertain. Had they been killed or taken prisoner? Had they escaped and were hiding somewhere? The news hit them hard. Missing airmen were not uncommon, but a dead colleague strengthened the realization that each mission, including the first, could be the last.

Between 1300 and 1400 hours[2], 34 crews at Wendling, including nine of the 579th BS, received their main briefing. The highlight of the briefing was the revealing of the mission map. While the crewmen held their breath, a curtain was drawn from left to right, first revealing England and the home bases and then the flight routes and targets. The men were told that the mission was part of Operation Cobra. The 392nd BG would support this operation by bombing an oil refinery near Lens, in the French department Pas-de-Calais. The mission would involve 482 Liberators, escorted by 178 Mustang and Thunderbolt fighters, stationed at various air bases in England. No secondary target was designated. In the event the primary target was not visible, they were often given a second option. Two target options maximized the efficiency of the mission. It was also dangerous for the crew to return to home base with a full load. If something went wrong during the landing, (these accidents did happen) the bomber could catch fire and the bombs could explode, causing considerable damage to the air base. If no alternative target was found during the mission, the bombs were dropped into the sea, if possible. Since there were no secondary targets on this mission, the crews were ordered to bomb any enemy airfield, camp, railway, bridge, column or convoy, concentration of troops, or equipment they could find. The crewmen were also told about the mission procedures, weather conditions and the expected danger of flak and fighters. During the briefing they also received instructions on emergency landing spots and what to do after bailing out over enemy territory: *"Instead of wandering around to find the lines yourself, keep your head down and hide until the allied troops have reached you. Retreating Germans have a habit of evacuating people and to investigate every house that they encounter. If you're outside, you must behave as inconspicuously as possible, like a citizen. If you're hiding, do it as carefully as possible. It is very dangerous if you are found while you're hiding. If you manage to escape, do not tell any war correspondents or any unauthorized person whatsoever."* The briefing came to an end after a *time hack* to synchronize the watches.

After the crew briefing, navigators and bombardiers went to additional briefings for map planning, marking flak positions and developing a flight plan. The gunners had their own briefing where they were instructed about the target and the route and when they could expect the escorting fighters. Radio operators were instructed about the codes and frequencies that were used that day.

After briefing, Gerow's crew first went to fetch their flying equipment in the personal equipment room. They were given escape kits with foreign money, maps, matches and other items useful in case of evasion. The moments between briefing and mission were emotionally difficult. They knew their mission and were eager to act, but now they had to wait. During these moments, doubt and fear kicked in. They realized all too well, the odds were they would never see their families again. Army chaplains tried to ease their minds. Senior officers arrived to boost their morale. The crewmembers were relieved when they finally got the order to assemble at their Liberator, *Our Gal*. The ground crew had loaded this bomber with twelve 500-pound general-purpose[3] bombs, known as M64. Liberator crews did not always fly the same aircraft. They flew any available bomber. Sometimes they were assigned a brand new and improved aircraft. They were just as likely to fly an aging and refurbished airplane that had logged many hours in the air. While the ground crew were working on the bomber to be ready for the mission, the men stared in amusement at the painting on the nose of the bomber, a scantily dressed blonde looking coyly over her shoulder while stepping into a mailbag.

Waist gunners Ely and Ben had to install their own guns, while the guns in the turrets were installed by the ground crew.

The crew first walked around the bomber for a visual check and went to their positions. Meticulously they checked their instruments and weapons, and carefully read the mission orders again. Assisted by the ground crew, flight engineer Gene Kieras checked the entire aircraft for technical defects. After these preflight checks were complete the men put on their flight suits. Because they would fly at high altitudes, they dressed for the extreme cold. They wore long underwear under the pants and the shirt. Over the basic uniform, they wore a thick, electrically heated jacket and pants that limited their mobility and responsiveness, but were essential to protect them from freezing at high altitude. Over that they wore a bomber jacket and wide trousers. Finally, they put on a yellow, inflatable lifejacket called a *Mae West*, named after the famous and generously endowed diva.

The men also wore a parachute harness. There was little room in the plane especially in the turrets, for the crew and their equipment. While boarding, the belly parachute was hand carried and not immediately hooked to the harness. Because it restricted their movement, the crewmembers placed it nearby, in the hope they had enough time to grab it and hook it up in an emergency. Pilots and co-pilots often wore flat parachute bundles on their backs that covered the buttocks, so they could sit on them during the flight.

Gunners wore a flak jacket, a type of bulletproof vest, made of ballistic nylon with metal slats underneath. This armor offered limited protection against bullets and flak shrapnel. Over thick socks they wore heated felt shoes, over which they wore thick lined boots. They wore gloves to protect their hands and, depending on their flight position, a second pair of mittens. A leather helmet with a built-in headphone protected the head. They wore goggles and an oxygen mask with a microphone to allow them to communicate with each other. Because off the loud noise of the engines, communication was only possible through the interphone, an open circuit, so everyone could hear what the other said. When the interphone was damaged by flak or fighter bullets, men positioned far from the damage were sometimes not aware that the bomber was in trouble until they saw the smoke and flames.

After they had checked the parachute harness, the parachute pack, the Mae West and the flak jackets, the crew was ready to board the bomber. Pilot Jim Gerow, co-pilot Fred Vallarelli and engineer Gene Kieras climbed through one of the doors of the bomb bay and took their positions in the cockpit. Jim took his place in the left seat. It was his job to control the aircraft and command the crew. Fred sat in the right seat. When necessary, he would take over for the pilot.

For takeoff Gene was positioned between Jim and Fred. The flight engineer was in charge of all technical operations. He was required to fix all technical defects and, if necessary, act as top turret gunner, operating two machine guns. When a crewmember was killed or got injured, the engineer was required to take over any position in the bomber. He also manned the top turret when needed. The top turret was located behind the cockpit and above the radio operator desk.

Bombardier Joe Sulkowski, Navigator Dave Grandon, and Radio Operator Morton Baker wriggled through the narrow, front wheel opening. For takeoff Dave and Joe were positioned on the flight deck. During the mission Joe's position was in the nose of the aircraft. It was his job to determine when to drop the bombs. He used a bomb targeting system called the Norden Bomb Sight, a device named after the Dutch inventor Carl Norden. The device was highly classified and the bombardier took an oath to protect the device with his life. When the bombardier neared his target, he took command of the Liberator from the pilot, and, with the press of a button, dropped the bombs. In addition to this task, Joe manned two machine guns in the nose turret. He was trained to take over any gunner position as well as the task of navigator.

During the mission Dave Grandon, the navigator was positioned in the front of the aircraft, near the cockpit. Dave had a table, lamp, various maps and charts, compass, radio, and other equipment at his disposal. A glass dome, the astrodome, was mounted overhead, for use in navigating by the stars at night. This he rarely needed because most American bombing missions were conducted during the day. It was Dave's responsibility to determine the whereabouts of the aircraft and to calculate the flight route to the target and back to Wendling.

During takeoff radio operator Morton Baker was at his desk behind the co-pilot, where also his radio equipment was located. He established a radio link with other aircraft in formation and the home base. To avoid revealing their location to the enemy, he used code names during communication. For example, the code name of the Wendling control tower was *BUTTERMILK* and the code name for the 14th Combat Wing was *HAMBONE*. The Crusaders were designated as *NOT NOW*.

The numbers and letters painted on the aircraft were an identity code. On the tail rudder of the Crusaders was a *D* inside a circle (the light blue *D* for the 392nd BG and the white circle for the 2nd Bombardment Division). Gerow's 579th BS was designated as *FACE UP*, with *GC* painted on the tail. A letter indicated an individual aircraft, sometimes with the addition of a dash or a plus, for example *B* or *Z+*. The last three digits of the aircraft serial number were visible on the rudder.

Both sides used codes and nicknames in battle. The Americans called the enemy fighters *Bandits*, while the Germans called American fighters *Indianer* (Indians) and bombers *Kuriere* (Couriers).

Gunners Ely, Ben and Frenchy climbed through the rear hatch or the opened doors of the bomb bay to the waist. While Ely and Ben stayed in the waist, Frenchy climbed into the tail turret so he could watch for planes coming too closely while taxiing. The B-24 had two Plexiglas side windows with rotating devices for their guns. From these positions on each side, gunners fired their .50 machine guns. Loyce operated the left side gun, Ben the right one. Frenchy in the tail turret, defended the vulnerable rear of the aircraft against approaching enemy fighters.

In the control tower the Group Operations Officer directed the takeoffs. After all squadrons had started their engines, a green flare was fired from the control tower as a signal to start taxiing. Jim signaled to the ground crew to pull away the wheel chocks and started taxiing to their place in the queue on the taxiway. The noise of all these engines and squeaking of the breaks was deafening. At 1620 hours a green light flashed from the checkered Flying Control trailer, a go-ahead signal for the leading bomber to takeoff. After the bomber before him took off, it was Our Gal's turn to get in position. Pilot Jim released his brakes and headed down to the runway while co-pilot Fred set all the throttles for maximum power and engineer Gene checked the instruments. It took about 3,000 feet for a B-24 to takeoff, but most of the time they used the whole runway to gain maximum speed. Once in the air the crewmembers moved to their assigned positions. Our Gal kept straight for about two minutes before heading to the group assembly area. The squadrons of the 392nd BG formed the formation behind their strikingly painted assembly ship, *Minerva*, which orbited a radio beacon at the prescribed altitude and fired colored flares. This aircraft was painted with two additional noses, creating an optical illusion of three Liberators flying together.

The 8th Air Force used various formations schemes known as *Combat Box Formations*. These consisted of a number of smaller formations. In 1944 the B-24 crews often used this variation: (from small to large):

1: *Element Formation*: (aka *Flight*) three bombers flying next to each other: high, lead and low bomber.
2: *Squadron Formation*: two Elements.
3: *Group Formation*: three Squadrons: high, lead and low squadron.
4: *Wing Formation*: three Groups: high, lead and low group.

The formation varied depending on the number of aircraft available. Assembling and flying in a formation was not easy for the bomb and fuel loaded bombers; even the slightest mistake could cause fatal collisions with another bomber. During the war 89 men of the Crusaders were killed in action while forming up.

Once the formation was in place, *Minerva* returned to Wendling and the Crusader formation headed to the Wing and Division assembly areas to team up with the other bomb groups. After all the bombers were gone, the ground crews took their rest, for when the bombers returned they had a lot of work to do.

Ely, who was assigned to be the armorer-gunner, hooked himself on a portable oxygen tank while the bomber was flying over English Channel. Wearing his bulky suit he went through the small door and walked over the narrow catwalk past the two bomb bays, to remove all the safety pins and serial number tags on the bombs. Because doing this with an oxygen bottle in your hand was very difficult, most armorer-gunners simply learned to hold their breath. Walking over the narrow catwalk was not easy, when Ely would misjudge a step and fell onto the doors he could easily fall through them, because they could only hold about 90 pounds.

After he returned he and the other gunners test-fired their air-cooled Browning .50 caliber guns, cautious of not hitting another bomber of course. They only fired with short burst so the gun barrels were not overheated.

The sky over the sea was partly clear that day, but over French territory, heavy clouds severely limited the view of the primary target. Thirteen aircraft returned unsuccessfully, two due to technical defects and eleven due to the weather. Because they crossed the Channel and flew over enemy territory, the mission was considered a complete mission. This meant crews could add this one to their number of required missions.

Two squadrons of 21 aircraft opted for an alternative objective. One of these aircraft was Our Gal.

Dr. Kees Griep was on his way home after checking on a patient in Kruiningen. Although skies in France were overcast, it was a beautiful summer day in the Netherlands, 68 degrees F, a gentle breeze and clear skies. He drove his gas fueled Fiat over the Vlake Bridge, the main connection between Zuid-Beveland and the rest of the Netherlands. The bridge, consisting of a railway bridge and a road bridge, connected the two banks of the Canal through Zuid-Beveland. It was an important link to the Netherlands, and was strictly controlled. Kees was a doctor and he had a special permit, so he easily passed the German roadblock. At the end of the bridge he passed a second roadblock and drove quietly toward Heinkenszand. Suddenly he was startled by humming in the distance, followed by artillery fire and heavy explosions behind him. Kees checked the bridge in his rearview mirror, stepped on the gas, and thanked God he had not left a minute later.

Radio Operator Morton Baker learned over the radio the secondary target was a strategic bridge in the Netherlands. Destroying this bridge could seriously impede the German transport of equipment and troops to German fortifications on Walcheren, a part of the heavily fortified Atlantic Wall. Walcheren also allowed access to the deep-water port of Antwerp. On July 8th, the Vlakebrug was initially bombed. Due to the many flak positions around this important bridge, they had to fly on a high altitude, causing the bombing to be a moderate success. There were, however, four people dead and two wounded in other crews. These two lost a leg. Although the Vlake Bridge was a secondary target, it was important the Crusaders succeed this time. As the 579th approached the bridge, Gerow's crew experienced flak fire for the first time. During training they had been warned for the seemingly innocent, but deadly black smoke plumes that suddenly appeared around the aircraft and also for the flak shrapnel that tore through metal and flesh and could ignite the fuel tanks in the wings. Their training however could not prepare them for the experience of being under fire during battle. German anti-aircraft artillery was a feared weapon. Most flak guns had a caliber of 88 mm (3.46 inch). Mounted on X-shaped cruciform, they could fire 15 to 20 rounds a minute from both stationary and mobile platforms like flat rail cars. A flak battery usually consisted of four flak positions. During the night, when the RAF usually flew their missions, searchlights accompanied the flak. The flak lacked the proximity fuse technology, so the timing mechanisms on the flak shells were only effective when accurate range and altitude was calculated. For this purpose, the flak positions were also equipped with radar. The German goal was to zero in on the bombers without firing multiple salvos. Once the range and altitude of a formation was detected by radar, the four flak positions started to fire so the shells would burst in a *box* around the formation. They would then fine-tune their aim so the shells burst in the middle of the formation. To avoid flak, the bombers within a formation flew at different altitudes and also varied their collective altitude. Cloudy weather and headwinds were a disadvantage to the allies. The head winds could be so strong that the relative ground speed was only 80 knots. This meant the bombers were exposed longer to the flak gun positions and faced a greater threat of being hit. To confuse the radar signals, the waist gunners threw chaff, bundles of small strips of aluminum foil out of a side window of the aircraft. The British called this countermeasure *Window* and the Germans called it *Düppel*. Chaff appeared as a cluster of targets on the radar screens and confused the flak units.

While the smell of cordite filled the crew's nostrils and they could see the red bursts of the exploding flak shells, the waist gunners were throwing the chaff out of the windows. Our Gal shook dangerously through the explosions, while shrapnel struck holes in her belly. The bombardier on the lead aircraft set his bombsight. The bomb bay shutters opened, exposing their destructive cargo. Looking through the telescope eyepiece of the Norden Bombsite, the bombardier of the lead aircraft guided the bomber to the target. When the telescope crosshairs of his Bombsite centered on the bridge, he released the bombs with the push of a button and a *"Bombs away!"* After the drop, the lead plane continued straight ahead for a few seconds to allow the other bombardiers to drop their bombs and close the bomb bay doors. After all bombs were dropped the radio operator of the lead plane sent a *"target bombed"* signal to headquarters. The crew felt relief, for flying without the twelve bombs on board was much safer than with the bombs. A single hit could ignite them, with disastrous consequences The group had dropped a total of 264 500-pound bombs. The general-purpose bombs destroyed both the Road Bridge and Railway Bridge. The bridges came down in the channel, stopping car and train traffic, as well as boat traffic on the channel that ran from the Eastern Scheldt to the Western Scheldt. In addition, a nearby building used by the Kersten family as railroad station-coffee shop and hotel called *Vlake* was destroyed. The family lived downstairs, while German soldiers were billeted on the upper floor. The Americans bombed the building because their bombers were under fire from German flak from the roof.

There was one casualty in the bombing. It was a close call; Kees Griep could easily have been the second.

They did not encounter enemy fighters during this mission, so the gunners did not have to take action. In the summer of 1944, they rarely encountered enemy fighters. Because German aircraft factories and oil refineries were frequently bombed, the Luftwaffe suffered from a serious shortage of both fuel and flight equipment. Intense air battles and dogfights were sporadic and took place only above major German cities. Nevertheless, every mission was perilous. During this mission, flak damaged 20 Crusader aircraft. One of the bombers succeeded in reaching England, but was so badly damaged the crew had to bail out before it crashed near Wendling. One crewmember broke his ankle after he landed in a tree.

Because of the bombs gone and less fuel Our Gal flew faster on the return trip. The squadron returned that evening. After Gene confirmed that the wheels were down and locked, Jim could start landing. After touchdown, Our Gal followed a checkerboard painted truck with a large sign *FOLLOW ME* guided the airplane to its place on the ramp. Their debut in the European war theater was a success. Takeoff to landing lasted no more than five hours. No men were killed. After the adrenaline rush during battle, fatigue began to take its toll. The crew took off their flight gear and the guns were removed for cleaning. Jim, Fred and Gene reported all mechanical problems and damage, while the ground crew visually inspected the bomber. A truck took the crew to the briefing room where a S-2 clerk interrogated them about every detail of the mission. Only after they had turned in their flight gear, the exhausted airmen could rest from their combat debut. The Red Cross personnel served them coffee, juice, sandwiches, donuts and a double shot of whiskey.

1: Failure to follow a lawful order of an officer one faced from that day of 45 days of imprisonment and a fine of $25. On drunkenness and disorder were a 60-day prison sentence and a fine of $ 35. Desertion and evading imprisonment was three months hard labor and a fine of $120.
2: In 1940, the Germans introduced *Central European Time* in the Netherlands, which still applies. The first mission of the crew was in the summer. *Central European Summer Time* is one hour ahead of *Western European Summer Time* in England, but during WWII the English used *British Double Summer Time*, which was the same as the summer time in the Netherlands.
3: The term general-purpose (GP) bomb is used for an airdropped bomb intended as a compromise between blast damage, penetration and fragmentation in explosive effect.

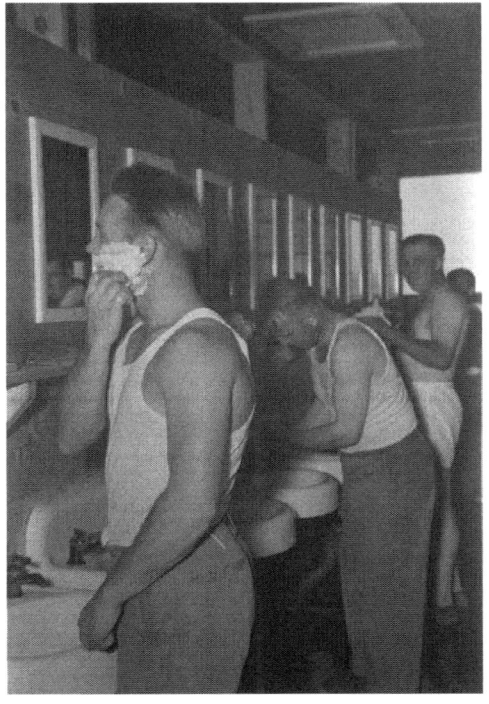

A 579th Bomb Squadron Nissen hut. In the front, are bikes crewmembers used to ride to the pub in Beeston. Behind the pub is the farm where the men did chores in change for milk and eggs. (061 – www.b24.net)

A wash room on Wendling. (062 – www.b24.net)

The map that was used at the briefing on August 3, 1944. (063 - www.b24)

The nose art of the Liberator *Our Gal*. (064 – www.b24.net)

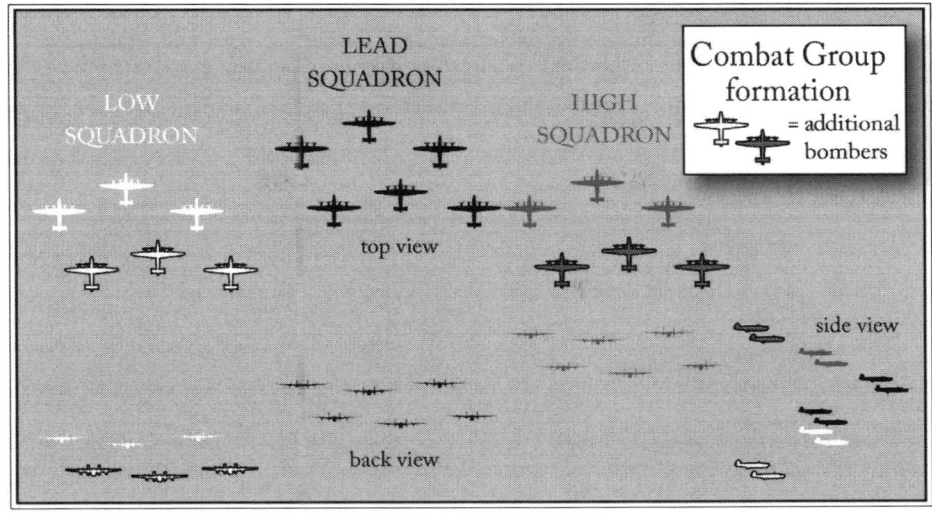

(065)

The B-24D *Minerva* of the 392nd BG, painted with an optical illusion. (066 - U.S. Air Force)

Left: The Crusaders fly in formation. (067 – U.S. Air Force)

The Vlake Bridge (068 – Beeldbank Rijkswaterstaat)

An aerial photo taken on August 3, 1944 of the Vlake Bridge, just before it was bombed. (069 – www.b24.net)

The bombing of the bridge. The circles indicate: 500, 1000 and 2000 feet from the target. (070 – www.b24.net)

The destroyed Vlake Bridge. (071 - Zeeuwse Bibliotheek/Beeldbank Zeeland)

The train station coffee house and hotel *Vlake* which was destroyed during the bombing. (072)

Bombers of the 392nd BG fly over the North Sea. (074a – U.S. Air Force))

Bombers of the 392nd BG in formation. (074b – U.S. Air Force)

Debriefing after the mission. (073 – U.S. Air Force)

The snack bar at the Red Cross Aero Club at Wendling. (074 – www.b24.net)

Chapter 6

Factories and traitors

Jim and his crew did not have long to recover after their first mission. The next morning, August 4, 1944, they were again awakened early. From 0630 to 0730 hours they were briefed on their next mission. The crew was assigned the aircraft *We'll get By*[1].

After a fog delay, all 29 Crusader crews were ready for takeoff. A total of 446 Liberators and 209 fighters, both Mustangs and Lightnings, flew this mission. The target was the northern German port city of Kiel. Near Kiel was the Friedrich Krupp Germania Werft, one of the largest shipyards in Germany. This industrial complex manufactured submarines for the Navy. In 1944, more than 10,000 men worked at the plant; 11% were forced laborers. During the flight over the Netherlands and Germany, the Liberators dealt with the expected flak. The bombers flew toward this unmistakable landmark, both visually and on radar.

When the lead bomber reached this *Initial Point* (IP) it alerted the formation to make the final turn toward the target by signal flares or by opening the bomb bay doors. When the formation reached the target, they saw the Germans had placed a smoke screen around the complex. This move proved effective, for the crews could not see the result of their bombing. The formation also managed to bomb the railway facilities of Kiel, one mile south of the target. A total of 348 500-pound M64 bombs were released during this mission. Just like he did on the previous mission, bombardier Joe Sulkowski dropped a load of twelve bombs on the target. Again, no enemy fighters were identified, but the flak at Kiel was very accurate and caused severe damage and injuries. During the six and a half hour mission, two airmen were killed by shrapnel (both members of the Crusaders), two men were wounded and 40 were missing in action. Four Liberators were lost and 114 were damaged.

The next morning, Saturday August 5th, Gerow's crew was awakened for a bomb mission to the German garrison city of Braunschweig (Brunswick). Their target was the Mühlenbau und Industrie Aktiengesellschaft (MIAG), a factory that manufactured armored vehicles and parts for the dreaded Messerschmitt BF110. This was the fifth time the Crusaders flew a mission to Braunschweig.

After the 0600 hours briefing, Gerow's crew was assigned to the aircraft *Mairzy Doats*[2], loaded with six 1000-pound general-purpose bombs, known as M44. Despite the rising dense fog, 27 crews were ready for takeoff at 0910 hours. A total of 452 Liberators and 172 Mustang fighters flew this mission.

Just after takeoff, an unfortunate accident occurred within the Crusaders. The lead aircraft, piloted by 1/Lt Owen Filkel from the 576th BS, crashed near East Dereham, cause unknown. The entire ten-man crew perished. Another aircraft took the lead and the formation dropped 156, 1000-pound bombs over the target in Braunschweig. Eighty percent fell within 600 meter radius of the target. The MIAG factory, the Braunschweiger Dom cathedral and the train station were hit. There were 36 deaths that day, in and around Braunschweig.

Although the bomber crews could see the destruction, the number of deaths remained an abstract concept. Unlike the American army who fought on land, they did not witness the suffering they caused. However, they saw their own bombers and fighters shot down. On the radio, they heard the death cries of fellow airmen as they plunged to their deaths. They saw their crewmates hit by shrapnel. After each mission, it was a shock to discover the empty beds and places at the breakfast table.

During the six and a half hour mission, there were several deaths among American aviators, ten casualties within the Crusaders. There were a total of five wounded and 55 men missing. Again, the bombers observed no enemy fighters. The accurate and heavy flak over the Netherlands and Germany caused damage to 149 Liberators, two of which could not be repaired. Seven aircraft were lost. The remaining aircraft returned at 1620.

The next morning, the Crusaders were assigned a mission to target oil refineries and oil depots near Hamburg, one of the largest cities in Germany. The Germans heavily defended this strategically important port city with its extensive industry, shipyards, submarine bunkers and oil refineries. During the war, Hamburg was attacked 69 times. In the last week of July 1943, during Operation Gomorrah, the city and its industrial complex outside the city were almost completely destroyed by British and American bombers, resulting in one of the largest firestorms of World War II in Europe. During the August 6th operation, more than 42,600 civilians were killed. By the end of the war, Hamburg suffered the most air strikes of all the cities in Germany.

Gerow's crew was part of a formation of 445 Liberators, escorted by 196 Thunderbolts and Lightnings. That day the crew flew the aircraft

YMCA Flying Service[3], loaded with twelve 500-pound M64 bombs. Despite heavy flak shelling, 27 of the 28 Crusaders aircraft flew a successful mission. One Liberator was shot down. The crew bailed out in time, but one crewmember was killed. The rest were captured and transported to prisoner of war camps. All other aircraft landed safely in England. There were a total of 13 deaths during this mission, 16 wounded and 38 men missing. Eight Liberators were lost, 293 damaged, three beyond repair.

After their first four missions, Gerow's crew was given two days of leave. The railway station near Wendling was crowded with soldiers who wanted to spend their leave in the city. They could have fun in Norwich or Kings Lynn and spend their wages on good food, drink, clothing, and souvenirs to bring home. When they had seven days off, it was possible to travel further, to London or another large city in England or Scotland. But visiting a large city became less desirable due to constant attacks by German V1 flying bombs.[4] Since June 13th, the first day a V1 fell on London, 5,000 people were killed and 35,000 homes destroyed. Despite the threat, American soldiers continued to spend their leave in London. They witnessed how the British were coping with the devastating attacks that ruined their city. Many of them then began to understand why the Royal Air Force (RAF) was less restrained than the USAAF when bombing German cities.

With or without a hangover, Gerow's crew was awakened before dawn of the morning of August 9th, for the next mission. They were assigned an unnamed Liberator, loaded with twelve 500-pound cluster bombs, known as M17A1. The target was the Daimler-Benz factory in the southern German city of Sindelfingen, as well as factories manufacturing military vehicles, aircraft, and aircraft engines. During this mission, 247 Liberators, and 165 Mustangs, Lightnings and Thunderbolts were deployed.

That day they encountered heavy clouds over the mainland, forcing the heavily laden Liberators to climb high above the clouds. This caused some of the aircraft to be separated from the formation and return to base without reaching their target. Gerow's crew was also separated and joined bombers of the 453rd BG from Old Buckenham. As a result, Joe did not drop bombs over the target. The remaining Crusaders flew a successful mission. The mission to Sindelfingen lasted seven hours and twenty-five minutes, killing one and wounding ten. Twenty-nine men were missing. Four Liberators were lost, 128 were damaged, two beyond repair.

The 8th Air Force boasted that neither enemy fighters nor enemy flak ever turned back a mission. The same could not be said of European weather. Many missions were scrubbed, aborted, or recalled because of poor weather conditions en route or over the target area. In late 1943, the radar device called *Mickey* changed that. Mickey, the USAAF *H2X* radar platform, was developed at the Massachusetts Institute of Technology Radiation Laboratory in Cambridge, Massachusetts. This was a *TOP SECRET* project that developed and deployed American aircraft equipped with Air to Ground Radar. The *Mickey Navigator* in the lead aircraft operated the radar, located behind the co-pilot. Radar signals were collected in a rotating *radome* (radar dome) mounted below the airplane, in the hole where the ball turret used to be. The Pathfinder Force (PFF) provided accurate route information, helped avoid flak, located the IP and the target and marked them with flares and other target indicators. Using Mickey, bombardiers aimed their Norden Bombsites at the target indicators, increasing the accuracy of their bombing. This was the first time the Crusaders used their own newly trained radar operators from the Pathfinder Force (PFF.) Before this date, these men were provided by other groups.

And so it went. On Tuesday, August 15th, the crew flew *Idiots Delight*[5], loaded with 52 100-pound general-purpose M30 bombs. They flew to Wittmundhafen Air Base, where many Messerschmitt BF101's were stationed. Gerow's squadron did not release their load because of cloud covering above the target. The next day they were assigned to *Pursuit of Happiness*[6], a bomber equipped with a radome. The crew flew this aircraft most often and considered it their own. It was loaded with twelve 500-pound M64 bombs. In this Liberator they flew missions to factories at Köthen on August 16th and the French Nancy-Essey airport, 199 miles east of Paris, on August 18th. The Luftwaffe used this French airport primarily as a base for transport and combat gliders. Radar Technician S/Sgt J. P. Meyers supplemented Gerow's crew on this mission to France.

The next day the weather was so bad that the entire 8th Air Force stayed on the ground until Thursday, August 24th. During this interval, engineer Gene Kieras was promoted from to Sergeant to Staff Sergeant. To pass the time, the men sometimes went to the makeshift cinema on the base. This bizarre alternation of war and entertainment illustrated why many airmen called their job a rollercoaster of emotional peaks and valleys. One day they saw their buddies die in combat, the next day they could relax and dream during a movie like *The Amazing Mrs. Holliday,* a comedy drama starring Deanna Durbin.

On Saturday August 19th, a ball was held in the officers' mess. Ladies from the neighboring towns were invited. From Norwich, Kings Lynn, and East Dereham, they took a bus or train, to the station, where military trucks picked them up. After the ball, they returned to the station. It was ordered that only officers, who were responsible for the trucks, were allowed to return the ladies. On Wednesday, August 23rd, the film, *Follow the Boys,* was screened to boost the morale of the troops. The film starred George Raft, Dinah Shore, Vera Zorina, Marlene Dietrich, Orson Welles, WC Fields, the Andrew Sisters, and many others.

After several days of forced leave, on Tuesday August 24th, the crew successfully bombed Evershorst, a major military airfield near Hannover, now called Langenhagen Airport. The next day, on August 25th, the same day Paris was liberated after a long siege, the crew got time off. On that day Glenn Miller[7] and his sixty-piece band gave a concert at Wendling. In a large hangar, Gerow and his men enjoyed an hour of musical favorites like *In the Mood* and *Chattanooga Choo Choo*. On August 26th, the crew watched the comedy *Make Your Own Bed* with Jack Carson and Jane Wyman.

On August 27th, the primary target was the Heinkel aircraft factory at Oranienburg, near Berlin, but due to dense cloud cover, the crew bombed a secondary target on the German island of Helgoland, an important naval base.

For the next five days the weather was so bad, no Wendling aircraft flew. The crews kept busy with extra training and were put to work repairing runways.

While the crew was grounded in Wendling, the weather in Zeeland was also gloomy. Like the bad weather, German oppression increased. The Allied troops approached Belgium faster than expected, requiring German soldiers stationed in Zeeland to move south to halt the advance. German troops confiscated horses, carriages, cars and bicycles for use as transport to the front lines. Soldiers of the Magen Division were shipped across the Western Scheldt. Due to the absence of this division from parts of Zeeland and the lack of replacement troops, German forces eventually disappeared completely. The Occupier became increasingly nervous. The Germans increased restrictions on the local population because they were beginning to feel trapped by Allied and Russian troops. About a month earlier, on July 30, 1944, after the attempt on his life, Adolf Hitler issued the *Niedermachungsbefehl,* an order to abolish all military courts and charge all opposition with terrorism and sabotage. Anyone arrested by the Germans or the Landwacht faced execution. Granted such power, the hated Landwacht became bolder and crueler.

In his spare time, Kees Griep was chairman and director of the local art theater, *Kunst naar Kracht* (Art to Strength). Kees Klap, painter by profession, was a member of the theater group and often visited Kees Griep. When Kees Klap joined the NSB and also became leader of the local Landwacht, Kees Griep expelled him from the theater group.

By doing so, Kees Griep made a dangerous enemy. Kees Griep owned a secret radio, a dangerous possession. Citizens possessing an illegal radio risked confiscation of their homes with all contents and imprisonment at *Konzentrationslager Herzogenbusch* also known as Camp Vught, the only SS-Concentration Camp in the Netherlands. During German occupation, at least four Zeelanders were killed for possession of a radio.

On a drizzly Tuesday evening, someone knocked on the door of Clara's Pad number 12 in Heinkenszand. As soon as he opened the door and saw men in their gray field jackets standing in the rain, Kees Griep realized he was in trouble. The men from the Landwacht walked directly to the cabinet and pulled out a hidden radio. Kees was arrested and handed over to the German police. A friend of his daughter Iet, Geert van Dijke, was also present and arrested. After interrogation, they carried Kees off to the prison in Middelburg. German authorities confiscated his house and furniture at Clara's Pad, and his wife and children were evicted. Fortunately, the family of Mayor Mes sheltered them. The Mayor himself was in hiding somewhere else.

Piet van den Dries was more fortunate. After his friend, Kees, was arrested, a member of the NSB came to his home. He told Piet a night raid would take place and that they would look for a secret radio in the headmaster's house. The man asked Piet if *"something should go wrong with the war"* and the Allies would win, would Piet put in a good word for him. Piet strongly denied he had a radio. He thanked the man and promised him he would remember him when the time came. After the NSB agent left, Piet buried the radio in his garden. That evening the Landwacht searched his house but did not find anything. After liberation, Piet kept his word and told the authorities about the NSB agent who warned him.

Nico van Biezen, the blacksmith from Heinkenszand, also faced the consequences of his resistance work. Kees Klap, lived in the Dorpsstraat, not far from Nico's house. He noticed strangers working in Nico's blacksmith forge, but when the Landwacht checked their papers, they seemed authentic.

Nico: *"Everything went fine at first, but the last year everything seriously went wrong. Twice I was picked up for questioning by a German commander, and the second time I had received a heavy beating. I was once picked up for questioning by the NSB mayor, and I had a fiery argument with him. As punishment, I got twelve soldiers billeted in the downstairs rooms and a call for inspection to work in Germany. I got two searches, but the people that were hiding in my house always had good false papers."*

Nico realized that he had to be very careful. His forge stood at the junction of the three main streets in the village. This allowed him to check in all directions at once, which gave him time to flee whenever he saw agents of the Landwacht nearing his smithy. At night he didn't have this advantage, so he was forced to sleep overnight in a dry ditch in one of the polders.

The Group Griep realized they were in a difficult situation. One of their leaders was arrested and the rest were under surveillance. In Kees' house, now occupied by German soldiers, a list of the names of people in the OD was hidden. It would only be a matter of time before the Germans found this dangerous information, with grave consequences for their group and other groups in the area. The men realized they had to act. One stormy night, Nico van Biezen ignored the curfew and went out. He and his friend, the accountant, Cees Paauwe, stayed in the shadows as they carried a ladder towards the doctor's house. Due to the heavy rain, the home was not guarded. They crept carefully around the house and silently put the ladder against the wall. Cees stood guard and held the ladder while Nico opened a window and climbed through. Knowing German soldiers were sleeping in the house, Cees shook with fright. Nico searched the doctor's office and finally found the incriminating document, put it in his overalls and crawled through the window into the rain.

For now, the danger had passed. Nevertheless, the group knew the Germans were suspicious of Kees Griep and were afraid he would talk if tortured. They could only hope and pray this would never happen.

During those early September days, the Landwacht continued to harass Nico. Three times he found a threatening letter in his mailbox. Kees Klap had written these threats and insults on pieces of paper and on an old envelope:

> *"BASTARD*
> *HIDER MUST LEAVE*
> *HOUZEE"*[8]
>
> *"WE WILL PUT YOU IN VUGT*
> *WE WILL TAKE YOUR HOUSE AND SEIZE YOUR PROPERTY*
> *TO HELL WITH YOUR WIFE"*
>
> *"YOUR SERVANT HIDER MUST GET THE HELL OUT*
> *IN 2 DAYS WE WILL SMOKE OUT YOUR RESISTANCE NEST AND*
> *PUT YOU IN MIDDELBURG IN THE CELL WITH YOUR FRIEND*
> *DR GRIEP*
> *HOUZEE"*

On the back of this threatening letter Nico wrote: *"Such a friendly letter I found in my mailbox... My servant remained, but it worried me, because it was at the end of the war*[9]*. I was actually still in hiding at night. In the evening, I loaded my revolver and went to see Klap (Landwacht). I gave him two choices: to have his brain blown out right now, or to leave my family and me at peace. I won. After two days he had fled, with the mayor. I could feel free in my own home again."*

1: Inspired by the song *I'll Get By*, sung by Dinah Shore in the film *Follow the Boys*, in 1944. On August 23, 1944, this film was featured at the cinema in Wendling.
2: A name without a clear meaning. It was based on a popular song from 1943. *Mares eat oats and does eat oats and little lambs eat ivy* was in child language: *Mairzy doats and dozy doats and liddle lamzy divey*. In May 1944, it became a number one hit by the Merry Macs. It became a popular song among American soldiers abroad; the strange words in the song sometimes were used as a password.
3: Named after the truck that brought tea around the airfield in Wendling. *YMCA* stands for *Young Men's Christian Association*. It assisted in providing sport and relaxation for the American airmen during the war. The 392nd BG had at least two and perhaps even three bombers named *YMCA Flying Service*.
4: *Vergeltungswaffe 1*(Avenge Weapon 1): a flying bomb, powered by a jet engine.
5: Named after a movie musical from 1939.
6: Based on a famous phrase from the American Declaration of Independence of the United States in 1776: *"We hold these truths to be self-evident,*

that all men are created equal, that they are endowed by Their Creator with Certain unalienable Rights that among these are life, liberty and the <u>pursuit of Happiness</u>."

7: This famous American jazz trombonist and big band leader had enlisted in the U.S. Army in1942, after which he was appointed Captain. As leader of the Army Air Force Band he toured the various U.S. military bases in Europe to boost the moral. On December 15, 1944, during a flight from England to Paris with a single-engine UC-64 Norseman (Canadian), the plane disappeared from radar and never made it to France. The aircraft, its crew, and passengers were never heard from again. There is a theory that claims the aircraft was hit by excess bombs from British Lancaster bombers that were unloading over the English Channel on that same day.

8: The greeting of the NSB. The NSB were Dutch nationalists, so instead of using the German *Heil Hitler*, they used an old Dutch word. There is some discussion about the origins of Houzee. It has some relation to the old English word *Huzza (*hurray*)*, but some say it is an old Dutch maritime yell, used by sailors to encourage each other in stressful situations. The NSB liked Houzee because it reminded them of the glory days of the famous Dutch naval heroes like Michiel de Ruyter and Maarten Tromp.

9: As we will see in the next chapters, the German occupation in Zeeland ended much earlier than it did in the Dutch provinces north of the Great Rivers.

The Liberator *We'll Get By*. (075 – www.b24.net)

One of the bombers called *YMCA Flying Service*. (076 – www.b24.net)

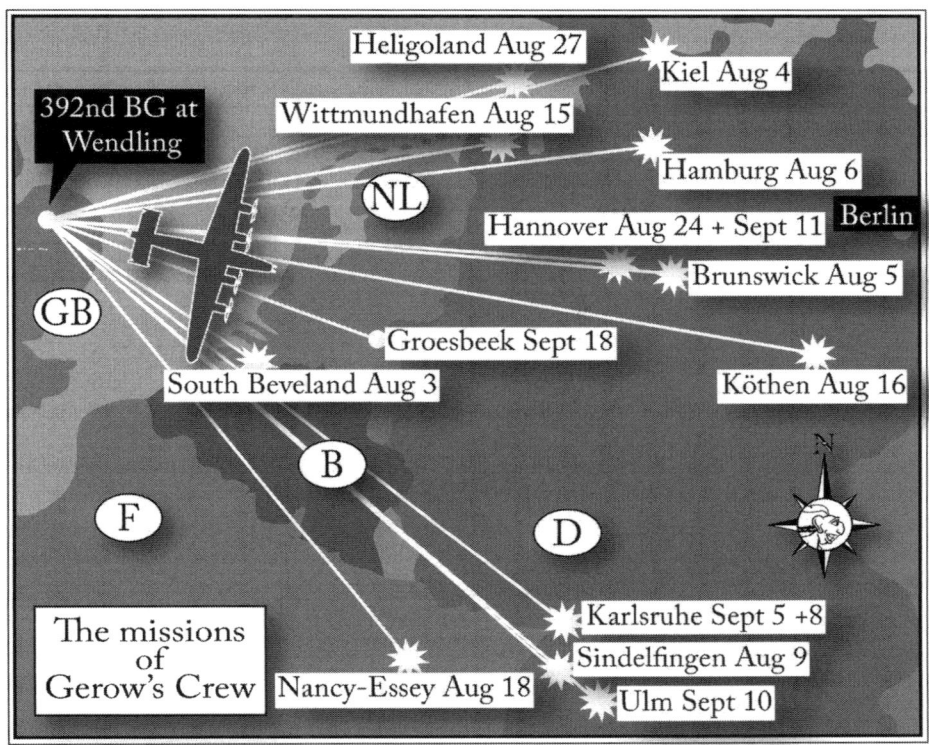

(077)

Jou KNECHT ONDERDUIKER MOET
OPDONDEREN OVER 2 DAGEN ROKEN
WIJ JE VERZETNEST UIT EN
DONDEREN JOU IN MIDDELBURG
IN DE CEL BIJ JE VRIENDJE DR
GRIEP

HOU ZEE

One of the notes that Nico received from Kees Klap. (078)

The Glenn Miller concert in a hangar ar Wendling on August 25, 1944. (080 - www.b24.net)

The famous trombonist and big band leader Glenn Miller. (079 - U.S. Air Force)

The house of Kees Griep. (081)

The improvised cinema at Wendling. (082 - www.b24.net)

Left: Gene Kieras (082a)   Right: Loyce Ely (082b)

Normand Hebert (082c)

Chapter 7

From Hope to Despair

Heavy showers plagued the European continent during the early days of September. In the Netherlands on September 3rd, there was cautious hope when the BBC and Radio Oranje reported that Brussels was liberated. The population anticipated Zeeland and North Brabant would be free in a matter of days, then Rotterdam and the rest of the Netherlands would soon follow.

The wonderful news had the opposite effect on the Occupiers. All border guards east of Zeeland disappeared and many NSB members in Zeelandic Flanders fled across the Western Scheldt to Walcheren. Shortly after, NSB leader, Jan Dekker, fled Goes and called upon all NSB members in Zeeland to follow his example and take their families with them. When the Belgium cities of Antwerp and Leuven were liberated, the citizens of Goes located in South Beveland saw their NSB Mayor flee. The German and Dutch high-level collaborators closely followed after them. Mayor Kole and Landwacht leader, Kees Klap, also fled Heinkenszand. It was reported they were in such a hurry to leave their homes that the villagers found their bowls of porridge still warm on the breakfast table. Most traveled by train to the east of the country, or to Germany, where they hoped for safety. This journey was not without risk because the Allied fighters attacked every moving train.

To hide their collaboration, the NSB burned many documents and destroyed a lot of information about the resistance groups. At last the Group Griep could breathe freely. Finally, German soldiers had something better to do than hunt for local rebels in insignificant Heinkenszand. Long columns of battle-weary German soldiers, driving stolen cars, horse carts, bicycles, or on foot, fled across the Western Scheldt and staggered through Walcheren and South Beveland. They were harassed by Allied fighters and the roads were littered with burned-out cars and horse carcasses. In Goes, ragged gangs of drenched, hungry, and wounded soldiers were loaded on overcrowded trains and transported east.

Euphoria increased among the people of Zeelandic Flanders on September 5th due to false information broadcast on the BBC, claiming the city Breda in North Brabant was already liberated. Assuming the Allies were on the verge of liberating Zeeland, the citizens braved the rainy weather and celebrated in the streets. They adorned themselves with orange ribbons and red, white and blue decorations. Hardly anyone worked that day. A few people flew the Dutch flag and brought out their secret radios to follow the news. People hiding from the Occupiers crept out and joined the celebrations. In Zeelandic Flanders and North Beveland, some resistance groups even dared to arrest German soldiers, NSB members, and other alleged traitors. To prevent chaos, men of authority in their community took over as mayor. Festivities were modest in South Beveland. Hope for a quick liberation was celebrated with an extra cup of ersatz coffee. September 5th, 1944, was later called *Dolle Dinsdag* (Crazy Tuesday) because of the chaos and confusion.

On that day two police officers arrived at the prison in Middelburg. They handed the German jailer an order to retrieve the terrorist doctor, Kees Griep, for execution. After he read the order, the warden handed him over to the police. Kees Griep, who was already ill, realized the end was near. Pale and somber, he climbed into the police car with the two agents. At a sufficient distance from the gate, his agony disappeared when the agents told him they were OD men. They explained they took advantage of the chaos on Crazy Tuesday and *borrowed* police uniforms. The agents handed Kees false travel documents, wished him good luck and, before he could thank them, drove away. He still felt sick, but new hope gave him strength, so he ignored the rain and began to walk home. Through the city of Arnemuiden, he reached the heavily guarded Sloedam[1], the only road to South Beveland. The Germans were afraid the Canadians would cross the Western Scheldt into Walcheren, and issued emergency decrees to the inhabitants of Walcheren to evacuate to South Beveland. Very few people complied and many received permission for exemptions, but some did evacuate. This may be why Kees was able to cross the Sloedam without being arrested. Not long after reaching Lewedorp, 6 miles from Heinkenszand, Kees met one of his patients who lent him a bicycle. After he reached Heinkenszand, Kees went into hiding, joining his family at the house of Mayor Mes.

The night before Crazy Tuesday, Gerow's crew was briefed for the next day's mission. During their days on the ground, radio operator Morton Baker was promoted from Staff Sergeant to Technical Sergeant. They were again assigned to the Pursuit of Happiness, loaded with twelve 500-pound M64 bombs. After pre-flight check, 24 Crusader aircraft took off. Accompanied by other bomb groups, they flew to the marshaling yards around the city of Karlsruhe. The weather was terrible and the formations had to fly through heavy storm clouds. This was dangerous because formation was tight and collisions could easily occur. However, they managed to leave the clouds behind them without incident. The bombing of the marshaling yards was successful. A combination of Flying Fortresses and Liberators dropped 224 500-pound bombs. No enemy fighters were seen, but, as usual, there was much flak damage. After they returned to English soil, it was discovered one Liberator was missing. The crew had to make an emergency landing on Le Bourget Airfield near liberated Paris and returned to Wendling the next day.

Disillusionment followed the euphoria of Crazy Tuesday. Allied troops had indeed liberated Antwerp, but the Scheldt estuary was still under German control. It would be weeks before the Allies set foot in Walcheren. The citizens of South Beveland were dismayed to see fresh German troops marching to the west. Zeelanders discovered their actions were premature and unwise. These new soldiers were hardened men, who had witnessed all the horrors of war. Many of them remained in Zeeland and, in reprisal, imposed depressive conditions on the inhabitants. Severe punishment awaited those who celebrated German losses too exuberantly. Resistance fighters who dared to arrest Germans soldiers, collaborators, and traitors were hunted down, arrested and executed without mercy. The Germans also hunted down everyone who came out of hiding. Zeeland remained a *Sperrgebiet* (Prohibited Area) and became increasingly isolated. German troops seized all public transportation. There were no telephone, no telegraph, and no official newspapers. Import and export of fuel and food halted. Food shortages were somewhat mitigated by the slaughter of exhausted horses left behind by the Germans.

Rinus Geschiere, the 14-year-old son of a milkman from Heinkenszand, said[1], *"Around that time, you saw them pass with the strangest vehicles. Just after Crazy Tuesday there came a bunch of Krauts to us. It was only twelve men, led by a sergeant, a real asshole. He had fled France with an old farm wagon. An uncle of mine had a beautiful horse cart with rubber tires. He hid one of the wheels, so the krauts could not take the cart. The Sergeant who had been looking for it for a few days, kept asking 'Wo ist das Rad (Where is the wheel)?' I, a kid who only spoke a few German words, told him that two weeks back one of his comrades had already taken 'das Rad.' He bought my story and left."*

The weather remained volatile. On Thursday, September 7th, a rainstorm with 40mph winds raged. Northern Europe was impacted and English bombers were again grounded. Despite the bad weather, Jim

Gerow was assigned to the next day's mission, Karlsruhe. On Friday, September 8th, pre-flight briefings were given to 36 Wendling bomber crews before dawn. The crew was assigned a familiar bomber, We'll Get By, loaded with twelve M17 incendiary bombs. Due to heavy clouds, the bombers could not stay in their formation. They regrouped above the mainland. Thirty three aircraft dropped 380 500-pound bombs on targets in Karlsruhe. Some of the Crusaders' crews joined a formation of B-17s and bombed Ludwigshafen. Results looked promising, but aerial photos showed no damage to the target area. One plane was shot down by flak with six men killed, two men taken prisoner of war, and one man evaded. One bomber landed at an emergency airfield in Lignerolles, France, to refuel and returned to Wendling later that day. Again, gunners saw no fighters, but the flak at the target site caused much damage.

On that same Friday, the Germans began to use V2 missiles[2]. The first two of these unmanned short-range ballistic missiles were launched from Wassenaar in South Holland, targeting West London's Cheswick suburb that night. It left three dead and 17 wounded.

On September 10th, in the aircraft *Little Joe*[3], with twelve M64 bombs, Gerow's crew bombed railway marshaling yards at Ulm. Flak damage was significant but the Crusaders reported no fatalities.

That same day, trains overcrowded with German troops were mercilessly bombed by the British RAF bombers. They previously bombed Terneuzen, on the southern shore of the Western Scheldt estuary and also the Sloedam. Because railway personnel refused to work in such dangerous conditions, German personnel replaced them.

Mission # 166

On Monday morning September 11th, the same day the U.S. 5th Armed Division reached the border between Luxembourg and Germany for the first time, Gerow's crew was briefed for another mission. This time S/Sgt. Matthew A. Bartnowski was assigned to them, who was specially trained in Radar Counter Measures (RCM). It was his job to focus on German radar and jam the signals that revealed the bomber location.

What follows is part of the briefing for 24 Crusader crews, led by leading bombardier 1/Lt J.S Lawrence of the 579th BS.

LOCATION AND IMPORTANCE OF TARGET:

Hanomag[4] engineering works formerly specializing in locomotives and steam engines. Later converted to include trucks, tractors and agricultural machinery. They have recently become very important builders of tanks, heavy military vehicles, medium caliber guns, and other heavy armaments products. It has been reliably reported that in one month this plant produced over 321 tanks in addition to its other products. The target is located on the southeast outskirts of Hanover in the suburb of Linden. To the south of the target is a plant producing aircraft components.

PAST RAIDS

Severely damaged on RAF mission on 22 October 1943. Nothing recent.

The formations consisted of 396 Liberators, escorted by 164 Mustangs and Lightings. Their target was Hanover, capital of Lower Saxony, an important transportation hub for military and industrial traffic. Throughout the war, the city endured 88 air attacks, resulting in the deaths of 6800 people and the destruction of 90% of the city.

Gerow's crew once again boarded the Pursuit of Happiness, loaded with eight 1000-pound M44 bombs and equipped with a radome. They took off at 0730 hours. While crossing the Rhine River, somewhere between near Koblenz and Giessen, Germany, the crew encountered enemy fighters for the first time. Between 1140 hours and 1145 hours, twenty to thirty Messerschmitt Bf 109s and other enemy aircraft attacked the American formation.

The 392nd BG Teletype reported: *"Most enemy aircraft were camouflaged with light colored bellies and dark on top. A few were noted to be painted olive drab, and some had black and white stripes on their wings to simulate P-51s* (Mustangs.) *- Most of the attacks were from level or below and in general from the tail. Enemy aircraft attacked singly or in small groups of 2-4 echeloned[5] up, or queued up in a line. The enemy aircraft sat high above our formation and queued up for about 5 minutes before attacking. – Attack occurred at a time when we were temporarily without fighter cover. When called, escort came to our assistance. – One report of a radial engine plane, very similar to a Zeke[6], with a large red circle painted on the fuselage. – A P-38* (Lighting), *painted black, no other visible markings, picked up our formation about 10 minutes before fighting attack, and left when attack began; crews believe it to have been enemy operated. Mention should be made of an unknown P-51 pilot who accompanied one of our crippled* *ships back (aircraft 764), but ran out of gas and bailed out somewhere over the continent."*

Flying at an altitude of 23,000 feet Gerow's crew was among the first attacked. The startled gunners faced the reality of battle with formidable German fighters. Rattling volleys were fired at the German fighters from the turrets and waist positions. The attack wounded one on board the Pursuit of Happiness. A flying piece of Plexiglas[7] cut bombardier Joe over his eye when the nose turret was hit.

Tail gunner Frenchy managed to shoot down a Messerschmitt attacking from behind. Frenchy wrote on a Combat Form[8]: *"Left waist gunner called enemy aircraft at 8 o'clock and I was on 4 o'clock on enemy aircraft. Then left waist gunner called one at 7 o'clock low, I turned my guns on 7 o'clock and he was about 200 yards from me, attacking our left element[9], and I fired on him as he dove down towards the ground. When he dove towards the ground, he passed me and no one on right or left was there because we were flying No. 4 [10] and no one was there to fire on him, and I fired about 400 rounds and shots kept flying off and he caught on fire and went down. My right waist gunner saw him go down. Right waist gunner saw pilot bail out as ship passed his line of fire. Expect pilot was killed by shots from right waist gunner."*

Left waist gunner, Ely, damaged another one. Loyce's story on a Combat Form: *"The enemy aircraft attacked our left wing ship and then came on by our ship which was leading the element at about 50 yards when the gunner opened fire on him. The enemy aircraft turned up his right wing and gunner fired about 30 rounds into him and tracers could be seen going into his belly then he went down smoking and flaming. Out of control straight down to ground. Navigator witnessed this."*

Liberator damage was enormous. Within five minutes, German fighters brought down three Crusaders. Five crewmembers died in the first bomber crash, four were able to parachute safely and were taken prisoner. In the second aircraft, eight died and two were taken prisoner. The third bomber was a member of Gerow's squadron. The entire crew survived but was taken to prisoner of war camps. In addition to the crashed airplanes other bombers sustained heavy damage. Five Crusaders returned to base due to mechanical problems caused by the shelling.

Frenchy and Ely were not the only gunners who eliminated a Messerschmitt. Eleven enemy fighters were shot down that day.

Despite considerable losses and significant damage, the squadron crews accomplished their mission. At 1245 hours, about an hour after the fighter attack, Pursuit of Happiness managed to drop all her bombs. In all, 90% of the 186, 1000-pound bombs were dropped from 23,600 feet within a 600-meter radius of the target, achieving excellent results. On their return trip, one of the Liberators performed an emergency ditching in the English Channel between France and England, resulting in the death of two crewmembers. Air Sea Rescue (ASR) of the RAF picked up the survivors.

Because of battle damage, Pursuit of Happiness landed at the 458th BG at Horsham St. Faiths, Norfolk, where Joe was treated for the cut over his eye.

The mission lasted six and a half hours. There were three additional casualties, bringing the total number of deaths for that day to fifteen. In addition, there were 13 wounded and 102 men missing. Ten Liberators were lost, 181 were damaged, two beyond repair.

That Monday was also a harsh day for Zeeland, not because of the Germans, but because of the British RAF. They heavily bombed the harbor town of Breskens and the surrounding area to prevent shipping traffic on the Western Scheldt and the crossing of German units. Many homes were destroyed or damaged. There were 199 civilian fatalities and many injuries.

1: From an interview by Willem Visser and Hans Vergeer on August 28, 2010.
2: In all, during the war 1,115 V2s and 2.419 V1s came down on London and the surrounding area. These numbers were only surpassed by the liberated Antwerp, where 1,712 and 4,248 V2s and V1s came down.
3: Named after a gambling character in the film musical *Cabin in the Sky* from 1943.
4: Hannover Machinenfabrik AG
5: An *echelon* is a formation in which the aircraft are arranged diagonally.
6: *Zeke* was the Allied nickname for a Japanese Mitsubishi A6M Zero.
7: Joe's son John still owns this piece of Plexiglas.
8: The document where airmen described the enemy fighter attack and what damage their bullets did plus other airmen who witnessed the incident. From these Combat Forms the 2nd Air Division allocated credit to the shooter: Destroyed, Damaged, Probable, or No Credit.
9: An *element* consists of three aircraft, stacked from high to low.
10: Pursuit of Happiness was the fourth aircraft in the *Lead Squadron* that consisted of six aircraft. It was the middle bomber in the second element.

An aerial view of a B-24 and the bombing of Karlsruhe on September 5, 1944. (083 - U.S. Air Force)

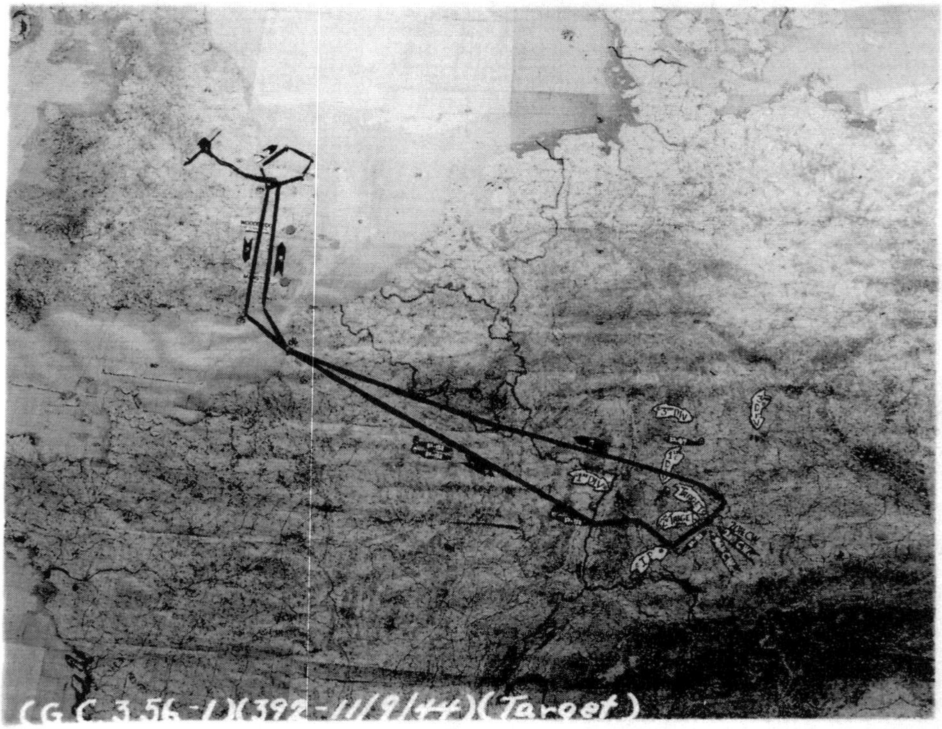

The map that was used at the briefing at September 11th. (083a – www.b24.net)

A Liberator is shot in half over German territory. (084 – U.S. Air Force)

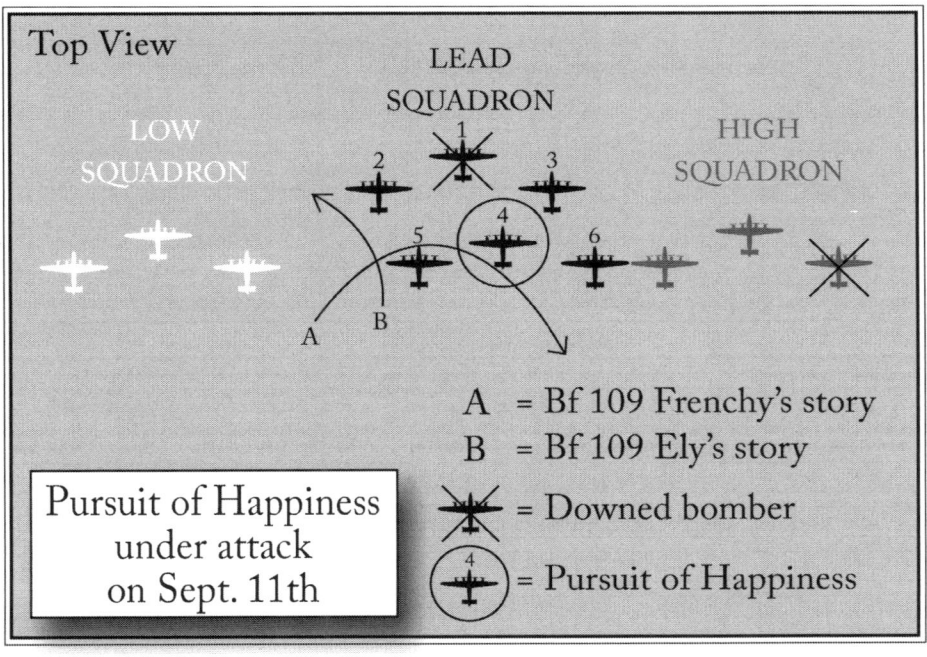

(084a)

DECLASSIFIED
Authority NND745005

HEADQUARTERS
392ND BOMBARDMENT GROUP (H)
OFFICE OF THE INTELLIGENCE OFFICER
Station 118   APO 658

22 September 1944

SUBJECT: Claims for E/A.

TO : Awards Section, S-1.
     Group Operations
     576th Operations
     578th Operations
     579th Operations
     Capt. Felheim
     Capt. McCammond

1. The following is a list of E/A claims allowed by 2d Bombardment Division for the Mission of 11 September, 1944, HANNOVER:

SQUADRON	NAME	DESTROYED	POSITION
576	S/Sgt. Robert J. Scott	FW 190	Left Waist
576	S/Sgt. M.E. Roberts	ME 109	Tail gunner
576	S/Sgt. John D. Huba	ME 109	Right Waist
578	2nd Lt. Harold J. Clark	ME 109	Nose
579	S/Sgt. Normand B. Hebent	ME 109	Tail Turret
579	S/Sgt. John R. Moore	ME 109	Tail Gunner
579	S/Sgt. Delmar J. Carter	ME 109	Tail Gunner
		PROBABLE	
576	Sgt. S. Luciano	ME 109	Tail Gunner
578	Cpl. Judson Markle	ME 109	Right Waist
		DAMAGED	
576	Sgt. R.P. O'Kane	ME 109	Nose Turret
579	S/Sgt. Joyce E. Ely	ME 109	Left Waist

LETCHER B. HUNT
1st Lt., Air Corps
ASST. S-2

Claims for enemy aircraft: tail gunner Normand B. Hebert destroyed a ME 109 and left waist gunner Loyce E. Ely (misspelled) damaged another one. (025b – www.b24.net)

Chapter 8

Holland Supply Drop Zone

After their first air battle, Jim Gerow and his men were granted five days of *Rest and Recuperation* (R&R.) The damaged Pursuit of Happiness needed less time to recover. The plane was back in the air in three days.

Zeeland was given no rest. While fleeing German units overran Walcheren, Allied bombers and fighters continued to bombard strategic targets in Zeeland. In their attempt to disable German army escape routes, the RAF bombed both the Kreekrakdam[1] and the Sloedam on September 12th. There were few German casualties, but the Sloedam was heavily damaged. Electricity cables and water pipes were destroyed and traffic was impossible. A day later, the men of Walcheren and South Beveland were ordered to make the Sloedam passable again. The heavy damage increasingly isolated the province and shortages were becoming acute. On September 13th, Maastricht became the first Dutch city to be liberated and all drinking water was rationed in Zeeland.

The prospects for German forces in Western Europe were grim. The Allies in France and Belgium seemed unstoppable and a few high-ranking German officers already spoke of surrender. But surrender was not an option for Adolf Hitler. He was convinced Germany could still win the war. To reinforce this, in September 1944, *Reichsführer* Heinrich Himmler issued a warrant ordering the immediate execution of all families of deserting soldiers. This applied equally to the families of German soldiers who were too easily inclined to surrender to the allies.

That same month, Hitler developed a bold plan. A number of Eastern Front hardened armored divisions would secretly be sent to the Ardennes to supplement the troops stationed there. He planned a massive surprise attack to recapture an area of 95 km between the Ardennes and Antwerp. If successful, supplies to the Allies would be cut off and Allied defeat would be only a matter of time. Hitler hoped the major Allied losses would force them to the negotiating table. On September 16th, Hitler outlined this plan to his staff. Not all were convinced it would succeed, but Hitler did not tolerate any contradiction. He gave the order to prepare.

Operation Market Garden

Instead of focusing on the conquest of Walcheren and South Beveland, to allow the Allies to use the Scheldt to supply the armed forces from Antwerp harbor instead of distant Normandy, British commander, Field Marshal Montgomery, came up with a different plan. On Sunday September 17th, he launched *Operation Market Garden*.

Market Garden was divided into two phases. Phase 1, called *Market*, was the largest-scale airborne operation ever devised. Troops would land by parachute or glider behind the German lines near the Dutch cities Arnhem, Nijmegen, and Eindhoven. The first drop would be conducted by the U.S. 101st Airborne Division (*Screaming Eagles*), the U.S. 82nd Airborne (*All American*) and the British 1st Airborne Division (*Red Devils*).

Phase 2, called *Garden*, and consisted of a ground offensive of 150,000 men, mainly from the British XXX (30) Corps, advancing from Belgium to the Netherlands to assist the paratroopers. Their purpose was to capture major bridges in the provinces North Brabant and Gelderland so the airborne divisions would be able to push through to the IJsselmeer, a large lake in the central Netherlands. This would isolate the German army in the west of the Netherlands. When bridges over the Rhine, the Meuse and the Waal were taken, they would push through to the German Ruhr area and paralyze the enemy's war industries. Little resistance from the Wehrmacht was expected at the American and British drop zones. The Allies assumed the German troops in the area consisted only of teenagers and old men. The remainder would be on the Eastern Front fighting the Russians. Montgomery told his troops they would be home by Christmas.

The first aircraft took off on Sunday morning, September 17th. The fleet consisted of 1,073 troop transport aircraft[2]. Most of them were used for towing 500 gliders[3]. Another 1,500 fighters[4] participated in this operation. A total of 20,000 men, 511 vehicles, and 330 artillery pieces were transported by air to the Netherlands. Before their departure, flak positions on the route were bombed. Weather conditions were good, with a light breeze from the north and few clouds. With a mixture of hope and fear, the people of Zeeland saw an endless armada flying inland from the sea. Once these aircraft were above Dutch soil, 10% were destroyed by German flak. Under heavy fire, American and British airborne divisions landed around Eindhoven, Nijmegen and Arnhem. It appeared the Wehrmacht soldiers in the area were not the weak troops the Allied expected. Instead, two armored divisions awaited them.

The American 101st Airborne Division, led by General Maxwell D. Taylor, landed near Eindhoven. His regiments captured Veghel, St. Oedenrode, Son, and the major bridges within a few hours. The bridge at Son was destroyed by the Germans, so the Americans had to wait for the British XXX Corps to build a temporary bridge.

When the men of the U.S. 82nd Airborne Division flew over the Netherlands, they encountered heavy flak, resulting in paratrooper fatalities and aircraft damage. Unfortunately, a German reconnaissance unit discovered a complete plan for Operation Market Garden in one of the destroyed British Horsa gliders. The Germans now knew what the Allies were up to.

37-year-old Brigadier General, James M. Gavin, the youngest general in the U.S. Army, led the *All American* forces. One of his regiments captured the Maas Bridge at Grave, the longest bridge in Europe. Another regiment captured Nijmegen, abandoned by the Germans. They also initiated a surprise attack on the Waal Bridge, where they encountered heavy resistance from the 9th Panzer SS.

Allied fighters attacked flak positions near Arnhem causing considerable damage. Major General Roy Urquhart led the British 1st Airborne Division. His troops landed successfully near Heelsum and Wolfheze with no interference from German troops. However, immediately after landing, the troops discovered their radio was inoperable and communication with other units was impossible. The British began an eleven-mile march to Arnhem. They left a regiment to guard the drop zone so other troops could land there the next day. During the advance to Arnhem, two battalions, including Urquhart's, were delayed by heavy German resistance.

A third battalion, led by Major John D. Frost, took a different route and reached Arnhem without incident. This handful of soldiers opened the attack on the bridge at Arnhem. After several attempts, it became clear to Frost that assistance from other battalions was necessary. But reinforcement was slowed down due to heavy German shelling. The British XXX Corps, led by Lieutenant General Brian G. Horrocks, prepared to cross the border between Belgium and the Netherlands. They were surprised by strong opposition from German forces, seriously impacting their ability to reach the airborne troops on time. The hard-fought corridor that ran from Eindhoven, Son, St. Oedenrode, Veghel, Uden, Grave, and Nijmegen to Arnhem was appropriately nicknamed Hell's Highway.

Holland Supply Drop Zone (DZ)
The mission of Monday, September 18, 1944

The Allies decided to use bombers to resupply the American and British troops. Instead of dropping bombs, they would parachute supplies in canvas-covered bundles and metal containers. The cargo consisted of parts and ammunition for howitzer guns, weapons, smaller ammunition, food, and medical supplies. All four squadrons of Crusaders were deployed to support mission number 169, called, *Holland Supply Drop Zone (DZ)* with forty bombers carrying 800 bundles. While airborne troops landed in the Netherlands, the Crusaders practiced above the English countryside, flying and dropping at treetop height. This Field Order reached the bomb groups from 2nd Bombardment Division Headquarters on September 17th[5]:

"This operation is one of furnishing supplies to the airborne forces now operating behind enemy lines, whose landing has been publicly confirmed this evening. It will be coordinated with a fighter operation and the Ninth Troop Carrier Command, which will precede us into this area tomorrow, attacking ground installations and dropping additional airborne troops. Interrogation will secure the special information required by Division Station Control on this mission. Group station officers have been informed of the information to be secured and should be consulted by S-2's[6] *at to what is desired. All crewmembers should be briefed as to the importance of observation and accurate reporting of all enemy movements in this area. The latest battle line will be passed to you tomorrow prior briefing.*

Initially, the airmen were not informed of the purpose for the training. This became clear the next morning on Monday, September 18th, during the briefing. While viewing the projected map, the aviators were informed of the paratroopers landing in the Netherlands and the supplies they desperately needed.

A total of 252 Liberators were tasked to drop the load, escorted by 374 Mustangs, 185 Thunderbolts, and 16 Lightnings. These were the fighters orders:

A: *8th Fighter Command will:*
   (1) *Escort the airborne forces and provide defense against air attack.*
   (2) *Attack and neutralize all flak encountered along route.*
   (3) *Escort the 2nd Bomb Division on resupply effort and provide defense against air attack.*

B: *One squadron (18 P-47's) of the 9th Fighter Command will attack and neutralize other flak positions and other specific positions along the route.*

To prevent damage to the dropped cargo and to ensure the cargo landed on the right spot, the bombers had to fly low at a maximum speed of 150 mph. Because this made them an easy target for flak, the bomber crews were not happy about this mission. But they were told it would be a *milk run*, an easy mission without significant opposition from fighters or flak. A field order on September 17th stated:

"Light flak and small arms fire may be encountered at any point particularly when crossing the battle line. However the following areas, which lie near the briefed routes, are known to be defended:

> *5126N-0525E considerable heavy and light flak* (west of Eindhoven, North Brabant)
> *5128N-0518E 6 light guns* (south of Oirschot, Brabant)
> *5124N-0456E 3 light guns* (south of Baarle-Nassau, North Brabant)
> *5145N-0544E 3 light guns* (north of Grave, North Brabant)
> *5148N-0539E 3 light guns* (west of Wijchen, Gelderland)
> *5148N-0558E 3 light guns* (north-east of Groesbeek, Gelderland)
> *5135N-0447E 12 light guns* (Breda, North Brabant)
> *5142N-0451E 9 light guns and balloon barrage* (Geertruidenberg, North Brabant)
> *5143N-0517E considerable light flak* (North of 's-Hertogenbosch, North Brabant)
> *5134N-0504E 6 heavy guns and slight light flak* (Tilburg, North Brabant)
> *5140N-0540E considerable heavy and light flak* (east of Uden, North Brabant)
> *5123N-0610N considerable heavy and light flak* (north of Venlo, Limburg)
> *5150N- 0552E considerable heavy and light flak* (Nijmegen, Gelderland)

The amount of flak encountered will be largely dependent upon the activities of our own forces in this area. It is very probable that many of the defended localities mentioned above will be operative, however main roads, cross roads, railways and bridges are all likely to be defended and such points should be avoided as far as possible after the target areas have been left.

The flak at 5126N-0525E and at 5140N-0540E has been strafed and bombed and will be attacked again for at least 1 1/2 hours before our operation. It is therefore hoped that most of it will be out of action."

The RAF bombed four nearby airports and several flak positions on the night of 16 and 17 September. On the morning of the 17th, B-17s also bombed enemy targets around the area of the operation. This is another Field Order about the flak danger:

"The flak positions along the whole route are being thoroughly strafed just before this operation takes place. Troop transports have so far encountered only meager oppositions in this area. The chief danger from flak will therefore probably lie in the immediate vicinity of the battle line, but crews should be briefed to keep strictly to the briefed routes in order to keep within the prepared corridors."

So there was not much to worry about. There were advantages to flying at low altitude. Heated clothing and oxygen masks were unnecessary. All ball turrets were removed from Liberators that still had one, so the supply load could be dropped through the round hatch. To ensure the supplies were dropped accurately, another man was added to each crew, a *drop (or load) master*, from the 2nd Air Cargo Resupply Detachment[7]. The waist gunners of the Crusaders would assist these forty specially trained men in dropping the load. To mitigate risk to the aircraft and save fuel, the drop masters also ensured the load in the aircraft was well distributed.

Johan and Johannes

Johannes Schipper, Piet's father-in-law, worked as a coffee roaster at the firm Kriense-Wessel & Co. His wife, Pauwtje, managed the Museum of South Beveland in Goes built in 1533. They lived on the ground floor of this monumental Gothic building and now a national monument, in the old harbor of Goes. Johannes and Pauwtje took care of their grandson, Johan, who lived with them. The museum building, also known as the *Charles V House*, closed in 1970 and is now a restaurant.

Johan was a lanky boy of 16. Together with a gang of friends, using iron pipes, he attacked some NSB members because they were parading down the main street of Goes. The Germans arrested Rudolf Fassaert[8], the leader of a *knokploeg*, a fighting gang that attacked NSB and other pro-German groups, and found a notebook on him containing the name of J.J. Schipper. On Monday, September 18, old Johannes was arrested and transferred to the prison in Middelburg. Dismayed, Piet van den Dries hurried to Middelburg on his bike that same day, to explain to the authorities they had captured his father-in-law instead of his nephew. The authorities recognized their mistake and freed Johannes. When the two men were asked where J.J. Schipper was, they could only reply that the rascal was in hiding at an unknown location. Betrayed by a NSB member who had not yet fled during Crazy Tuesday, Johan was later arrested and sent to the transit camp *Polizeiliches Durchgangslager Amersfoort* (PDA) in Amersfoort, where he was forced to work in the surrounding forests. Because Johan was very thin from malnutrition, he easily removed his handcuffs and managed to escape at the first opportunity and caught the train back home. Just before he reached Goes, he was accidentally noticed by the same NSB agent who betrayed him. Johan was put back in irons and sent back to Amersfoort. He was transported from Amersfoort to a camp in Germany, where he remained until the liberation.

Morton Baker

On September 16th, radio operator Morton Baker was admitted to the US Army Hospital Plant at Morley Hall in Norfolk for abdominal pain. During his training in the U.S. he was treated for this same problem in several military hospitals. The doctors in Norfolk initially diagnosed appendicitis, but during examination they could not locate the source of the pain. Morton did not fly a mission again until November 5th.

Elton Southwell

While Morton Baker was recovering from abdominal pain, 22-year-old S/Sgt Elton E. Southwell from Lyons, Nebraska substituted for Gerow's radio operator. Elton was raised on his parents' farm. He had an older sister, an older brother, and a younger brother. His older brother joined the Army and later died of a ruptured appendix. His younger brother joined the Navy. In high school, Elton worked as a butcher for McMonies grocery. He also worked there after he graduated in 1940 and before he enlisted in the army. He began boxing and even participated in prestigious Golden Gloves competitions. Elton was recruited on June 1, 1942, in Fort Crook, Nebraska. He trained as a pilot at an airbase in Fort Wayne, Indiana. After a few weeks, he was rejected from pilot training when a neglected injury in his shoulder was discovered, probably sustained during boxing. He continued working at the grocery while waiting to be recalled. When Elton was finally called back, he trained as a gunner at the Harlingen Army Gunnery School in Texas and as a radio operator at the Army Air Force Technical Training Center (AAFTTC) in Sioux Falls, South Dakota. He ended up in England at Wendling airbase. He flew with the crew of pilot 2/Lt. J. W. Bell, who, like Gerow's crew, was part of the 579th BS. Elton replaced the radio operator, W.T. Cheshire, and flew five missions with this crew. When Cheshire returned, Elton was available for Jim Gerow's crew and replaced Morton Baker.

Feathered Injun

The 392nd BG lost a lot of bombers in September, especially on September 11th during the mission to Hanover. As a result, the Crusaders had seven Liberators on loan from the 466th BG[9] from nearby Attlebridge Air Base. Jim Gerow and his crew were assigned to one of the bombers, called *Feathered Injun*[10].

Seven months earlier, this aircraft was manufactured at the Ford Motor Company, in the Willow Run Assembly Plant in Michigan, where a B-24H rolled of the assembly line every hour. *Feathered Injun* bore the serial number 42-94886. The bomber was assigned to the 787th Bombardment Squadron. On August 15, 1944 the bomber flew its last mission for this squadron. Because the aircraft was a loaner aircraft from the 466th BG, it bore the squadron letters *6L* on the fuselage just in front of the tail and had a circled *L* on the right wing instead of a circled *D* of the Crusaders.

The original name of the Liberator was *No Feathered Injun*. A cartoon character was painted on the nose of the aircraft, a grinning Indian with a long braid, sitting on a falling bomb. Initially, the Indian warrior wore no feather on his head, but a previous crew had painted one on top his bald head and crossed out the *No*. *No Feathered Injun* was a name with a double meaning. *Injun*, a derogatory corruption of the word *Indian*, sounds like engine. Feathering was a term used for fixing the blade position of the propeller after engine failure to improve aircraft control. Feathering was common. And this aircraft, which had flown about 60 missions, would certainly have experienced it a number of times. Therefore, the name was unofficially changed to *Feathered Injun*.

The upper half of the Liberator was painted an army green color called *olive drab*. To camouflage the bomber in the air, the belly and underside of the wings were painted a gray-blue color with a wavy separation to the green. The propellers were painted black with yellow peaks at the tips of the blades. When the propellers became a blur while rotating the ends of the blades were still visible.

Elton Southwell wrote:[11] *"We were briefed about 8 o'clock in the morning and we were to take off at about eleven, but something happened, and after pre-flighting our ship from stem to stern, the tower called us and told us to return to the mess hall for our noon meal. We were then to return to our ships and prepare for takeoff at one o'clock."*

After they had eaten and returned to the aircraft, they saw that the ground crew was almost finished loading it.

Ed Yensho

A young soldier came up to them and introduced himself as Pvt. Ed Yensho, drop master from the 2nd Air Cargo Resupply Detachment. The young man was nervous. This would be his first mission. Instead of a chest parachute, he wore a back parachute, like the pilot and co-pilot. The 19-year-old Edward Yensho was from Lakewood, Ohio. His family emigrated from Czechoslovakia. He had three older brothers and a sister. Before the war, his ancestor's land was already occupied by the Germans. This was the reason Ed's brothers all fought in the war. His brother, Andrew, served in the Navy in the Pacific. Jay was in the Army in Africa and Nick was in the Army in Europe. Ed was fond of baseball and it had always been his dream to pitch for the *Cleveland Indians*. He was talented and left-handed, a plus for a pitcher. Scouts for the *St Louis Cardinals* invited him to play for them. He pitched remarkably well during his first game but afterwards he told the coach that he, like his brothers, wanted to join the army. The astonished coach asked him why. Ed shrugged and said that he just wanted to prove that he was a good pitcher. Moreover, he only wanted to play for his favorite team, the Cleveland Indians. A few days later, on November 27th, 1943, Ed enlisted at Fort Hayes in Columbus, Ohio. In December, he was stationed at Jefferson Barracks in Lemay, Missouri, and in March 1944 he transferred to Seymour Johnson Air Base in Goldsboro, North Carolina.

On this Monday, September 18th, 1944 Ed loaded twenty bundles on the four bomb racks, on the catwalk and in the waist. The top of the bundle was hooked to a fixed static line that pulled the parachutes open as soon as the bundle was dropped. There were large signs painted on them to inform the soldiers what was in the bundles or containers. Drop parachutes were different colors. Blue could mean drinking water, orange for ammunition, and green for food. This color code changed several times during the war to confuse the enemy. Feathered Injun was loaded with ammunition boxes wrapped in canvas and at least one tubular metal ammunition container, both connected to yellow orange parachutes.

That day the Crusader's formation consisted of five squadrons:

(1) Lead Squadron, with eight bombers of the 578th BS. The commanders of the formation, General L.B. Johnson and Colonel J.A. Duke (Duke was from Headquarters, 9th Troop Carrier Command), flew in the lead bomber *Jolly Duck* with the crew of pilot Capt. A.B. Alexander.
(2) High Squadron, with eight bombers of the 577th BS.
(3) Low Squadron, eight bombers of the 576th BS.
(4) Low-low Squadron, eight bombers of the 579th BS.
(5) Compilation Squadron, a mix of eight bombers from the four squadrons.

Feathered Injun was the Low (left) Aircraft of the Low Element of the Compilation Squadron and was thereof the last and lowest flying bomber in the formation. This was not a preferred position. By the time the crew flew over enemy flak positions, the flak operators already had enough time to aim their guns and adjust timing fuses on the shells.

At 1220 hours, the Lead Squadron bombers started their engines, followed by the other squadrons, each with five minutes in between.

Feathered Injun started its engines at 1240 hours and taxied to the runway five minutes later. The aircraft took off at 1355 hours and climbed 1500 feet to join the formation behind the assembly ship, Minerva. At this height, thick clouds limited visibility, but the mission continued. After the formation was assembled, the first bombers crossed the English coast at Clacton at 1425 hours. At 1458 hours, they reached the coast of Goeree-Overflakkee, an island in the province of South Holland. The weather on the continent became favorable. There was a light breeze from the northeast and it was dry, with a few clouds. At a low height they had a good view of the beautiful farms and large areas previously flooded by the Germans in February and March.

Elton: "We would fly over a small village and friendly Dutch people would wave at us and it looked as if they were cheering us. It seemed this way, because at this time, we were at two hundred feet and one can see things fairly well at this height. But on the other end of the village, the Jerries would shoot at us with everything, including small arms. About this time, we decided that this wasn't going to be such an easy flight as we had planned."

That suspicion was realized when, after passing over the third village, they were again under fire. While exploding flak shells formed black clouds around the aircraft, the number 2-engine (to the pilot's immediate left) was hit and had to be feathered. Flying on three engines, they managed to stay in formation. The crew was startled by a number of hits in the bomb bay, but damage was minor. Within a few minutes, the bomb bay was hit again, resulting in gas leaks. Flight engineer Gene, who was just promoted to the rank of Technical Sergeant, had to open the bomb doors slightly, so the toxic, flammable fumes could escape.

After turning over the Initial Point (IP) in the vicinity of 's-Hertogenbosch, the formation split up into three sections headed towards their targets. At 1548 hours, the first Liberators finally saw purple parachutes, highlighting the designated area near Groesbeek. When the Feathered Injun neared their target area, radio operator, Elton, looked out through the crack of the opened bomb bay door and saw the British Horsa gliders crisscrossed in the fields and parachutes everywhere around them. This drop zone was on the Knapheide, a piece of farmland southwest of hilly Groesbeek, near Nijmegen and was called Drop Zone-N (DZ-N).

Now all hell broke loose. It seemed the enemy knew exactly where the squadrons were to drop their cargo because they concentrated their flak just above the drop zone. It was a miracle that no one was hurt, because Feathered Injun was hit many times, not only in the back and the bomb bay, but also in the side. The fuel leak expanded, filling the bomb bay with gas and fumes. Because they were close to the target, but also because they wanted the gas and fumes to escape, they completely opened the bomb bay doors. Ed, who was trained to recognize the exact drop zone, gave the signal. At an altitude of only 250 feet, Ed, aided by Ely and Ben, managed to drop most of the twenty bundles on the drop zone. Because they were constantly under fire, the crewmembers did not have time to watch the orange parachutes hit the ground. Flak fire became so intense that Jim decided to get out of their range before they could drop the whole load. With flak grenades exploding around them, the Liberator began to climb and headed for England. The plane was hit again. This time the number 3 engine (to the copilot's immediate right) began to leak oil. Before this engine was completely lost, Gerow decided to gain more elevation. He was careful not to fly too high, because the crew's clothing did not protect them against the biting cold at high altitude. Feathered Injun was hit again in the bomb bay. They had to close the bomb bay door and the fuel leaks were becoming unbearable.

Navigator Dave Grandon suggested they leave the formation and fly to liberated Brussels. The decision was Jim's, but it was a terrible dilemma. The damage to the aircraft worried him, but flying in a formation had its advantages. Like a flock of birds or a school of fish, an individual is less likely to be singled out in a large group. A lonely aircraft out of formation was an easy target for flak batteries or enemy fighters. Jim decided to stay in formation and hope he would be able to keep this *flying coffin* safe. But halfway to the coast, tail gunner Frenchy reported the rudder cables were shot in half. Jim tried to fly on autopilot, which proved defective as well.

At 1655 hours radio operator Elton reported the aircraft damage to the airbase via the ultra-short wave. Flying above the sandbar called *Hompels* (northeast of Vrouwenpolder, 5 miles north of Middelburg), the crew saw the North Sea before them. Jim realized that under these circumstances, he could not cross the North Sea without risking an emergency landing in the water. He decided to follow his navigator's suggestion and fly to Brussels. Engine failure at a lower altitude would definitely result in a crash, so he decided to gain as much elevation as possible. Jim ordered flight engineer Gene to go to the tail and try to fix the rudder cables. The crewmembers began to use the oxygen masks to protect themselves against the toxic gases in the bomb bay. Gene wore a mask, supplied by a portable oxygen bottle. He met Elton on his way back and told him what he was up to.

Dave calculated the route to Brussels. As they flew, Gerow gave his crew instructions to exit the aircraft in case of an emergency. Everyone reported they heard his command, nobody was hurt, and everyone would be able to jump. The sputtering engine broke down and the propeller could not be feathered. It is possible to fly with a propeller that rotates randomly, but with only two engines operating, a windmilling propeller and a feathered propeller, it is virtually impossible.

Feathered Injun flew at an altitude of 1,700 feet when it was suddenly hit by flak grenades, fired by the *3./ Flakscheinwerfer-Abteilung 369th V*[2]. According to a German situation sketch[13], Feathered Injun was attacked by six C/38 Flaks, from two positions in the Ankerverepolder, designated *I/3/369* and *II/3/369*[14]. The Germans fired a 20 mm caliber with 809 grenades. The bomber fuselage and wings were hit, igniting escaped gases in the bomb bay, which spread rapidly. The air gunners fired several volleys into the II/3/369 positions and a German column, but they hit nothing. The situation was hopeless. Jim rang the alarm bell and gave the order to bail out.

1:     The dam that forms the connection between the mainland of North Brabant and the peninsula South Beveland.
2:     During the operation, the USAAF, the RAF and the RCAF (Royal Canadian Air Force) participated. USAAF used the Douglas C-47 Skytrain (Dakota) and Curtiss-Wright C-46 Commando. RAF bombers used the Short Stirling and Handley Page Halifax. RCAF flew with both the Douglas C-47 Skytrain and the Short Stirling.
3:     The USAAF used the WACO CG-4A and the RAF and RCAF used the Airspeed Horsa I and GAL.49 Hamilcar.

4: The USAAF used Thunderbolts and Mustangs. The RAF used Supermarine Spitfires and Hawker Typhoons.

5: All orders in this chapter: Field Order No. 464 from 2nd Bombardment Division Headquarters.

6: S-2's = Officers of the Intelligence Section. They lead the briefing.

7: A logistic unit within the U.S. Army.

8: Resistance fighter, Rudolf Fassaert, was the leader of the Group Fassaert, a fighting gang from the Zeelandic Flanders village Lamswaarde. In the spring of 1944, they were engaged in a raid on the town hall of Vogelwaarde and an unsuccessful liquidation attempt of a member of the Landwacht. During Crazy Tuesday, under his leadership, a number of German soldiers were captured in a farmhouse in Spui. After it became clear they had acted too soon, they left the soldiers behind in a barn. On 17 September 1944, Rudolf was wakened from his bed by German soldiers who were on retreat. They took him to Middelburg, where he was sentenced to death. On the day of execution, he managed to escape with outside help and he hid himself in Grijpskerke and then in Domburg. After the war he became a captain in the Dutch Royal Army, and was commander of the 3rd Company of the 1st Guard Battalion. This battalion was given the name: Rudolf Fassaert Battalion, later: Battalion 1-14 (the 1st Battalion of the 14th Infantry Regiment).

9: The 466th BG was nicknamed *The Flying Deck*, with each squadron named after a different card suit. The 784th BS was the *Clubs*: the 785th was the *Diamonds*: the 786th was the *Hearts*: and the 787th the *Spades*. The Feathered Injun came from the *Spades*. On the nose art photos, the name Vincent L. reed can be read under the co-pilots window. Reed was the co-pilot for pilot Lt. John H. Woodnough. His 466th BG crew flew the bomber, No Feathered Injun, from April 26, 1944 until August 25, 1944. After the war John Woodnough was the founder of the 8th Air Force Historical Society and the writer of the book *Attlebridge Diaries*.

10: The other bombers on loan were: *Queenie, The Lemon, Big Fat Mama, Off Limits Again, Mama's Little Angel* and *Pale Ale*.

11: All quotes from Elton Southwell are from his memoirs: *Life of a German POW*, written in the early nineties.

12: 3. = *3rd Company, Flakscheinwerfer-Abteilung* = a unit whose task was to man the flaks and its floodlights. *369* = 369th Division, *V* = *verlegbar* (mobile). This *Luftwaffe* unit was part of the Flak-Brigade XX. It was one of seven *Abteilungen* of *Flakscheinwerfer Regiment 195 (V)*. This regiment was commanded by *Oberst* (Colonel) Hans Hübner. It was on August 26th, 1939 assembled in Wolfenbüttel in Hanover. From October 1940 Flakscheinwerfer-Abteilung 369 was in Dunkirk, from July 1942 in the Netherlands. By late 1943 the unit was deployed in Boulogne and from March 1944, in Lille. From September 1944, the unit returned to the Netherlands.

13: The German data is from the sketched outline: *Zielwegskizze Abschuß einer Liberator am 09.18.44 um 17.52h* and the corresponding German report from *Oberluitnant* (Lieutenant Colonel) Bracke.

14: At that time there were five German flak positions in the area: *I./3./369* and *II./3./369* were located at the Anker Vere Polder, *III./3./369* and *IV./3./369* were located at the railway north of 's-Heer Arendskerke and *V./3./369* north of 's-Heer Hendrikskinderen.

An ambulance with equipment at Wendling Air Base. (086 - www.b24.net)

The hospital at Wendling Air base. (087 – www.b24.net)

Johan, Johannes and Pauwtje Schipper at their home. (088)

The Museum of South Beveland. (089)

Radio operator Elton Southwell. (090)

Drop master Ed Yensho. (091)

Elton during his training as a gunner in Harlington, Texas. (092)

Elton during his radio operator training in Sioux Falls, South Dakota. (093)

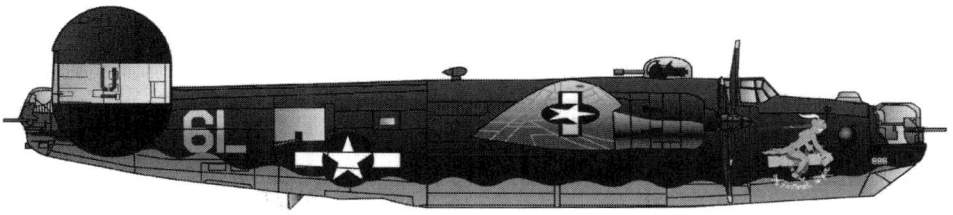

A reconstruction of Feathered Injun. (094)

The two versions of the nose art. Left: No Feathered Injun. (095 - b24bestweb) Feathered Injun. The stump of the feather is just visible. (096 – b24bestweb)

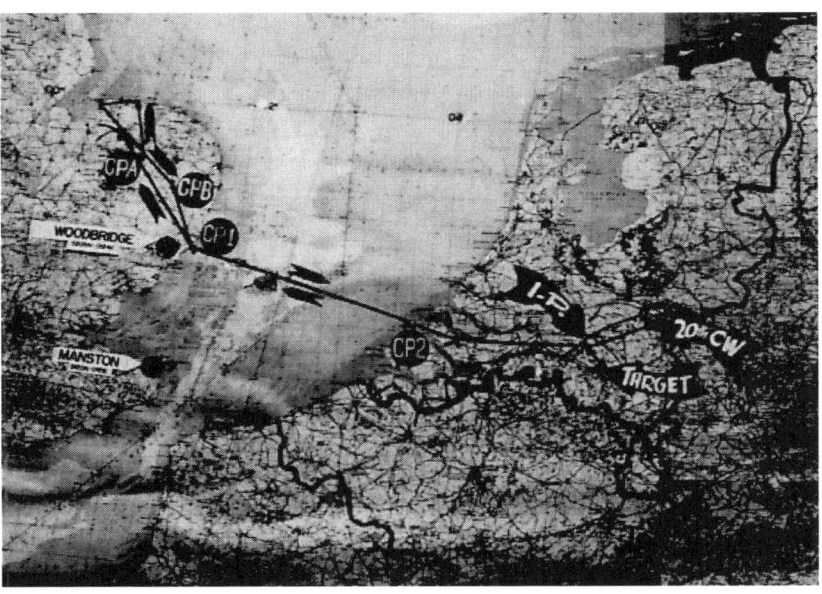

The map that was used at the briefing. CP = Contact Point, IP = Initial Point. (097a - www.b24.net)

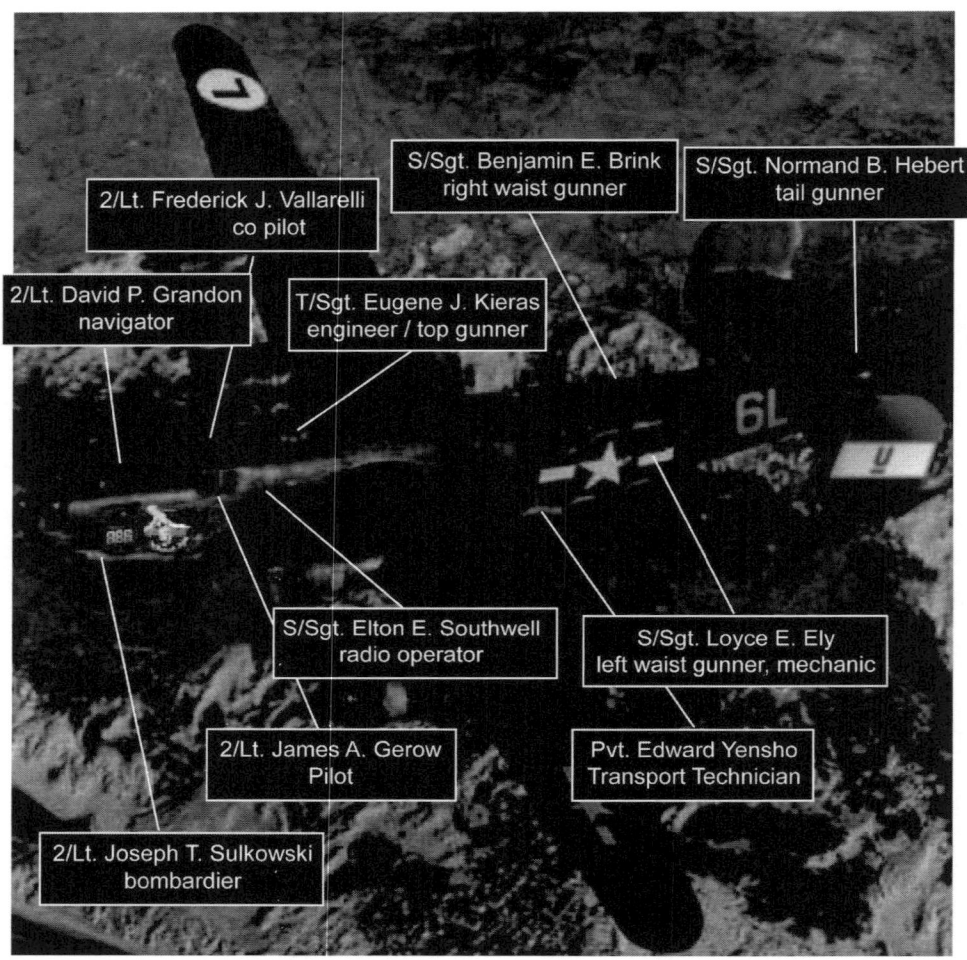

The positions in Feathered Injun. (097)

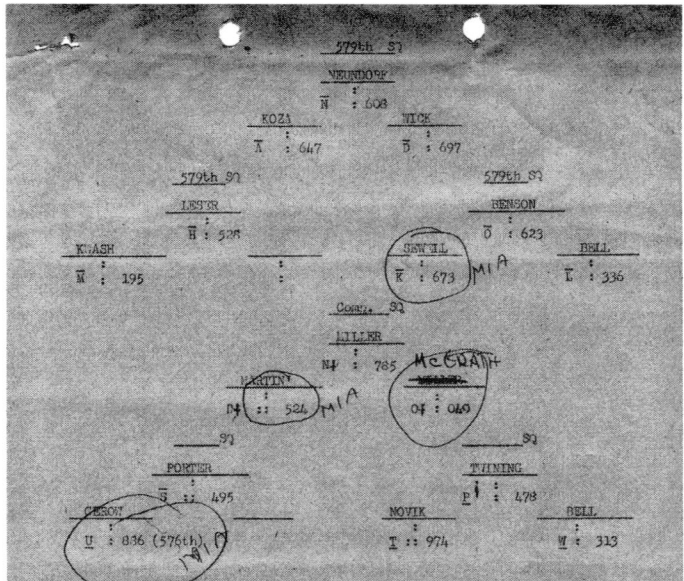

The position within the Low-low Squadron and the Compilation Squadron. Gerow's crew is bottom left. MIA = Missing in Action. (097b - www.b24.net)

A B-24 of the 466th BG drops cargo above the Dutch town Eerde on September 18, 1944. (097c - U.S. Air Force)

A bundle has landed. (098 - U.S. Army)

A plane's engines were numbered from left to right, from the pilot's perspective as they sat in the cockpit. In this photo, the #1 engine is burning and the #4 prop has been feathered. (099 – U.S. Air Force)

A Liberator is hit in an engine while flying between exploding flak grenades. (100 – U.S. Air Force)

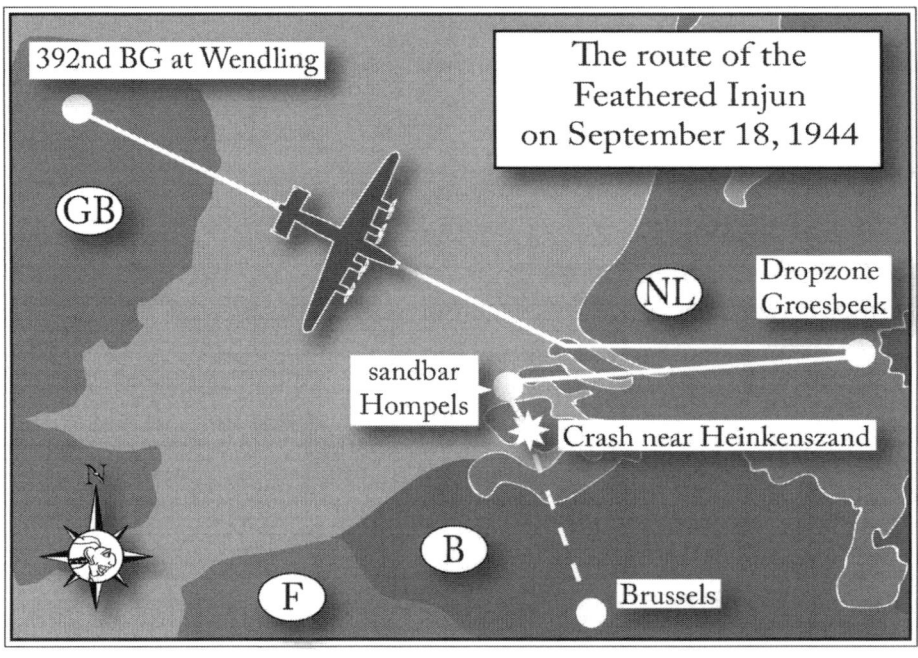

(101)

Elton Southwell (in the middle), with his sister Vera and brother Dale. (101a)

Ed Yensho and his brother Jay. (101b)

Chapter 9

Parachutes in the sky

On that bright Monday in September, Feathered Injun quickly lost altitude above the polders of South Beveland. They flew at an altitude of 1500 ft while the crew prepared to abandon the burning aircraft. As the bomber lost altitude, they wondered whether they would be able to parachute safely. There was no time to think. It had been less than three minutes from the first hits until the crash. Because everyone acted simultaneously, events at each exit will be described separately.

The Rear Hatch

Tail Gunner Frenchy jumped first. As left waist gunner Ely prepared to bail out, he saw Ed standing by the hatch. The young dropmaster was not an aviator and lacked the experience of the others. It is probable he had never jumped out of a plane. Although he wore a back parachute and appeared ready to jump, Ed froze. Ely realized the danger and tried to persuade the boy to bail out. Ely grabbed Ed to assist him with the jump, but Ed tore himself loose, screaming and kicking. Ely realized his efforts were futile and every lost second would put his own life in jeopardy. He made a difficult decision and jumped through the hatch before it was too late.

Flight engineer Gene was also in the rear of the airplane. He had no time to argue with Ed. Gene had his own problems. The *catwalk* in the bomb bay was very narrow and it was not possible to cross it with a parachute hooked on. Gene had therefore not brought his parachute with him because he carried a portable oxygen tank in one hand and tools he needed to fix the rudder cables in the other. He left his parachute near the top turret in the front part of the aircraft, but could not retrieve it because of the fire in the bomb bay. The crew had been taught how to deal with such emergencies during parachute training. Right waist gunner Ben told Gene to climb on his back and hold on, and they would jump together. Ben's parachute was hooked in front, so this plan had a chance of success. Gene realized the danger of such a leap at low altitude, but he also knew he had no other option. Gene clung to Ben's back and together they squeezed out the rear hatch.

The Bomb Hatch

Because the landing gear was retracted and it would take too long to let the nosewheel down, the bomb bay doors were the safest escape route for the men in the front of the aircraft. Radio operator Elton rushed to the burning bomb bay and hesitated, not knowing whether they had enough altitude to make the jump. He realized he had no choice, and, as the flames began to burn his clothes, he tried to manually open the two front shutters. As he struggled with the doors, his parachute harness became entangled. No matter how hard he tried, he could not tear himself loose. Suddenly, co-pilot Fred jumped from the catwalk to the rolling shutters and succeeded in opening one door so there was enough space to jump. Fred freed the radio operator and ordered him to jump. With fire scorching his face and clothes, Elton did not hesitate.

After Elton disappeared through the hatch, the co-pilot jumped after him, followed by navigator Dave and bombardier Joe. While his crew abandoned ship, Commander Jim tried to stabilize the aircraft, with limited success. After he assumed everyone had enough time to jump, he hastened to the bomb bay. The flames flared, fed by oxygen from the opened door, and burned Jim's face as he jumped.

Eyewitnesses

The first eyewitnesses on the ground to see the aircraft were German soldiers from the *Flakscheinwerfer-Abteilung 369 (V)* (Searchlights Department 369 (Mobile)).

Oberleutnant (First Lieutenant) Bracke reported[1]: "*It was shot from 500 meters. They fired back with their onboard weapons at our Flak II.3/369 and at a column of soldiers in the streets without causing damage. Their own aircraft was hit. Hits were observed in the engine, wings and fuselage. The inner left engine was stopped, the inner right engine showed plumes of smoke and was on fire. The fire quickly caught around them.*"

The next witness was in 's-Heer Arendskerke, a village north of Heinkenszand. Sergeant Vermeulen of the Dutch military police reported the following[2]: "*In compliance with your order to make a report about the burning plane which came down burning, I beg to inform you the following details: On September 18, 1944, about 1730 hours, I was in the municipal-*

ity of 's-Heer Arendskerke and saw a plane of American nationality coming from an eastern direction[3]. By the sound of the engines and the quick coming down I supposed the plane had already been damaged before it came over the municipality of 's-Heer Arendskerke. I heard some flak from the before mentioned direction just before. After that the plane had flown over this municipality and then came again within reach of German ac-ac, this post too fired at the plane. After some shots I saw that a flame started under the plane and that some eight pilots bailed out, after which no more shots were fired. Immediately after the pilots had left the plane I saw that the plane came down fast with a curve and crashed burning in the polder of De Poel. As I was on duty I could not go to the place where it had come down."

Koos van Iwaarden[4], the 16-year-old daughter of farmer Rienbouw van Iwaarden was on her father's farm Helenahoeve, on the south side of the Boerendijk, just north of the village Heinkenszand. She said: *"My sister and I just took the cows to the milking shed to get them ready for milking. We heard a roaring aircraft engine and saw a huge bulky airplane flying over. Where it came from, I do not know exactly, I think from the Postweg at Ankerverepolder, because they shot it with guns. They have just finished the plane off, for it was already hit before that."*

Rinus Geschiere[5] from Heinkenszand, the 14-year-old son of the local milkman: *"We had a piece of farmland. It was against the Westdijk and bordered about where the Roofvogelstraat is now. There was a mild breeze and it was beautiful weather. We were there in the afternoon with five men busy collecting the dried beans from the bean tepees[6]. Suddenly, we heard shooting from the north and a roar. The noise grew louder when the bomber emerged. It was a gigantic airplane. Black smoke billowed out and it was on fire. The engines were still roaring. When it came down toward us, we saw about six parachutes in succession drop from the plane. I think it was no more than 50 meters from the ground. It quickly lost altitude. We were shocked because we thought it would fall in the meadow. That's a weird feeling, because you cannot run away from it. You do not know which way to run. When it flew above us, it turned and lost a piece of metal, about 5 x 5 centimeters, with a number on it. It flew so low that, when it would fly over the church tower, it would have hit the peak of the bell tower. After the turn it came down. We heard a loud bang, but no explosion. I did not go there, but I did go to the village. Next to the Roman Catholic Church was a Catholic school with a unit of German soldiers. They immediately went searching for the men that bailed out."*

Jan Minnaard[7], the 5-year-old son of baker Adriaan Minnaard. Was at his father's shop playing in a small paved garden: *"When I saw the burning* plane coming, I thought that it came from the direction of Landlust estate. I thought it would crash at our house. When I saw the plane coming at me, a woman ran up to me: Mrs. Tienpont. She lived a little further down the street. She was at this time at our shop. She came up to me and dragged me inside and leaned over me to protect me from the crash. I still remember the fear on her face. Apparently, the aircraft was flying higher than I thought; it flew quite a lot further before it came down. I saw very clearly someone sitting at the place of the pilot. My feeling was that it was the pilot, but it may also have been someone else."

Han Nijsse[8], 14-years old, lived in the Dorpsstraat opposite Landlust. "We heard people on the streets shouting: 'There is one on fire!' So we came out our front door, my father and my brother and me. When we arrived on the street, we saw that huge plane coming over. I think I counted seven parachutes or so. We saw through the bombs shutters that the aircraft was burning inside. We saw a huge flame at the crash but no explosion. We immediately ran towards where it had crashed."

Dies Hannewijk[9], 14 years old, also lived in the Dorpsstraat opposite the Landlust estate. "We were picking potatoes in a field where the Guldenroedestraat is now. We heard guns firing. We were used to it, because that happened almost every day, especially at night. Then they came about in groups of 40-50 aircraft. They went at night to Germany and they came back in the afternoon or morning. Suddenly we heard a plane flying at us with smoke and fire. We saw it just above the farm of the wedding hall emerge and fly at the same height of the Heinkenszand church tower. It came in our direction. The engines were not working at that time. I thought it made a strange whooshing sound, like a zeppelin or a fan blade. After it soared overhead, we walked along in the direction of where that colossal thing would come down. At about 300 meters away from us it crashed right between two linden trees on the Grotedijk."

Marien Mol[10] was 24-years-old and and living in Nisse. "I was on the Thijs Hoekseweg, at which we had an orchard, southeast of Heinkenszand. Suddenly I heard flak, so my eyes were drawn to it. Then I saw that low aircraft appear. I did not see the grenades, but I felt and I heard them explode all around, because there was flak artillery firing at that low plane. I was close to a ditch, so I crawled in there because of the flak, but also because the low aircraft flew in my mind right at me. I would prefer not to bang my head! At the last moment I saw him make a turn and end up on the dike between the linden trees. I did not see the crew bailing out because I was too far away. At first I thought it went towards Heinkenszand, when it made a strange turn and then it went down. Of course, it all happened so fast. I didn't go to the *scene of the crash, it was a few kilometers of cycling and usually the Germans would have blocked the place off."*

Ko van 't Westeinde wrote[11]: *"We were busy, my brother and myself and a few farm hands, trying to pull a horse out of a ditch. The horse belonged to a farmer in Borssele. This farmer had his work horses in our area in a pasture near the motorway to prevent them from being seized by the Germans. We had a quiet corner over there. While we were doing our job, we saw an allied aircraft shot and hit by flak near the Ankerverepolder. The aircraft flew very low. It flew in a curve to the village Heinkenszand, and came straight at us, but hit the ground at the pool called de Brilletjes (the Glasses). One of the engines of the aircraft came to a stop only ten feet away from us. The plane flew just one meter over the head of Mr. W. Wisse, who was cleaning a ditch along the Grotedijk. He survived, but you could see at the color of his face that it was the shock of his life. We also saw parachutes coming out of the plane, but could not determine how many there were, given the heavy poplar plantations on the Grotedijk. The devastation was very large and the debris were scattered over a large area, just before a nursery for fruit trees and an orchard. Within a range of 200 meters it fried the apples hanging on the trees."*

After The Jump

The crew drifted in a southwesterly direction. They came down, scattered in Heinkenszand, in an area from the Stelleplas to the Stellepolder and to Julianastraat in the village. According to eyewitnesses, there was little wind that day and the aircraft was flying very low, so the distance from jumping to landing was not long.

Frenchy, who jumped first, broke his ankle upon landing and was arrested by soldiers of the Flak-Searchlight Division.

Jan Minnaard saw a man in the cockpit. This must have been Ed. In a desperate attempt to save himself, he must have run through the fire in the bomb bay to the empty cockpit. The report of Dies Hannewijk suggested that the two remaining engines had failed and the aircraft was only making a whooshing noise caused by the three random rotating propellers (the fourth was feathered and not moving). The Liberator arced almost 180 degrees to the left. Later, the Group Griep suspected the pilot of the Liberator tried to avoid the village and sacrificed his life to prevent civilian fatalities. In hindsight, this heroic theory was questionable. The only crewmembers who could control the aircraft were pilot Jim, co-pilot Fred, bombardier Joe, and flight engineer Gene and they had already left the aircraft. In addition, the German sketch indicated the plane's arc began over the Helenahoeve farm. If the plane had flown straight, it would have crashed in the meadows south of Heinkenszand rather than in the village. Others decided Ed wanted to extinguish the burning aircraft by landing in the pool called de Brilletjes that he saw shining in the distance. The turn could have been caused by pilot Gerow's attempt to stabilize the aircraft before he jumped. It is possible the fire caused a technical failure in the wings. That, combined with a possible shift in the load balance of the aircraft, could have caused the turn.

Once the burning Feathered Injun made this large turn, it skimmed the Grotedijk and hit some poplar trees. It crashed to the left of the *weel*[12], called de Brilletjes, on the border of the municipality Heinkenszand. Fragments were scattered over a great distance, but most of the plane ended up near two linden trees in a bend of the Westhofsezandweg. Both trees caught fire. The poplar trees on the dikes were later cut down but the two large linden trees that withstood the fire are still there. Three years after the crash leaves began to grow on the trees again. The crash ended the life of Ed Yensho on his first mission.

Ely gave the following statement[13] on his landing: *"I jumped out of the aircraft at about 1500 ft. and came down in the back of a farm near the village Heinkenszand in South Beveland, Holland."*

This farm was on the north side of the Boerendijk, where the Van Liere family lived. Behind their house they had an orchard with many berry bushes. Leny van Iwaarden, 12-years old, lived on the other side of the dike, in the aforementioned Helenahoeve.

Leny: *"When the bomber came over, I was playing in the orchard at the neighbors Van Liere. I was watching the parachutes from the aircraft coming down and suddenly a parachutist landed behind me. I was terrified and ran home through the orchard. While running I saw three parachutes hanging in the trees. When I was over the dike and ran to our own yard I saw another soldier walking there."*

Ely: *"I joined up with my pilot and navigator, and we started to walk away from the place though a dry ditch. From a distance we saw three German soldiers approaching. We had nowhere to hide, so we drew back and started to sneak the other way. We walked through the ditch when I suddenly realized that I had forgotten to hand in my wallet at the airbase. It was still in my pocket and I paused to bury it, but the pilot and the navigator kept on walking. When I began to bury my wallet, the krauts opened fire on the two that they had discovered. I began to crawl towards where we had come from and hid under some hawthorn bushes. The shelter was not much, but it worked. I heard the Germans open fire again, and heard the pilot shout*

"Kamerad!" (Comrade). *The three Germans walked with my pilot and navigator passing me just a few feet away."*

Ely was fortunate to escape detection. Crewmembers had to hand in their wallets before every mission. This rule was introduced to prevent the enemy from getting private information. In interrogations, personal data was often used to put the prisoner under psychological pressure. During a mission, an aviator was supposed to have only his dog tag and a picture of himself in civilian clothes. Airmen did not always obey the rules.

While Ely stayed behind, three soldiers of the Flak-Searchlight Division arrested Jim and Dave.

Jim wrote: *"A female German soldier[14] who was armed with a Schmeisser machine pistol warned me that they would not hesitate to shoot if we tried to escape."*

After their capture by the Boerendijk, Jim and Dave tried to appease the soldiers by offering them some American cigarettes. They were marched to Heinkenszand.

Ben jerked the cord to open his parachute and his fall abruptly slowed when his parachute opened. Gene could not hold on. He desperately tried to cling to Ben's legs but finally let go and fell to his death. The 20-year-old Gene Kieras landed in a meadow of the Molenhof farm. Several witnesses saw him fall. Cor Mallekote[15], a butcher's son, lived across the street at the Stationsweg. He stood among the tobacco plants playing with a friend. Cor saw the aircraft crash and he saw Gene fall without a parachute. Also the painter, Willem van der Linde, who was painting a home in the Stationsstraat, saw the whole thing and ran toward the body.

Another eyewitness, 18-year-old blacksmith Frans Bliek, later stated in a report by Sergeant Vermeulen: *"When these persons where coming down from the plane, I saw that one man came down without a parachute with turning movements and that in his vicinity one opened parachute, to which no person was attached was sailing in another direction. After the foresaid person had left the plane the German flak fired no longer. I have not seen if this aforesaid man without a parachute was attached to a parachute, but I suppose so. Aforesaid pilot came down thereupon in a meadow opposite to my house. After he had come down on the ground he overturned once more as far as a yard from the ground."*

Other witnesses claimed that the body bounced and turned sideways and you could see a cross shaped imprint in the ground for days afterward.

Frans: *"After that I went immediately up to him and saw that he gave no sign of life and that a thin blood stream ran along his nose. Further bruises* were not visible. On a disc, which he wore round his arm, I saw that his name was: Eugene Kieras, old 20 years. When the pilot had come down, the Germans were not long in arriving and we were compelled to leave the spot. Before I had to leave I saw that some soldiers immediately searched his pockets and took away the cigarettes, which they smoked together. After they had thoroughly examined him they put the corpse on a wheel barrow and covered it with some gunny sacks."

Jacob Koole, sergeant of the local constabulary, saw the crew jump and Gene fall. He stated in the report of his colleague, Vermeulen, that he had seen an unmanned parachute floating away. *"After I saw this happen, I hurried straight to the spot where the aforementioned aviator had landed, what appeared to be a meadow somewhere in the municipality Heinkenzand. Immediately after the Germans had arrived, they forbade me to see the aviator."*

Ben Brink, shocked by Gene's death, came down safely, but was arrested. He and the injured Frenchy were put in a car and taken to the town hall on Dorpsstraat.

While Joe drifted with his parachute, he saw a number of German soldiers on motorbikes riding toward where he would land, an orchard behind a large farm, Helenahoeve, on the south side of the Boerendijk. Here lived the 45-year-old, Rienbouw van Iwaarden, with his wife and their three daughters, Kaat, Koos, and Leny, the two youngest already mentioned. Rienbouw was born on this farm. On May 13, 1925, his twenty-fifth birthday he married Appolonia Lokerse. Ploo, as she was called, was from the Molenhof, the same farm where Gene was killed. Her father still lived there. Together, Ploo and her husband ran the farm on the Helenahoeve. Rienbouw was occupied with the cultivation of the land, while Ploo took care of the household, the horses, pigs, chickens, turkeys, dogs and cats.

Koos and Leny: *"We had Germans billeted in the so-called basement room, in the room above the basement. There were bunks where eight young Germans slept; the youngest was 17 and the oldest 21. They were sons of mountain farmers in Bavaria. They always wanted to help with the care of our animals. They thought the horses were beautiful because when our father came home from working the land, they ran shouting to see who could help unharness and take care of the horses. These guys would cry sometimes because they were homesick. Two officers slept in the so-called alcove, between a small room adjacent to our parents bedroom. They were real Nazi men. We no longer remember their ranks. They were very strict with those young boys.*

They often punished them and those guys had to perform various exercises until they fell down. During the day they all went to the village and at five o'clock they came back. What they did all day in the village, we do not know. On the morning of September 18th, this group of Germans left going towards the Sloedam. That's why the Germans were not there when Joe parachuted down near our farm."

Rienbouw was picking apples in the orchard behind the house when he saw a parachutist in the air. He ran to the spot where the man would land, and saw him fall into an apple tree breaking many branches - and his ankle. The parachute was draped all over the tree. Under the parachute, Joe rid himself of his harness and fell to the ground. Urgently, he shouted to the rushing farmer that the parachute had to be removed and then limped as fast as he could to hide in a pig barn. He soon realized this was not a good hiding place and, while Rienbouw tried to free the parachute from the tree, Joe fled in the direction of a large barn, meeting a shocked Leny on the way. She saw him limping toward the barn and ran to tell her father. Because Joe might be armed and the Germans in the village were in an uproar, Rienbouw dared not go look for him.

Koos and Leny: *"The Germans that were stationed near the cannons at the Ankerverepolder came to us every day to buy a few liters of milk. Some time (we think 5 to 10 minutes) after Joe had parachuted down here, some Germans came from the village to the Helenahoeve. They ordered our mother and older sister Kaat to tell them where the pilot was. Mother and Kaat said they did not know. The Germans drew their gun and put it on the breast of mother and Kaat and said they would shoot if they remained silent. Also, they threatened to throw grenades into the barn. Just at that moment the Germans who were stationed near Ankerverepolder and always came to fetch milk, walked into the yard. They said, 'Ha Mutti!' (Hi mom!) That was their salvation because the guns were put away. That same evening we got another twenty Germans to quarter in the same barn where Joe was hiding."*

That was another reason why Rienbouw did not dare look for Joe, even though he suspected he was hidden somewhere in the barn. The barn was so big that a company of about two hundred Germans was housed in it just before the liberation of Heinkenszand. The Germans had a good view of the village from there. It was also the last farm outside the village with electricity, which was necesary to communicate with other units.

Joe was lucky that he landed at the Helenahoeve when there was a platoon change. After he fled to the barn, he climbed up two rickety ladders as fast as his broken ankle allowed him. He reached a small attic and hid behind some hay. When he heard shots and dogs barking, he quickly pulled up the ladder. After the noise subsided, he calmed down. From the first shots above Goeree-Overflakkee, Joe had been running on pure adrenaline. Now that he was safe, he became very tired. He thought about all the images he had witnessed, including the gruesome image of the falling Gene. After he finally dozed off, he was rudely awakened when something heavy jumped on his face. He drew his revolver, looked wildly around, and realized it must have been a cat chasing a rat. Joe remembered this all his life. Many times he woke up, frightened, sweating and gasping for breath.

Meanwhile, Elton was having a difficult time. He wrote: "*I then jumped and reached for my ripcord, but as I had dove out, I was somersaulting over and over and couldn't reach it immediately. I finally grabbed it and gave it a healthy jerk, and then I was jerked roughly to an upright position. The right leg strap had broken, and therefore, let the chute harness slip up till the chest strap caught me in the mouth. Believe me, I really clamped my legs together and slapped my arms to my body and did some hoping that I would not fall through the straps. After doing that, I watched to see if the rest of the crew had gotten out and then, watched as the plane crashed and blew up. I saw eight[16] other chutes besides mine, which meant that there was one unaccounted for. The co-pilot was floating down close to me, but he was working on his chute so we could slip it away from one another. I could see the Jerries down below and they were coming in the direction that we were going to land. About that time, I landed in an apple tree in an orchard of some Dutch farmer. I believe I knocked every apple off the tree. I was caught there for a moment and by the time that I got out of my harness and dropped to the ground, the Jerries were so close that it was no use to try to hide. I reached for my billfold and took out my birth certificate, driver's license, etc., and tore them up, as we were told that we should always do that in the event that we were to be captured. The co-pilot came over to me and we then went to the farmhouse and asked the old lady that was there just where we were. She could not understand what we wanted so we turned back to the barn. About that time, the Jerries were hollering at us to put our hands up. Now all that happened in the preceeding paragraphs all took place in just a matter of a few minutes.*

We put up our hands and the Jerries came up to us and felt for guns. The co-pilot had his .45 revolver, but I had none. They were rather surprised that I didn't have one, but nevertheless, they continued searching us. When they finished, one man that could speak English told us to line up over against the barn. We asked him what they were going to do, but none of them would say a word. Of course, we were pretty darn scared and could imagine most anything, but when they lined us against the barn, we figured we had had it. The one soldier backed off a ways and took the safety off the machine pistol he was carrying. The machine pistol is something similar to our Thompson sub. The co-pilot asked if they were going to kill us and still they were silent. Boy, about that time, we were really sweating, and believe me, one can think of a whole lot when the chips are down that far. I thought, 'Just why should they kill us when they never knew us and ten minutes before that they had never seen us and we had never seen them.' It was something that one cannot express in words or writing. About the best way to express the feeling of one that is about to be killed, I guess, is to just say that everything you ever did and everyone that you have ever known comes into your mind."

-*"About the time that the Jerrie backed off a ways, a German officer came up the road and started yelling at the guys that were with us. It seemed as if they were catching the very devil for doing what they were doing. He then dismissed the man and he took charge. The officer could speak English fluently with an English accent. He made us carry our chutes and started us towards the village. The village was about two miles from where we were."*

1: The German data is from the mentioned outlined survey map and the associated report.
2: From his police report recorded on 18 July 1945 and compiled on August 2nd, 1945, addressed to the mayor of Heinkenszand. I own only a version that was translated by my grandfather into English.
3: The German sketch however shows the Feathered Injun coming from the north, rather than from the east.
4: The details by Koos en Leny van Iwaarden come from two interviews. The first was on April 27, 2011 conducted by Willem Visser. The second on May 5, 2011 conducted by Willem Visser and me.
5: The fragments of Rinus Geschiere come from an interview conducted by Willem Visser and Hans Vergeer on August 28, 2010.
6: A bean tepee (in Dutch *Ruiter*) is made of three upright, slanting poles tied together at the top. Horizontal three other horizontal beams connect the poles, forming a triangle. The bean plants are hung on these poles to dry, making the beans easier to remove from the pods.
7: The fragments of Jan Minnaard come from an interview conducted by Willem Visser on November 11, 2010.
8: The fragments of Han Nijsse come from an interview conducted by Willem Visser on November 17, 2010.
9: The fragments of Dies Hannewijk come from an interview conducted by Willem Visser on December 22, 2010.
10: The fragments of Marien Mol come from an interview conducted by Willem Visser on October 7, 2010.

11: From a letter of protest from Ko 1984 in response to the denial of the Resistance Memorial Cross to his brother Pier, mentioned later in the book.
12: A "*weel*" is a pond that is left behind after an old flood. De Brilletjes are a remnant of a dam disaster in 1404. It is called the Glasses because from the air the two ponds look like a pair of glasses. The water in the pool is salty.
13: From an Escape & Evasion report of the U.S. Army from 1944.
14: This woman was probably one of the *Luftnachrichten-Helferinnen* of the *Luftwaffe*, who could operate the flak.
15: Conversations between Willem Visser and Cor Mallekote in 2008.
16: Elton counted too many parachutes. Both Frans Bliek and Sergeant Jacob Koole saw an unmanned parachute drift away. Eyewitnesses have told me, that when the plane crashed a yellow/orange parachute was found. The eighth unmanned parachute that was seen floating, could have been a bundle parachute that was sucked from the hatch.

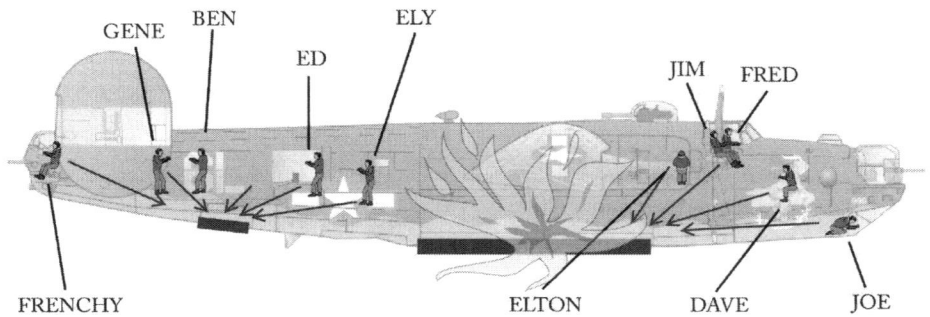

The positions in Feathered Injun. (102)

The catwalk, the narrow passage over the bomb doors to the tail, which the airmen only could cross sideways. (103 - www.b24.net)

How a tandem jump must be performed. (104 - www.b24.net)

Molenhof, the farm where Gene Kieras died. (105 – Mrs. Leu van de Swaluw-Faes)

Cornelis Lokerse, the father of Ploo van Iwaarden and the owner of the Molenhof. (106)

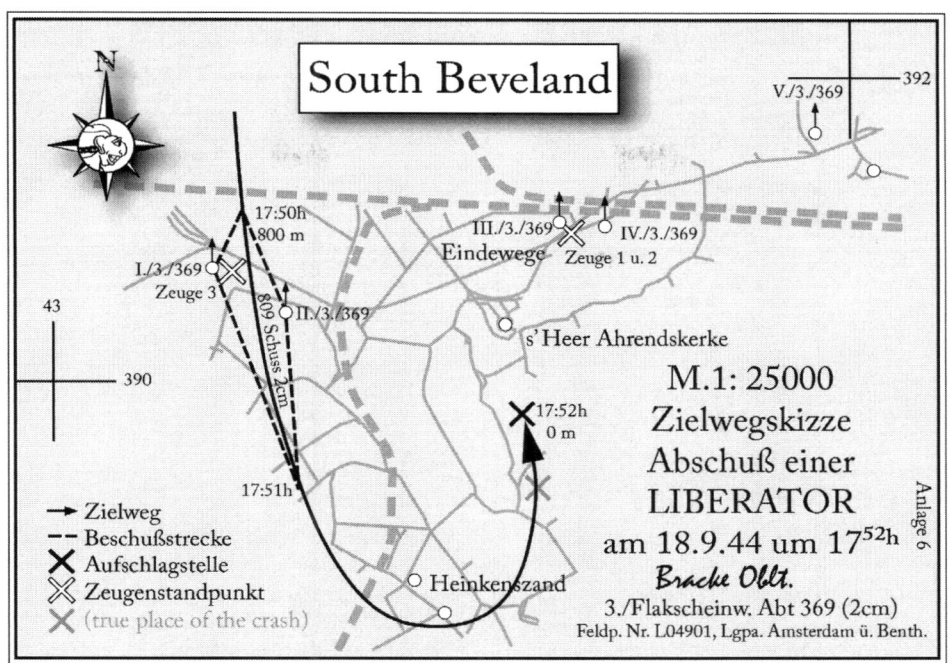

An adaptation of the German sketch. Translation: Route Sketch Shooting Down of a Liberator at September 18, 1944 at 1752 hours. Zielweg = Route, Beschuβstrecke = firing range, Aufschlagstelle = crash site, Zeugenstandpunkt = place of witnesses, Schuss = shots, Zeuge = witness. (107)

A photo from 2009 of the two linden trees that burned in the fire. (108)

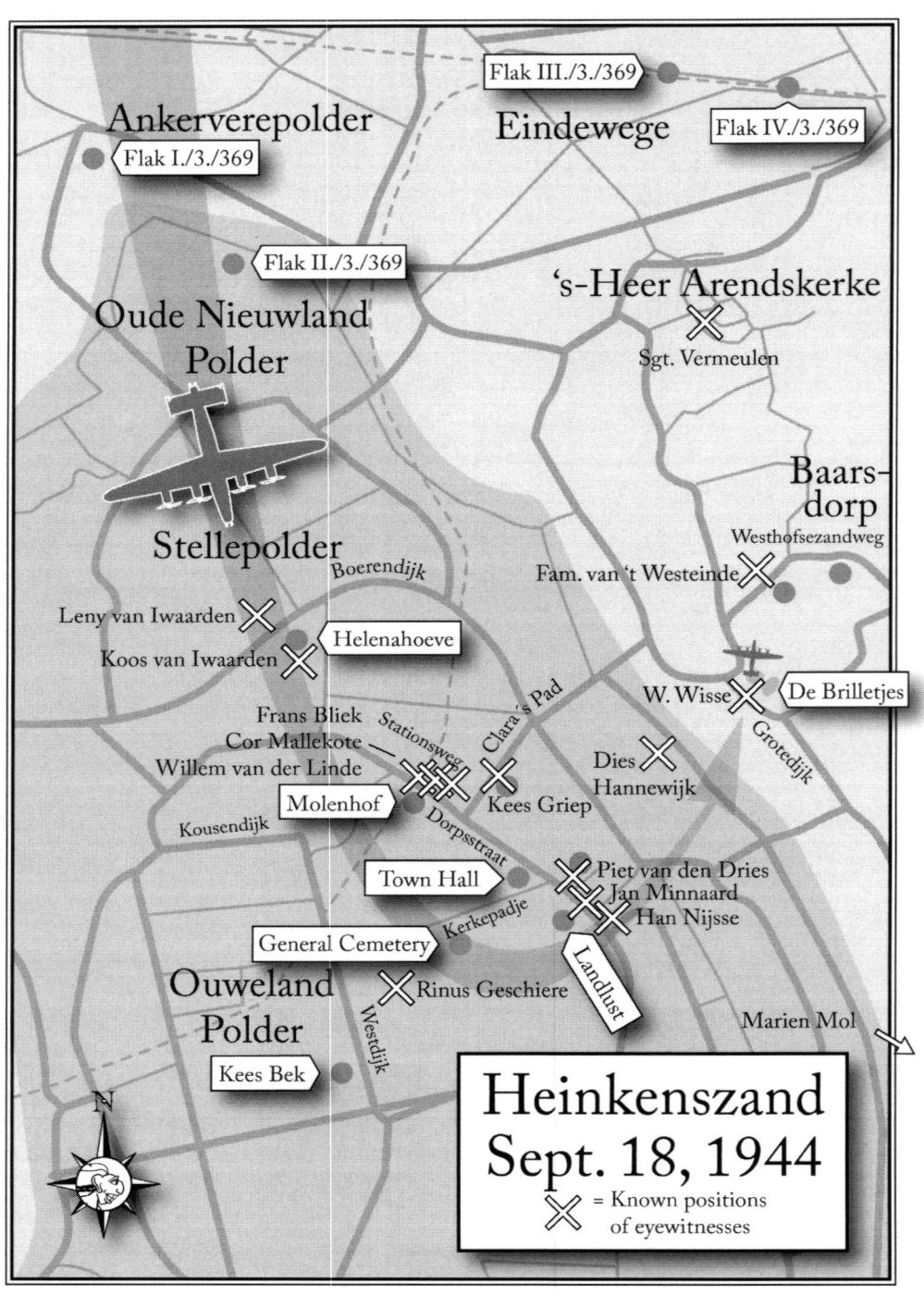

Helenahoeve at the Boerendijk. (110)

Rienbouw and Ploo van Iwaarden with their three daughters: Kaat, Leny and Koos. (111)

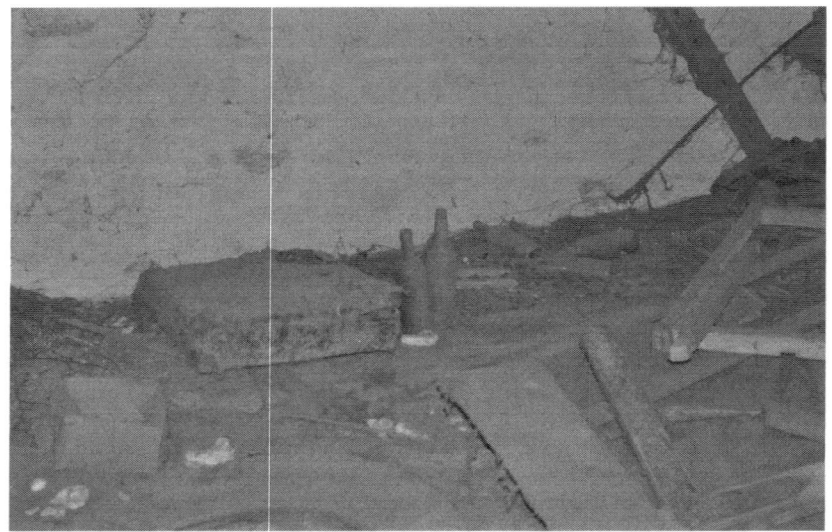

The hayloft at Helenahoeve, 67 years after the crash. The pillow that Joe used to sit on and the bottles from which he drank are still there, covered with a thick layer of dust. (112)

The barn where Joe hid. The hayloft was at the small top window. (113)

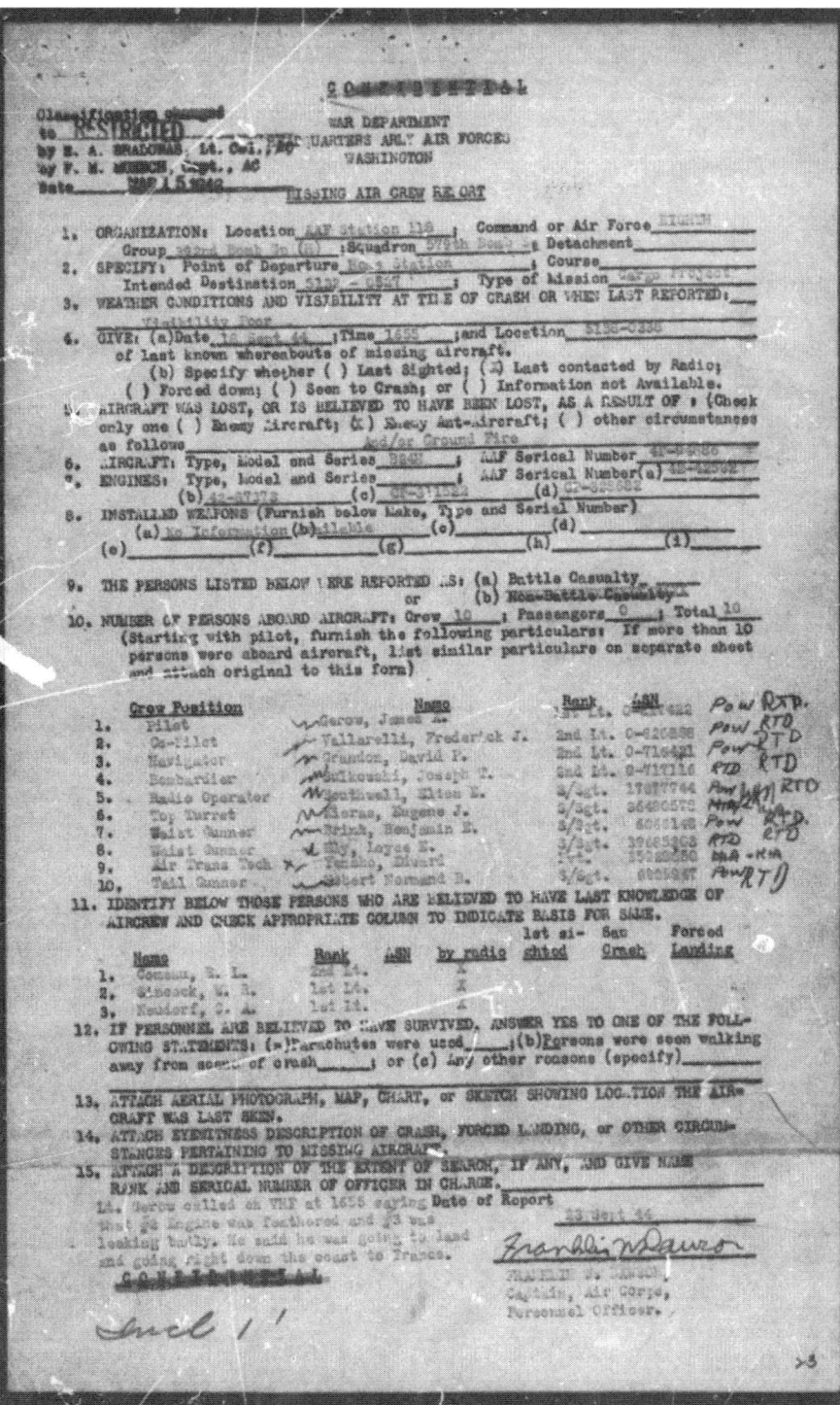

The American Missing Air Crew Report of the crash of Feathered Injun. (114 - National Archives)

Piet van den Dries and his family. (114a)

The St. Joseph School, billeted by a German unit. (114b)

Chapter 10

Hay Barns and Interrogations

At 1800 hours, less than ten minutes after the crash of Feathered Injun, the first aircraft returned to Wendling. The mission lasted five hours. Of 252 Liberators launched by the 2nd Air Division, seven were shot down over the Netherlands and six crashed due to damage caused by shelling. One aircraft was forced to ditch at sea and only three crewmembers survived.

Additionally, 154 bombers returned to England with flak damage. Four of these aircraft were so seriously damaged they had to prematurely land in unplanned areas like Woodbridge, in Suffolk, England. Their extra-long, extra-wide runways made it an ideal landing spot for badly-damaged aircraft. Another plane was forced to make an emergency landing near liberated Brussels to obtain medical help for injured crewmembers. They returned to England in a Dakota C-47 Skytrain the next day.

Another plane crashed in enemy territory in Belgium. After the crew abandoned the aircraft, three crewmembers died, five crewmembers escaped with the help from the local resistance and three others were taken prisoner. One of them subsequently died from his injuries. Corporal Nevin Johnson was one of the dead. Nevin was on board because he wanted to experience a mission. When the crew bailed out, he also jumped and broke his leg. Because of fierce ground fire, the other crewmembers could not get to him to give him first aid and Nevin bled to death.

Although three Crusader bombers were shot down and four others were so heavily damaged they had to make an emergency landing in the UK, the drop mission was successful for the 392nd, with 780 of 800 bundles dropped on target. Unfortunately, only a fraction of the bundles reached the Allied Airborne Divisions. Most of the bundles were seized by the Germans.

This was a difficult mission for escorts. Twenty Thunderbolts were shot down and another eight were lost in liberated territory. Thirty Thunderbolts returned home in spite of flak damage. The Mustang escort had better luck. Only one of the Mustangs was damaged beyond repair, while sixteen others were able to fly again a few days later. The 7th Photo Group[1] conducted photoreconnaissance over the Netherlands with seven F-5A variants of the Lightnings. One of these was lost above the Scheldt area.

On this same Monday, the 101st Airborne Division liberated Eindhoven and made contact with the XXX Corps in the afternoon. Together they were able to push through to Son to build an emergency bridge there. The Americans who previously liberated Veghel and Eerde were bombarded by German troops, while the 82nd Airborne Division tried to occupy the Waal Bridge at Nijmegen. All their attempts were unsuccessful. Meanwhile, the British 1st Airborne Division fought fiercely for the road bridge in Arnhem, but was unable to capture it.

After Elton and Fred were captured and narrowly escaped execution at Heinkenszand, they were marched down the main street.

Elton: *"As we started coming into the village, some Dutchmen tried to speak to us, but were chased off. The village was about as beautiful a village as I ever saw in Europe. People were bringing in potatoes, cabbage, apples, rutabagas and all sorts of vegetables and fruits for it were at that time of year when the harvesting of crops began. It made one homesick right then, for it reminded me of when we used to dig potatoes and bring them in when we lived on the farm. As we walked through the village, all the women would come out and look at us with a pathetic look. Some would make V-signs and others would shake their heads with pity. I am sure that, if we could have gotten away then, we would have been taken good care of and would have joined the American forces in a few days. But it was hopeless, for the town was filled with German troops. They then chased the people into their houses and would point their guns at them to frighten them. Right then and there, I decided that the only good German was a dead German. And still think that but of a few exceptions of whom I met later on. In about the center of the village, or on what seemed to be the main street, was a large building[2] into which they took us. Inside was a group of German officers and men of what I think was the intelligence section. They put the co-pilot and me in one room, which was filled with straw and had two large windows. They took our matches from us, but let us keep our cigarettes. We were told that, if we went to the windows we could be shot at, so we just sat down and tried to take it easy. In a few minutes, I asked the guard for a match and he gave me one but motioned for me to put it out if an officer came. I then asked to go to the toilet, so he took me outside. By that time it was getting dark and you could see the flashes of gunfire in the not too far distance. After he had brought me inside again, we began to wonder if they had captured the rest of the crew and if they were in the same building. Valleralli then started to whistle 'Jim'[3] (the song) and in the next room came the same tune, so we knew that the pilot was there for his first name was Jim. We tried to whistle and knock finding out how many were there, but all we could figure out was two were in the other room, so that made four of us accounted for."*

Hidden under a hawthorn bush, Ely had time to determine his strategy and to contemplate the day's events. Ely had seen Gene fall, his best friend on the team, and was very upset. But he also knew that he had to stop thinking about Gene if he wanted to stay out of the hands of the enemy. After dark, Ely left his hiding place and walked quietly south across fields and pastures. He came to a farm and climbed a haystack. Unlike Joe, Ely did not have an emergency kit. All he had was some cash. He was very hungry. He crept out of the haystack to dig potatoes and ate them raw. Years later, when he told this story to his family, he said he would have given a kingdom for a saltshaker. While nibbling on the potatoes, Ely tried to keep warm by covering himself with hay. It was mid-September and the temperature was just above 50^0 F at night.

After 14-year-old Dies Hannewijk saw the plane crash, he hastened to the spot.

Dies: *"The baker Adriaan Minnaard, Jan Naayer, Adriaan Braamse, Han Nijsse and I were there first. There were not even Germans, because they were looking for the parachutists. We could board the aircraft and walk through it, because the left wing was bent by the crash against those trees. The engines were still attached to it. It was sort of crushed between the two linden trees. When we looked in the cockpit, there was a dead man. In the fuselage were three, or perhaps the double number of rows with large ammo packs, wrapped in canvas. It was dark in the plane. We pulled the parachute that was loose and I think there was someone lying under it[4]. Outside we found another parachute. We brought it with us to the other side of the dike, because we knew the Germans would come to seal the area off. Meanwhile more people came to the site. They said: 'Get out! That thing might explode in a moment!' because it was still smoldering. But it didn't explode. There was a strange smell in and around the aircraft. This canvas and the stuff that was wrapped around the bullets smoldered and smoked. In the tree nursery, there was some panic, because the family van 't Westeinde were hiding a lot of people in the orchard and in their barns. They did not want us to stash the things we found in their orchard, so we were sent away by Ko van 't Westeinde. Jan Naayer was our leader, who told us what to do. Jan was the same age as us, maybe a year older. The baker Minnaard had a carrier with a large* breadbasket on his bike. He said: 'Guys, I'll help you, but I want a piece of canvas from those boxes for my breadbasket, because now it rains through. So the canvas was cut loose, large enough for Minnaard's basket and there were some long strips left. Then we could take the bullets out, wrapped in a kind of glass wool. Bullets were fine exchange objects among the youth, just like the aluminum that we could get loose. We did not have aluminum then because it was not yet available in 1944. Each time we loaded the breadbasket of the baker and brought it over to the company of Ko Rijk, who was building a hangar. The building of the hangar was stopped long a go, so there was no one to be seen. We were busy with getting all the stuff out from the plane. A half hour later, there were also a bunch of older boys at the plane: Arie Lammers, Gilles Geelhoed and Cor Schipper, who sent us away. These guys picked up everything that they could lay their hands on. They also took a propeller with a loose curved blade, which they brought into the barn of Lammers. Arie and Gilles, who were neighbors, were working to polish the propeller blade and tried to get it straight, but they didn't succeed. A day or so later a carriage with horses came to their house and servants of Van 't Westeinde took the propeller back. The boys were very angry because of this! I never knew who told Van 't Westeinde the propeller was at Lammers' house. But I think Mrs. Lammers wanted to get rid of that thing herself, because father Lammers was hiding in the barn and wanted no visits by the Germans. After we were sent away, we went to our own stuff at the hangar to share it. Only the baker had first choice, which was the canvas. This canvas was on his bakery basket for years after that. The parachute was cut into quarters. It was a yellow and orange-colored parachute. I also got a part. My piece is still at my cousins in 's-Heer Arendskerke. There were neat dresses made from it. But they had to wait until the liberation to wear them because they were too orange. Orange was the color of the Dutch Royal Family and was not allowed by the Germans."

Han Nijsse: "We were in that plane with some other boys, looking for something that we could swap. There was little left of it, you did not even recognizes it was a plane. The two linden trees were scorched and for three years after that no leaves grew on them. There were those flares we found. We took them with us and tried them later. A red colored light came out of it. We arrived there at the wreck and started digging with sticks into the ground. There was also a well in the dike. The baker, the father of Jan Minnaard, had just delivered his bread somewhere near our town. He asked while he was standing on the dike: 'Guys what are you doing?' I said: 'We're digging and searching.' The baker came down to the well and pulled on a ring, and then we saw a big yellow orange parachute was attached to it. The four of us jumped to the well and together we pulled up the parachute. The parachute came out quickly, but there was also something heavy attached to it, in a large container. It took quite some effort getting that thing out. We thought that perhaps it was cigarettes. The parachute was still intact, though there were burn marks on it. We removed the container and opened it. Therein we saw some smaller boxes, not filled with cigarettes, but with ammunition. That container was as big as me and those boxes were full of nice shiny machine gun bullets.

The baker had a basket on his bike, so we hid that parachute and some stuff in there. Nobody could see it. Then we drove a little further to the hangar of Rijk. It was still unfinished then, and we could just walk in. Later on we spread the parachute on the floor. Kees, the father of Jan Naaier, lived next door and we said to him: 'Kees, we want that thing fairly shared to make clothes of it'. Kees agreed and stood with the parachute in his hands with his back to us, so we could not look. He said then: 'Who wants this piece?' And then we picked blind a part of that thing. All four of us got a piece of parachute fabric."

Jan Minnaard, the 5-year-old baker's son: "When my father came home from his bread round, he said: 'Come, let's see where that plane crashed.' With my dad and my brother I went to the place where the plane went down, at the Brilletjes. There were people there, including children like me. We could just walk around and were not stopped. By now it was burnt out. I did not really see a plane, for my experience it was nothing but junk. The wreckage lay near those two linden trees. It was all black. And what I remember of it is that among the wreckage were all kinds of objects, for example, many small square zinc plates[5]. I saw very clearly a shoe with a foot in it. I will never forget that. I later heard from Han Nijsse, who was already present, that when the Germans were walking around, the body of the dead airman was lying on the ground. One of the Germans gave it a kick. My father looked at one point at a kind of ring from a pit. He began to pull it and pulled out an orange parachute. But he was not alone. There were several who were pulling the same parachute. Then they decided to take this parachute to a hangar of van Rijk, at the end of Clara's Pad. They have that orange parachute divided into four parts. Of the quarter that my father had, he made a shirt for my brother and me, and my sister got a dress. After this there was a piece left and my sister has always kept it. I did not know about her having a piece, but some time ago, after I told her that story, she showed it to me. I myself also have another piece and also have a piece of white ribbon from the parachute. It is attached to a sled and I have pulled both our children and grandchildren with it. It still looks new."

Koos and Leny van Iwaarden: "We went along with Dad to the crashed aircraft site. Our mother, our sister and uncle Cor stayed home. We saw Dad *running and just ran after him. 'We also want to see it!' We shouted to mother. It was a pretty long walk, but we didn't run on the road, but straight through the meadows. There were lots of people and there was a piece hanging in a tree that was completely black. It was was smoking, smoldering and smelly. After that the three of us walked quietly back home. We arrived at the farm and mother was a little mad at my dad. She said: 'Dad, you leave me here all alone to do the work!' We went back to our normal rhythm. The cows still needed to be milked. But at dinner we could talk about it. Mother said: 'That pilot, he is still there! He's still there!' We were curious, but Dad didn't allow us to go to the barn, because of all the Germans on our farm."*

Policeman Sergeant Jacob Koole, who saw Gene fall to his death, arrived at the scene of the crash and saw a completely destroyed aircraft. "When I arrived on the spot, I saw the aircraft was completely burned out and there was a charred body in the plane."

Municipality servant Kees Franse from Stationsstraat later stated[6]: "On 18 September 1944, after the aircraft crashed, I pulled the badly burned body of Edward Jennson[7] from the burning aircraft, which I thought was a B-17. His body was at the height of his waist torn in two."

The Germans did not want to get their hands dirty. They ordered old Piertje and his son Ko van 't Westeinde, who both lived in the nearby farms, to deposit the charred remains of Ed, previously removed from the aircraft by Kees Franse. With a pitchfork they had to deposit the remains in a basket used for horses. Ko saw the partially burned back parachute that covered the legs of Ed, the same the boys had seen before. Ko later gave the parachute to his maid to make a wedding dress out of it.

Rinus Geschiere said: *"I heard that after the bomber crashed, old Piertje walked up to the Germans. Piertje was a fierce little man. He was annoyed to death by those Krauts who didn't do anything to put out the fire or things like that. Then he gave a speech, with his traditional farmer's hat in his hand. I don't know what he exactly said, but the last line was: 'Well, this is what I had to say!' and he walked back home angry, without the krauts harming him."*

Sergeant Koole: *"This person who proved to be Edward Jensen (later it was found that his name name was Edward Yensho), expert in loading and unloading, was taken to Heinkenszand, where he was wrapped in a sheet and was placed in a coffin. On his body nothing could be salvaged because the Germans had stolen everything. I also saw how some Germans took the money from his wallet and divided it among each other."*

About two hours after Elton and Fred were caught and brought into the town, the guards took Fred out of the room.

Elton: "*In a few minutes they came and got me. They took me into a room that was lit up only by a small candle and the rest of the room was entirely blacked out. It was certainly spooky, as all you could see was three or four Germans with a deadpan expression of their faces. They started to ask me questions of all kinds, to which I told them I didn't know.*"

As ordered, the only information Elton gave was his name, his rank and his serial number. Gradually his eyes, which were affected by the fire in the bomb bay, became accustomed to the dark. "*Suddenly, I heard someone cough and when I looked around I noticed the other crew members were in the background, which made me more at ease. When the Germans realized that they could not learn much from me, they tied my hands behind my back, and the others were handcuffed.*"

Jim, Dave, Fred, Elton, Ben and Frenchy were loaded in a truck. This was the first time they knew who had been captured and that Joe, Ely, Gene and Ed were missing.

1: This unit within the 8th Air Force made aerial photographs of the affected targets to determine the damage.
2: In the more expensive part of the Dorpsstraat there were three stately properties that meet this description: the Dutch Reformed Presbytery, the house of Mayor Mes (both still there) and the town hall (demolished). Several residents of Heinkenszand think the prisoners were brought to the town hall, because there was also a prisoner's cell. This building served as the town hall from 1931 to 1969.
3: A song from 1941, sung by Billie Holiday.
4: The body of Ed was cut in two, so it seemed to the boys they saw two dead people.
5: These were probably metal slats from Ed's flak vest.
6: A document of the Municipality Heinkenszand dated 7 March 1946.
7: They didn't find an identity tag on Ed's body with his name. Presumably the German soldiers stole it. Joe had only heard the name of Ed Yensho when Ed was introduced to the crew. When the resistance fighters asked Joe to make a list with the names of his crew members, he guessed that Ed's name was written as Jenssen. This misspelling (and variations thereof) thus appeared more than once in documents from Heinkenszand.

The town hall of Heinkenszand where the prisoners were interrogated. (115 - Mrs. Leu van de Swaluw-Faes)

The Dorpsstraat with the town hall on the left. (116 - Mrs. Leu van de Swaluw-Faes)

A drop container in the Arnhems Oorlogsmuseum, topped with a pad to soften the landing. (117)

Dropped ammunition boxes removed from the canvas pack by ground troops. (118 – U.S. Army)

Jan Minaard, son of the baker, 67 years after the crash, with a piece of parachute from the Feathered Injun. (119)

This is what remained of the Feathered Injun: a pile of debri. In the picture is Nele, the wife of Ko with two of their children. (120)

Kees Griep and his family. (119a)

Kees Franse at the Town Hall. (120a)

Kees Franse making a rope. (120b)

Elton Southwell. (121a)

Chapter 11

Separate Ways

At 2300, a German soldier told Sergeant Koole the body of Gene Kieras was in Cornelis Lokerse's barn on the Molenhof farm.

Sergeant Koole: *"When I got there, I saw the body in a sitting posture in a wheelbarrow, covered with burlap sacks."*

That evening, headmaster Piet van den Dries received a secret message from someone in the LBD[1] concerning the whereabouts of Gene's body. Because he was a doctor, Kees Griep received a request from the Deputy Mayor to inspect the body. Kees Griep could come out of hiding without the fear of being arrested because most NSB members, including the mayor, fled earlier and destroyed many documents to cover up their crimes. Together, Piet and Kees walked to the barn and met Sergeant Koole, carpenter Piet Engelse and the man from the LBD, presumably Kees Franse, who previously helped to recover Ed's body from the crashed bomber.

Later, Kees Griep wrote to Gene's family: *"When I examined the body of your son, I saw that he had no wounds, but he had a fracture of his skull, a fracture of his neck, and of his right leg, so I can assure you that he was instantly dead."*

Sergeant Koole: *"Then the body was moved with the help of the man from the LBD to another more suitable area where it was washed, wrapped in a sheet and placed on a bier* (a stand on which a corpse is placed before burial). *In my presence he was then placed in a coffin. On the dog tag from the body of the crewman, I read that his name was Eugene Kieras, 20 years old, a flight engineer. I also took from the body two small pencils, a chain and a lock of hair, which was cut by me to send to his relatives. I brought all these items to the town hall of Heinkenszand."*

The next day, Gene's body was taken to the town hall, where Ed's body had already been placed in a coffin. The two coffins were manufactured and supplied by Piet Engelse. This carpenter later tendered this bill to the acting mayor. He also included two coffins for fallen German soldiers:

4	Wooden boxes with masking frame twice stained	
6	Medium handles	
10	Medium screws	
	Oil coated paper and cotton fabric garnished with printed tape	
4	Lace embroidered pillows	each f 45-[2]
4	Freight	each f 2,-
2	Administration	each f 6,-
4	Coffins and preserving the bodies	each f 5, -

That night, while Joe and Ely were hiding in the hay, the rest of the survivors were put into a truck. Their hands were tied and began to feel like lumps of ice due to reduced blood supply. A German guard noticed that Frenchy had injured his ankle. He kicked the tail gunner every now and then, when he shifted his weight to sit in a more comfortable position.

Elton: *"This gave us an even greater hate for the Germans. This proved again that all those stories about the brutality of the SS troops were true."*

They stopped at a train station in Goes. To their dismay, the crew was split apart. The officers, Jim, Fred and Dave were separated from the NCOs, Ben, Elton and Frenchy. Not much is known about the officers journey. They were loaded into a boxcar and taken to the German prisoner of war camp, Stalag Luft I[3], at Barth-Vogelsang on the Baltic Sea.

After they were separated from their Officers, Ben, Elton, and Frenchy were transferred to another truck. Their handcuffs were removed.

Elton: *"A German officer asked us if we had anything to eat and we said 'no'. Rather, Frenchy spoke in French, for none of us could understand German. The officer threw us in a loaf of bread. We tried to eat it, but were not hungry enough to eat that what they called bread. It was the most foul tasting stuff any of us had ever tasted up till that time, but we kept it and then tried to sleep, most of which we did in spells. We were too nervous to sleep very well. Finally I dozed off and when I awoke, it was daylight."*

Ben, Elton, and Frenchy saw gasoline cans in back of the truck labeled U.S. Army, probably stolen. They wondered whether they were in Germany, but a sign they saw on the side of the road indicated that this was not the case.

Elton: *"If one of us had to pee, we were told to stand at the back of the truck and they wouldn't let us do that until we were in town where all the people could see us. Then the guards would say to the people, 'Americans!' and laugh. The scenery in Holland is very pretty; the clothes that the people wore were a bit old fashioned. They wore wooden shoes, while doing work in the fields, etc. Every house that we saw was very tidy and almost immaculate in the surroundings. Of course, it was fall and the trees, grass, etc., had the touch of fall in them, which also made it seem a bit dreary. But to see the women shining the brass doorknobs until they sparkled showed that the people still had the pride that they were known for."*

The three Americans spent most of the morning in the moving truck. They saw a lot of damage caused by Allied bombing. They approached Fliegerhorst Soesterberg, a Dutch airfield used by the German Luftwaffe for bombing runs on England, and saw damage from multiple bombings. Prisoners from nearby Camp Amersfoort were clearing debris. Every day prisoners from this infamous transit camp traveled in a wood-fired truck to the airfield to work. It was very dangerous due to continuous bombing. The destruction was so vast that the Luftwaffe later declared it unusable and decided to abandon the field. This was the first time the American NCOs saw forced labor of citizens and prisoners of war. Looking at the prisoner's uniforms, they saw most were French and some Italian.

The Americans reached a village[4] and were taken to an old prison for a few hours. They were then taken to a large building in another part of the village where they were thoroughly searched and interrogated. They refused to answer any questions, so they were brought to another room. There were about seventy English soldiers there, captured during operation Market Garden the day before. They told the Americans their division had been completely destroyed by the German army. Frenchy's broken ankle finally got some medical attention. The Germans wrapped it with a paper bandage and allowed Frenchy to rest with a number of wounded British.

Elton: *"At first Ben and I were rather cautious of the English, because we weren't sure they were all English and maybe a German was in the group posing as an Englishman. Here we got a bowl of some kind of soup, which we all shared, and as I had a few cigarettes left, we had a smoke. This is where we first began to realize that we would not be getting any more smokes as soon as the ones I had were gone, for the English boys were after the butts as they had had their smokes taken from them and had been out for a day. There were two windows in the room, but we were up on the third story and when we would look out we could see the guards below us. There were some bullet holes in the room and we took for granted that some guard had shot at some former pris-*

oner, so we stayed away from the windows. That evening, about eight o'clock, they called out the names of thirty-four Englishmen, as well as my name, to be ready to leave right away. I tried to explain to the interpreter that I was not an Englishman, but he would not listen to me, so I had to go with them."

There was nothing else for Elton to do but say goodbye to Ben and Frenchy, his crewmembers he had only met two days before while training for the drop mission. Elton is the only crewmember who wrote a detailed report about his journey. Little is known about the journey of Ben and Frenchy except they ended up in the same prison camp as Elton.

Guards took Elton and the British soldiers down into the basement and gave them each a piece of liverwurst and a piece of bread. They were ordered outside into a small enclosed truck, camouflaged with branches. There was not enough room, but they were crowded and jammed in. None of them could sit down and the air became suffocating, while the Germans tried unsuccessfully to start the truck. They ordered the prisoners out to push the truck, but it would not start, so they ordered them back into the building for the night.

Although Rienbouw van Iwaarden was suspicious, he did not know where Joe Sulkowski was hiding.

Leny and Koos van Iwaarden: *"Every now and then, when the German soldiers were in the village, father walked into the barn and shouted: 'Psst, psst, Tommy, Tommy?!' But he got no response."*

Joe heard the farmer but was afraid to show himself. When the barn under his loft filled with German soldiers, he survived on the emergency rations he carried in his survival vest[6]. According to Koos and Leny van Iwaarden, Joe had a water filter to clean his urine in case he needed water.

Operation Market Garden initially went well. American ground forces constructed another bridge over the Son. They made contact with the soldiers of the 82nd Airborne Division between Veghel and Grave. But the Germans retook Veghel and Eerde and the bridge at Neftrik. In Arnhem, a handful of Brits who reached the Rhine Bridge suffered heavy losses. They did not succeed in taking the bridge. Paratroopers of the Polish 1st Independent Parachute Brigade, landed in a drop zone abandoned by the British, making them easy targets. Heavy German shelling killed many of the paratroopers and critical equipment was lost.

1: The man from the Dutch version of the Air Raid Precautions was Kees Franse, a member of the Group Griep.
2: f was the symbol of the Dutch Guilder. The former name was the Golden Florin and the f remained.
3: Stalag Luft: an abbreviation of Stammlager Luft, which in turn is an abbre-

viation of Mannschaftsstamm-und Straflager Luft, a POW camp specifically for aviators. The Roman numeral gave the military district in which the camp was located.

4: Elton wrote they were taken to a village where the old prison and the large building were located. This could also have been a *Waldlager*, one of the military camps in the woods surrounding the airport. The buildings in these camps were made of bricks, making the camp seem like a village.

5: Tommy was the nickname for British soldiers. It is possible that Rienbouw did not know Joe's nationality.

6: An emergency ration for crews of the Air Force was part of a C-1 survival vest that was worn over the jacket. Attached to this vest was also the holster for his Colt .45. Besides that, the ration included a knife, a signaling mirror, a first aid kit, fishing and sewing kit, a water filter and a booklet with survival instructions. The emergency package consisted of: sweet chocolate bars, candy bars, dried cheese and crackers, stock cubes, sugar, cigarettes, water purification tablets, instant coffee, chewing gum and a small plastic bag to keep the food in after the cans were opened.

A ruined hangar at Fliegerhorst Soesterberg. (121)

Elton Southwell. (122)

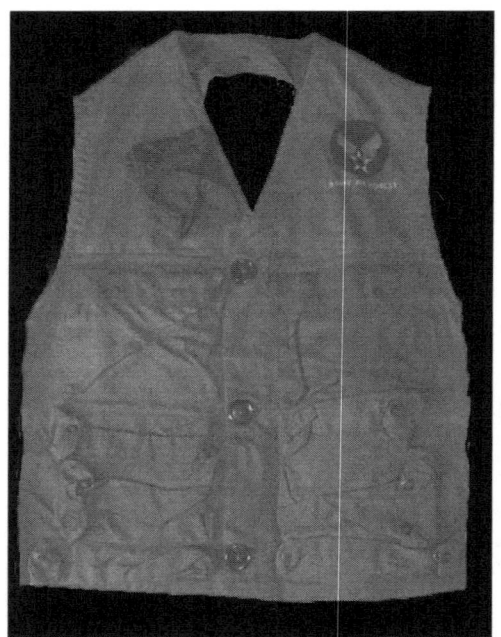 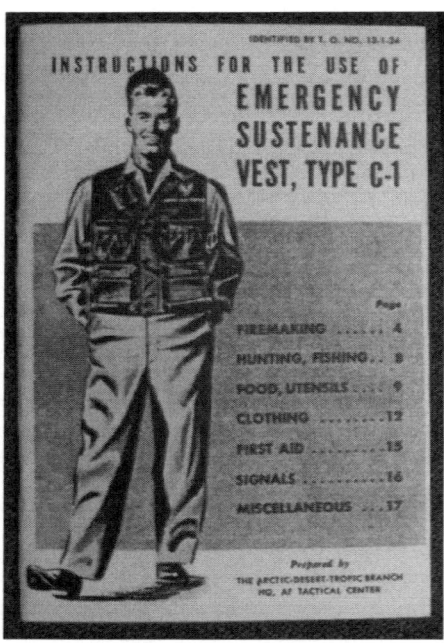

Left: An emergency vest, used by Joe while he was hiding. Right: An instructions booklet for the vest. (122a and 122b)

A name sign of the Helenahoeve farm where Joe was hiding. (122c)

Chapter 12

A Time for Reflection

On Wednesday, September 20th, at six o'clock in the morning, Elton and the other prisoners were forced to push the truck. This time they got it started. The engine began to smoke heavily and Elton understood that the truck ran on fire wood[1].

Elton: *"It was all covered with canvas and on the outside of that barbed wire crossed about four inches apart. We rode all that morning, stopping once in a while to get wood for the truck. Once when we stopped, there were a bunch of Dutch close by and they came over to the truck and tried to talk, but the guards chased them away. But not before they had gotten a few apples into the truck, however."*

That morning, while Joe was hiding in the Helenahoeve hayloft, Ely peered out from his hiding place in the haystack and saw a group of twenty men. They were uprooting potatoes from the tough Zeeland clay. The men discovered gnawed raw potatoes and wondered who was responsible. As they were preparing to leave, Ely decided to follow one of them. Silently, he crept through the dry ditch and followed him to a farm. When he saw the man go inside, Ely hesitated but decided to knock on the door. When the farmer opened the door, he saw a strangely dressed man on his doorstep desperate for help. Ely was fortunate the man understood English. The man grabbed Ely's hand and pulled him quickly inside.

While the hungry American was eating a meal they provided, the man and his wife discussed what to do about this dangerous situation. They decided to shelter Ely in their barn, whereupon the farmer made a shelter from straw bales in which he cut an opening. 46-year-old Kees Bek and his 44-year-old wife, Adriana, spoke English because they had immigrated to Greenock, Canada in 1927, where their daughter, Natalie, was born. She was now 17 years old. Because they could not adapt to life in Canada, they returned to Heinkenszand. Kees found a job as an assistant at the tree nursery of the Van 't Westeinde family and cared for a farm owned by this family. This was the same farm on the Westdijk that Piertje van 't Westeinde inherited from his father-in-law.

Rinus Geschiere, the son of the milkman, told about Kees Bek: *"Kees was a poacher. When I was a little boy and went to the orchard at night to cut some rabbit food, sometimes I sat very quiet in the bushes. Then I could see Kees walking around between light and darkness. You had to make sure he did not see you. He was always very careful."*

On this same Wednesday, Acting Mayor, A. Vermaire of Goes, who replaced the NSB mayor, called on the population to volunteer 200 men with shovels to restore the Sloedam that was damaged by allied bombers.

That same day, the 82nd Airborne Division finally managed to conquer the Waal Bridge at Nijmegen. While under heavy German gunfire, a unit first crossed the Waal River in rickety boats. Many never reached the other side. Later, the U.S. Army remembered this crossing as one of the most heroic acts of WWII. Their sacrifice gave the Americans the opportunity to attack the bridge from two sides, allowing victory. There was heavy fighting in Nijmegen and, at the Arnhem Bridge, more than five hundred British soldiers were desperately waiting for reinforcements. There were heavy losses that day. Fighting also continued around Oosterbeek and Eerde.

That afternoon, Elton and his new companions arrived at a military camp where a small number of German soldiers were encamped. This was probably the Maurits barracks in Ede, renamed the Kommodore Boute Kaserne[2] by the Germans during the war.

Elton: *"Here they unloaded us and we finally got some water, as it was still pretty warm and we were awfully dry from the ride. We stayed there that afternoon just laying around a big tree that was in the yard. All around this yard was a cement wall about nine feet high so we could not see anything that was going on outside the yard. We found that we were located in a town and that afternoon, some kids must have heard that there were some prisoners in the yard, for they crawled up on the wall and were peering over at us and waving to us. They were giving the old V-sign. That, more than anything else, gave me a rather inspired feeling. Knowing that if the children of an occupied country could make fun of the Germans that way and still not seem to fear them, then we surely could not or should not have too much fear of them killing us (which we were still thinking about, for none of them would tell us anything). But we felt reasonably sure that they would not kill us now, not the ones that were around us at the present anyway. That afternoon I met a German marine. Rather, he came over and found me and asked if it was true that I was an American. When I told him that I was, he told me that he had been in Washington State working in a shipyard during the first part of the war, but had returned home when it became imminent that we were to get in the war. He said he liked the U.S. a lot and he would talk of a lot of things that happened. It sure made me homesick. This marine had had his ship blown up, he said, and was waiting for orders now. He had a full set of chin whiskers, which made him stand out, but he was just a young guy too. That afternoon I saw a P-51 drop his auxiliary gas tank[3] over this town, and it came down almost into the yard where we were at. The people were all running for shelter, for they thought that it might be a bomb. That plane sure looked good and did I ever feel good about seeing that plane. It was about at that time that I started to think about what had happened so far and about the two guys that the Germans had shot from our crew, even though I did not know them, as the crew was new to me. One member had died from not being able to get to his chute. And he had clung to the back of another crewmember in an attempt to escape from the burning plane. He was, of course, jerked off when the chute opened. He was the engineer that had gone to the rear of the plane in an attempt to fix the control cables and had to leave his chute at the front of the plane. One could not go through the bomb bay with your chute on. Our chutes were the chest type that you hooked on to the harness in the front. All this made me feel very bad. It was about that time that I started to check my wounds and was concerned about my eyes that had been burned from the fire in the plane. I could not see well and my eyes were hurting and burning. The wounds on my hand and back were getting sore, but after checking them, I found that there was no flack embedded in the wound, but my eyes burned quite badly. One of the English soldiers kept getting me wet cloths to keep on my eyes. He was a man named Sidney Goldstein, a Jewish kid whose parents had escaped from Russia and had gone to England and changed their name to Goldstein. This kid kept helping me all the time, for which I am still grateful. He was rather shunned by the rest of the English, I think, because he was a Jew. They were all from the glider corps. Most of their outfit was captured or killed and a lot of them were wounded. One kid had one hole in his jacket and two bullets in his arms."*

Sidney Goldstein, the man who helped Elton, was a member of the 16th Platoon of the Polish 1st Independent Parachute Brigade, led by Polish General Stanislaw Sosabowski. Two days before Elton met Sidney, the young Russian landed by glider with the Anti-Tank Battery near Wolfheze and was arrested not far from there on the Ginkelse Heide, a heathland between Ede and Arnhem. His mission was to assist the British 1st Airborne Division. The antitank unit preceded the landing of the remaining Polish paratroopers who were delayed by fog. According to an eyewitness, his commander deployed Sidney to speak with the local population in Yiddish. It was hoped the Dutch locals would understand some of the German words that were part of Yiddish.

Elton: *"About four o'clock, they loaded us into a bus and started for somewhere. The bus was a wood-burner, so it could not go very fast, and every so often, they would stop, throw in some more wood, stir the coals, and then we would go for a few miles and stop again. Soon they ran out of wood, so they would get us off the bus and make us gather some wood. This happened all night, so it was a slow process."*

On September 21st, a cloudy Thursday morning, about half past nine, a silent procession walked from the town hall of Heinkenszand to the General Cemetery.

Kees Griep later wrote to the family of Gene Kieras: *"We have put the body in a coffin and also that of his comrade, and put the coffins on stretchers and then the funeral started. Each stretcher was carried by eight inhabitants: members of the underground action in our village. As the Germans had forbidden all demonstrations only a few persons could follow the procession: the burgomaster[4] and his staff, me and some other persons. It was also impossible to cover the coffins with flowers. As we went through the streets, most of the population stood before their houses, the women with a tear in their eyes, the policemen saluting when the procession passed, and the men with grim faces. You could see that they now hated the Germans more than they had ever hated them. In the churchyard, when the coffins were in the grave, the burgomaster made a speech in which he thanked your son and his comrade for what they had done for the free making of our country, giving their lives for it and he hoped that our village should never forget it. When the speech was ended, one of the other persons prayed 'Our Father.' I hope you will forgive us that there was no priest, but we did not know that your son was Roman Catholic. The following morning, the grave was already covered with flowers, which the inhabitants had brought there in the evening and night and I know that there are always fresh flowers on the grave."*

On that Thursday, Elton came to an abandoned camp. By his description, this was probably the infamous Camp Vught, which the Germans called *Konzentrationslager Herzogenbusch*. This was the only SS concentration camp in the Netherlands. Between January 1943 and September 1944, more than 31,000 men, women, and children were interned there. The Germans imprisoned Jews, gypsies, homosexuals, political prisoners, Jehovah's Witnesses, tramps, black marketeers, criminals and many resistance fighters. Approaching Allied forces caused the evacuation. As of 14 September, it was no longer officially classified as a concentration camp. The only prisoners who remained behind were hostages or the seriously ill. These hostages, helped by nurse Aleida Hulsman of the White Yellow Cross, a Catholic association, were ordered by the Germans to keep the camp clean. On September 17th, the last hostages were transported elsewhere or were released. After that, the Germans imprisoned only allied troops captured during Operation Market Garden. Sister Hulsman remained to assist the prisoners.

Elton and his companions were imprisoned in the Bunker[5], a complex with 150 individual cells around a square courtyard and spread over two floors. The Bunker previously held prisoners waiting for trial or execution.

Elton: *"We were housed in an old jail-like barracks, individual 5x8 foot cells with a small window about 8" by 10" which was about 8 ft. from the floor, and a cell door of wood and iron, locked by a large iron bar on the outside. There was no cot or bed, but we were given a German blanket with lots of fleas. They put two to a cell; my cellmate was Sidney Goldstein. It was not so cold yet, so we put one blanket on the cement floor and used the other to cover us. No lights were in this cell, but being very tired with little sleep since my capture, I slept quite well the first night, except for the fleas."*

On this Thursday, British resistance on the Arnhem Bridge was broken. The Germans captured all remaining British paratroopers. Arnhem was now a ghost town, destroyed by the fighting and looted by the Germans. The bridge over the Rhine was immediately used to supply German troops fighting the British who held Oosterbeek, about three miles west of Arnhem. Paratroopers from Sidney's unit who had been held up in England by flak, finaly landed at Driel and endured violent attack the next day. The British in the isolated Oosterbeek were still standing, but there was a critical lack of food, medicine and ammunition. Drop zones were in German hands, making the dropped material unavailable to the Brits. The Poles crossed the Rhine in rubber boats to reinforce the Brits at Oosterbeek.

Operation Berlin was launched. It was a massive evacuation to rescue the trapped British troops in Oosterbeek and help them escape across the Rhine. This happened under heavy artillery fire, with many fatalities.

Operation Market Garden was a fiasco. The largest airborne operation ever, involving 30,000 Allied soldiers, cost the lives of 18,163 American, British, and Polish troops, more deaths than during D-Day. Thousands of other soldiers were captured and transported to the various POW camps. This failure coincided with the September 17th General Railway Strike, organized by the exiled Dutch government. In reprisal, the Germans blocked all food and fuel shipments to the west of the Netherlands. While the area of the Netherlands below the main rivers celebrated liberation, over 20,000 Dutch citizens died from starvation and cold during the infamous Hunger Winter in other areas.

The hay that was stored in the attic where Joe was hiding, was cut from the sides of the dikes. It was used to feed small cattle. On Saturday, September 23rd, after Joe's fifth night in hiding, Jaap IJzerman, the Van Iwaarden family servant, climbed two ladders to the attic for some hay. Instead of hay, he accidentally grabbed Joe's hair. Startled, Joe sat up and drew his service pistol. Jaap uttered a cry of terror, hurried down the ladders, and ran to his boss to tell him what he had found. Later that morning, 12-year-old Leny Iwaarden saw her mother in the kitchen baking onions and tomatoes. When she and her sisters got none of the food, she realized it was meant for their mysterious guest. Rienbouw assumed the American would be very cold and ordered his servant to bring the hot tomatoes with onion and some tea to the hayloft.

Rienbouw did not know what what to do with Joe and decided to talk to Kees Griep in confidence. Kees Griep knew Joe could not stay in the barn. The Helenahoeve was like a small village, accommodating the family, a number of evacuees, a boarder, the servant, and a platoon of German soldiers. Rumors about the hidden American soon buzzed around the farm and it was only a matter of time before someone talked. Furthermore, the farmer was already under suspicion because Rienbouw's brother was a member of the NSB and many people in the town thought the Van Iwaarden family was far too friendly to the Germans. Kees organized a meeting with other members of the resistance. They decided to move Joe.

On Sunday September 24th Kees Griep and Piet van den Dries went to the Helenahoeve. German soldiers were in the village, so it was safe to bring out the American airman. They met an anxious Joe. They shook hands and Piet told Joe about the decision to move him. While Kees set Joe's broken ankle, he didn't realize this was the same bombardier who almost had killed him on Joe's first mission when he and his squadron bombed the Vlake Bridge on August 3rd. Joe was not very happy with the plan to move and said he preferred to stay at the Helenahoeve. Kees and Piet told him that was out of the question. Billeted soldiers would soon notice him. If he were caught on the farm, he would be sent to a POW camp where there was a slim chance he would survive the war, but Rienbouw and Ploo would pay with their lives.

The doctor and the headmaster convinced Joe and explained their plan. Meanwhile, Joe was to keep a low profile and was definitely not to leave the hayloft. The family Van Iwaarden took care of their guest. Every day, their servant secretly brought Joe bread, cheese, coffee, and bottled water.

Koos and Leny van Iwaarden: *"One day everything almost went wrong when a German officer saw our father walking with food and drink in his hand. The Officer stopped him and asked him for whom all that was intended. Father looked hastily for an excuse, and saw his servant with a horse in hand walking past. Father gestured with a sad face to the man and told the German that the poor man had a large family, but they barely had enough to eat. The faithful servant spared the bread from his mouth to feed his family, so he could have something extra. 'You are a good boss,' said the officer who was very moved and patted father on his shoulder."*

According to Elton, the prisoners at Camp Vught left their cells only for limited exercise, to go to the bathroom or for questioning. Eventually, they were allowed to walk outside during the day and went back to their cells in the evening. While walking around the barracks, they found a lot of personal belongings.

Elton: *"Coins, toothbrushes, combs, shoestrings and all sorts of assorted things. This made us think that maybe we now were going to be eliminated, for this pile of stuff looked like things that had been taken from prisoners who had no future. Sidney, he being Jewish, thought that this was a sign of it for sure. He felt like we were all going to be searched and our belongings put in this pile along with the rest. Part of his thinking was right, for we were all searched and things taken from us, but I hid my watch and my rings and they never got them. I had picked up a few of the coins from the pile and they took them, but never found my rings and watch, as they concentrated on things in the pockets."*

The belongings Elton found could have been from other prisoners of war, but also from executed camp prisoners. Every prisoner had to surrender his property upon arrival at the SS concentration camp. Items were sorted, stored, and transported to Germany. On July 30th 1944, Hitler ordered that resistance members were to be executed without trial. In August and September 1944, many prisoners from both Camp Vught and the Oranje Hotel, the prison in Scheveningen, were shot at the execution site in Camp Vught. On 5 and 6 September, the confusing days of Crazy Tuesday and the beginning of the evacuation of Camp Vught, over a hundred resistance fighters were executed.

It is also possible the belongings Elton found were carelessly thrown aside because the Germans were in a hurry to evacuate. The prisoners evacuated in early September ended up in German concentration camps, the men in Sachsenhausen and the women in Ravensbrück. Many of them did not survive. A year earlier, on Sunday, June 6, 1943, all Jewish children under sixteen years were put on trains and transported via the

Dutch transit camp, Westerbork, to the Polish extermination camp, Sobibor. Here, 1269 children were gassed.

Elton and the other prisoners were permitted to turn the old barracks into a dormitory. They refurbished and cleaned it. Because anything was better than their small and oppressive cells, the prisoners worked hard and moved to the barracks. They did not enjoy that luxury very long. After the first night, they were told that they would be leaving.

Vught railway station was a few miles away. It rained as they were loaded into a boxcar and the doors locked. There was dirty straw in the cramped car and only a small vent window at the top of one of the sidewalls. One of the English soldiers spoke German and shouted to the guards to unlock the door so they could relieve themselves. After much complaining, the train finally stopped and a small tin was thrown inside. The men used the can and emptied it through the vent window. Suddenly, they heard shouting and swearing outside the boxcar. A German soldier was found standing under the vent window, smoking a cigarette.

To complicate the Allied advance, the German 70th Infantry Division began flooding various polders in the tail of South Beveland. They placed heavy barricades on roads that were still intact.

1: Due to the lack of fuel, because of the bombing of oil refineries, this truck was equipped with a generator that worked on gas produced by burned wood. In the Second World War, wood gas was commonly used as fuel for cars. This wood generator was located at the rear of the vehicle.
2: I tried to find out which German barracks Elton had visited. Given the various clues he provided, as the route from Soesterberg, the presence of the German marine, and the proximity of the Ginkelse Heide where Sidney and his comrades had landed, I suspect he went to the Kommodore Boute Kaserne in Ede. In this merger of Maurits barracks and Johan Willem Friso barracks, Germans troops were trained for the Kriegsmarine. The Ginkelse Heide lies nearby, between Arnhem and Ede.
3: Fighter Pilots did this to lose the excess burden of an empty tank.
4: The archives do not tell who the mayor (or deputy mayor) was. The NSB mayor Kole had already fled to the east and mayor Mes was reinstalled in November 1944. Because Kees Griep also held his post again after Crazy Tuesday, I suspect that Alois Mes had ventured out of hiding for this ceremony.
5: In this same prison complex on the night of 15 to 16 January 1944, the infamous Bunker Drama occurred. The Bunker Drama is an example of the atrocities in the camp. When one of the women from 23B barracks was imprisoned in the Bunker, other women protested against it. In retaliation, Camp Commandant Grünewald had put as many women as

possible in one cell. In cell 115, 74 women were pressed together on an area of nine square meters, with little ventilation. On Sunday January 16, after 14 hours the door of the cell was finally opened. Ten women had been suffocated.

Today, Penitentiary Vught occupies a large part of the grounds of the former camp, where the Bunker is still located. Because the Bunker cannot be visited, the National Monument Camp Vught has built a replica of a prisoner cell at the former camp crematorium. In this replicated cell the killed women are memorialized. Penitentiary Vught is now a heavily fortified prison for very dangerous criminals. Willem Holleeder, one of the kidnappers of Freddy Heineken (the chairman of Heineken Beer), was imprisoned here. Mohammed Bouyeri, murderer of Dutch film director Theo van Gogh is still imprisoned here.

A P-51 Mustang with two drop tanks. (123 – U.S. Air Force)

A reconstructed barrack in the National Monument Camp Vught. (124)

A reconstructed cell in the National Monument Camp Vught. (125)

Behind the small upper window of the barn was the loft where Joe was hiding. (126)

The identity pass of Rienbouw. (127)

The identity pass of Ploo. (128)

Left: The interior of a barrack in Camp Vught. Right: A furnace in the crematory of Camp Vught. (128a en 128b)

A reconstructed watchtower of Camp Vught. (128c)

Chapter 13

Some Kind of Disease

On Wednesday, September 27th, after two days and a night of traveling, the freight train finally stopped. Through the window vent, Elton saw they had arrived in a large rail yard with much railway traffic. This implied they were in a large city. Suddenly the prisoners heard the sound of sirens and the roar of approaching planes in the distance.

Elton: *"We could feel the train unhooking our car. We yelled to the guards outside, for we knew that it was a bombing raid. The guard yelled back, 'It's your Americans, they won't hurt you!' Then all was quiet, except for the sirens. Very soon the bombs started coming and our rail car would shake and the noise was deafening. We all were lying down and covered our heads with our arms. This kept up for quite a while, wave after wave of planes were heard coming over and dropping their bombs. It was a big raid from what we could hear, then all at once it was over and it was quiet, but we could hear fires burning. About an hour later, the guards came back and opened the doors and got us out. Everything was in shambles around us and we were the only rail car in the rail yards. The trucks were all blown up and no way could a train move in this mess. We found out that we were in Cologne. They marched us across the city to another rail yard and we could see the whole city was on fire. It was, we later found out, a very big raid and involved all American planes. How we came not to be hit, no one will ever know. Just lucky, I guess. We were then loaded on another rail car and started moving again. I don't remember how long we were on this train, but I think it was the rest of that day and night and then got to a camp sometime the following day."*

On Thursday, September 28th, Elton and the British arrived at Bergen-Belsen, the infamous concentration camp in Lower Saxony where more than 70,000 people died during the war. Many of them died from Typhus. This was also where Anne Frank[1] and her sister Margot died. Elton and the others stayed in the *Sternenlager*, a part of the camp set aside for transit prisoners.

Elton: *"We found out from guards that this camp was called Belsen. It did not mean anything to me then, but later (after the war) I found what this really was. The prisoners were mostly kept away from us, but we could see their* striped funny-looking clothes and their shaved heads. Some of the prisoners were around us, and they looked like walking skeletons, so we thought they had some kind of disease. Just a few of them could talk to the German-speaking English soldier and one could speak some English. He found out that I was an American and one of the guards said that I was the only American that had ever been in this camp. They treated the prisoners with utter contempt, and after finding out the prisoners were mostly Jewish, we could understand why. Some claimed they were various nationalities, but I guess they were mostly Jews. Some were political prisoners. Just a few could get near us. We could see so many bodies being piled up in another yard and each day more being added to it. We thought that it was some sickness and really did not think that they were dying of starvation or being gassed. That was in front of the crematoriums, where the bodies were being piled up. Later I found out that the crematoriums were not working very well."

They stayed in Bergen-Belsen for a week. Elton kept telling the guards and anyone who would listen that he was an American, not English. The Germans told him they did not know his identity because he had no dog tag and no wallet in his pocket to identify him. They suspected he was a spy. Elton knew spies were executed so he hastened to deny he was a spy and kept a low profile.

Elton: *"The few English that were still with me had identification that was not very good either. That is the only reason I can think of for sending me to this camp. Very little food was given to us, just a cup of ersatz coffee[2] in the morning and a cup of some very weak soup made of kohlrabis or some sticks of something that looked like branches off a bush or tree. There was no water to bathe or wash with and very little to drink. We still thought that maybe they were going to eliminate us, but held out hope that they would not. It was a very depressing time. But I was not alone and that helped some. It's funny that when you have company, the thought of dying doesn't seem as bad when you are with someone in the same circumstances. We were also concerned that if the prisoners had typhus or some other disease that was killing them, that we would catch it, also."*

In Heinkenszand, on Friday, September 29th, the moment for Joe's transfer arrived. It rained periodically and stayed cloudy. Earlier that week Nico van Biezen asked a local tailor to give him some civilian clothing. The man was afraid of reprisals and refused to help. This was disappointing, but Nico didn't give up.

Late in the afternoon, Nico embraced his pregnant wife, looked at her a moment longer and gave his daughter a kiss before he got on his bike. Dressed in his overalls and with a stovepipe under his arm he rode through the drizzly weather to the Helenahoeve. In the farm kitchen, Rienbouw introduced the blacksmith to Joe. Leny and Koos van Iwaarden still remember they were not allowed to enter the kitchen. Everything was kept secret from them, because children could easily give away information without realizing it. The plan was that Nico and the American would bike to the Westhof-farm, the nursery of the Van 't Westeinde family, about 1.5 miles away. The bombardier was asked to remove his bomber jacket and leather boots. Nico gave him a dirty overall to cover his uniform. Because American soldiers wore shorter hairstyles than was usual in Zeeland, Nico gave him an equally dirty cap. The blacksmith also gave him a pair of clogs, but Joe was unable to walk in them because of his broken ankle. They hoped his army boots would not stand out under the legs of the overalls. Then Nico took a handful of black soot from the stovepipe and smeared it on the boots and on Joe's face and hands and laid the pipe on his shoulder. *"Now he looks exactly like a blacksmith servant!"* Nico said to Rienbouw. *"If they check us, I will tell the Jerries that he was evacuated from Walcheren and he is now temporarily my servant."* After Rienbouw indicated it was safe to leave, Nico and Joe got on the bikes that were waiting for them. Joe owned a rusty bike at Wendling and could ride a bike very well, but he still had many problems with his ankle. But there was nothing for it but to try. Nico and Joe thanked Rienbouw and went on their way.

The Helenahoeve was located under a dike and Joe had great difficulty riding up the slope with his sore ankle. When that failed, he pushed the bike. At the top of the Boerendijk, he got back on, ignored the pain and rode with the blacksmith on the dike, between the rows of poplars. They passed a German roadblock on the dike that surrounded the nursery. Joe was worried because the legs of his overalls crawled up while riding and revealed his boots. But there was nothing he could do. Nico rode ahead. Nico, who spoke no English, used gestures to tell Joe that he must ride on when Nico was stopped at the roadblock. Joe was very worried this would arouse suspicion. Nico made it clear he had a loaded pistol under his coat and would not hesitate to use it should something go wrong. Nico was indeed stopped at the roadblock and Joe, just a few yards behind him, rode by. Nothing happened. Extremely nervous, Joe rode on, just slowly enough to stay on the bike. He did not know a single Dutch word, and although he knew the farm was close by, he had no idea where it was. A little later, he saw Nico behind him. Relieved, the men cycled to the Westhof farmhouse, where old Piertje was waiting for them. Nico gestured to Joe to wait in the kitchen for the other members of the underground, and left. Piertje and the American bombardier waited silently. Piertje only spoke a little English and Joe knew no Dutch.

Joe's son, John Sulkowski, later wrote: *"The farmer looked at my father and said, 'Tobacco?' and asked with gestures if he wanted to smoke. My father nodded, the man disappeared through the back door and came back with a leaf tobacco from his garden, which he put in the oven to roast. Then he rolled a cigarette for my father. My father told me the tobacco was so strong that it almost blew the top of his skull."*

After his rescuers arrived, Joe relaxed a bit. He could finally wash and shave, get new and spare clothes and enjoy a good meal. Piet van den Dries told Joe an unknown American was killed in the crash and Gene Kieras had fallen to his death without a parachute. Joe nodded. He had seen Gene fall. They told him they also saw six men being arrested and transported to the town. At least one of them showed burns on his face and another had a broken ankle. Joe revealed how many crewmembers were on board and they realized there was one missing.

That night, Joe lay in a hayloft, wondering who the missing crewmember was and what was happening to him and the others. Joe slept in a barn belonging to Ko van 't Westeinde, above a beet storage area where the family Ford was hidden. In the loft, an enclosure of hay bales was made, complete with a hay-camouflaged door.

As the nights grew cold, the Group Griep decided to move Joe to a more comfortable place. Through an official who worked at the building inspection in Goes, they were told a hiding place was available in the neighboring village of 's-Heer Abtskerke. It was in the rectory of St. John the Baptist Church, a spacious villa-style house on the *Kerkring* (Church ring) where Pastor André Evelein lived with his wife and children.

In December 1940, André and his wife Cor (Cornelia) moved to 's-Heer Abtskerke when André was appointed pastor of the Reformed Church of John the Baptist. At the time the Group Griep decided to bring Joe to 's-Heer Abtskerke, the couple had a two-year-old daughter, Hanneke, and a year-old son, Freddy. The rectory already housed several evacuees, so there was little room available.

On Saturday, September 30th, Piet van den Dries put on his hat and looked at his wife with mixture of concern and encouragement. *"Katrien, I'm going to do something dangerous"*, he said. *"If this goes wrong, you might never see me again."* Katrien nodded, embraced him and watched him leave. Nico van Biezen and Joe walked three miles to the 's-Heer Abtskerke. Halfway there, Piet van den Dries joined them. The guards at the roadblocks to 's-Heer Abtskerke were billeted in the school behind

Piet's house. These men really appreciated the kind headmaster because he spoke flawless German. It was Piet's job to guide Nico and Joe through the two roadblocks. He told Joe to look down as much as possible and, if they were stopped, he should answer only *Ja* or *Nee* (Yes or No). Soon the first roadblock appeared. They tried to remain calm. When the German guards recognized Piet, they saluted him and allowed all three men through. At the second checkpoint, the guards also recognized Piet. "*Guten Tag, Herr Haupt Meister*", (Good day, mister headmaster) they said kindly. Piet took off his hat and saluted them back in the fluent German they appreciated so much. Once in the little village, Joe was quietly smuggled into the rectory to keep the new guest apart from the other refugees.

Joe was given a small room with two beds on the top floor, a small window overlooking the neighbor's yard. Piet advised Joe not to show himself in the window and to keep a low profile so nobody would notice him. If the Germans conduct a raid in the rectory, Joe would get a signal to hide in the attic, in the space between the roof and the roof tiles.

On this same Saturday, a nervous Kees Bek knocked at Ko van 't Westeinde's door. Kees told his boss a man was hiding in his barn. Ko suspected this had to be the missing American. He went with Kees to the house on the Westdijk to see for himself.

Ko: *"When I got there, I saw immediately this could not go on like this. Mr. Bek and his wife were very nervous. Their legs were shaking. The American was happy to hear his comrade Joseph had escaped, but also knew that his best friend had fallen to his death. He had seen this happen himself."*

That same day, Ko's younger brother, Pier, came to the Westdijk and brought the gunner, Ely, civilian clothes. Because Ely had never ridden a bike before, he had to practice before he got the hang of it. When Pier was convinced Ely rode well enough to avoid detection, he brought him to the Westhof.

Ko: *"This aviator was much freer and easier than Joseph. While cycling to my home he insisted on seeing what was left of the plane."*

Just as Joe had done the night before, Ely spent the night above the beet storage. The next day he and Nico van Biezen were accompanied by 17-year old Nathalie, daughter of Kees and Adriana Bek, walking safely to the rectory in 's-Heer Abtskerke. To his relief Ely met Joe in the little room. Kees Griep and Piet van den Dries were also waiting for him and explained the safety rules.

At the request of Kees Griep, Joe again told them the names of the crew of the Feathered Injun, so the resistance group knew the name of the second deceased man. Piet wrote these names down for them.

During this stage of the war, a lot of products were still scarce in Zeeland. To support the pastor couple, brothers Ko and Pier provided them with necessary items like butter, meat, and cigarettes. Headmaster Piet occasionally brought a bag full of English books to the rectory to give the men something to read. Once, when he was stopped while German guards inspected his bag, he declared he came to give English lessons to the pastor. His excuse allowed him to continue on his way. While Joe and Ely waited in their small room, Joe often read his Catholic prayer book, a momento from home. Ely noticed the usually nervous Joe was at peace when reading his book and became interested. During their stay at the rectory, he and Joe had many conversations about religious matters.

On Sunday October 1st, Joe and Ely were in their room in 's-Heer Abtskerke when suddenly the lights went out. This was a punishment for the villagers not showing up to repair the Sloedam that morning as ordered. The electricity was shut down in the whole area. The adventurous Ely who was bored in the oppressive room seized the opportunity to sneak out for a breath of fresh air in the village, shrouded in darkness. When he returned, he was met by the angry pastor who asked Ely how he could be so stupid. In a small village like 's-Heer Abtskerke, people would immediately notice a stranger, especially the American haircut. He had not only risked his own life, but also that of Joe and all resistance fighters who helped them. If Ely were caught, he and Joe would be sent to a POW camp, but the pastor and his wife would be interrogated and executed. Startled, Ely promised to keep a low profile.

Material supplies were crucial for the Allied conquest of Europe. They flowed through a long and dangerous route from two artificial harbors at Arromanches in Normandy. Later, the ports of Dieppe and Le Tréport were used. On September 4th, the major port of Antwerp fell into Allied hands, virtually intact. With 27 miles of quay to load and unload ships, 600 cranes, and 900 warehouses, Antwerp gave the Allies a significant advantage. However, the Allied forces could not use Antwerp as their main port, because areas across the Western Scheldt were still under Nazi control and the water was full of floating mines. Western Zeelandic Flanders, Walcheren, and South Beveland were still occupied territory.

On Monday, October 2nd, the Battle of the Scheldt began. The battle consisted of four large-scale operations:

1: *Operation Switchback*: the liberation of the western part of Zeeland by the 3rd Canadian Infantry Division, assisted by the British 5th Assault Regiment of the Royal Engineers.

2:    *Operation Vitality*: the liberation of South Beveland by the 2nd Canadian Infantry Division and the British 52nd Lowland Division at Baarland.

3:    *Operation Infatuate I*: the liberation of Walcheren from South Beveland by the 2nd Canadian Infantry Division and the British 52nd Lowland Division, in conjunction with British landings from the Scheldt via Breskens by the British 155th Infantry Brigade and No. 4 Commando.

4:    *Operation Infatuate II*: British landings from the sea on the beaches of Westkapelle by the 4th Special Service Brigade, 48 Royal Marine Commando and No. 10 Inter Allied Commando (consisting of Belgian, Dutch and Norwegian troops), preceded by bombing from the RAF and the Royal Navy.

The 2nd Canadian Infantry Division marched north from Antwerp to take the Kreekrakdam and access South Beveland. On October 2nd, while the Canadians pushed through to the village Woensdrecht in North Brabant, Allied aircraft dropped warning pamphlets on Walcheren. The civilian population was told to leave the peninsula immediately before the dikes were bombed. A stream of refugees fled to South Beveland. Nico and Suus van Biezen offered their home and forge to the Hildebrand family from the village of Sint Laurens at Walcheren. The father of the Hilderbrand family was also a blacksmith and he helped in Nico's workshop during the evacuation. Many Walcheren residents, however, thought the bombing would not be very dangerous and decided to stay home.

The following day, Piet van den Dries managed to obtain a *Sonderausweis* (special permit) to travel to Middelburg. He explained he wanted to study the German language in there. In reality, he was under orders to locate and record information concerning enemy reinforcements and pass it to the Allies. With the permit in his jacket, he crossed the partially ruined Sloedam and returned the same day. This trip was not without risk because the bombing on Walcheren began the same afternoon. Two Hundred Forty Seven British Lancaster bombers attacked the sea dike at Westkapelle Zeedijk because Walcheren was part of the Atlantic Wall and reinforced with a network of heavily armored bunkers. It would take too long to destroy all these fortresses one by one, so they decided to flood the entire peninsula. The bombing destroyed 400 feet of the Westkapelle sea dike. The village Westkapelle was almost completely destroyed by the flooding seawater and more than 120 people, including 47 residents who had taken refuge in the basement of a mill, drowned that day.

At the same time, members of the resistance gave the two Americans false identity passes in case the Germans raided the rectory.

Joe later wrote to his brother Ted: *"The Dutch identity was provided to us by the Dutch underground. One of the things we had to do before we flew a combat mission was to make a picture (of the passport type) in civilian clothes. That was one of the few things I took on a combat mission. Also, I took a small pocket prayer book that mother gave me when I left the house to go to the Air Force. My name was chosen in this way: I was given a list of names to pronounce and they picked the one I could pronounce the easiest. This information was on my identity card:*

1) *My name (Piet Smit)*
2) *My date of birth and place of birth (May 10, 1918, Zaamslag Z)*
3) *My job was a clerk at the auction (fruit and vegetables)*
4) *The date on which and the place where the pass was made (July 18, 1941, St. Laurens) with a forged signature of the mayor.*
5) *My current address (Noordweg 15)*
6) *My signature.*

Also, I've put my index finger print on the back of my passport. That picture was covered with a transparent seal, in order to ensure the image could not be removed. Also the stamp of the mayor had to be put in the right place, again so the card could not be altered. The stamps were real and were put on by the night janitor of the mayor who had stolen them from his office. He was a member of the underground."

It is not difficult to deduce who provided the false information. Nico van Biezen was from Zaamslag and had just employed a worker from St. Laurens.

On October 5th, the same day all German boys aged 16 were called to enlist in the army, Elton and the British were marched to a train station. They were put in a passenger train with German citizens and told to stand in the back of the train car, so the guards could protect them from German passengers, who yelled *"Terror Flieger!"* and *"Luftgangster!"* (terrorist flyers and air gangsters) and threatened to lynch them. Several times, angry German citizens hanged Allied airmen from lampposts or beat them death, in revenge for the bombing of German cities After the war, Allied prisoners of war have stated that when they were at the train station in Berlin, they could see an airmen hanging from each tree on the Unter den Linden Boulevart. German soldiers had orders not to deter the citizens. Only officially declared prisoners of war were protected. This is why downed airmen preferred to surrender to soldiers rather than to civilians.

Elton: *"It was evening and after awhile it got dark. With the cars not very light, we looked around and saw that we could open a window at the end of the car. I and another guy talked of escaping while the train was moving, for we were small enough to crawl through the opening. It was all set, when the train stopped and we were made to get off. So there went our escape plans. When we got off the train, we saw that on top of the car were a machine gun and some soldiers. The cars behind us were all military equipment and guns and large anti-aircraft guns. If we had crawled through that window, the floodlights on the top of the train would have spotted us and that would have been it."*

Elton was right. During mass transport by train to various camps it was common for fleeing prisoners to be shot dead by German guards. Only a few managed to escape in this manner.

The prisoners were transferred to another train, into a boxcar again. They spent the night and next day on this trip. The journey was slow because other trains carried important equipment and troops for the battle and were given priority.

On October 6th the family of Ed Yensho was notified of his death.

On that same day, despite heavy opposition, the 2nd Canadian Infantry Division approached the village of Woensdrecht. Defying floods, rain, landmines, booby traps and fierce German defiance, the Canadians attacked and endured heavy losses. The Germans would not cede access to Zeeland easily.

As part of Operation Switchback, the 7th Brigade of the 3rd Canadian Infantry Division crossed the Leopold Canal to the Western part of Flanders, while the 9th Brigade performed amphibious landings. The 3rd Canadian Infantry Division faced fierce resistance and suffered heavy losses. Operation Switchback ended on November 3rd, after Knokke and Zeebrugge were liberated and all Flanders and Zeelandic Flanders were in Allied hands.

After they left the train, Elton and the other prisoners were forced to march to a transit camp at Limburg an der Lahn in Germany (Stalag XII-A). They were imprisoned in a building with no light or heat. They had not had food and water since Bergen-Belsen, so they shouted for something to eat or drink, but to no avail. It was freezing and snowing outside, so they curled up together on the floor and tried to get some sleep.

The next morning Elton and his companions were taken to the center of the camp for interrogation. They still had nothing to eat or drink. After standing in line for some time, an American Sergeant came up to them and told Elton he might as well tell the Germans all he knew, for they knew it anyway.

Elton: *"This made me mad, for here was an American collaborating with the Germans. I saw quite a few of these bastards later on and it was all for the good of themselves. They would get more food and were treated better than the rest of the prisoners. When I hear some say they weren't treated so bad, I begin to wonder about them, if they were some of these turncoats."*

Elton was still with the Brits, but now he also saw Americans in the camp, including many airmen. Most of the Americans were paratroopers from the 82nd Airborne Division, the same division Elton and his crew had supplied just three weeks earlier. Limburg camp held about four thousand prisoners of all nationalities. Each prisoner was issued an old, dirty German cup and cutlery. There was no water to wash anything. They were given water at four o'clock in the afternoon after waiting six hours for it. When Elton's turn for water came, the Germans delivered soup to the rest of the men. That was depressing, but he had at least got his cup and cutlery clean and had a drink. A German guard came for Elton, and said he had to go to another building because he was an American. Finally, the radio operator would join his countrymen. However, that also meant he could not continue traveling with Sidney Goldstein. Sidney and Elton had become good friends and they supported each other through this misery. They did not know how much longer they would see each other.

The prison for the Americans was no barracks, but a paltry, drafty cabin with beds only half equipped with bed boards. There were no mattresses. Everyone had to share his bed with someone else. Elton shared a bed with Sgt Ralph Tyson, a paratrooper from Florida. They warmed themselves with each other's body heat, because nobody had blankets. They were often rousted out of bed at night for roll call. They tried to fool the guards by changing positions, so the Germans repeatedly had to recount.

It began to rain wet snow, so everything in the camp was wet and muddy. Elton caught dysentery from the dirty environment and poor diet. It would stop for a few days, but always came back. Meager rations consisted of watery soup with some vegetables and very little fat. They drank a coffee substitute made from roasted barley and sometimes surrogate tea made from vegetables. There was no bread. Occasionally they received a few packs of cigarettes from the Red Cross. They also got Polish cigarettes, which tasted awful, but they smoked them anyway to distract them from the hunger cramps. Cigarettes were also useful to exchange with the guards for a bit of bread. Elton often heard artillery in the distance and hoped he would be freed soon. But his liberation would be long in coming. The roar he heard was from German guns bombarding General Patton's troops, whose advance was slowed by a lack of material. Elton remained at Camp Limburg for two weeks.

On Saturday, October 7th, 59 British Lancasters bombed the Nolledijk at Flushing, leaving a 65 ft gap in the dike. Simultaneously, the dike at Rammekens was attacked, leaving a 130 ft gap in the dike. Seawater flooded most of Walcheren. A few days later, sixty Lancasters bombed the Oostwatering dike at Veere. Many attacks on the coastal batteries followed.

At the same time, another dangerous situation occurred in 's-Heer Abtskerke.

André Evelein wrote [3]: *"Early in the morning the doorbell rang. I was still shaving in the bedroom upstairs. My wife was downstairs and opened the door. Two German soldiers were conducting a billeting search for an officer. Oh, horror! No one could warn Joseph and Ely! In case of an emergency they were told to flee to the attic, but now we could not warn them. My wife remains calm and says the house is full of our own family and some guests. Still the quartermasters want to take a look inside. Downstairs is all easily viewed, in the rectory all was in use. Then they went to the rooms upstairs. Quietly, my wife generously opens the door to the guest room and bathroom to show them. 'Here our children sleep.' At that time, our small children and a twelve year old were lodged there. 'Ah, die kinder...!'(Ah those children...!). Quickly they went to the room above the front door. My wife keeps the door shut. 'Here a few guests sleep.' That was true! A young married couple from the village stayed in there temporarily, in waiting for their own house. Immediately, distracting them, my wife opens the door to a junk room. To show them: 'No secrets behind these doors'. But this room won't do either! At the next door: 'This is where we sleep ourselves. My husband is still shaving.' They did not want to witness that. Finally with a look of: 'What a mess!' they came to the airmen's room... a door in a narrow corner of the floor next to a toilet. Still my wife didn't panic. 'Another young couple is staying here...' But the Germans already decided: 'This floor has no room for an office' and claiming the whole house? No, too much trouble. The quartermasters left. Although they were not looking for people who were hiding, but for a room for an officer, it was a dangerous situation. The coolness of my wife at that time spared many lives! It may well be said. Had it gone differently, we would probably never be able to celebrate liberation afterwards."*

This was not the only threat they endured in the rectory. Ted, a younger brother of Joe, later wrote[4]: *"They were in the same room when a German unit made a surprise search of the village. The Reverend's family was taken by surprise and there was no time to warn Joe and Ely. In such a case the pastor had told them, to lie in bed with the covers drawn over them and they had to pretend to be asleep. This is what they did. To the shock of Joe and Ely one of the officers entered their room and had some lengthy minutes at their bed, as if he doubted. If he had pulled back the bedcovers, he would have found two fully clothed men with their shoes on. But to their relief - and surprise - the officer left the room without any further action. Joe later told that he felt the German officer was aware of what was going on, but he deliberately ignored it. Looks like not all German soldiers were True Believers."* Years later Joe told his brother he regularly woke up sweating after a dream about a German soldier standing in his room gazing at him.

Friday, October 13th was a black day for the Canadian troops who fought for the small, but strategically important, town of Woensdrecht. That day, regiments of the Black Watch Battalion of the 5th Infantry Brigade were wiped out. However, on Monday, October 16th, the Canadians finally managed to capture Woensdrecht, separating South Beveland and Walcheren from the mainland.

Also on this day, General Montgomery made the liberation of the Scheldt estuary his highest priority.

1: The Jewish Anne Frank is still one of the most discussed victims of the Holocaust. Her impressive diary about hiding in a house in Amsterdam has been the basis for several plays and films.
2: A substitute for coffee made of chicory.
3: The story André Evelein wrote about his experiences during the war has been previously published in an extra edition of a small village paper in 1994 in 's-Heer Abtskerke and then partially reflected in the book *Slagveld Sloedam* by René Hoebeke.
4: Joe was always reluctant to tell his children about his experiences. However, after the death of his wife, he told a few things to his younger brother Ted. After Joe's death, Ted put those memories on paper, along with his own memories of that time.

The barn at the Westhof tree nursery where Joe and Ely slept. (129)

The hayloft above the beet storage. (130)

The family of Pastor André Evelein after the war. (131)

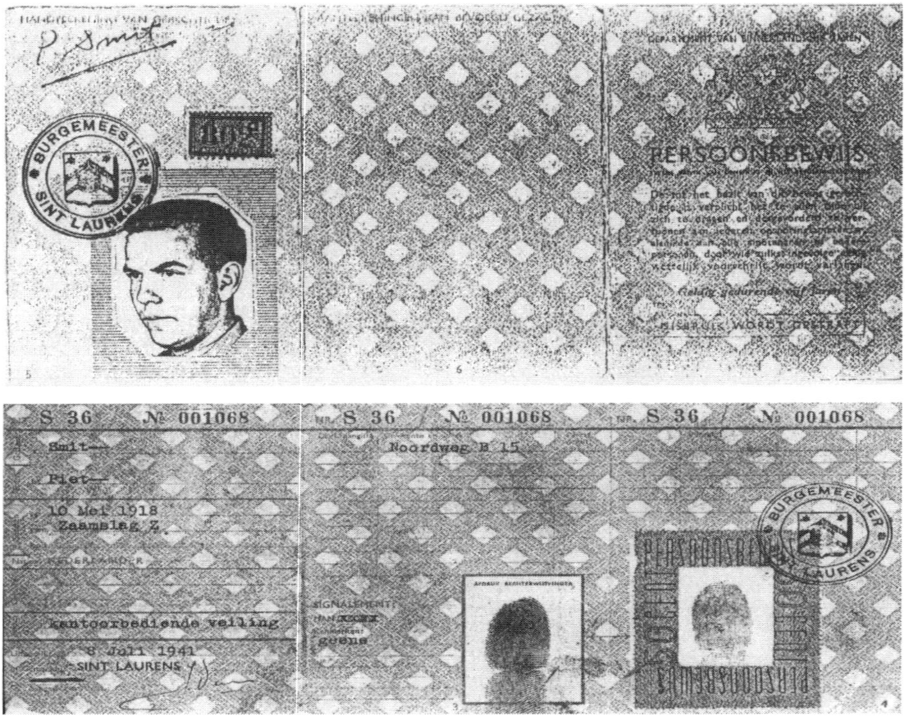

P. Smit

BURGEMEESTER SINT LAURENS

PERSOONSBEWIJS

MISBRUIK WORDT GESTRAFT

S 36 № 001068 | S 36 № 001068 | S 36 № 001068

Smit

Piet

10 Mei 1918

Zaamslag Z.

kantoorbediende veiling

8 Juli 1941

SINT LAURENS

Noordweg B 15

SIGNALEMENT

geene

BURGEMEESTER SINT LAURENS

PERSOONSBEWIJS

The forged identity pass of Joe alias Piet Smit. (132 and 133)

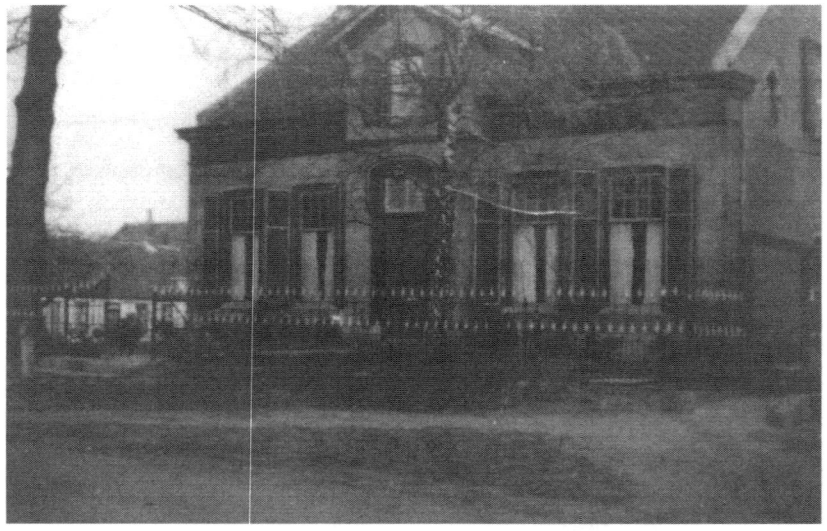

The rectory of ‘s-Heer Abtskerke in 1944. (134)

```
                    S o n d e r a u s w e i s  Nr._____

Der                            Pieter Jacobus Willem van den Dries
Die  ─────────────────────────────────────────────────────────────
         (Beruf, Vor - und Zuname)  mit Begleitperson
geboren am  26.9.09              in Houten
wohnhaft in  Heinkenszand A 97
                  (Wohnort, Strasse u. Hausnummer)
ist berechtigt, zur Durchführung  seiner
                                  Ihrer
Dienstobliegenheiten in der Zeit von   20    Uhr bis   22    Uhr
in Strecke Middelburg-Heinkenszand die Strasse zu betreten.

Gültig bis    3.Oktober   1944

                           Middelburg, den  3.Oktober 1944
                           Der Beauftragte des Reichskommissars
                               für die Provinz Zeeland
                                 - Polizeioffizier -
```

The *Sonderausweis*, which Piet van den Dries could use between 2000 hours and 2200 hours for traveling from Heinkenszand to Middelburg. (135)

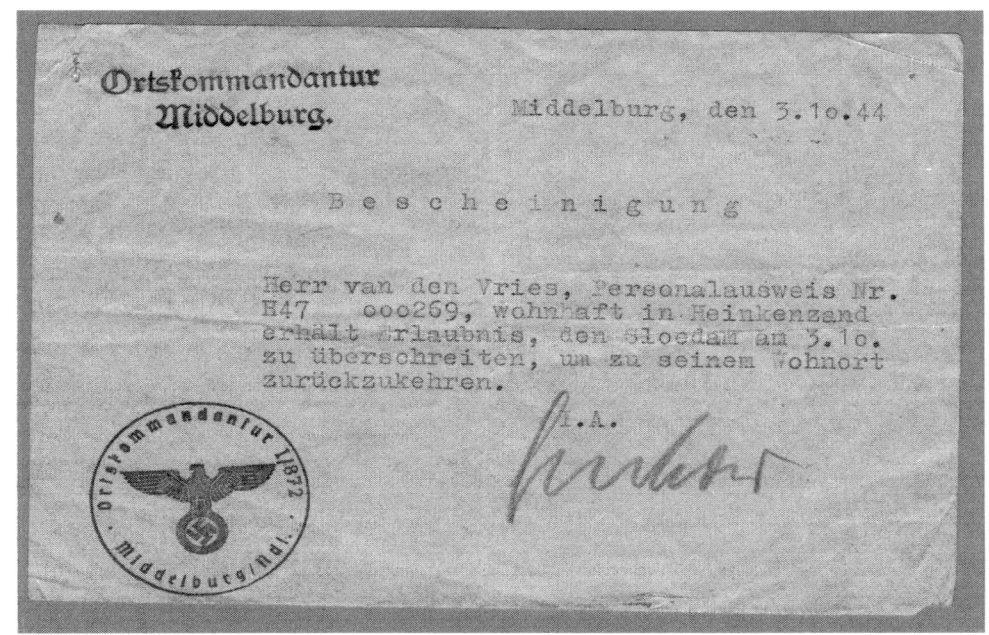

The *Sonderausweis* for coming back across the Sloedam. (136)

> **C. GRIEP**
> ARTS
> HEINKENSZAND
> POSTGIRO 91326
> TEL. No. 260 's-HEER ARENDSKERKE
>
> HEINKENSZAND, *september* 194 4
>
> Edward Jenssen
> × Eugene Kiras S 20 1st engineer R.C.
> Brink sidegunner
> Hebert tailgunner
> Southwell wireless oper.
> Grandow navigator
> Jerow 1st pilot
> Valleralli 2nd pilot
> Joseph Sulkowski bomb aimer (Pittsburg)
> Ealy Loice mechanic (California)
> Bemanning vliegtuig, neergestort te Heinkenszand

The list of crew names written by Piet van den Dries on a sheet of paper from Kees Griep's office. The name of Ed Yensho is misspelled. The attached photo of Joe in civilian clothes was unusable for the false identity because it was taken from the front. Instead, another photo taken from three quarters of the side was used. (137)

Chapter 14

Life and Death

On October 20th, Elton and the other American prisoners of war were loaded on a freight train. This was the last time Elton saw his friend Sidney Goldstein. They said goodbye and wished each other a good homecoming[1]. The rail cars transporting Elton and his fellow prisoners were packed. The guards treated them like animals and stabbed them with bayonets. With 60 people to a rail car, there was no place to sit, so they were forced to stand the entire trip.

By that time, Frenchy and Ben had spent a few days at Stalag Luft IV in Poland. According to an American newspaper, Frenchy's wife, Juanita, from Pueblo, CO, received a letter from her husband from Stalag Luft IV, dated October 19th. Frenchy and Ben did not have to suffer through cruel marches like Elton did. However, they certainly visited the camp where Elton and the English would end up, the infamous transit and interrogation camp for aviators, Dulag Luft Oberursel, near Frankfurt am Main. Dulag Luft derives from the German *Durchgangslager der Luftwaffe* (Transit Camp for the Air Force).

Dulag Luft Oberursel was the main interrogation center in Europe. Here psychologists systematically questioned all aviator prisoners. Sometimes, the interrogators were Germans who had lived in America or Canada for many years. They spoke English very well and understood the prisoner's cultural background. The interrogation was often accompanied by threats, sometimes with reward, according to the Good Cop/Bad Cop method.

After arriving at the camp, Elton and his fellow prisoners were taken to a 25 square foot room containing only a few chairs. Like the train, the room was so full that no one could sit down. The Americans pounded on the door when they wanted to go to the bathroom, but there was no reply. Some of the men had dysentery and the room soon became a smelly mess. Eventually, the men were allowed to the bathroom in pairs. Here they could finally get off their feet and sit down. The Germans began to retrieve five men at a time from the room and the remaining prisoners heard machine gun fire outside. They did not know if their comrades were shot or whether it was a trick to frighten them.

Elton remained in the room with 35 to 40 people until the next morning. He tried to get some sleep while huddled under a chair. Elton: *"I would pound on the door to go to the bathroom and a guard would escort me. You would hear the machine gun fire all the time as if they were executing some people. I did look out the window in the bathroom and did see some men being shot, so it was not all bluff. One felt pretty well discouraged about this time, but didn't let on to the Germans, but I was pretty mad at them at this time."*

Early in the morning, Elton was given a cup of ersatz coffee and then taken to a cell containing a single cot in it and a light in the ceiling. He knew he was going to be interrogated.

Elton: *"I also knew that there were microphones in the cell, in case I would talk if someone came to me in the cell. This person would speak English, but would no doubt be a planted German or a turncoat American trying to get information from you. They would ask about your outfit, bomb group, where you were from in the states, what your mission was, or where you were going or where you were coming from, where you were stationed at your base, and also, a lot of stuff of a personal nature. Sometimes it was obvious that the guy was a plant, for he would have an accent. They would ask about football games or baseball games, dates you had been on and all kinds of stuff that was normal talk among G.I.'s. I didn't talk much, I pretended to be sleeping."*

The Germans asked these questions to learn about America. Every piece of information was important. Hundreds of airmen, each telling small details, revealed a lot.

Eventually, Elton was ordered from his solitary cell and taken to a room where a German officer waited. This would be the most brutal interrogation Elton had experienced. He gave them only his name, his rank, and his army serial number. Elton was surprised by the amount of information the Germans already knew about the prisoners. They knew the names of their crew, the name of their unit and where it was located. Amazingly, they also knew many personal matters. This made some prisoners think that it was useless to conceal anything. Yet most still gave only their name, rank, and army serial number.

Because Elton had no identification on him the officer shouted that he would be shot for spying. The increasingly devastating raids by the RAF and 8th Air Force frustrated Hitler, so he declared that captured airman with no identification were to be treated as spies and terrorists and must be executed. Captured airmen dressed in civilian clothing and with false passes were also to be treated as spies. This meant that men in hiding, like Joe and Ely, were in serious danger. If caught, they could end up in a concentration camp and be executed. Hitler also ordered the execution of fighter pilots suspected of attacking civilian targets.

Elton: *"I just told him that I didn't like his country good enough to be a spy and would rather be back in the states, and he would just have to believe me that I was just an airman doing what I was told to do, the same as he was doing. I also told him it was his people that had separated me from my crew that would prove that I was an airman. He at last called a guard and dismissed me. The guard took me down a long hallway and to the outside. It was at this point that I thought maybe I was going to face that firing squad, but he took me outside and then to another building where there were other prisoners."*

Elton was luckier than many other airmen in Oberursel. Although he didn't have any identification, he did wear a uniform. After reading the report of the crashed bomber near Heinkenszand, it was clear to the officer that Elton was indeed an American airman who had bailed out of a burning bomber. His stay at Dulag Luft did not last long for two reasons. First, the Germans could not hold the large influx of prisoners for very long and, second, they knew prisoners lied under long interrogation.

Elton was put on the next train with fifty other prisoners. After a short ride, they arrived at camp Dulag Luft Wetzlar, a few miles from Frankfurt am Main. There they were welcomed by the American prisoner, Colonel Darling, imprisoned after his Mustang was shot down. After the crash, citizens and German soldiers attacked the Colonel and the marks were still visible on his face. He had been at camp for a while and was respected by the Germans, so they put him in charge of orienting new prisoners.

The men were finally allowed to take a shower and shave for the first time since they left England. They were given two blankets, an American Army shirt, two pair of socks, a sweater, a G.I. overcoat and a pair of long underwear. Just getting into some clean clothes after a shower raised everyone's spirits. They also received a toothbrush, some toothpaste, a razor blade, a piece of soap, a scarf, and a woolen hat. The starving men were finally presented with a meal, sent by the Red Cross. They were given barley flakes for use in soup or cereal. Even the German bread began to taste better. It was not nearly enough to satisfy their hunger, but it was more than they had since their arrest. This was due mainly to the courage of Colonel Darling, who constantly reminded the Germans to respect the Geneva Conventions.

That night they came together to encourage each other by singing. The Americans sang *America the Beautiful* and *The Star Spangled Banner*. The English sang *God Save the Queen*. The men swore loyalty to their homeland and did everything they could to annoy the Germans, encouraged by Colonel Darling, who knew exactly how far to push it.

Here, Elton met a Polish man, captured by the Russians and handed over to the Germans. He managed to escape and somehow reached England, where he joined the 1st Polish Armored Division to fight against the Germans. During the fierce battle of Operation Market Garden, he was again imprisoned.

Elton: *"I sure hope he made it OK. He could speak several languages, so I was able to visit with him quite a bit. He didn't think that his chances would be too good, if they found his record; but he had changed his name and was still hoping. He had no use for the Russians or the Germans and wanted only to fight them."*

Elton: *"We were loaded into rail cars again; this time in stock cars that were used for cattle or hogs with the slat siding. We rode the rest of the day in these cars, almost freezing to death, and then we stopped and were loaded into boxcars. This was luxury compared to the cattle cars. I think we rode in these cars for about three days. There was no way to relieve oneself, only in a can that we had to empty out along the door by throwing it out through the window air vent at the top of the car. Not many of us had the dysentery these days, but it was a mess, nevertheless. The train would stop quite often to let other trains pass and about once a day, they would let us out for a drink and to relieve ourselves. Guards were all armed with machine guns and rifles. There was no chance to escape and it was useless to try, for we were deep in Germany and no help could be gotten in Germany."*

Meanwhile, the people who stayed in the rectory of 's-Heer Abtskerke were startled again.

Andre[2]: *"In the middle of the day a Dutch military policeman on a motorcycle drove up and parked it in the front garden near the living room window. Another person accompanied him. They knocked on the door... When it appeared the officer was to be 'trusted', he said he had brought a third aviator to our two Americans from 'somewhere'. This man suffered from loneliness and he wanted to see the two that were with us. The pilot was indeed very happy to meet our guests and after they had a good time, the officer and the pilot left us. Fortunately they never came back again! To which crashed plane he belonged, we never found out. Sitting on the back of the motorcycle he was disguised as a blacksmith servant with a stovepipe under his arm, like he went to us to 'fix' something. But at the opposite of our rectory was our own village blacksmith's workshop that had a shoeing stock in front of the door. Imagine that this real blacksmith had seen what was going on and in his ignorance had told someone of these two unexpected guests! 'Don't come again!' we told them."*

The visiting aviator probably was the Polish Spitfire pilot Jerzy Mazurkiewicz of the No. 308 Squadron Krakowski. On September 11th, 1944, his plane crashed in Nieuwdorp, in the west of South Beveland. When the local policeman, Daniëlse, saw the Spitfire crashing, he immediately jumped on his motorbike. Ille Rijk, a miller's son, dressed in dusty flour stained overalls, jumped on the back of the motorbike. They passed a few Germans on their way to the landed aircraft. When they reached the Vleugelhof farm of farmer Boonman, they quickly dressed Mazurkiewicz in the dusty overall, so he would look like a miller's servant. They put him on the back of the motorcycle and brought him to safety. The Polish pilot remained in hiding on the Landlust farm owned by the family Vermue in Nieuwdorp. Mazurkiewicz was not easily frightened. The farm housed many refugees and he often walked among them in civilian clothes, even when German soldiers were present. The military police officer who brought Mazurkiewicz to the rectory probably was this same Daniëlse. Given the clothes the Polish pilot wore and the stovepipe under his arm, it's easy to figure out that Nico Biezen had a hand in his disguise.

On October 25th, after the 2nd Canadian Infantry Division cut off the route of North Brabant to South Beveland and Walcheren, Canadian troops crossed the Kreekrakdam, connecting the island of South Beveland with the mainland of Brabant. This was after exhausting battles with many casualties on both sides. *Operation Vitality*, the plan to expel the Germans from South Beveland, had begun. The 2nd Canadian Infantry Division initiated an attack on the German 70th Infantry Division and pushed into the west after Rilland-Bath was taken. A day later, the village Krabbendijke was captured. There were many civilian casualties in these villages, a devastating side effect of liberation.

At the same time, hundreds of soldiers from the British 52nd Lowland Division boarded Water Buffalo amphibious vehicles[3] to cross the Western Scheldt to South Beveland. They made shore near the town of Baarland. Other troops followed and, although the Germans focused most of their attention on the tail of South Beveland, the Canadians and the British found much opposition. A fierce battle broke out. Civilian casualties were high and much damage was done, including the destruction of the church of Ellewoutsdijk.

At the command of the Wehrmacht, all male residents between 17 and 45 years from Goes, Wemeldinge, and Yerseke were ordered to report for work. They were to bring warm clothing, blankets and food enough for three days. This was intended to be a large assembly, but barely thirty men reported for duty. In Goes, over two thousand men fled to the countryside and went into hiding. Police officers also went into hiding because they did not want to arrest objectors. The employment project failed.

There was heavy fighting in South Beveland. Those wounded by bullets or grenades were brought to Wolphaartsdijk, converted to a Red Cross hospital village. Pressure on the Zeeland Occupiers was increasing. On Friday October 27th, it appeared that the *Grüne Polizei* (German Green Police) had fled. On the same day, Yerseke was freed and the first Canadian troops reached the Kanaal door Zuid-Beveland (Canal through South Beveland). This canal was spanned by the Vlakebrug, the same bridge destroyed earlier with help from Gerow's crew. This bridge was again blown up by the Germans to stop the Canadians. But this did not stop the Allied advance. During the night of 27 to 28 October, the Canadians crossed the canal in boats and occupied the village of Hansweert.

The battle was approaching Heinkenszand and the village experienced destruction from air strikes and shelling. Several were injured. Nico van Biezen's pregnant wife was in shock from the violence. On October 27th, a rainy Friday, Piet Stavermans, with two other doctors and a nurse, managed her difficult labor in the basement of the forge. After a long struggle, Suus gave birth to their son, Sjaak. Initially they thought the child died, but Nico discovered, just in time, that the baby was moving. Although the child was healthy, Suus endured a long illness.

Nico: *"We came out of the war very unhappy. My wife was affected the worst. This beautiful, courageous woman was a wreck for many years before her death."*

On the birth announcement of Sjaak van Biezen was written:

<u>We call him Sjaak</u>
With great gratitude and joy we wish to inform you of the birth of a son and baby brother
Jacob Adriaan,
at Heinkenszand during the crushing defeat of the aggressors
and under the roaring canon thunder of the liberation army
date 27 Oktober 1944.
N.J. van Biezen
S. van Biezen-Geensen
Rietje

Piet Staverman suffered from stress and a resulting ulcer, so Kees Griep decided to help his deputy. While Piet was busy with the childbirth, Kees went on the road to care for the wounded outside the village. His journey was uneventful until his return to Heinkenszand under intense shelling.

He was hit by shrapnel that broke his leg. With great difficulty, Kees was transported to a hospital in Goes, but there were no surgery facilities. After another dangerous journey to a hospital in Middelburg, he had surgery to set his leg.

That night, André Evelein's rectory was in turmoil.

Andre: *"Boommm, boom, boom in the distance ... And then again not so very far away. Then immediately: the screeching sound of an approaching shell. Will it fly over our village or will it explode near our house? Where? Whose house will be hit? Do they have shelter? Some have followed the advice to dig a shelter next to their house. But what good is it when you are lying in the firing line? On the night of Friday, October 27th to Saturday, October 28th someone is ringing the brass bell of our rectory in the bowl of 's-Heer Abtskerke. What is going on? It is clear that the Allies (Canadians) are here in South Beveland. What is this alarm at the door? One of us unlocks it. There are neighbors in a panic outside! 'Why didn't you open the door in such dreadful night?' No time for discussions. We understand: our basement under the high-lying kitchen, that's the safest bomb shelter now! The windows on the garden level are shielded with thick straw bales. This must be a place where everyone can hide! Together we run through the long corridor. In the face of these emerging bombardments, how many can we hide there? Still more candidates are ringing our bell. Mattresses are dragged to the shelter.*

The next day and the second night the basement was completely full. Our youngest Fred was lying there in a corner in his crib. Hanneke, our oldest of two years, lies on a mattress in the living room, protected against any shards by the table top, which we had put on the side. The shutters outside were closed, because ugly jagged shards of a grenade already tore up the study of the rectory. In the basement we could sit on the mattresses. For an older neighbor this position was impossible so she sat in a straight chair. One of our young refugees was ill and remained lying on a mattress: Quinten Remijnse. To spend his time well, he had brought a part of an encyclopedia with him. At home he had studied the book systematically and kept on doing that in the basement. 'You can always learn something from that!' After fifty years my wife can still remember that it was the letter 'N' he was studying. The basement was so full. And despite the open door to the corridor it was also stuffy. My wife and I stayed on the ground floor trying to make it all a bit more comfortable for everyone. Only when we heard the boommm, boom, boom, we ran to the cellar door, just to hide on the stairs. We could not go inside any further than that.

Yeah, and then we had the two roommates. Nobody knew of their presence. They didn't want to hide in the basement. They had their reason... They hardly ever came out, but sometimes they rummaged in the barn. For exam-

ple, they sawed the Rommel Asparagus into firewood. The citizens collected these poles after Crazy Tuesday. But these days the two Americans kept in their narrow alcove: four walls with small barred windows on the side. They did not want to face the 'cellar dwellers'. Safety was first. You never know. So during those days my wife and I moved between these two and the others. We were quite used to it, because especially in the last years of the war the rectory was often shared with more or less homeless families and individuals for short or long periods. Being the young people as we were, we learned quite a bit of managing because of this. But at the same time we also had a great time."

While this was going on in 's-Heer Abtskerke, Elton and his fellow prisoners arrived at Kiefheide railroad station, about two miles from Stalag Luft IV at Gross Tychow[4] in the German province of Pomerania. This camp was located 12 miles from the city Belgard, (now *Białogard*) in a forest clearing. Stalag Luft-camps[5] were specially created to intern aviators. At the station, heavily armed camp guards with dogs were waiting for the prisoners. This was a special ritual that fell upon any new inmate. The leadership of the Stalag Luft camps consisted of Luftwaffe officers who considered it an honor to guard Allied airmen and treated the enemy airmen with a certain respect. But when the tide began to turn against Germany, the second in-command of the German Empire, *Reichsführer* Heinrich Himmler, decided the prisoners were not only a burden to feed and house, but they could also be used as hostages, in subsequent negotiations with the Allies. Himmler had the Luftwaffe guards replaced by elite SS officers and Gestapo police. Elton and the other prisoners would personally experience the consequences of that decision.

The German guards were led by a fierce commander in a white coat. His aide was a thin man in horn-rimmed glasses. They ordered the camp guards to put their bayonets on their rifles and line up along the road. The commander chose guards who lost family members during Allied air raids. He yelled that these prisoners were criminal terrorists, Chicago gangsters paid to kill women and children. The Nazi in the white coat began shooting his pistol into the air and at his command, the columns of prisoners were ordered to run. Driven by biting dogs and prodding bayonets, the prisoners were forced to run two miles to the camp. Those who fell were mercilessly attacked by the dogs and stabbed by the angry guards, fired up by the two commanders who were running up and down the column, screaming and yelling. Many prisoners were severely wounded and bleeding, which made the dogs even more aggressive.

Stalag Luft IV was in the middle of a forest and the two miles to the camp seemed endless. Some men claimed they saw a guard with a machine gun in a tree, to ensure no one would escape into the forest. Running and stumbling they reached the camp, surrounded by watchtowers and barbed wire. They were driven like cattle through the gate, forced to undress and strip-searched. Their mouths, noses and their anuses were inspected to make sure nothing was smuggled inside.

Elton: *"One of the guards who we later would call Big Stoop[6] almost knocked me through the wall of a building while we were naked and being searched. He was very cruel. My mate Russ Martin drew back his arm like he was going to hit him after he poked Russ very hard at his searching. Big Stoop then proceeded to just beat the hell out of Russ. Russ was a big man and very athletic but he didn't dare hit back, or he would have been killed. Big Stoop would do this to any prisoner who even thought about defying him. Russ's beating was very rough and he was marked up real good. His eyes blackened and swelled shut. He also had cuts on his eyes and cheeks and mouth."*

After a brutal body search, the prisoners were assigned to a room and allowed to treat their wounds. They were interrogated again and assigned a prison number and a barracks.

On Saturday, October 28th, there was a rumor in 's-Heer Abtskerke that the Canadians were already in the neighboring 's Gravenpolder. Canadian troops, advancing from the tail of South Beveland, met with Canadian troops that came ashore on the banks of the Western Scheldt. The residents of 's-Heer Abtskerke heard the rumble of cannon fire and did not know what to expect. Would the liberators come to the village first or would they advance to Kloetinge and Goes?

Andre: *"Now one of our airmen couldn't wait any longer. Joseph was the most careful, but Loyce felt the necessity to explore the situation. Maybe the long-awaited hour of their deliverance was finally there! I told him: 'Okay, but we will go together and I will show you the way. Maybe we can quietly make contact and report to them that there are no German soldiers left in 's-Heer Abtskerke. Maybe they will come to our village.' Together we walked out of the village, towards 's Gravenpolder, a white handkerchief in hand to give signals. Not far from 's Gravenpolder we suddenly came to see a camouflaged Canadian tank in an orchard. We didn't see any movement. Near us, along the side of the road, there was a wooden storage shed under some trees. Loyce quietly climbed on the sloping roof to see the tank better and signaled with the white cloth. Suddenly shots whistled past us, presumably as a warning. Look out! Going back along a ditch, we saw a dead German soldier lying. We jumped out of the road, took cover in the deep ditch and hurried out of sight as quickly as we could. In the village we reported: 'The vanguard seen on walking distance!' Joseph and Loyce were highly tensed!"*

Loyce Ely's family owns a German 7.65 mm *Ortgies* pistol Ely took from the dead German soldier. Ely must have taken the weapon to arm himself, when he and André took cover in the ditch.

1: After their farewell Sidney was brought to Camp Mühlberg (Stalag IVB) in Brandenburg.
2: From a letter dated 8 October 1997 from André Evelein to René Hoebeke, the author of the book *Slagveld Sloedam*.
3: The LVT (Landing Vehicle Tracked) Water Buffalo (often called *Buffalo*) was an American made armed amphibious vehicle that could deliver up to 30 troops to the beach.
4: Now *Tychowo* in today's Poland.
5: The main Stalag Luft camps were: Stalag Luft I in Barth, Germany, where Jim, Fred and Dave were, Stalag Luft III at Sagan (now in present-day Poland: Żagań), known from the book and the movie *The Great Escape*), Stalag Luft IV at Gross-Tychow (where Elton, Ben and Frenchy were), Stalag Luft VI to Heydekrug (now in present-day Lithuania: Šilutė), Stalag Luft VII Bankau (now in present-day Poland: Bąków).
6: The POWs gave each guard a nickname like: *Trigger Happy*, *Crowbar Pete*, *Green Hornet* or *the Spider*. *Big Stoop's real name* was *Feldwebel* (Sergeant) Hans Schmidt. The prisoners of war named him after an eight foot Mongolian from the popular American newspaper comic strip, *Terry and the Pirates*. Schmidt was about fifty years old, a bear of a man. He hunched a bit, what made him look like a caveman. He was fat, had blonde hair and large ears. He was also known as *Ham Hands* or *Slap Ears* because his hands were abnormally large. He was feared because he used to hit the prisoners on the ears so hard that it broke their eardrums. Big Stoop was notorious for randomly molesting numerous prisoners and stealing their goods. There were rumors that he had lost a daughter who was killed during an Allied bombing raid. Schmitt was the right hand of security officer *Oberfeldwebel* Reinhard Fahnert. Together with Fahnert Big Stoop performed many nightly raids. They ransacked barracks and they stole everything they found of value.

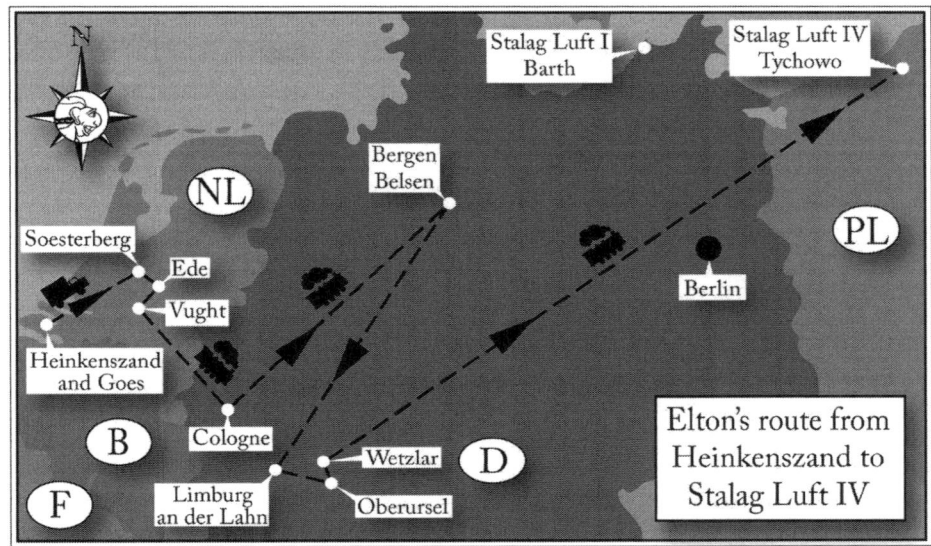

(138)

Dulag Luft Oberursel, as seen from a watchtower. (139 – www.b24.net)

Dulag Luft Wetzlar. (140 – www.b24.net)

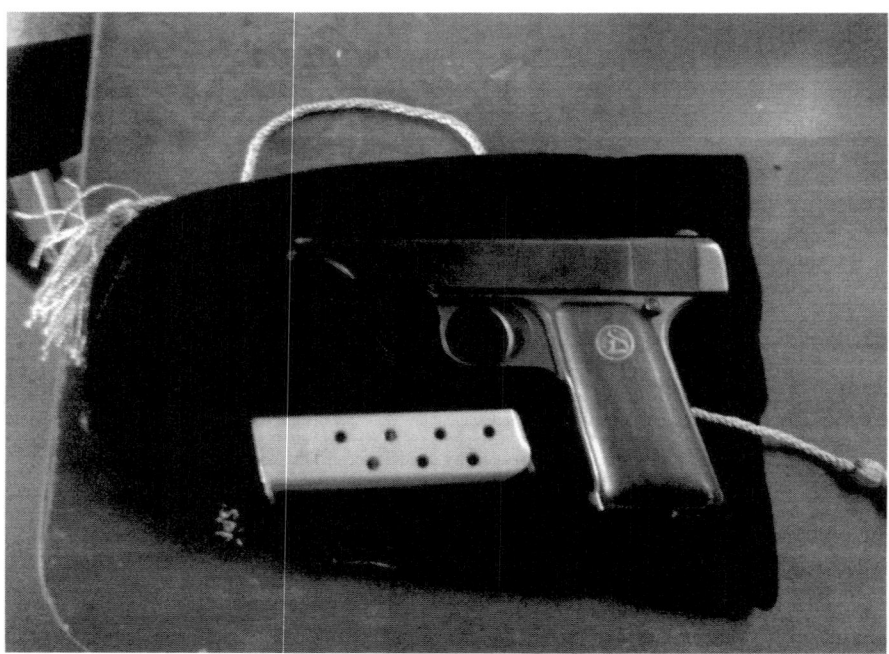

The *Ortgies* pistol Ely took from the dead soldier. (143)

Wij noemen hem Sjaak

Met groote dankbaarheid en blijdschap geven wij U kennis van de geboorte van een Zoon en Broertje

Jacob Adriaan,

te Heinkenszand tijdens een verpletterende nederlaag der dwingelanden en onder het kanongebulder van het bevrijdingsleger d.d. 27 October 1944.

N. J. van Biezen
S. van Biezen-Geensen
Rietje

K 937

The birth card of Sjaak van Biezen. (141)

Allied planes dropped photos like these of the Dutch Royal Family to encourage the people in the Netherlands.

L-R: Queen Wilhelmina, Crown Princess Juliana (142 and 142a)

Princess Juliana's family. (142b)

Chapter 15

Freedom and Captivity

The other survivors of the crash were also exposed to harsh conditions in the camps. The officers, pilot Jim Gerow, co-pilot Fred Vallarelli, and navigator Dave Grandon were transported to Stalag Luft I at Barth-Vogelsang, a small German village on the Baltic Sea, 23 km from the city of Stralsund.

Stalag Luft I opened in 1942 to intern British airmen, but American aviators were also held there. Initially, the camp was divided into two blocks: South and West, each with seven barracks. Blocks North 1, North 2, and North 3 were added in December 1944. North 1 was a former Hitler Youth camp where the three officers of the Feathered Injun were located. As a former youth camp, the prisoners benefited from a communal dining room, internal latrines, and running water. Prisoners in the other blocks had to make do with a much inferior kitchen and sanitation facilities. By September 1944, Stalag Luft I held almost six thousand men, a number rapidly increased by the failure of Operation Market Garden.

The Allied prisoners of war called themselves *kriegies*, an abbreviation of *Kriegsgefangener* (prisoners of war). Guards were called *Goons*[1] by the prisoners.

While he was a prisoner of war, Jim Gerow was automatically promoted to the rank of First Lieutenant (1/Lt) because he met the Army Air Force time in grade requirement. Jim wrote about Stalag Luft I: *"We were housed in a large wooden building, in one very large room, approximately 120 men, with double bunks, a couple of tables and a latrine at one end of the building. There was a fireplace in the center that heated the room that could also be used to cook turnips and toast black bread —the main foods provided. There was some kind of ersatz coffee and the men made "turnip jam" for the bread. Once a week, we would go to a central mess hall and be served small portions of potatoes and meat. Within the prison, there were people who were able to pick up news of the progress of the war by secret radio. They in turn got the word, usually weekly, to all of the barracks."*

Once a new aviator arrived in the camp, he was asked to hand over his electrically heated suit. The prisoners tore all copper wires out of the suit, and used them to make secret radios.

Until October 1944, the daily rations totaled 1200 to 1800 calories per man, far too little for the average man. When food shortages arose, rations were reduced to 800 calories. Malnutrition affected the entire body, as wounds healed slowly with increased risk of inflammation. The Red Cross was permitted to give the prisoners additional food parcels, but many parcels never made it to the POWs. Often hungry German guards plundered these packages. The small medical staff present did their best with an acute shortage of medical supplies and facilities.

The camp leadership of Stalag Luft I appointed American prisoner, Colonel Jean R. Beyerly, as Senior American Officer (SAO). An SAO was often called *Old Man* by the kriegies. In poor health due to stomach problems, Beyerly was respected as someone who really tried to help his men and alleviate their suffering.

The camp Stalag Luft IV at Gross Tychow, in modern day Poland opened in May 1944 when only 25% complete. Eventually, 6400 non-commissioned officers were interred there, brought by ship and train from Stalag Luft VI in Lithuania. On July 13th, VI was evacuated before the approaching Russian army. Stalag Luft IV was led by camp commander *Oberstleutnant* (Lieutenant Colonel) Aribert Otto Bombach (also known as *Snaggletooth* or *Big Wheel*). The Nazi's black hair was combed back and he had thin features. It was rumored he was a spy in France before the war. Before he commanded Stalag Luft IV, he was deputy commander of the evacuated Stalag Luft VI.

The commander of the run was *Hauptman* (Captain) Walther Pickardt (also known as *Ice Cream Man*, *Mad Captain* and *Butcher of Berlin*). He was a fanatical Nazi who wanted to separate the Jewish prisoners from the others. That never happened in Stalag Luft IV. Pickardt was guilty of physically abusing the men and stealing their belongings.

His thin sidekick was security officer *Feldwebel* (Sergeant) Reinhardt Fahnert (also known as *Iron Cross*). He was as abusive and aggressive as his boss and organized nightly looting raids in the prison barracks. Like Bombach, it was rumored Fahnert was also a spy before the war.

Hauptman Sommers was the Chief medical officer. Sommers didn't do anything to relief the suffering of the POWs. He only cared for German personnel.

Stalag Luft IV consisted of five blocks, the prison blocks *Lager* A, B, C, and D and a *Vorlager*, a block with billets for camp personnel, a small equipped hospital, and several store rooms. Barbed wire fences separated the blocks. One block was fully English, two were for American, and one held a mix of American, English and other nationalities. Because the men in Stalag IV were NCOs (non-commissioned officers), they were represented by a Senior NCO. The Senior NCO was Sgt. Richard M. Chapman, who lead Lager A, assisted by Sgt. Francis Paules from Lager D. Paules was elected by the prisoners, but not recognized by the camp commander. Other leaders were Sgt. Victor R. Clarke, who represented the British and the Commonwealth, Sgt. Willard C. Miller from Lager B and Sgt. Francis Troy from Lager C.

Germans in charge of the Lagers were: Lager A: Major Gruber who wore an eye patch (also known as *Medals*, *Hollywood* or *Snake Eyes*), Lager B: Hauptman Wolf, Lager C: Hauptman Weinert, and Lager D: Major Zallman.

The census on 15 July 1944 noted the camp held 7,089 Americans, 886 Britons, 147 Canadians, 22 New Zealanders, 8 South Africans, 1 Norwegian, 2 Frenchmen, 58 Poles and Czechs. The different blocks had no contact with each other. They could only communicate through improvised signal flags or sign language. Elton never had contact with Ben or Frenchy. Each camp consisted of 40 wooden barracks. Each barracks housed 20 to 25 men. Not every room had a heater, nor were there enough beds and many of the prisoners slept on the floor. Each camp had two open latrines and the barracks had a night latrine which several men could use at the same time. These were rarely emptied and cleaned. The prisoners didn't have many opportunities to wash themselves. There were no washbasins or showers and all of the water was carried by hand from the water pump. Due to poor sanitary conditions, fleas and lice infested everything. Among the common camp diseases were diphtheria, pneumonia, erysipelas, gastric enteritis, and typhus.

Elton: *"Our room is where we spent most of our time, although we could go outside and walk around. But we were never to get close to the warning wire, for the guards would fire at you. We did not have to work, but you could volunteer for work once in a while, if you wanted to. We would get morning ersatz coffee or tea, and sometimes a barley cereal. For supper we would have some potatoes or sugar beet soup, carrot soup or bean or pea soup. We would get a loaf of bread to split between seven men about every four to five days. A Red Cross parcel would be given to us about every 10 to 12 days to be split up between seven men. If it had not been for the Red Cross, we would have probably starved to death. The cigarettes from the Red Cross were used mainly to trade with the guards for bread or something to eat. Once in a while, they would be used to trade for something special that we needed, like parts to build a forbidden radio. We sometimes had soap, but later after the war we have learned that the soap in an extermination camp was made from human* fat. I've heard that in that same camp lampshades were made of tattooed human skin².*"*

The atmosphere in the camp was always anxious and tense because the guards in the watchtowers had a habit of indiscriminately firing at the prisoners for target practice.

Elton: *"Stalag Luft IV was also the headquarters of the Gestapo and the camp guards were the S.S. troops, so we had to answer to both of these creatures. They would call an inspection of the rooms during the night, and come in and tear up everything and look for anything that might be used for escape purposes, or as a threat to the guards. They would have a roll call in the mornings and that would take forever. They would keep us out in the cold for as long as an hour or so every roll call. This was just to count the prisoners and it seemed they couldn't come up with the right number. The guards were afraid of the SS and the Gestapo goons. One of the guards that everyone hated was the man who had beaten Russ when we just arrived in the camp: Big Stoop. That was a sadistic guy who liked to hurt prisoners. He was an SS man with a high squeaky voice, a product of Hitler's youth. He and the other guards held their room inspections preferably at night, where they stormed in and the whole room was in havoc, looking for anything that could indicate attempts to escape or a threat to the guards. In order to count the prisoners they called everyone out in the morning, which could last forever. Sometimes we were an hour long in the cold waiting. We played cards a lot and read, if we could get anything to read. We always had to send some men to peel the potatoes every day. Most of the potatoes were culls, of which most were designated for hog feed, but they would get some for the prisoners. In our room, there were bunks three high with a straw mat. One slept on the table and the rest of us had to sleep on the floor with a straw mat for all of us. We did get two more German blankets, which were very coarse and rough, but they helped with the cold. I slept on the floor, which was as good as the bunks, for the bunks did not have slats. The fleas were terrible, but you got used to them after a while. The bites didn't bother once you went to sleep, but when you woke up, one's legs and arms and eyelids were covered with bites and would become infected until you became immune to the infection or the bite. That was a daily chore, to try to get the fleas out of your clothing. It was an endless task and also useless, for the fleas were everywhere because the soil around the barracks was very sandy. So sandy, in fact, tunnels could not be dug because they would cave in. Many were tried, but none were successful at this camp. We had a light bulb in our room, but it could not be turned on until we had put on the shutters over the windows in the evening and the electricity was turned off. The guards strolled through the barracks at any time, so there was a warning sounded by anyone seeing them, by yelling, 'Goon Up!' Each compound held about 2500 prisoners with about 300 to each barracks. A kitchen building that also had room to house the few books that we could read was also used to put on plays. In the kitchen part were big vats that were used to cook what we had to eat. Also, in this building was a place for the doctor of our lager and the operating room. The medical staff did not have much to work with, but they did the best they could do with what they had. Mostly, they had just bandages, little else, except what the Germans would give them in emergency cases. An amputation was made here and a few operations. One was an appendectomy of a guy who had to walk to the rail station the following day."* This medical staff was led by Senior American Medical Officer, Captain Henry Wynsen, and Senior British medical Officer Captain Robert Pollack.

In South Beveland the Canadian troops advanced west. After the reverend and the waist gunner returned to the village, the two Americans stayed in the rectory one day and one night before the Canadians came through.

Andre: "*So now and then it's quite exciting, this shelling. The church tower seems to serve as a target; it's one of the junctions on the road to Goes. Fortunately, in retrospect, there is no excessive damage to the church, nor damage to the houses. Obviously on that Sunday morning, October 29th, there was no church service, although I think I remember that there were still a few people from Sinoutskerke* (a hamlet nearby) *that had walked through the meadows to see what was going on in our village. But in the afternoon, we think about two o'clock, suddenly everyone runs out. There is a Canadian tank rolling into the village center! Afterwards you cannot really put into words what you've experienced together. Among the first ones to come out of the rectory are of course our two pilots. They make themselves known immediately to the tank crew and ask about the possibility of a quick escape behind the line. In our silly enthusiasm schoolmaster Deurloo and I consider to climb the church tower to wave our Dutch red, white and blue flag over the area. By wise men, we were convinced to not do so. Imagine: if every village which the Canadians had come through had a flag flown from the tower, the Germans, who undoubtedly had nested in and around Goes, would find an easy trail to the Canadians. And then what? 'Yes, now what?' We ask ourselves, when in the evening the Canadian tank returns back to its base. The Americans could not go with them. What if somebody would betray us who saw the two? What if the Germans would come back again? Who it was, I can't remember afterward, but some of the Canadians pushed a big revolver (or something like that) into my hands*[3]*. 'You might need it in case of danger…' With friendly thanks I give the thing back. If you have no idea how you should operate it,* you better should not carry something like that in the house! Fortunately, after the 29th there was no more direct threat. On this day, everyone was surprised not to have noticed anything. The most dumbfounding was perhaps our immediate neighbor in the bowl of our village: P. Braam, the jovial blacksmith. From his cozy forge with a shoeing stock in front of the door he had a full view of the entrance to the rectory. We made sure he had not seen anything! He was quite surprised that he hasn't noticed what was going on."

On that same afternoon, around two o'clock, the Canadians approached Goes from the south and east. They were hardly opposed by the battle-weary Germans. A number of people from the OD, including Nico van Biezen, went to meet the Canadians. They successfully disabled the explosives the German placed under various bridges and guided the Canadian tanks to Goes. The Canadians, together with the OD-men, rode their tanks to the main market square accompanied by loud cheers. The harvest month was over, so the soldiers were offered all kinds of fruit. They had to refuse because they had already accepted so much fruit from surrounding villages. The German soldiers still present in Goes were disarmed and the tricolor flag was raised again. A few skirmishes occurred resulting in several civilian fatalities. It was not long before all local German resistance was broken. The revelry was again disrupted by shells, fired at Goes by a German battery in Heinkenszand, resulting in more fatalities. All OD members wore an orange band around their arms identifying them to both the military and civilians as auxiliary forces of the Allies. It was their job to keep order, to prevent NSB and other accused persons from being lynched, and to monitor non-military property and the internment camps for traitors.

While the OD gathered all remaining NSB members in Goes and brought them to the Beursgebouw (Event Center), a bridge in the neighboring 's-Heer Arendskerke was destroyed.

Twenty-four-year-old Marien Mol from Nisse said: *"There came a girl to us on a bicycle because her brother was wounded by a grenade. I got on the bike to get to a doctor in 's-Heer Arendskerke. When I was near the Grote Dijk the Germans were there to lay mines on the road. So I maneuvered between them with my bike. I rode past Westhof (the tree nursery of the van 't Westeinde family) to 's-Heer Arendskerke. When I was in 's-Heer Arendskerke the first thing I saw was a policeman with a bunch of captured Germans. When I was at the doctor's home, I saw a large Canadian officer washing his feet. 's-Heer Arendskerke was liberated on the 29th. That evening there was still some shooting in the distance and people advised me to not go back. But you know how it is: at home they did not know where I was. I wanted to prevent that I was missing, so I went home trough Baarsdorp, and not on the Grote Dijk with all those Germans with their mines. When I arrived in Nisse, the first Canadians arrived. There were many casualties in the village. Overnight we cleaned up the debris into piles of rubble. Near us, there was someone who crawled under a table and was killed. I believe he bled to death. From the Zwaakweg* (street) *came the first motorized Canadians forces. We waved our hands in the air, for they kept their guns pointed at us, for it was in the middle of the night. You were happy when that thing was pointed in another direction. Then they stopped and started handing us cigarettes. That was our acquaintance."*

There were battles in and around various villages the rest of the night. Heinkenszand was shelled by the Canadians, who fired from both 's-Heer Abtskerke and 's Gravenpolder. While the shells flew over their house, the family of Piet van den Dries, together with the sexton's family, took refuge in the basement. Little Peter slept through everything. He was startled only when the cellar door was blown inside. On Canadian maps, the school was regarded as a German barracks and endured three hits, leaving big holes in the roof. After an anxious night, everyone was unharmed.

In the morning on Monday October 30th, there was a sudden pounding on the door. *"The Canadians have arrived!"* Peter remembers that he was awakened to welcome the Liberators. The Canadian soldiers were marching in two columns toward the center of Goes. They gave Peter something, a piece of paper with a brown strip in it. The boy had never seen chocolate; he thought it was a bar of soap. After his father convinced him it was edible, Peter dared to take a bite. Peter munching on his delicious chocolate, watched the Royal Hamilton Light Infantry (Wentworth Regiment)[4] of the 2nd Canadian Infantry Division, commanded by Lieutenant-Colonel William Denis Whitaker[5].

There was considerable damage in Heinkenszand. That night, eight people died when a shell destroyed a shelter. Despite this, there were celebrations throughout the town. A merry masquerade paraded in the Van Cittersstraat. Canadian soldiers were dressed in the costumes of Zeeland farmers, while citizens, including Piet van den Dries, wore Canadian uniforms.

Members of the Group Griep gathered and wore their orange armband, which made it clear they were OD-men. In Heinkenszand, the OD began arresting collaborators and transferred them to the fort at Ellewoutsdijk. Anyone who was suspected of treason had their identity cards taken and many of them were put to work removing the remaining Rommel Asparagus or cleaning up debris from the battle. Some were interned and some were put under house arrest.

Koos and Leny van Iwaarden: *"When Heinkenszand was liberated and we heard the cheers, we had still about 200 Germans on our farm. And if the Canadians had advanced to our farm, it would have become a war of its own here. Luckily the Canadians stayed in the village to wait for another day. There was one tank that rode on the Plattedijk and shot in our direction. A shard went through my father's pant leg. A little window in the barn was smashed and there was a grenade in the chestnut tree. The Germans who were with us were very fanatical guys. Before they came, there were only older Germans, from which two wanted to surrender. Dad had hidden these two. The leader of the fanatics suspected something and he didn't let father out of his sight for a moment. He always stood next to him. Throughout the night, when they were shooting, he stood next to the cistern. We were in the basement. In the house was a room above the basement, there were always Germans, ten or twelve. On the night of liberation there were only wounded Germans in that room. Those were from Baarland, where there was some fierce fighting. Of that unit, there were only 29 left, and my father hid two of them. I have briefly seen the wounded that were very drunk because they got schnapps to relieve the pain. Father said to the commander: 'Let them stay here, I will deliver them to the Tommies', but they didn't allow him. The wounded were loaded on wooden carts and went towards the Sloedam. The liberation night was a beautiful clear night. The Germans left in groups. They had a canteen attached to their knapsack that we heard clattering. I still can picture this scene and hear the sound of the departing Germans. In the morning all the Germans were gone, and then came the Canadian storm troopers. Dad brought the two Germans who were in hiding to the Canadians. Those two were quite badly beaten by the Canadians. But okay, now we were also liberated. Many large vehicles arrived at our farm and one was laying electric cables. Everything was wet and the whole yard was muddy. The basement room where the wounded Germans used to be located was now a Canadian headquarters with telephones and cable etc. Behind the Boerendijk, 24 cannons were placed to fire shells at the Sloedam and Walcheren. In the basement room they gave the command: 'FIRE!' They shot a lot of grenades. Then a soldier told my mother to take a cork and cut it in half. She had to open the windows slightly and put the corks pieces in between, so the windows would not shatter. I remember: when you stood on the dike and they started shooting, your clothes would flutter on your body by the air movement. Our father for a moment was tempted to ask if he could shoot only once. But then he changed his mind because he did not know who or what that he would hit. I can remember those iron cases with all the grenades inside.*

There was thick felt inside that we could have. We sewed it together to make a kind of slipper. The copper shell cases were also preserved and someone in the village carved the liberation date on them. One night the Germans slept in our straw, the other night the Canadians."

Like in other villages, Heinkenszand residents sought revenge. So-called *Moffenmeiden* (Kraut girls) were put on farm carts in the Dorpsstraat and shaved bald, often by those who never helped anybody during the occupation. The eldest daughters of Rienbouw and Ploo were also under suspicion. Weren't they too friendly with the Germans soldiers at their farm? Wasn't their uncle a leader of the Landstand, one of the NSB affiliated agrarian organizations? Didn't their father hide two German soldiers? Kees Griep did not allow the girls to become victims of the mob. Many townspeople were unhappy with his intervention. Koos: *"Because all those Germans in our farm, in the village my father was sometimes called pro-German also because we were quite isolated. But when they heard that we had hidden an American pilot they came around."*

On Tuesday morning, the day after liberation, Joe Sulkowski and Piet van den Dries visited the Helenahoeve. Joe wanted to visit his hiding place and thank the family for caring for him. He also wanted to retrieve his bomber jacket that Rienbouw had saved for him.

That afternoon, Joe and Ely walked two miles to 's-Gravenpolder with two armed resistance men from 's-Heer Abtskerke, farmer and trader, Bastiaan Markusse, and police officer, Boidin. They transported five German prisoners to the Canadians. Once there, the prisoners were interned in the fortress at Ellewoutsdijk. A Canadian Major was very impressed with Joe's warm bomber jacket. Because it was a cold autumn, Joe offered it to him. In exchange the Major gave Joe a German Waffen-SS winter coat[6]. Joe and Ely went to Antwerp in Belgium with the Canadians, where they reported to the U.S. commander. He sent them to Brussels, where the mayor arranged a place for them to sleep. On November 2nd, they returned to England in a B-17.

While waiting for a long debriefing with the Allied military intelligence in England, Joe met another American aviator. The aviator asked if the resistance gave him false identity papers. Joe confirmed and the man advised him not to mention it during the interview. The identification card would be confiscated and Joe would never see his souvenir again. During his interrogation, the intelligence officers were particularly interested in the Resistance and how they operated in German-occupied territory. Joe told them everything he knew, but was silent on the passport. His son, John, still possesses this forged document.

Back at Wendling Air Base, Joe discovered all his belongings were gone. The only thing left untouched was his rusty bike, which he rode on the base. It was still chained where he left it before his last mission. During their stay at Wendling, Joe and Ely gave survival classes, sharing their experiences with other crews about survival in an occupied country after a crash. On November 8th, they received their back pay. With money in their pockets, they visited London's Hobson and Son and each bought two black and silver emblems. The first was called the *Winged Boot*. The RAF introduced this emblem for British soldiers who escaped the enemy and came home on their own. The second was the *Caterpillar*, a caterpillar-shaped emblem representing the *Caterpillar Club*, for soldiers whose lives were saved by a parachute jump. Although these were not official emblems, they were popular with American soldiers. They usually wore them under the left lapel of their jacket, but a photo of Joe shows that he wore his Winged Boot on his left breast pocket.

In December that year Joe and Ely were allowed to return home for R&R (Rest and Recuperation). They were provided with an Honorable Discharge Emblem, which they wore above the right breast pocket of their uniforms. It displayed an eagle within a circle. The emblem was called *Ruptured Duck* by the troops because the eagle looked more like a duck. The emblem was to show the Military Police they were honorably discharged, currently on leave, and not on active duty. Due to clothing shortages, they also had the right to wear this emblem on their uniform thirty days after dismissal.

Ted Sulkowski, Joe's younger brother, wrote: *"Joe was at an airbase in England, Vince was in the South Pacific, Cec was on her way to the South Pacific, and Walt was nearing the end of Navigator training. I was 13 at the time and Tom was 9, the remaining family at home. Nearly every family in Everson had one or more family members in war zones. It was an extremely stressful period. Families were notified of 'events' by very terse War Department telegrams: 'We regret to inform you that so and so was killed in action, was missing in action, or was wounded in action…' no other information. We only knew that Joe was missing in action. Within a week, we were contacted by Preston Grandon, the father of David, who was the Navigator in Joe's crew. Preston Grandon was the publisher of several newspapers around La Salle, Illinois. Through professional contacts and coordination with crew families, he kept everyone informed of all available information. I remember this well because I was the family correspondent. The six crewmembers that were captured were eventually identified, but the remaining crewmembers were 'Status Unknown'. We knew nothing more about Joe until a few weeks after he was liberated on October 29'. What is not generally known in the family is the immense toll that this period exacted from our mother. Joe was her Favorite Son. Not because he was the first son, but because he was extremely caring and considerate of his mother. During this period our mother simply ceased to function in all of her usual capacities as wife and mother. Fortunately, this was reversed when Joe finally came home. Both mother and first son did well and another son made a quantum leap in maturity."*

In U.S. newspapers, people read articles about the fate of Jim Gerow's crew. These papers relied on news circulated by Preston Grandon, father of the Navigator Dave Grandon, resulting in errors which persist in books and on websites to this day. For example, the Pursuit of Happiness was named as the aircraft that crashed, not the Feathered Injun. It was even suggested the Feathered Injun was later renamed the Pursuit of Happiness. This rumor was probably based on crewmembers' letters to their families about the Pursuit of Happiness, an aircraft they flew only four times. This aircraft was damaged on a mission prior to the crash of the Feathered Injun. The Pursuit of Happiness was later repaired and flew a few more missions.

Not long after the liberation, Lou Mes was reinstated as Mayor of Heinkenszand. Living conditions were still poor. Instead of German soldiers, Canadians were now living in Piet van den Dries' school. The Canadian Commander, Lieutenant-Colonel Whitaker, claimed Piet's office. To thank Piet for the accommodations and his help as an interpreter for the OD and the Canadians, Whitaker gave him an ordnance map of South Beveland, highlighting all German positions. After all, the information on similar maps were collected by OD-men like Piet and sent via secret channels to the Allied forces.

The Canadian liberators were not always friendly. Katrien, Piet's wife, didn't mind the Canadians using her house as a command center, but when they interrogated and brutally tortured German soldiers, she stormed into Whitaker's office to protest. The Canadian soldiers also stole from local residents and from dead Germans. A Canadian soldier showed Piet a handful of German wedding rings. Piet didn't want to know how he acquired them. Brothers Pier and Ko caught a Canadian soldier stealing bottles of liquor from their barn at Westhof. The two blocked the door, captured the soldier, and handed him over to a Canadian officer. The soldier was punished. Their car, hidden from the Germans for years, was found and confiscated within a day by the Canadians. Later on the Canadians returned the car. According to the following list by Ko van 't Westeinde, they didn't return everything:

14 November '44. **Stolen by the German Wehrmacht:**
*1 horse (recovered with a receipt), Harness for 3 horses,
1 car tire, 4 bikes (2 men and 2 ladies bikes)*

Stolen by the Allies:
*1 trailer for car, 1 car jack (oil pressure jack), 2 pairs of rubber boots,
1 pair of work boots, 3 trimmers, 1 wrench key.*

Piet showed the Canadians the graves of Gene and Ed and the place where the Feathered Injun crashed.

In spite of the conquest of South Beveland, the battle for the Scheldt was not over. Allies controlled the mouth of the river, but they needed to beat the Germans in Walcheren. The German 70th Infantry Division withdrew across the Sloedam, the only connection between South Beveland and flooded Walcheren. They were followed by the Allies who were only a mile from the Sloedam by late afternoon. The next day, the 4th Brigade captured all the German positions in South Beveland and the last Germans were expelled.

The final phase of the Battle of the Scheldt, *Operation Infatuate,* began. On Thursday November 1st, heavy artillery bombardment of Flushing began when two landing units from Breskens tried to take the city. At the De Schelde shipyard, the Germans attempted to destroy the ship, Willem Ruys but were thwarted. The battle for Flushing lasted until November 3rd.

At the same time, more Allied units landed on the beaches of Westkapelle, Domburg, and Zoutelande. At the beginning of the war, the Allies suffered a staggering eighty percent loss of men and equipment here.

The Allies managed to take Westkapelle and Domburg. Zoutelande followed a day later.

The Canadians, Scots, and English advanced on Walcheren from the east, but they had to capture the Sloedam first. Initially, the Allies were unable to conquer it and suffered heavy losses. It was not until Friday, November 3rd, that they managed to take the dam. The road to Walcheren was open. The 70th Infantry Division was stuck between two enemy forces and could no longer move. A message from the Resistance arrived. *Generalleutnant* (Lieutenant General) Wilhelm Daser, the German commander of the 70th Infantry Division at Walcheren, headquartered at the Dam in Middelburg, was willing to surrender.

On Sunday, November 5th, a service was held in the Reformed Church of 's-Heer Abtskerke. Pastor André Evelein conducted this thanksgiving service in honor of the liberation of South Beveland, Psalm 126 and Isaiah 35 were read.

The Scheldt was stripped of land mines and it was again possible to use it as a troop supply port. The Allies assumed they would soon conquer the weakened German army. The Germans were threatened from the east by the Russians, from the south by the Allies who conquered Italy, and from the west by the Allies on the banks of the Rhine. Moreover, Hitler's war industry was destroyed by Allied bombing. But Hitler, encouraged by the German victories during Operation Market Garden, gave orders to initiate *Wacht am Rhein* (Watch on the Rhine). He planned to defeat battle-weary American troops in the Ardennes, then recapture the important port of Antwerp, advance on Brussels and cut off Allied supply routes. In secret, he ordered 25 German divisions, the most hardened warriors from the Eastern Front, to the Ardennes. There were four American divisions stationed there, tired, weak and not alert, supplemented with inexperienced troops. Through dense forest they saw nothing of the massive troop movements in an area they regarded as safe and quiet.

In England, people at the Government Code and Cipher School[8] at Bletchley Park were alarmed by large troop movements in Germany. They knew that something big was about to happen, but allied Commanders ignored their warnings.

Morton Baker, the original radio operator of Gerow's crew, recovered from his abdominal pain. On Sunday, November 5th, he flew his first mission since the air battle of September 11th. He was assigned to the crew of 1Lt R.J. Benson. They were ordered to bomb a fortress in the city of Metz, but because of heavy clouds, they chose a rail yard in Karlsruhe as a secondary target. They dropped their bombs, but could not assess the damage because of the low clouds.

Lieutenant General Wilhelm Daser, commander of the 70th Infantry Division, was only willing to surrender to an Allied senior officer of a tank unit, but there was no tank unit available in Walcheren. The Allies decided to send the eleven existing Buffaloes to Middelburg. Major Johnston was the only high ranking officer present. He was the commander of the 7/9 Battalion Royal Scots. Johnston was temporarily promoted to Colonel so he could accept the general's surrender. Daser's demand was the result of pressure from the German high command. If a German officer surrendered to an inferior unit, it was viewed as treason and endangered his family.

Once the German soldiers and their collaborators were imprisoned, Zeelanders who did not collaborate with the Germans received a certificate of good conduct. But they could not leave or enter the province without special permission from the Allied powers. The OD was disbanded not long after the liberation of Zeeland. The members, together with the members of the fighting gangs and the Council of Resistance, became the *Nederlandse Binnenlandse Strijdkrachten* (Dutch Interior Military Forces). The BS[9] was part of the Dutch Royal Army and under the command of Commander in Chief, Prince Bernhard.

On November 27th, Piet van den Dries, as a member of the OD of South Beveland, registered with the BS. He was given a machine gun and bullets, but he had no time to monitor strategic buildings. Three Allied shells had damaged the school roof and all the windows were shattered, including those of Piet's house. Piet repaired the holes so that, once the Canadians left, the students could return to school. However, it was not until January 1945 that Piet could welcome the children back again.

It was December and the American troops in the snow-covered Ardennes still had not noticed the massive enemy reinforcements in their area. On December 16th, all hell broke loose. At half past six in the morning, the massive German tank army attacked. The Battle of the Bulge[10] began. The Americans of the 28th Infantry Division were completely surprised. To make matters worse, they could not expect any assistance from the 8th Air Force or the RAF because of the dense clouds covering the Ardennes. Yet the Americans, despite heavy losses, were better at defending themselves than the Germans expected. The battle took place under extremely harsh conditions, dense forests covered with a thick layer of snow.

A large number of American soldiers were taken prisoner during this offensive. Hitler instructed his men to be as cruel as they were on the Eastern Front, where it was not unusual to completely ignore the law of war, and to execute prisoners. On September 17th, in Malmedy, Belgium, 120 unarmed American prisoners of war were forced to walk into a field, where they were mowed down with machine guns. Only a handful of soldiers survived the hail of bullets. Most were killed with a shot to the head. The bodies of the Malmedy Massacre were covered with snow and were not discovered until January 14th.

The Americans gained reinforcements and engaged in bloody battles for places like St.Vith and Bastogne. Gradually, they got the upper hand. On December 23rd, the weather cleared and U.S. ground troops received air support from fighter-bombers. It was not until December 28th that Hitler realized his plan had failed and his troops could be of better use on the Eastern Front. Stalin's troops marched with alarming speed towards the west, and the Germans decided to evacuate camps around the harbor of Königsberg[11] in Prussia. There were many evacuations in the following months.

1: This name was inspired by Alice the Goon, a character from the popular Popeye comic strips. Initially it was prohibited to call the guards this name, but when they were told it would mean *German Officer or Non-Com* they accepted it.
2: This was a persistent rumor during and after the war. However, no evidence was found that soap from the fat of human corpses was industrially produced by the Germans, but there is evidence that the Nazis where experimenting with it and produced it on a small scale. In Buchenwald concentration camp Ilse Koch, the wife of the camp commander, had indeed made lampshades from the skin of prisoners. She also collected the tattooed skins of prisoners and had them framed.
3: Joe and Ely were also armed: Joe with his Colt 45 service pistol, Ely with the German Ortgies pistol.
4: This unit came from Hamilton, Ontario and was nicknamed *the Rileys*.
5: William Denis Whitaker was from Toronto. Before the war he was a quarterback on the football team the Hamilton Tigers. Afterwards, he joined the Royal Hamilton Light Infantry in 1937. As a token of appreciation for his courageous actions during the Battle of Dieppe in 1942, he was promoted to Captain. After the war, he was promoted to Brigadier General and he later wrote several books about World War II.
6: Because the inside of this green camouflage jacket was white, it could also be worn inside out as a camouflage jacket in the snow. Joe's family still owns his jacket.
7: According to a telegram from the U.S. Army on November 13th Ely's mother received the liberating message that their son had safely returned to his unit.
8: The British intelligence that had cracked the German coded radio messages.
9: Initially, the Dutch Interior Forces abbreviation was NBS, but because the comparison with the NSB was obvious, this was changed to BS.
10: Also known as the Ardennes Counteroffensive.
11: Now the city of Kaliningrad, the capital of the eponymous province, a Russian enclave between Poland and Lithuania.

A barracks at Stalag Luft IV. (144 - www.b24.net)

A sports field at Stalag Luft IV. (145 – www.b24.net)

This was photographed by André Evelein on the day of liberation. Loyce and Joe in civilian clothes. In the background is a Canadian armored vehicle. (146)

Loyce and Joe with residents of 's-Heer Abtskerke and some Canadian soldiers. (147)

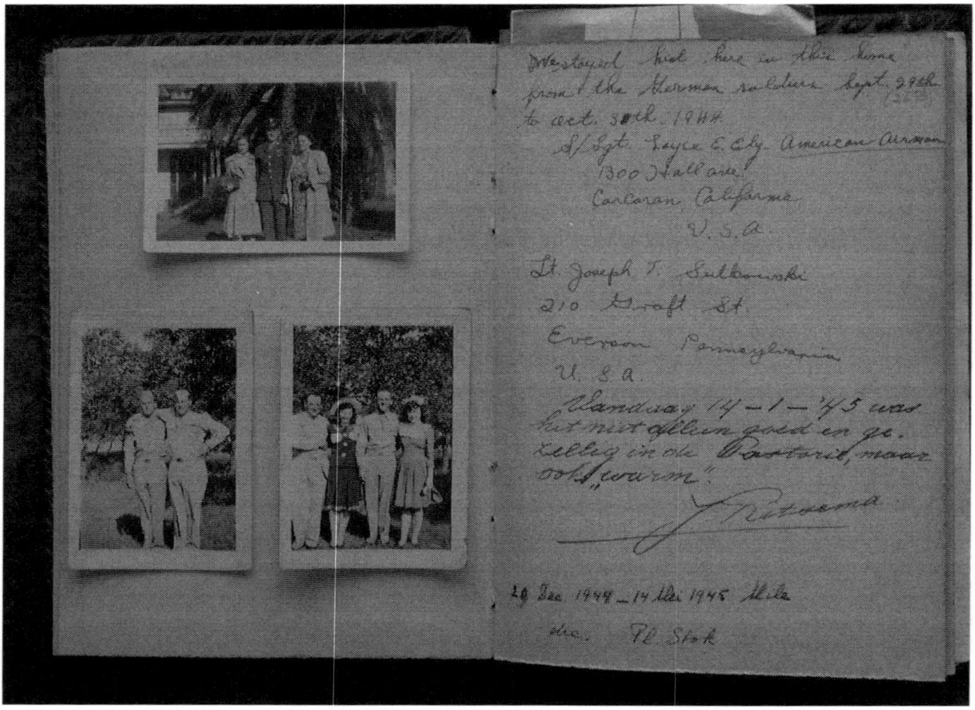

The guestbook of the family Evelein in which Joe and Loyce wrote a message. On the other page are some pictures of Loyce and his brother Gene. (148)

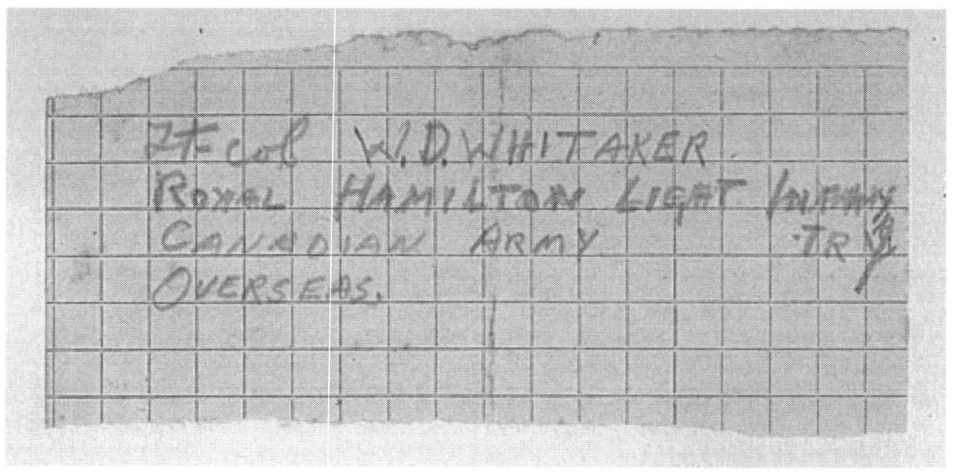

A piece of paper on which Lieutenant-Colonel Whitaker wrote his name and unit for Kees Griep. (149)

A costume party was held just after the liberation of Heinkenszand. Piet van den Dries is on the far right in a Canadian uniform. The boy with his hand in his pocket is his son Peter, and the girl with the white bow is his daughter, Paula. The two men in black farmer's costumes are Canadian soldiers. (150)

The liberators of Heinkenszand: the Royal Hamiliton Light Infantry. (151)

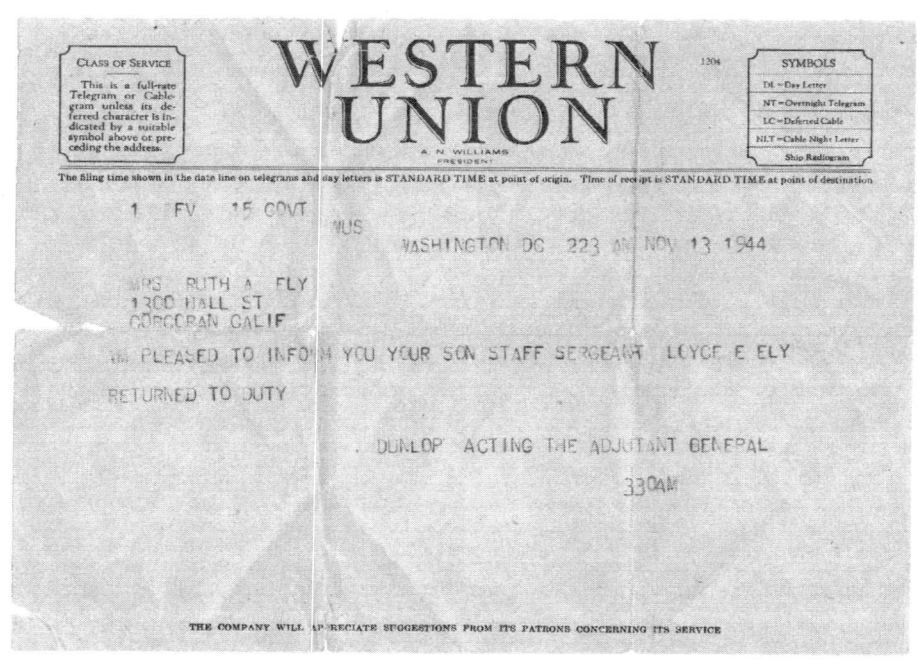

A telegram of November 13, 1944 from the U.S. Army to Ruth Ely about the safe return of her son Loyce Ely. (152)

SGT. HEBERT NOW IS WAR PRISONER

S/Sgt. Normand B. Hebert, 26, husband of Mrs. Juanita J. Hebert, 828 Jackson, was taken a prisoner by the Germans on Sept. 18 and now is interned in that country. He has been in the Army for nine years and has been overseas since June 29, 1944. He was a tail gunner on a B-24 Liberator. He is the son of Mr. and Mrs. J. Arthur Hebert who reside in Woonsocket, R. I. Sgt. Hebert's wife received a letter from him recently dated Oct. 19 from the prison camp.

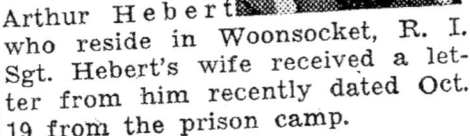

A newspaper article about the captivity of Normand Hebert. (153)

'Correspondence Pool' Writes Parents Of Missing Crewman

A Woonsocket man, reported missing in action in Europe, was tail gunner on a Liberator bomber shot down in the heroic attempt to relieve the British paratroops trapped at Arnhem, according to details learned by his parents here today.

The member of the Liberator crew is Staff Sgt. Norman B. Hebert, son of Mr. and Mrs. J. Arthur Hebert, 499 Willow street, who was officially reported missing in action Sept. 18.

Mr. and Mrs. Hebert have received their information through a unique community of interest formed by parents or next of kin of all members of the lost bomber's crew, pooling their information by correspondence.

Preston F. Grandon, publisher of the Post-Tribune, La Salle, Ill., whose son, Lieut. David P. Grandon, was navigator of the ship, was the originator of the correspondence pool. He obtained the names and addresses of all parents or next of kin and sent a list to each of them, with the suggestion that information be exchanged.

In a letter received from Mr. Grandon, Mr. and Mrs. Hebert learned that the plane, which was carrying supplies to the troops at Arnhem, was last seen going down with one propeller feathered and an engine leaking oil badly.

He said the area in which the Liberator was operating was limited in size which brought the planes in close touch with guns of the enemy.

The letter contains detailed information about the possibility of rescue of the fliers through the underground and also the assurance that if captured by the Germans they will receive good treatment, which is usually accorded to fliers.

Sergeant Hebert was on his 13th mission when his plane was shot down. He has two brothers in the service, Lieut. Edgar, aviation instructor at Selman field, Monroe, La., and Seaman 1/c Paul who is at sea. His wife, Juanita, lives in Pueblo, Colo., where they were married while he was in training.

A newspaper article about Norman and the correspondence pool of Preston Grandon. (154)

Sgt. Eugene Kieras Killed in Action

Met Death when Bomber Crashed In Holland, Sept. 18

T/Sgt. Eugene J. Kieras, son of Mr. and Mrs. John Kieras, 1353 Porter ave., La Salle, who served as an engineer-gunner on a Liberator bomber based in England, has been reported killed in action on Sept. 18, the date he had been reported as missing.

The message was received Monday afternoon in a telegram from the war department culminating many months of anxious waiting regarding his status. He was a member of the same crew with which Lt. David Preston Grandon, son of Preston F. Grandon, La Salle, was serving.

The bomber, on which the flier served, was downed Sept. 18 over Holland while on its 13th mission. Both fliers were listed at that time as being missing in action, but later Lt. Grandon was reported as a prisoner, and only recently liberated. The plane was engaged in dropping supplies to the Allies airborne army in Holland.

When the bomber was struck, the crew was forced to bail out but flak from German anti-aircraft guns tore the rip cord of the La Salle gunner's parachute resulting in his death as he plummeted to the ground.

Other members of the crew who witnessed the action reported that Sgt. Kieras was killed instantly. Since that time it has been disclosed that the body of the flier was interred in Holland near the site of the crash.

A monument is to be erected in memory of Sgt. Kieras near his grave, a tribute arranged for by the residents of the Holland community. crew members have since related.

Four Brothers in Service

Sgt. Kieras, who was one of four brothers in service, left April 9, 1943, to enter the air corps. In June, 1943, he was promoted to private first class at Keesler Field, Miss., where he was in training with a technical school squadron. Oct. 31, 1943, he was graduated from the B-24 Liberator bombardment school...

(Turn to Number 2, Page 1)

NUMBER TWO
(Continued from Page 1)

mechanics school at Keesler Field after which he attended the army air force flexible gunnery school at Tyndall Field, Panama City, Fla.

At the completion of this course Jan. 18, he was awarded his "wings" and promoted to the rank of corporal. After a furlough he reported at Pueblo, Colo., where the bomber crew was formed.

The crew was later moved from Pueblo to Topeka, Kan. While there he was given a three-day pass to visit his family before reporting to an eastern port of embarkation.

Late in June, 1944, Sgt. Kieras wrote of his arrival in England and since then had been participating in bombing missions over Germany, on a Liberator, "The Pursuit of Happiness."

While overseas he had two promotions, the first being to staff sergeant and the second to his present rank, that of technical sergeant.

On May 21, 1945, parents of the flier received an Air medal with Oak Leaf cluster in a ceremony held in the La Salle American Legion headquarters, with members of the Romulus Meehan post participating.

The young flier was educated in La Salle schools.

Surviving are his parents, four brothers, M/Sgt. Edward J., stationed at Brookfield, Tex., Stanley, S2/c, Albany, Calif., Ernest, TM3/c, New York, and Raymond, La Salle, and his paternal grandmother, who also resides in La Salle.

Memorial Mass

A memorial mass will be held at 9 a.m. Tuesday, June 26, at St. Hyacinth's Catholic church, La Salle. During the service the 17th gold star will be placed on the church service flag signifying that 17 young men of the parish have sacrificed their lives for their country.

The firing squad of the Romulus Meehan American Legion post is to take part in the service and members of the post and its auxiliary are to attend the mass.

Lt. David Grandon Is Prisoner of War

Reports Show Two Of Crew Got Back To Base in England

Missing in action since Sept. 18, 2nd Lt. David Preston Grandon, 21, son of Mr. and Mrs. Preston F. Grandon, 1108 N. Marquette st., La Salle, has been reported a prisoner of war in Germany. (A picture of the crew of Lt. Grandon's plane, "The Pursuit of Happiness," is shown in today's Stars and Stripes column.)

A telegram was received from the war department Thursday morning by his parents. However, no word has been received concerning T/Sgt. Eugene J. Kieras, one of the four service sons of Mr. and Mrs. John Kieras, 1353 Porter ave., La Salle, a member of the same bomber crew who had also been previously reported missing in action.

In an Associated Press report carried Oct. 25 it was explained that the two airmen went down over Holland, Sept. 18, on the same bomber while on their 13th combat flight.

Lt. Grandon was serving as navigator aboard the Liberator while T/Sgt. Kieras was the top turret gunner. Supplies were being dropped to the Allied airborne army in Holland.

Ship Seen Going Down

According to the AP report the ship was last seen going down with one propeller feathered and an engine leaking oil badly. At that time the last word from the radio operator was that they would try to land.

Both Lt. Grandon and Sgt. Kieras wore the Air medal with one Oak Leaf cluster. Other members of the crew, of which there were nine, have not all been accounted for, although telegrams received this morning divulged the fact that the pilot and the nosegunner are also prisoners of war.

Two others are also known to be back at the base in England.

A short time after the Associated Press report there were conflicting releases in news broadcasts which were later reported to have been misinterpreted by listeners.

The reports suggested that the airmen "might" have walked back from...

Two newspaper articles from the Daily Mail Tribune dated 1944. It was the newspaper of editor Preston Grandon, Dave's father. It erroneous mentions the Pursuit of Happiness as the crashed bomber. (155, 156)

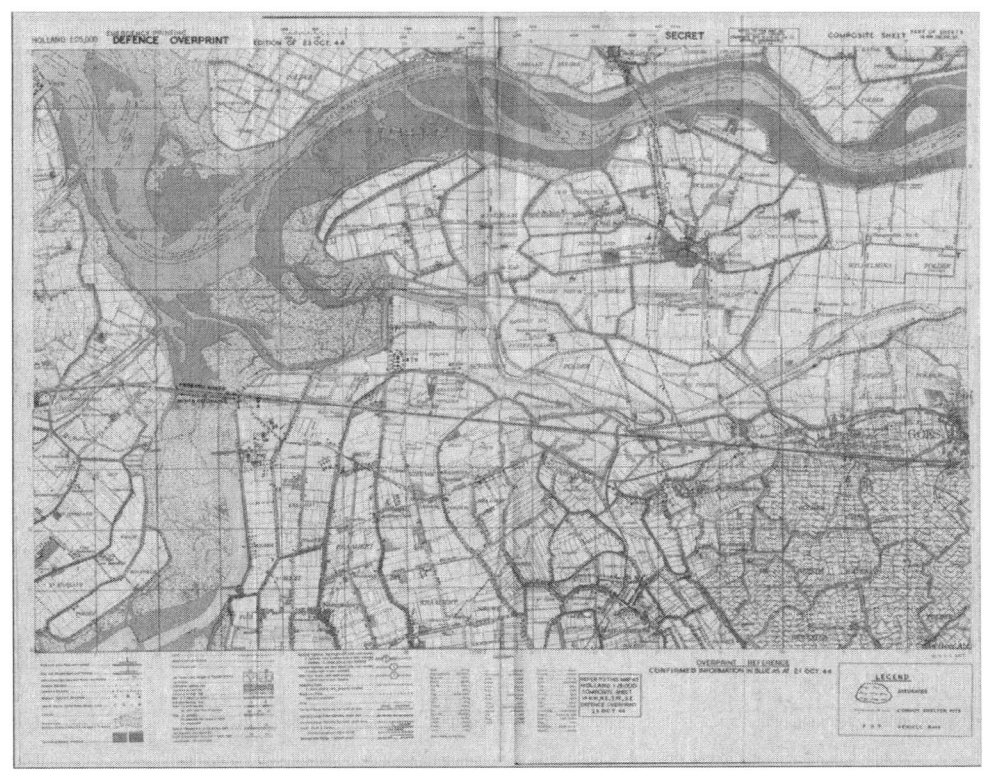

The topographical map that Piet received from Lieutenant-Colonel Whitaker. (157)

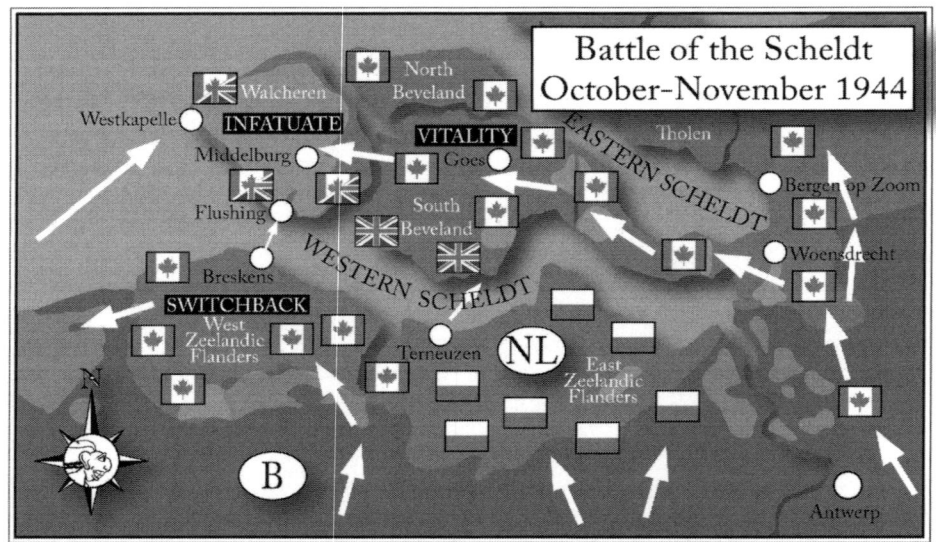

(158)

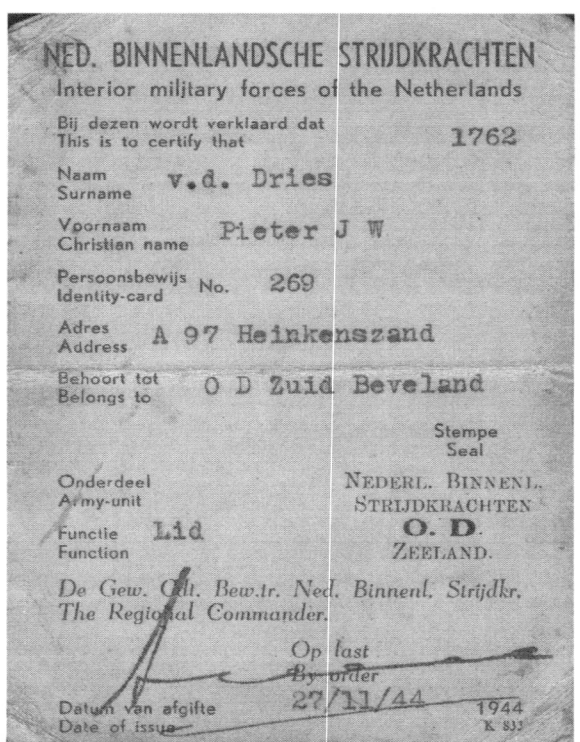

Piet's proof of membership of the OD, included in the BS. (159)

Chapter 16

The Russians are coming!

Although the Zeelandic lion[1] was released from the claws of the German eagle, citizens could not fully enjoy their freedom. Many Canadian soldiers were billeted with residents. They were more accommodating than their German predecessors, but the curfew remained and people still had to cover their windows overnight. Traveling was permitted only with the consent of the Canadian military command. Coastal areas and ports were not accessible to citizens. Many homes were uninhabitable due to bombing and flooding. Homeless families were sheltered in Nissen huts made of corrugated iron. Kees Bek's family was temporarily housed in a Nissen hut, because his house was given to Ko and Pier's sister, Kee, and her new husband.

Shortages continued in Zeeland. Soap and water were still rationed, causing lice infestation, scabies, and diphtheria. Despite hardships and shortages, the men of Group Griep spent a hopeful Christmas with family and friends. Spending the holidays in a free country made the hardship bearable. While the small Southern part of the Netherlands was liberated, the situation north of the rivers was increasingly grim. There, the infamous *Hongerwinter* (Hunger Winter) began. The German occupiers felt cornered by the Allies and took their frustration out on the local population.

The stark contrast between liberated and occupied Netherlands was similar to the situation in which the survivors of Gerow's team now lived. Joe and Loyce were liberated and spent the holidays at home while the remaining survivors of the crash endured hunger and fear. For them, the suffering continued. They endured harsh conditions in the prison camp, including skin diseases, dysentery, pests, oppression, homesickness and boredom. Day after day, they experienced hunger and depression. They woke up and went to bed with it. Then there was the winter cold, severely affecting starving men who had almost no fat left on their bodies.

The mail they received from family and loved ones helped alleviate their suffering. In order to send and receive mail, prisoners had to give their home address to German authorities. Although they were ordered not to reveal personal information, most men yielded, for it was their only link with home. If the railroads were in service and permitted the transportation of mail, the men received personal packages from home containing necessities like food, vitamins, and toiletries. Camp leaders carefully checked the packages to ensure they did not contain items that could be used to escape. Clothes were permitted, but only of a military nature, because civilian clothing could be used as a disguise. The kriegies were permitted to write home on specially printed sheets of paper, and both incoming and outgoing letters were heavily censored. The letters could reveal nothing about the harsh conditions in the camp. The Red Cross visited the camps sporadically and they were subtly deceived when presented with an alternative reality. People at home were led to believe their boys were in good hands and a prisoner of war camp was like a summer camp, where prisoners waited while the real heroes fought the war.

Despite the bitter cold and a thick layer of snow, the Christmas season brought some relief from hunger and oppression. On the day before Christmas in Stalag I, Jim, Fred and Dave enjoyed songs played by the camp orchestra, supplemented with pieces from Handel's *Messiah*. There was a midnight mass for the officers of Catholic faith and the next afternoon a Christmas service for the Protestants. Special Christmas[2] packages were distributed by the Red Cross and kriegies received larger portions of better food than usual. This sudden abundance was too much for many prisoners. Their stomachs, shrunk from chronic hunger, resulted in severe abdominal cramps.

Elton about Stalag IV: *"At Christmas that year, we were given an extra portion of food and a little more bread. A loaf of bread was cut in the days before Christmas to feed sometimes 21 men for about 4 or 5 days. Try dividing up a loaf equally between 21 men and get all slices equal. They also gave us more Red Cross parcels than ever before. We hoarded this for better days, but it was a treat to have that much food all at once. We were allowed to put on a play for Christmas and to sing Christmas songs on Christmas Eve. On Christmas night we were allowed to be outside and to walk the compound in the beautiful night with a full moon. After coming inside about nine o'clock, we had to go to bed under the orders of the guards. About three hours later, after the best day we had had as prisoners, the lights came on and guards came in yelling at us and made us get dressed. They then proceeded to tear up the room; throwing all our stuff in a pile with the food that had been saved on top of that, opening cans and dumping them out and just destroyed everything. They made us stand outside for roll call and, all in all, just raised hell with us. The following night, we had the same thing happen and the following day and night the same. We had been told that an officers' pass had been lost Christmas night and they thought that someone had found it. This pass allowed the officer to go from country to country. They told us then that unless this pass was found, things were going to get worse for us. With our food now gone and not able to get any sleep, one guy told them that he had found the pass, but had destroyed it. He was taken to solitary confinement and kept for about a week. When he returned, he was a mess from the beatings he had endured. We never found out if he had found the pass for sure, or had just told them that to stop the raids on our barracks."*

On January 12th, during the worst winter in years, Stalin's troops began a major offensive in Poland and East Prussia, advancing toward POW camps in present Poland, Stalag Luft VII Bankau (now in Polish Bąków), Stalag 44 in Lamsdorf (Lambinowice) and Stalag 20-B at Marienburg (Malbork). The camps were evacuated under severe winter conditions. The British prisoners ended up in Stalag Luft IV. A day later, they were forced to evacuate because of advancing Russian troops. This gave the prisoners some hope. That hope was also fueled by the news of the Allied victory. Two days earlier, the Allies ended the Battle of the Bulge. On January 27th, the Polish death camp, Auschwitz, was liberated. The kriegies of Stalag Luft III at Sagan were evacuated and began an exhausting winter march through Poland to Germany.

S/Sgt. Matthew A. Bartnowski, the radar operator who had joined Gerow's crew on their mission on September 11th, was killed in action when his bomber crashed in Germany on January 28th.

On January 31st, the Russians crossed the German border for the first time.

Elton: *"It was clear that the guards were nervous. They seemed to realize that they were heavily in the vice grip of the Russians. It showed in their eyes and you could tell by their behavior."*

The planes flying overhead displayed both the American stars and the British circles. Almost never did they see swastikas. This suggested the German air force was virtually eliminated. But how long would Elton's own liberation take? He felt hope, but also fear. What would the Germans do once the Russians closed in? Elton had witnessed the cruelty to prisoners of war in Dulag Luft in Oberursel, so he feared the worst.

The kriegies went from room to room to whisper the news they heard on the secret radio. News could not be passed every day, nor could it be at the same time or to the same person. When guards searched for the radio, the kriegies would let them find a fake one and the searches would stop for a while. The radio was moved every day and few men knew where it was.

The British always carpet bombed German cities, while the Americans used precision bombing on manufacturing facilities. It seemed the war would drag on for months. On Sunday, February 3rd, 1945, the Americans were persuaded to join the British and bomb the nerve center of Nazi Germany. The British assured them a massive attack on Berlin and other large cities would break German morale. They initiated a plan for August 1944 called *Operation Thunderclap*. The joint attacks that followed had a devastating effect. After unprecedented attacks on Berlin, they bombed Dresden, Chemnitz and Leipzig.

In the Ukrainian resort of Yalta, Churchill, Roosevelt and Stalin held a summit to further discuss war strategy. During the seven-day conference the contours of postwar Europe were visible, with Europe divided between the largely parliamentary democratic countries in the West and the communist countries in the East. They also discussed plans to establish the United Nations.

At the end of January, the sick and wounded NCOs of Stalag Luft IV were loaded on a train and transported under terrible circumstances, to Stalag Luft I in Barth. With his broken ankle, Frenchy may have been one of them, but his family reports that he stayed in the camp.

On Monday, February 5th, 1945, Lieutenant-Colonel Bombach told the 6000 prisoners of Stalag Luft IV they would be evacuated the next day. In the east, the Red Army was less than thirteen miles away. In the south, they already occupied the city of Breslau (*Wrocław*). It would only be a matter of time until Gross Tychow was enclosed by what the Germans would call, "*The Red Plague of Stalin*". The only way to escape was through a strip of land fifty miles wide, along the Baltic coast. Bombach did not tell the Allied prisoners they would not be liberated by the Russians, because Hitler and his deputy, Himmler, chose to deport them to Germany for use as hostages and human shields during the merciless bombing. The evacuation march would soon begin. The kriegies jokingly called it *The Shoe Leather Express*. Soon they would come up with other, grimmer names. The prisoners were concerned about the German plans, but made no plans to evade the march. There was simply no time to organize an uprising and Bombach told them the march would take only three days. Even if they did have time for rebellion, Big Stoop and his men would have beaten it out of them.

Elton: *"We tried to make some things out of the tops of our underwear to carry things in. Then early the next morning, they called us out of our barracks. We thought that maybe a few days would be all we would have to walk, but we could hear the gunfire off in the distance. We knew that this had to be the*

Russians because we were very close to the Polish border. Danzig, Poland was less than 100 miles from us. They marched us past the kitchen to receive a Red Cross parcel all by ourselves. As we went by the vats in the kitchen, we dropped in cascara pills (laxative) that had been given to us by the Red Cross, in the vats that had a lot of food in them cooking. We figured that must be for the guards. The night before, we left some bars of soap in the barracks that we had embedded with broken razor blades. We left quite a few bars of soap because we knew that the guards would take them when we left. When they went to use them, they would cut their hands and especially when they would try washing themselves with the bar. It was just a little remembrance from us."

It was freezing and snowing when the column began to move, but that did not matter. The prisoners were relieved to see the hated watchtowers and barbed wire behind them. Although they were not free, they finally found themselves outside the camp. Most had been there for years. This positive mood would soon change.

Elton: *"The Red Cross parcels were bulky and hard to carry, and as the day wore on, we tried opening them and putting part of them in our pockets. We were traveling at a fast pace and could hardly keep up while carrying the Red Cross packages. We could not handle it, for we were told not to lag behind or we would be shot. We started dumping part of the package, the bulky things, on the ground. The civilians were wild to pick these up and the faster we were forced to march; the more we had to get rid of. It was like cutting off ones leg, for we had not had that much food since becoming prisoners. But the guards were poking us with bayonets and slamming us with rifle butts and putting the dogs on us, so we had no other choice. They kept increasing the pace until we were at our limit, but they never let up. They kept us going all day until about 9 o'clock that night. From the signs on the road and in asking the guards, we traveled close to thirty miles that day. My legs hurt so badly and my feet were sore, not being used to that, and besides that, it had snowed all day and we were wet and miserable. All in all, it was a terrible day, thinking of all the stuff we had to throw away just made us sick. Finally, they marched us into a yard on a farm and showed us a barn that we would have to sleep in. They had broken the column of prisoners into small groups of about 200, so the barn was full, but at least we were able to lie down and rest. We slept as best we could."*

To survive the march, it was essential for every prisoner to team up with one or two friends, so they could protect, support, and encourage each other. They shared rations and blankets. These comrades swore to never abandon each other and to drag each other through the misery at all costs. Elton always walked with Russ (Russell) Martin from Rhode

Island, a man he knew well. It was very cold and the floor of the barn was freezing, so Elton put his two blankets on the ground, and they covered themselves with Russ' blankets. Their body heat helped keep them warm.

Elton: *"The next day, after some ersatz coffee, I traded a German a few cigarettes for a piece of bread. Then it was back on the road again. This day wasn't quite as bad as the first day. We had moved far enough away from the Russian line so we would not be able to be liberated by them."*

The route took them through the region Farther Pomerania (*Pomorze Zaodrzańskie*), east of the Oder River. The column was usually three or four man wide. The endless, gray parade curling its way west consisted of Americans, British, Canadians, Poles, Czechs, Australians, New Zealanders, and South Africans. They were driven like livestock through the cold and snow. The men trudged along frozen, slippery roads. At night, they slept in barns. They ate soup from powdered milk cans.

Elton: *"We certainly looked like tramps. I had the top of my winter underwear tied around my neck with the bottom tied so it would hold some of my stuff. We looked better than we would look later on. I tied the arms of the underwear around my neck and the bottom of it was tied shut with a shoestring so as to make a sack. The weather was rather cold and it was snowing off and on all day again. We were wet again and our shoes were wet. That night I took off my shoes and put them under my blankets next to my body so they might dry out some. This I did every night from then on."*

On the third day, Thursday, February 8th, the prisoners faced another long march. Fear of the Russians was visible in the eyes of the German guards as they increased their abuse of the kriegies. The prisoners had to cross the river Swine (Świna) near the city Swinemünde (Świnoujście) as quickly as possible before Russians took the only bridge. Swinemünde was a funnel-shaped estuary of the Oder River. Along the Baltic Sea, this estuary was formed by the islands of Usedom (*Uznam*) and Wollin (*Wolin*), separated by the Swine River. The men were force marched throughout the day and a large part of the night. Not all kriegies from Stalag Luft IV walked the same route. Some marched towards the city Stettin (*Szczecin*), south of the estuary. It is unknown which route Ben and Frenchy walked.

The prisoners of war were not the only ones who made the trek west. Elton: *"Throughout the march, we saw a steady flow of elderly citizens who had fled the war. All young people up to the age of sixty, after all, had to fight at the front. All possessions of this ragged gang were piled on wagons drawn by horses, but also piled on carts, in strollers and hastily assembled carts. Other elderly were carrying their belongings on their backs or whatever they could carry. These were clearly the poorer inhabitants of the region."*

All concentration camps in the path of the Russians were evacuated, an exodus of prisoners of war, guards, civilians, slave laborers and prisoners. All had to endure the Baltic winter, driven by fear of Russian revenge.

Elton: *"We walked all day and into the night again. We had to stop once and they made us get over to the side of the road, for the Germans were bringing a bunch of Russian slave laborers up the road, running them as much as they could. Some were almost barefooted with rags tied around their feet. Some could hardly run and were falling down. The guards would hit them with rifle butts and with bayonets and they tried to get up, but the force of the blows would knock them down again. It was a mess. Some of them could not get up, but would crawl on all fours until they could get up. One old guy (he looked old) fell by me and couldn't get up. He was just worn out. The Germans yelled at him a few times and he still could not get up. So this one guard shot him in the head. There were some more that were shot, for I could hear the shots and others told about it. It was dark so one could not see very far from where you were standing. One of the Russians jumped into our ranks and was immediately given a cap and other clothes to hide his identity. He stayed with our bunch the rest of the time. Everyone helped to cover for him. He was a surly guy and never talked very much or mixed in very much."*

After the Germans and the Russians passed, the guards marched the kriegies over the bridge to the island of Wollin. The guards destroyed the bridge behind them. They marched until 2300 hours and bunked in a barn for the night. They got nothing to eat that evening and only a cup of ersatz coffee in the morning. Elton and Russ nibbled on a few sugar cubes they saved from their Red Cross packages.

Elton: *"We could see right then we had to trade or steal, and had to be very careful and ration anything that we got, for it was uncertain when we would be fed by the Germans."*

On February 9th, the same day the Allied forces in the west crossed the German Siegfried Line[3] for the first time, the kriegies from Stalag Luft IV crossed the Swine River to the island of Usedom in Western Pomerania (*Pomorze Przednie*). When they arrived at the river, a ferry took them across. The Germans seemed more at ease after they burned the ferry. Elton and his companions marched until 2000 hours when the Germans found another barn and locked them in. The guards told them they had some cooked potatoes for them, but they would have to come to the barn door and hold out their cans.

Elton: *"We were all so hungry that we could hardly wait to get something to eat that was warm. It was dark in the barn, so when I got mine, I started to eat them right away. I spit it out as soon as I tasted it, for it was not the potato I knew. So I put them away until morning and found out what I had bitten into was a horse turd. Horse turds were mixed in with the potatoes. We heard the guards laughing outside the barn and that is what they were laughing about. Our hands were so cold that we couldn't feel the difference nor could we see in the dark barn, but you sure as hell could taste the differences. They were potatoes with skins on and they were dirty like they had been harvested from the field and were all about the size of horse turds."*

On the nights of Wednesday and Thursday, February 13th and 14th, the German city of Dresden was struck by a joint attack of British and American bombers. Seventy percent of the city was destroyed. This controversial attack created a huge firestorm resulting in a large number of casualties. The explosive and incendiary bombs killed more than 25,000 people, including many refugees from other parts of Germany. At least 75,000 houses were bombed and destroyed.

On this same Thursday, the B-24 Liberator *Pursuit of Happiness* flew a mission to Magdeburg in Germany. Visibility was poor with a lot of flak shelling. Due to a damaged engine and a shortage of fuel, the pilot, 2Lt John Kelley, made an emergency landing between Wendling and Shipdham, collapsing the landing gear. No one was wounded, but the damage was too great, and the bomber, which Gerow's crew flew four times, never flew again.

1: The coat of arms of Zeeland shows a lion half-emerged from water, with the text *Luctor et Emergo* (Latin for *I struggle and I emerge.*)
2: This package contained canned food like turkey, sausage, cheese, ham, honey, jam, nuts, cherries, sweets, Christmas pudding, packets of tea, chewing gum, bouillon cubes and fruit slices. Also, there were useful things like a washcloth, a deck of cards and, then it was a necessity of life: a pipe, pipe tobacco and cigarettes.
3: Also known as the *Westwall*, a defense line that ran from the German town Kleef (near the Dutch border) to the Swiss border.

It was a snowy December in 1944. Joe and his sister Celia, 2nd Lt in the Army Nurse Corp are both on leave and spend the holidays at home. (160)

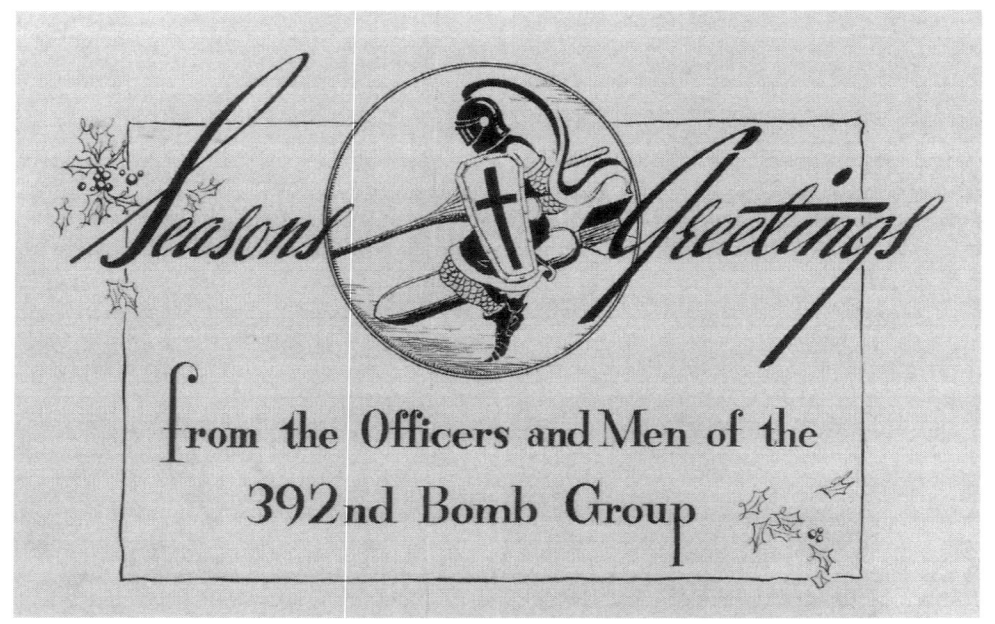

Also on Wendling Air Base Christmas was celebrated. (161 - www.b24.net)

One of the few pictures of the Black March. (162)

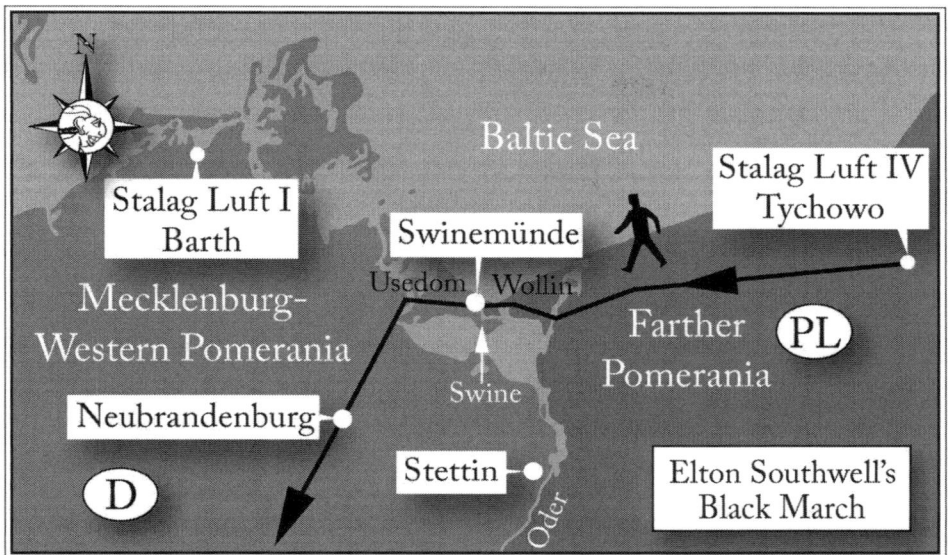

(163)

B-24 Liberator *Pursuit of Happiness,* in which Gerow's crew flew four missions, after the belly landing. (164 – www.b24.net)

Elton Southwell. (164a)

Chapter 17

Fire and Snow

During the last weeks of February and the first week of March, the Black, or Death March, continued. Elton, Ben, Frenchy and the other kriegies stumbled across frozen roads and slept in musty barns and smelly pigpens at night. The men were plagued with trench foot, dysentery and tuberculosis, as well as continuous hunger and thirst. Later, the prisoners stated that they ate too little to live and too much to die. Eating snow slightly alleviated thirst, but only the men in front benefitted, because the snow behind them quickly became polluted. Once the column began moving, the men were given no time to attend to their needs. Lagging behind was not an option and resulted in a couple of hefty blows with a rifle butt. So the men did what they had to do as they walked. Their dysentery became dispersed in the snow behind them.

The ragged procession passed through the area known as the German federal state of Mecklenburg-Western Pomerania. The men were becoming weaker from fatigue and hunger, so the guards had to stop more frequently. They walked shorter distances, but still covered 15 miles per day. Distance from the Red Army increased, so there was less need to hurry. But the SS and Gestapo officers remained alert and the prisoners were not allowed to build a fire because the smoke might reveal their position.

The Germans were also apprehensive about something else. During the march they frequently saw Russian, American and English bombers and fighters fly over, sometimes in combat with German aircraft. When an allied unit flew over, everyone was forced to run to the side of the road for cover, but the guards could not prevent the prisoners from cheering.

The lack of food was a constant concern. Surviving meant trading their few possessions for food, a bar of soap, a razor blade, or whatever. They traded with the guards and sometimes with civilians, if they could do it without the guards seeing them. Elton swapped his ring and watch for a piece of bread.

Elton: *"Once when we stopped for a day's rest, a guy stole a chicken from the farm we were at, and some ate it raw because we could not start a fire. I tried the chicken, but as hungry as I was, I could not eat it. I had an instant coffee can from a Red Cross parcel that I filled with what I think was peat moss. I rubbed it real fine and filled the can with it and got some other empty cans of coffee and made it smell like coffee, and I traded it to a German guard for some bread. Boy was he mad when he found out what it was. It's a good thing he could not remember who the guy was. He was one of the dumb guards and just a corporal. One time some guys were trading cigarettes to this one guard for some bread, and as he would put the cigarettes in his overcoat pocket, I got behind him and picked his pockets of three packs of cigarettes and threw them to Russell and he put them in his pockets. We then had trading material for a while. The guards were not supposed to trade with us, so they could not say too much to their officers. But they could take it out on all of us in some way. This was the only way we could survive. The Americans were not as organized as the English were in trading for food. The English had a barter deal that they held to and therefore, got better trades than the Americans. Americans were all for themselves and to hell with the other guy. This made trading harder for the Americans."*

Not everyone persevered in these inhumane conditions. The men who could not walk were loaded into a horse carriage and sometimes nothing more was heard of them. The Germans guards decreased the size of the columns, splitting the men into groups of 100 who went in different directions. The snow kept the prisoner's feet wet all the time, causing trench foot and terrible infections, often resulting in fatal gangrene. Gangrene was also caused by freezing. Men succumbed to this infection during and after the March. The two doctors present, the American Dr. Leslie Caplan and English Dr. Robert Pollack, were reluctant to perform amputations, because they just did not have the instruments for it. They tried to make surgical instruments by breaking off razor blades and fixing them between twigs.

During the hellish march, Caplan and Pollack seemed invincible. They saved the lives of countless men who would not have survived without their tireless care. Both were seen everywhere, walking the columns from the front to the rear and back, encouraging the men not to give up and trying to help everybody in need. They must have marched twice the distance the other kriegies walked. They assisted the stragglers with pep talks and medical help. They tended the men who were not able to walk and were loaded into the sick wagons, first pulled by oxen or horses, and later by the men themselves. It is said that Big Stoop was also at the rear, beating sick and wounded men in the wagons and sometimes throwing them off. In the evening, while the prisoners rested, Caplan, Pollack, and the other medics performed primitive surgery in improvised field hospitals, mostly old barns. They begged the German staff to allow the men more rest, more food, water, and medical equipment. Although Dr. Caplan was Jewish, he seemed to get some respect from the German guards. The only German medic present was *Stabsartz* Sommers from Stalag Luft IV, but he only treated German guards, not the prisoners.

Although Elton tried to dry his shoes and socks every night, he still had problems with his feet. After his blisters broke, new blisters would appear in the same place. His wet shoes shrank from drying them, and getting his swollen feet into shoes that were too small was a painful job. But he had to. Walking without shoes was unthinkable. The first few miles were like walking through fire, but once the shoes expanded and the swelling decreased, walking became more tolerable. As if this were not enough, Elton still suffered from dysentery.

Elton: *"On top of it all, I got the dysentery so bad that I had to strip down and turn my underwear inside out and put them back on. One had to shit on the run, drop your pants down and go while you were marching, for once you were marching the guards would not let you stop. They finally got so they would let us go, but hurry up and get back to your place in the formation. One time, in walking through a city[1], I had to go and the guards would not let me go, but I did anyway, and a guard got after me with his bayonet and there I was with my pants down trying to get the job done and a guard poking me and I trying to keep ahead of him. I got it done though. The dysentery would come and go, but it was always with you to some degree. I saw some that would get so bad that their intestines would telescope outside the rectum and the doctor that was with us, Dr. Pollack, would poke it back in by hand. No rubber gloves or anything, just his hands. He was no better off than the rest of us, but he would try his best to help. He was an English doctor. He would make charcoal by burning wood and putting water on it. This he did at night, after we had stopped marching. Charcoal was then eaten by the patient against the dysentery."*

While the NCOs staggered westward, Gene Ely, the younger brother of Loyce Ely, visited Heinkenszand in March 1945. The 23-year-old Gene was an officer in the 783rd Military Police Battalion, which was launched after D-Day in Europe. It was Gene's duty to identify dead American soldiers, buried in graves scattered throughout Europe after the war. These soldiers were reburied in various military cemeteries in Europe or, if the family wished, in a grave in their place of birth. In March, Gene was stationed in Tienen (in French = Tirlemont) in the Belgian province of Flemish Brabant. From there, he traveled to Zeeland to investigate circumstances surrounding the deaths of Gene Kieras and

Ed Yensho and to register their graves. Piet van den Dries escorted Gene to the graves and the places where the two Americans were killed. During this stay, Gene met with the other members of the resistance who helped his brother and Joe. He also spoke with eyewitnesses of the crash and local officials.

In mid-March, when the Dutch Queen Wilhelmina arrived in Eede in Zeelandic Flanders and set foot on Dutch soil again, Margot and Anne Frank died in Bergen-Belsen from typhus, almost six months after Elton left this same concentration camp.

On March 16th, Queen Wilhelmina visited the Grote Markt (Grand Market) of Goes.

Andre Evelein: *"As members of the former resistance it was something very special to be allowed to see her now so near, from the front rows where we stood – really face to face!"*

On March 19th, Hitler issued his infamous Nero Decree[2], named after the Roman Emperor Nero who is believed to have deliberately set Rome ablaze in 64 AD. He ordered the destruction of all remaining German industry and infrastructure, leaving nothing for the advancing Allies.

On Thursday, March 22nd the Crusaders experienced a tragic accident. T/Sgt Morton Baker, the original radio operator of Gerow's crew, flew a mission in a Liberator called *I Walk Alone*[3], with the crew of pilot Captain R.B. Grettum of the 579th BG. Their orders were to bomb jet aircraft in an airfield near the Swabian town of Hall, in the German state of Baden-Württemberg. I Walk Alone was the lead aircraft of 30 crews. Squadron commander, Major L. J. Barnes, was on board. There were twelve crew members in the lead crew.

The Liberators left Wendling at 0800 hours. On their way to Germany, they saw no enemy fighters and flak-fire was negligible. The weather was clear so they had a good view of their target and the effects of their bombs. The mission was a success. I Walk Alone returned to England and flew to Great Yarmouth, 30 kilometers west of Wendling. It was Bombardier Captain R.E. Good's responsibility to fire a flare gun to signal the airbase they were coming. For some reason, the flare gun went off by itself. One of the two flares landed in a box with other flares behind the pilot's seat. The box immediately caught fire and exploded. Smoke and fire blinded the pilots, causing the aircraft to dive and crash near the village of Horstead. Four crewmembers were able to parachute to safety, but eight crewmembers, including 24-year-old Morton Baker, were killed.

In late March, Elton's column spent four days in a barn in Mecklenburg-Western Pomerania, far from civilization. In the evening, they were fed potatoes and ersatz coffee in the morning. They were not told why they stopped marching. It was not until after the war that they learned a possible reason. The man responsible for the mass evacuation of the Polish POW camps, SS Lieutenant General Gottlob Berger, stated during the Nuremberg trials that Adolf Hitler was planning to hold 35,000 prisoners of war as hostages in the Bavarian mountains. According to Berger, if peace negations failed, all POWs would be executed. Hitler executed this command on March 22nd. Berger told the tribunal he delayed this monstrous task and intended to ignore it. Many considered Berger's story an attempt to wipe his own slate clean. Other sources told of a death warrant for prisoners of war, but it is not certain whether it was ever officially issued. It may be that, during their four-day stay in the barn, a high stakes game was played with the lives of Elton, Ben, Frenchy and their fellow prisoners. Because their German guards were needed at the battlefront, old infantry soldiers replaced them. Only a few SS officers were left to lead the evacuation. Because the new guards were ordinary soldiers, they were less abusive to the prisoners than their predecessors.

Elton: *"They allowed the chaplains to move outside where we were camped, if they would promise not to try to escape. We had one, a padre, Jackson, who would go and raid the smokehouses if he could find one, and steal sausages and anything that he could find. We used to ask him if it was not a sin to steal. He would answer, 'No, not if you are starving'. He could steal very well and not get caught, and he shared his loot with other prisoners. He stole too much one day, so they put a stop to his moving about. One day we were promised potatoes of which they brought and dumped into wooden hog troughs, and you never saw men act more like hogs than at that time. Everyone was on their knees trying to get their share. It was very degrading, but when you are starving, people will resort to any level to try to exist. Another day, when they rested us for a day, we were told we could buy a horse and they would cook it for us. We got enough cigarettes to buy the horse and it was butchered and thrown into a large kettle to cook. That was the best meal we had had for a long time. It was a small horse and I think it was sick. It was pretty tough, but it sure tasted good."*

As time crept by, the column had to rest more often as the kriegies became weaker. Moreover, the leaders of the guards didn't know where to bring the captives. Their only connection with headquarters came through phones they happened to come across. Sometimes they marched in a circle for days and returned to the place where they started.

Elton: *"We must have been a sight to see with our pack, our tin cans, blankets slung over our shoulder, clothes dirty and filthy, unshaven and long* hair. One day we were marched to a prison camp[4] and told that we would have a shower. All of us were skeptical at going into this building for a shower, for we had heard of the gas extermination centers. Russ and I held back and let others go ahead of us to make sure it was not gas that was coming out of the showerheads. We had to take off our dirty clothes, put them in piles separate from each other. It really was a shower and it really felt good, but it was of short duration. When we had to find our clothes and put them back on again, it was the same old feeling. This camp was later thought to be an extermination camp, for we saw very few prisoners and they were all dressed in striped clothes like we had seen at other camps as we passed by them. Some of these people were operating the showers under the supervision of S.S. officers and the Gestapo officers. At least we must have smelled somewhat better."

It kept snowing, so their feet never dried. The prisoners discovered they were less plagued by fleabites. One day, when the sun came out, they saw why. Their hair and bodies were covered with lice. Lice and fleas cannot live together on the same body. The lice were preferable to the fleas, because they didn't bite. However, lice were not that harmless, as they spread typhus. During World War II, lice killed many inmates. As the days grew warmer and longer, the prisoners were allowed to make small campfires during the day and cook the food they had stolen or swapped. They often slept outside, but it was still very cold at night. They could not build fires to warm themselves because they had to be put out before dark.

Elton: *"As the spring came and the grass started to grow, also, the dandelions started to grow. I guess not many knew about eating them, but I remembered eating them as a kid, so I showed Russ what they looked like and we would gather them and cook them over the fire when we stopped. It was not very long until everyone was doing it and we had a hard time to find them. One day we stopped at a farm that had a lake beside it, so we poked a hole in the ice and some fish came to the opening and we caught them by hand. They were just very small carp, but we dressed them out cooked them. Another time, we were stopped at a barn and I found some old ground feed in a bin. I took this and cooked it and as it cooked I stirred it and the bugs would come to the top and I could skim them off. We ate this and it tasted not too bad.*

Another time that still stands out is the day we had stopped at a farm and I found two large sacks of oats that was for the horses of the officers and the horses that hauled the sick in the wagons. I took a can of these oats and we tried to cook them. We cooked them all day and we still could not eat them, for the hulls would not come off. So I dumped them out. That evening, we were all called to formation by an SS officer. He informed us that two bags of oats had been stolen from the barn and that he would not stand for this. He was going to give us a chance to confess to save the others or he was going to have 10 men shot. Nobody owned up to this and he got very mad. He started to pick out 10 men and I was one of them. We were only 90 men to start with. After picking the 10 men, he had us marched over to some buildings and ordered the guards to check their guns and picked out five guards for the execution squad. I started thinking that having come this far and to be shot for some oats that were for horses was getting to the bottom of things that did not value life very much. I was very scared for this officer was mean and he meant it. All of us were pleading with him and the guards that spoke English told us that he meant it. About this time, a guard, that was an infantry soldier, come up to the officer and told him that the oats had been found. The officer gave the guard hell and yelled at all of the guards, cussing them out. The guard told him that he had fed the horses and had used the oats. I still don't know if the guard was telling the truth, or if he was lying to save us from the firing squad, but I was very much relieved to say the least. There were 10 men that were very thankful, but I learned right then that all we had heard about the S.S. troops was true and they did not value life very much. Russ and I started talking about trying to escape at this time, but we were so far inside Germany and the way the civilians felt, it was pretty dangerous."

1: Possibly Neubrandenburg.
2: Officially *Zerstörungsmaßnahmen im Reichsgebiet* (Destruction Measures in the Empire Area).
3: Named after a song from the movie *Follow the Boys* from 1944, sung by Dinah Shore. On August 23rd, 1944 this movie could be watched in the cinema of Wendling.
4: Given the route of the March, I think this must have been camp Ravensbrück. There were more camps on the route, but at Camp Wöbelingen near Ludwigslust they were only equipped with a primitive hand pump and did not have showers. Oflag-67 at Neubrandenburg was a POW camp, where, as far as I know, there were no prisoners in striped clothes. The Ravensbrück camp was initially established for women, but was later expanded to include a men's department and a department for teenage girls. Because Elton does not mention women, I assume that he was in the men's camp, with a high fence of barbed wire separated from the women's camp. The men section was officially an outer sector of the nearby Sachsenhausen camp. The fear of Elton and Russ for showers was not entirely unfounded, in the female part of Ravensbrück there were indeed gas chambers, where during the war years, thousands of women and children were gassed. In total, 153,000 people were imprisoned in Ravensbrück, between 90,000 and 92,000 of them died in the camp.

Gene Ely, brother of Loyce Ely, pictured with the family of Peter van den Dries and some other children. (165)

Queen Wilhelmina visits Goes, on her way to Bergen op Zoom. (166 – Zeeuwse Bibliotheek / Beeldbank Zeeland)

The wreck of the *I Walk Alone*, the Liberator in which Morton Baker died on March 22, 1945. (167 – www.b24.net)

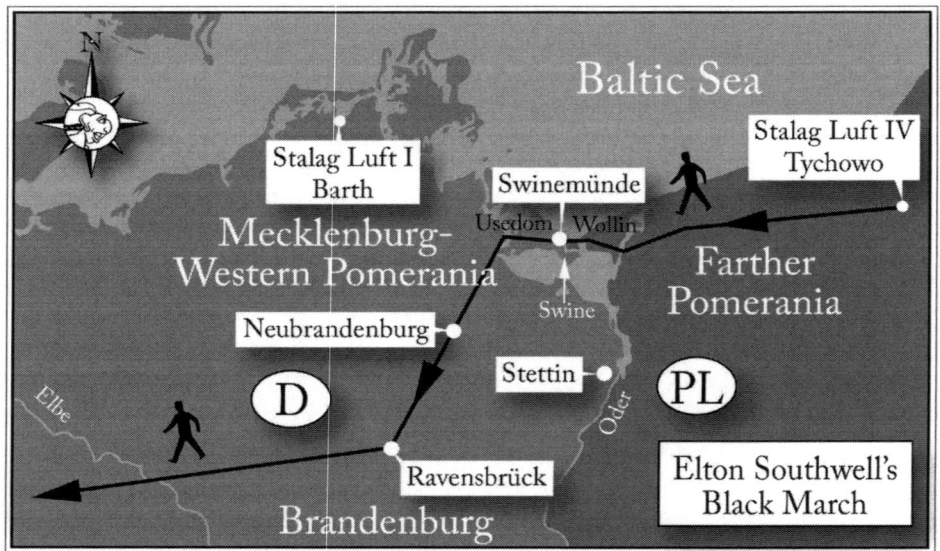

(168)

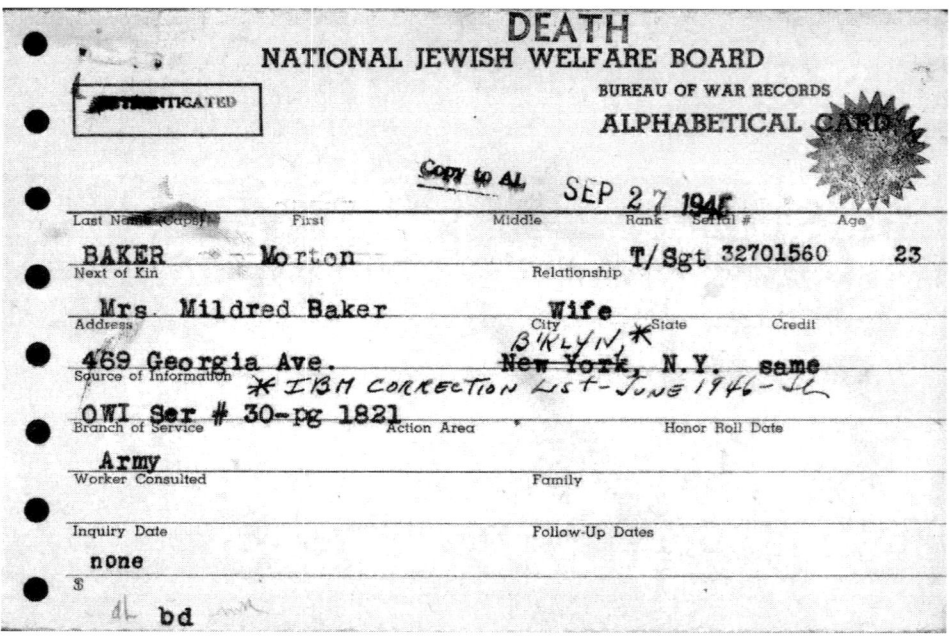

A registration card of the National Jewish Welfare Board, about the death of Morton Baker. (167 a)

Chapter 18

The Forest

On 28 March 1945, the same day Benito Mussolini was killed by Italian partisans, Canadian and British troops advanced from Germany to the Dutch border. The liberation of the Northern Netherlands, above the rivers, had begun. On April 1st, the Canadians and British liberated two cities in the east of the Netherlands, Doetinchem and Enschede. Around this time, after weeks of walking, Elton's column arrived at the overcrowded camp, Fallingbostel[1]. This former camp was not far from Bergen-Belsen and the city of Celle in Lower Saxony.

Elton: *"Here we were put in tents and this camp had all kinds of prisoners, a lot of them were English. While here, we got word that the war was going very well. I also found out what tough guys the English were and how they made everyone adhere to the unwritten rules of prisoners set up by their men. Amount of cigarettes to be traded for bread or any other thing to be traded was set up at a certain amount and not to exceed that amount. They were very strict about this and it was something that the Americans learned and it helped a lot."*

The peace and order within the English group was attributed mainly to the efforts of two men. Senior NCO Sergeant, Jimmy *Dixie* Deans, had been in several Stalags and became the leader of the prisoners. He could negotiate with the Germans without any fear for his own life. The strict Sgt Major John Lord was responsible for English discipline that prevailed. Lord, captured during the battle of Arnhem, considered it his personal mission to bolster the morale of the British prisoners. He demanded his men wash and shave daily, salute German officers, and do daily physical exercises to stay fit. Those who did not obey were punished.

Elton: *"For instance, if anyone got caught trading for more than the set amount, the English cut off any food that the Germans gave them. Also, one man was caught stealing some bread from an American, and he was taken to a slit trench (place where we all used for our toilet) and shoved headfirst into this crap up to his waist. Water was only turned on in the morning for 15 or 20 minutes and in the evening the same amount of time. It took him a long time to clean himself. The Americans, also, caught a guy stealing, but all they did was bring him before the formation each morning as we were counted by the Germans, and tell us all what a damn thief he was, and ridicule him before the entire bunch of prisoners. That was bad enough, but the English made sure that no one in their group ever stole again. This camp was close to Hanover, about 15 to 30 miles. We got very little food here, but it was no worse than any other camp. We, also, got word of the progress of the war and the movement of the troops. It sounded good to us and we could tell by the Germans that they were very upset."*

Fallingbostel also held Russian prisoners of war. The Americans and British noticed the Russians were cruelly treated. The Russians were systematically humiliated and abused. They received but a fraction of what the others got for food, which was already not much. One day, Red posters appeared on the walls of the camp. It was a desperate attempt by the Germans to convince the British and the Americans that the Russians were the real enemy, and there would come a day when they would fight together against the Red danger.

Elton: *"We stayed in this camp about 5 or 6 days, and then were told we were going to have to move[2]. We were not surprised, as word had come from the outside that the allies were moving pretty good. This had come from recent prisoners that had been captured and had been moved into the camp. We had walked all the way from eastern Germany to about Hanover, and now we were going to have to start walking back east again. The guards were now mostly older men, as the young ones had to go to the front. Guards were very afraid to have to go to the Russian front. We were herded into groups to start marching again, but Russ and I tried to hide out at the camp and not get into the groups, but we were found by an English-speaking officer and under threats of being shot, we entered the group to be marched out."*

Elton and Russ reluctantly joined the endless procession, which was again divided into columns. They were all so weak from the long march that they could not walk far without rest. They had been on the march over 60 days, all of February and March and now it was April. Again they were not fed, but the guards promised they would get some Red Cross parcels. This was the same lie they heard many times before. The Germans gave them only foul tasting ersatz coffee or tea. There was no snow to melt for water. The guards, a combination of old and wounded army, navy, and air force men unfit for the eastern front, told the airmen they were marching toward Lübeck, a city 160 kilometers northeast of Fallingbostel.

Elton: *"During the march Russ and I had a whole day of carrying a dead prisoner because we were not allowed to bury him along the way. On another* day a Mustang fighter flew repeatedly low over us. Suddenly there came from behind some forty or fifty German officers on motorcycles. All prisoners had to step aside to let them pass. The Mustang came back and started shooting. We dove to the ground and crawled into a ditch. The Mustang came back three times and hit mainly the front of the column. Our convoy was lucky, there was no one hit, but when we started to march again, we saw that the motorcyclists were affected. There were also some prisoners of war hit."

On the march towards Lübeck, the kriegies were often faced with friendly fire. Dozens of men, who narrowly escaped the horrors of the Stalags and the Black March, were now slain by allied fighters who mistook them for marching columns of German troops. The prisoners walked a few more days, then rested for a day at a lake, where they finally had clear water to drink. While the prisoners walked north, Arnhem was finally liberated on April 12th, nearly seven months after the start of Operation Market Garden.

Elton: *"One day, as we were marching by some French slave laborers, they told us the news that President Roosevelt[3] had died. We hardly believed them at first, but we got more of the same story from other French and also, the Germans. That night, Russ and I decided that we were going to escape the next day, if the chance came. We also talked to Mike Seiberling, who was from Mitchellville, Iowa, and was in the same group as we were. He was interested also. We decided that we were getting so weak that we had better do it while we could. Our intent was to try to get back to the lines, but we didn't know whose lines they were, American or English. We had no food though, but were sure that we could get to some mounds that the German farmers had their potatoes and carrots and sugar beets buried in. We had seen them at different places, and the farmers uncovering them to get at the goods, so we thought that we could do the same. The next day we kept watching for our chance, and at last, we came to a forest area. It was a large forest, for as far as we could see, was trees. We told some of the other guys what we had in mind and for them to cover for us, if they could. Distract the guards, especially the ones with dogs and machine guns. We walked for quite a while, so as to be far enough into the forest before we attempted it. At last, we decided it was far enough. It was about 4 p.m. and would get dark soon in this heavy a forest. I told the guard that I had to go to the ditch to relieve myself, for I still had the dysentery. Russ told him the same, as well as Mike. When we got to the ditch, we started to run into the forest as fast as we could, zigzagging so the guard could not shoot us so easy. We ran as far as we could go, trying to be as quiet as we could, but we heard this loud noise of someone running with their cans rattling and bumping the trees. We looked back and saw two other guys coming that had gotten away in the turmoil of our escape. We stopped and gave them hell for making so much noise and told them to get rid of their cans that were making the noise. The forest was so thick that once back in it a few yards, you could not see the road or any distance at all. We got rid of the cans of those guys and then started running again."*

Elton, Russ, Mike, and the other two soldiers were not the only prisoners who decided to escape. Everywhere in the procession men chose the danger of escape over a fate in the hands of nervous German guards. Some managed to escape while others were captured again and executed. Elton and his mates zigzagged as they ran, so they were difficult for the bloodhounds to track. They ran as far as they could. Eventually, they stopped to rest and decided it was better to leave more weight behind. They kept one blanket each and buried the rest. Suddenly, they heard machine guns rattle and they began to run. The landscape sloped sharply down. It was their salvation, because the bullets whistled above their heads.

After resting, they began walking, but not for long. They were afraid they would walk in circles and return to the same place they had just fled. During training, they learned if you could not find your way in a forest, it was better to rest first. Therefore, they waited until they saw the night sky through the tree canopy. The North Star, in particular, was of use because it always points north. The night was clear and the escapees could see the stars, allowing them to walk west all night. After the sun rose, they rested a bit, still in dense forest and they tried to sleep. The ground was still cold, so they broke spruce twigs to make mattresses. They covered themselves with blankets and laid them over the twigs. The pine branches isolated them from the cold ground and they soon warmed up. After a few hours of rest, they began walking again. They walked until morning and slept in the same way as before. The next day, they followed the sun west and came to a high fence in the forest. It was 12 feet high with the barbed wire on top of the woven wire. The men followed the fence, hoping to find an opening somewhere, but there seemed to be no end to it. Elton and his companions tested it to see if it was electrified. After they discovered it was not, they climbed over it. They walked for some distance and began hearing explosions, like artillery shells. The men came to a clearing and saw aircraft and soldiers doing something to the planes. They heard loud explosions and realized the soldiers were blowing up the aircraft. The men saw planes landing on a long airstrip in the forest. All types of aircraft were flown in to be destroyed. This made them feel good and they knew then the war was not going to last much longer. Getting rid of the planes was an indication there was no fuel to fly them.

Elton: *"This gave us the hope that the war would be over quickly, because the Germans were getting rid of the planes. This was an indication that they had no more fuel to let them fly. We watched for a while, after which we gently began to pull away. We did not like to be caught in a place like this. We went around this airplane graveyard and walked on till we came to a fence. We climbed over it and continued to walk towards the west."*

The forest thinned, so they hid and rested for the night. Because the forest was thinning and they saw more German soldiers walking through the forest, they decided to walk only during the day. It was easier for them to hide when they saw any German soldiers. From the forest, they saw the buildings of a good-sized town or city in the distance. After they circled the town to avoid detection, they found a stream and gratefully drank the water. They had not anything to drink for at least two days, maybe more. The escapees were used to thirst so even a puddle of water was enough to satisfy them. The men saw road signs off in the distance. Elton waited until all was clear and made his way to the signs. The sign said "*Lüneburg*", and he knew they were going in the right direction. After walking around the city, always staying in the forest, they kept going. Again, they bedded down for another night in the woods. Once it got dark, they tried to ignore hunger cramps and sleep.

Elton: *"Man, we were hungry! All we had eaten since taking off was a little bread that those other guys had and a few sugar cubes that Russ and I had. But, you can go a long time, if you can get some water."*

Continuing west the next day, they had to cross a road in use by a lot of army trucks, military equipment, and troops. The Americans hid until all Germans had passed by and were out of sight, and then crossed the road, hid in the trees on the opposite side, and watched more military vehicles and soldiers go by. Based on the number of troops, the men knew the Germans were preparing to fight a battle very soon.

Later that day, the men moved deeper into the forest and suddenly found themselves in a clearing. They walked cautiously and saw more military vehicles moving towards them. All five of them jumped behind brush, 3 feet tall and 5 feet long.

Elton: *"We all could not hide behind it, so we had to lie on top of each other to be covered at all. Then five German soldiers decided to take a rest from their motorcycles and rested not 50 feet from us. They talked and ate and drank from their canteens, all the while we hardly breathed. Mike Seiberling had a cough and we all knew this. I was lying on top of Mike so I just cupped by hands over his mouth and damn near smothered him, but at least it suppressed the cough. At last, the soldiers got up and moved on, but* they were there for at least half an hour, maybe longer. If they had been very observant, they could have seen us for sure, but we sure didn't move a muscle. We all were so afraid that Mike would cough; for he had a bad cough and that was the longest he had not coughed for a long time. He told me that he thought that I could smother him, and I told him that he was lucky, for I had thought about choking him."

When the soldiers left, they ran across the road as fast as they could and into the forest again. They traveled on, making sure they kept under forest cover. The men traveled close to the edge of the trees so they could see what was going on. Finally, they saw a mound that farmers used to store their potatoes, carrots, etc. They decided to stay there and dig for food. The men were on the north side of the mound, which hid them from a small town in the distance. Elton tried to dig into the mound, but it was frozen and he could not make a dent in it. Exhausted, tired and weak, he gave up. After dark, Elton slipped out and tried again to dig on the south side this time, because that side was exposed to sunshine. Luck was with him as he discovered a soft spot that he could dig in and found a few potatoes. He could not see very well in the dark and could not get many, as they were frozen. He brought them back to the rest of the men and they ate for the first time in five days. They had to eat them raw, but Elton liked raw potatoes. They thought they could dig for more the next day, so slept pretty well that night. The next morning, they awoke to gunfire and saw tanks moving about, surrounded by lots of military troops.

Elton: *"We also heard some noise in the trees and voices. We crawled over to see what it was, and it was some civilians bringing a tractor out to the forest and hiding it in the forest. They were about 200 feet from us, but were so interested in hiding the tractor and about the battle that was starting, that they didn't see us. A little after that, we saw a German soldier coming through the trees and he looked very nervous. He was just a little way from us, so Russ and I decided to jump him. We sneaked up on him and all at once jumped at him and grabbed him. He was so scared, when he saw us, and then the other three came up and helped, but he didn't put up much resistance. Once we had his gun and let his arms go, he threw up his hands and acted as if he was ready to die. We told him we were prisoners of war and then he was so relieved. He told us he was deserting the army and the war. After it all settled down, he was very friendly and offered us some bread that he had. I kept his gun all the time, but he was not about to try anything. He was just happy to be in our company and out of the battle. About this time, machine gun fire started hitting the trees we were in and branches started falling, so we hit the ground and lay down in the furrows. This kept up for quite a while, and then slowed up and finally stopped, only to start up again every few minutes. How we kept from getting hit, I don't know, but we stayed close to the ground all that morning and part of the afternoon."*

When the noise stopped, Elton crawled over to the edge of the forest, looked out at the town, and saw tanks and vehicles moving about. There was a lot of fighting going on. It became quiet by mid-afternoon, but they stayed put. About 1800 hours, Elton crawled to the potato mound to dig more potatoes, but he saw movement off in the distance and retreated back into the trees to wait until morning. They did not sleep very well even though one man stayed awake at all times. They did not know who won the battle or even if it was over. It was mostly quiet all night with occasional gunfire and some blasts they thought were from the tanks. By morning, all was calm, so Elton crawled out to the potato mound and tried digging again. He found a few before hearing gunfire close by. He was scared off and crawled back to the forest. They talked about what they should do, for they were certain it was the allies that were in control of the town.

Elton: *"Russ and I decided that we were going to take a chance and take off walking to the town, for we were all so hungry and were going to get weaker, if we just stayed where we were. We came out of the forest and made ourselves very obvious, so maybe whoever was in the town or if the Germans saw us not being armed, we would not be shot at. We walked our way over toward the road, which was about a mile. About half way to the road, we saw some German machine guns abandoned and some dead Germans by some of the guns. This made us real confident that in the town were Americans or English. We came to the road and just walked down the middle of the road, so we were visible to anyone. The walk to the town by taking the road was about half a mile. We could see men in the town watching us and then we could see some tanks. We started yelling to them that we were Americans and prisoners of war. They just stood there, and when we could see that they were the English, we started to run to them, as we were so happy that we were finally free. After telling them about being former prisoners and we were Americans and how glad we were to see them, we wanted to hug them, but as filthy as we were, we could see that they didn't care about that. We must have smelled bad, too, for although they were friendly, they still didn't get too close to us. They stayed rather distant. We told them about the other three and the German that was still out there. We pointed to where they were at and the one guy said, 'Were you out there all the time? We saw someone moving out there by the dirt pile and fired shots at him. Guess we weren't too good a shot'.*

That's what those shots were at me getting the potatoes. They were firing with the tank guns. I was almost slain by our English cousins."

Around the time Elton and his mates were walking west through the forest, the kriegies who remained in camp Fallingbostel were liberated by British troops. A day later, on April 17th, the nearby camp Bergen-Belsen was liberated.

1: This camp (Stalag XI-B) was initially set up as labor camp, but from 1939 on it became a prisoner of war camp. Initially, ten thousand Russian prisoners of war were interned here, of which thousands died during a typhoid epidemic. In October 1944, English soldiers who were captured during Operation Market Garden and from December also American soldiers who fought in the Battle of the Bulge arrived here.
2: Mainly soldiers from Stalag Luft camps were evacuated again, the rest stayed behind.
3: Franklin D. Roosevelt died on April 12, 1945 of a cerebral hemorrhage.

Chapter 19

Behind the Lines

Because it is known the district around Lüneburg was conquered by the British 2nd Army on April 18th, we know that Elton joined the English around that time. The British commanding officer ordered four of his men to drive an armed half-track[1] and take Elton and Russ along to get the rest of the men. The British soldiers were apprehensive for they thought Germans were still hiding in the forest. Even though the Americans told them otherwise, they would not take their word for it. They reluctantly mounted the machine guns on the vehicle and drove out to the edge of the forest. When they arrived, the other Americans cautiously emerged from the trees. The German prisoner stayed hidden, afraid they were going to shoot him. Elton finally convinced him they would not, so he joined them. The German was taken to a field with other prisoners and the Americans were taken to a house to clean up.

The German family that lived there was ordered to get hot water and soap. They didn't have soap, but the English were happy to give them some, anything to get rid of the smell. The Americans stripped off their filthy clothes to wash themselves. Since Elton's transport to Stalag IV the images of the starving prisoners from Bergen-Belsen were etched in his mind. Now, after seven months of hunger, he didn't look much different in the eyes of the English. After they washed, they had to put their dirty clothes back on.

The English gave them some of their rations and the starving ex-prisoners could not get enough. They felt very lucky because the Germans also fed them. Elton and his friends did not know it could be fatal to eat so much after a prolonged period of starvation. After the liberation of the camps, many starved ex-prisoners died from cardiac arrest and other severe reactions after over eating. But Elton and his mates did not know this and ate as much as they could, until the officer in charge came to tell them they would be brought to headquarters by truck. When they arrived, they were able to shower and eat again. Elton drank 21 cups of hot tea and ate a lot of crackers from the British rations.

The next day, the Americans were taken by truck to a much larger camp, farther behind the lines. The camp was two kilometers from Bergen-Belsen, where Elton had been imprisoned in the fall. The British liberated this camp a few days earlier. Upon entering the camp, the British were shocked to see mass graves and thousands of unburied bodies. The survivors looked more like gaunt skeletons than men.

The following incident concerning the commander of the Berger-Belsen camp, *Hauptsturmführer* (Captain) Josef Kramer, was unknown to the historians of the Bergen-Belsen museum until they read Elton's story.

Elton: *"They had the commandant of Berger-Belsen camp, prisoner and tied up by his wrists and hanging from a hook in the ceiling with his toes just barely touching the floor. They had taken Berger-Belsen prison camp a few days before and found all the dead prisoners piled up and the ones that were alive, walking skeletons. This made the commanding officer mad and he was holding the German commandant liable, with no mercy shown. The guard told me to go in and take a swing at him, after I told him I had been there in the fall. I looked at him, but didn't take a swing at him. He was a pathetic looking man, but I had no feeling for him^2. They were dozing holes or pits to bury the mound of corpses that were in the camp. Some of the corpses were almost mummified. Starved corpses, there is not much left to decay. I think that the prisoners that were left alive were just let go and they were being taken care of by the English."*

The British forced both male and female camp guards to bury the hundreds of dead prisoners in the camp. Citizens from the surrounding villages were also forced to help dig.

Elton: *"It was here, I believe, that there was also an S.S. school for training troops. When we went through the school, all sorts of weapons were in the rooms for training, just like a campus of a university. We took some weapons and carried them with us. I kept mine until I got back to St. Louis, where I got rid of it. I just dumped it in a trashcan"*

Elton and his mates were at Bergen-Belsen for two days. On April 21st, they were transported further west and started picking up prisoners that the English had released from other camps.

Elton: *"One day we picked up in the truck a soldier that was captured during the Battle of the Bulge. He came from the group that was executed by the Germans in a field at Malmedy. The man told me that he was left for dead in the snow, among the many corpses. He managed to escape the murderers and was later picked up by the British. They took him to a hospital to recover from his injuries. The scars of machine gun bullets looked terrible.*

After we were behind the English lines, I myself witnessed a massacre. There was a small forest that was surrounded by the British. They knew that a German unit was hiding, but they would not surrender. Every now and then there a negotiator was sent to the forest, but he was immediately shot. Time after time the British tried to persuade the Germans to surrender. After three or four negotiators were hit, the British commander ordered the flamethrowers to the forest opening. The forest was a major conflagration. When they came to inspect the dead, they appeared to be all boys of fourteen to sixteen years old. They were members of the Hitler Youth, who were so indoctrinated that they had sworn never to surrender. The English were very upset when they discovered the boys."

The boy's had acted out of fanaticism and fear. During their training, they learned that it was shameful to surrender without being wounded. If you did this, you were regarded as a traitor and your family faced heavy reprisals.

Constantly on the move and eating anything they could lay their hands on, the Americans finally ended up in Belgium. The British thought it was funny to see how much they could eat and still remain hungry. They threw them loaves of bread and watched them devour it all in seconds. The Americans remained in Belgium for a day before they boarded a plane to England.

Elton: *"Here we were met out on the runway, way off from everything and everyone. A group of medics met us out on the runway with clean clothes and dusting powder with a bellows to dust us with. We were getting out of our clothes and being dusted and the Salvation Army girls were getting us food and tea. Just the few medics and the Salvation Army girls were all that were permitted out there. After taking all of our clothes off, and dusting our hair and body with powder and getting into the clean clothes and drinking tea, all at the same time, I was so damn happy to be back. It was something I will never forget. They piled all of our old filthy dirty clothes that we had worn for months, some ever since I had been captured, into a pile on the runway, poured gas on them and touched them afire. Then they took us off the runway to the hospital. Here I was kept in bed a few days and treated for my dysentery. We also had been getting sick from eating, but thought nothing of it. I don't know what I weighed, when I first got liberated, but it must have been around 100 lbs., for they weighed us at the hospital after we had been there a few days and I weighed 122 lbs. On a Tuesday, and by Sunday, I weighed 149 lbs. I gained 27 lbs. from Tuesday until Sunday."*

About this time, a rumor circulated about the fate of Big Stoop, the hated camp guard at Stalag IV. On April 29th, General Patton liberated the prisoner of war camp in Moosburg (Stalag XIIA, in the German state of Bavaria). Four ex-prisoners climbed through the fence and stole a ham, some beer and some schnapps. After partying, they decided to return to the camp. Along the way, they saw something lying by the side of the road. As they approached, they saw a large corpse with no shirt, shoes, or belt and ... headless. The prisoners reported it was almost certainly the body of Big Stoop. Others in the camp told about two ex-prisoners of war, triumphantly displaying the head of Big Stoop in a basket.

Although Joe Sulkowski, Loyce Ely and Elton Southwell were free, the other members of the crew were still prisoners of war. Ben Brink and Normand *Frenchy* Hebert were still walking the Black March.

Ben's cousin Jackie Rhoades wrote: *"I have been told by Aunt Norma that on the Black March if you could not walk or have help from another soldier you were shot. Ben became so ill at one point and could not go on. A man by the name of Louie Flair (he was also from Clearfield County – Ben knew him before the war – they meet up on the march) took a wheel he found, 2 poles and canvas and somehow made a crude wheel barrel to transport Ben until he was able to move on his own."*

On their route north, allied fighters repeatedly attacked Ben and Frenchy's column. They killed both the prisoners and guards. The Germans realized they were being gradually enclosed by the allied troops and were extremely tense. The column from Fallingbostel slowly fell apart in all the chaos. Many prisoners managed to escape in the confusion during the shelling. The rest were driven towards the River Elbe. On April 18th, around the time Elton and his friends reached the English line, the prisoners crossed the river via the bridge at Lauenburg, constantly at risk of being shot at by British Spitfires. The next day, a part of the column remained at the river, while others continued marching towards the town of Gresse. Once there, the prisoners rested and were finally given the promised Red Cross packages that Sgt. Dixie Deans had managed to get from Lübeck. While devouring the contents of the packages, the hungry prisoners saw a group of British Typhoons coming towards them. Most kriegies rushed to the roadside, others tried waving their coats to signal they were prisoners of war. However, this did not deter the Typhoons. Sixty prisoners lost their lives. After the massacre, the march was more chaotic than ever. More and more prisoners escaped and German guards deserted. The long procession, was already divided into smaller fractions, fell apart. Here and there, prisoners were liberated by British troops, while others were driven further north by German guards.

On April 27th, the American and the Russian armies met each other at Torgau on the River Elbe. By joining forces at Elbe, the American and Soviet troops successfully cut the German army in two.

In the German Stalag Luft I, where Jim Gerow, Fred Vallarelli and Dave Grandon were imprisoned, they had also heard of the approaching Russians. At night, the cry "*Come on Joe!*[3]" was frequently heard in the barracks. On Monday, April 30th, the camp received an order from Reichsführer-SS Heinrich Himmler to evacuate the camp within 24 hours, before they fell into the hands of the Red Army, located forty kilometers away. The guards were ordered to march the prisoners westward toward Hamburg. The SAO in charge was American Colonel Hubert (Hub) Zemke, the successor to Colonel Beyerly. Zemke, an American fighter pilot, was the son of German immigrants and could successfully negotiate with the camp leaders because he was of their ancestry and spoke German. Moreover, after his arrest, he rescued two German girls during a fighter bombardment. The Germans respected Zemke.

Because he thought it was possible that the guards would shoot their prisoners rather than allow their liberation by the Russians, Zemke formed a camp gang armed with homemade knives and grenades. Once the camp leaders ordered him to prepare his men for the march, Zemke let the camp commander, *Oberst* (Lieutenant-Colonel) Warnstadt, know that they would never cooperate. Although Warnstadt commanded two hundred armed guards, he was opposed by an army of nine thousand men who would rather fight than march. Zemke threatened to order the prisoners to overpower the guards and kill them if the evacuation order was not rescinded. He told Warnstadt the guards could easily get away before the Russians arrived. Several meetings between Zemke and the camp commander followed before Warnstadt finally gave in. That night, at 1000 hours, all barrack lights and streetlights suddenly went out. Not long after, all the German soldiers marched out of the camp, leaving the gate wide open.

Colonel Zemke took command of the camp. As the Senior American Officer, Zemke was now responsible for the orderly evacuation of the prisoners to their home base. In order to ensure discipline, he organized an internal police force to maintain order and ensure no one left the camp before the evacuation. Where hated German soldiers had once stood, he stationed armed MPs on the watchtowers and forbade anyone to leave the camp.

Not only in Stalag Luft I did the Germans abandon all hope. On April 30, 1945, a few hours after Hitler married Eva Braun, the disillusioned couple committed suicide in his bunker. Hitler shot himself in the head. His wife ingested cyanide. The next day the Minister of Propaganda Joseph Goebbels and his wife also committed suicide after they had killed their six children. As soon word surfaced, that Hitler was dead, Grand Admiral Karl Donitz succeeded Adolf Hitler and accepted the office of President of the German Empire.

The next day Colonel Zemke sent a delegation to inform the Russian troops all Germans had left and there was no need to attack the camp.

Jim Gerow wrote about this first day in May: *"The next day a dozen Russian Cossacks on horseback came into the camp, some with a woman behind them. At that moment we knew we were free."*

These Cossacks were soldiers of the 2nd Belarusian Front. They didn't like the fact that the camp gates were closed and tried to convince Zemke the ex-prisoners had been locked up long enough. They did not wait for Zemke's approval and reluctantly he watched the Russians and ex-prisoners tear down the fences.

Jim: *"The Russians brought cattle with them, that they slew in the fields for us to eat. We roamed the nearby village as if it was ours."*

While groups of former prisoners pillaged the village, there was a celebration in the camp. The women who accompanied the Russian soldiers proved to be a dance group. They gave the ex-prisoners a spectacular show. Men who did not want to obey Zemke's command to stay in camp began to walk westward toward the Allied troops. Some of these men were killed by shellfire.

On May 2nd, while the ex-prisoners of Stalag Luft I feasted with the Russians. German troops in Berlin saw Russian soldiers plant their flag on the Reichstag after fierce battles.

That day, a column of Fallingbostel was still at the Elbe. When their guards received the message their Führer was dead and Berlin was lost, they abandoned their prisoners. British troops arrived and told them to walk west. They eventually joined Allied troops and the Black March was finally over for them.

On February 6, 1945, approximately 8000 prisoners of war, mainly sergeants from various air forces left Stalag Luft IV. On May 2, 1945, after 86 days and 600 miles of forced marching, 1,500 men died due to disease, cold, malnutrition and German aggression.

In the Netherlands, events quickly succeeded each other. Although Queen Wilhelmina in March had already visited liberated South Netherlands in March, she officially returned from exile on May 3, 1945. On May 4th, in Lüneburg, Field Marshal Montgomery accepted the military surrender of German General-Admiral von Friedeburg for all forces in northwest Germany, Netherlands, Schleswig-Holstein and Denmark. A day later World War II officially ended in the Netherlands. In the presence of Prince Bernhard, at Hotel *De Wereld* in Wageningen, General Foulkes presented the surrender terms to German commander, Colonel General Johannes Blaskowitz. The terms were accepted the next day. On May 6th, Colonel General Jodl at Reims offered to surrender to the Allies of all armed forces. He signed it the next morning. In Berlin, General Field Marshal Keitel signed a similar document in the presence of the Russian General Zhukov. The next day, Europeans received news of the surrender and there were many mass celebrations.

Colonel Zemke, along with two officers from the British Airborne Division, flew to England to report on the state of Stalag Luft I. On May 8th, the massive evacuation operation of Stalag Luft I began, with bombers and cargo planes picking up thousands of men to transport them to France. The operation ended on Wednesday, May 16th.

In Europe, the end of the war was celebrated on May 4th. Elton was still in a London hospital. Elton: *"We were kept here at the hospital for a few days, maybe a week or two, and then we were sent to London to wait being sent home. On our way in to London, in trucks, we met the procession of Winston Churchill, greeting the people, for the war was just about over. We had to stop, and he came right by our truck, waving to everyone. We stayed in London about three weeks, helped celebrate the end of the war in Europe, but we had no money to do anything, only ride the buses, which they gave a pass for. We got some money a few days before we left London. It amounted to about $2.00 (10 shillings)."*

Jim Gerow wrote: *"After a few weeks had passed since the liberation of Stalag Luft I, we were taken to Camp Lucky Strike[4] on the French coast. We had still a few weeks waiting for the ship that would take us home. It took so long because there were thousands of soldiers who had to be transported by sea."*

Dave Grandon wrote from France to his family[5]: *"At the moment it seemed that we will never come home. I've never seen anything as stupid as this. They say that the transport commands think that the 8th Air Force has flown us all home and that the 8th Air Force believes that the RAF has solved everything. It seems that we are prisoners of the U.S. Army now. Maybe the colonel wants us to celebrate the 4th of July over here. The Russians however are damn good guys, the ones I've seen anyway. I hope they are released on the Japs. I'll be home in a month, even though I have to go via Moscow."*

Jim Gerow: *"My wife Delphine was waiting for me in New York. We stayed at the New Yorker Hotel and visited many sights. The picture you have of us was taken at that time at the Rockefeller Center."*

Not long after, Gerow's Sergeants: Elton, Ben and Frenchy were shipped to the United States. Ben landed at Fort Dix, in Trenton, New

Jersey, where his sister, Norma, met him. Ben weighed only 98 pounds. The first thing he had to eat at home was shrimp with shrimp sauce.

1: A half-track armored vehicle, fitted with wheels in front and continuous tracks at the back.
2: For his role in the horrors of Bergen-Belsen, Josef Kramer was hanged in Hamelin on December 13, 1945 by the famous English hangman, Albert Pierrepoint, who was flown in specifically for this execution.
3: With Joe they meant Joseph Stalin and his troops.
4: Like all camps for freed Pows, the camp near Janville France was named after a popular cigarette brand.
5: A month later published in The Daily Post-Gazette by Dave's father.

An American half-track. British troops used these as well. (169)

Jim Gerow and his wife Delphine at the Rockerfeller Centre in New York. (170)

Norma Brink, who took her starved brother Ben back home by train. (171)

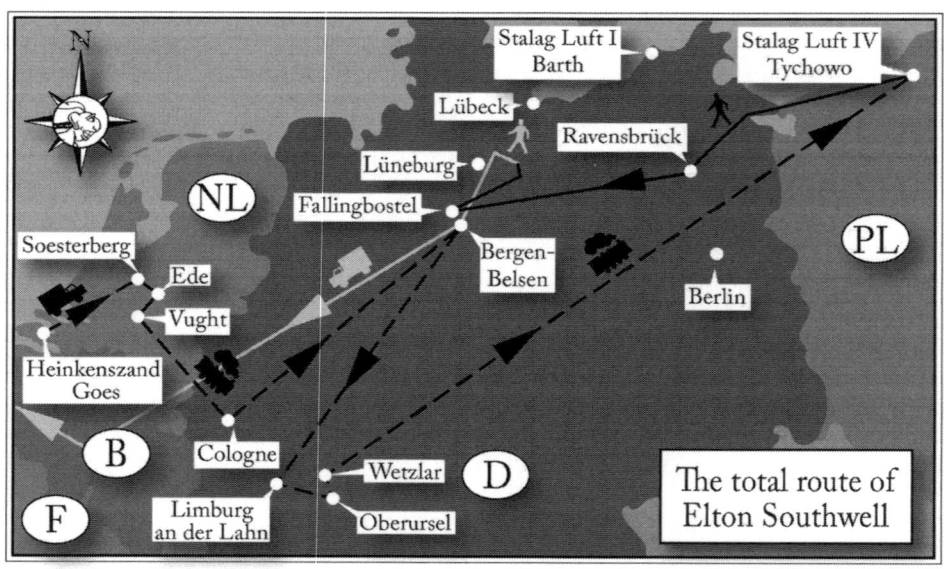

(172)

Chapter 20

The Aftermath of the War

While families of the ex-prisoners were finally embracing their loved ones, the families of Gene Kieras, Ed Yensho, and Morton Baker could only mourn. According to a report in The Daily Mail Tribune on Tuesday morning, July 26, 1945, a memorial service was held in St. Hyacinth's Catholic Church of La Salle, with the family of Gene Kieras present. During the service, a 17th golden star was sewn on the church service flag to commemorate the 17th parish soldier to sacrifice his life for his country.

Zeeland

In July 1945, my grandfather, **Piet van den Dries** and his family, moved to the nearby city of Goes, where he became headmaster of a Roman Catholic primary school. After the war he taught English in his spare time, usually for Zeelanders wanting to emigrate to Canada or Australia. In that same month, the Commissionership Military Authorities granted Piet permission to travel to Belgium.

On August 2, 1945, Sergeant Vermeule wrote his report on the crash of the Feathered Injun. Piet van den Dries translated it to English and brought the report with him to Tienen, where Loyce Ely's brother, Gene, was stationed. The report was not the only thing Piet took with him. He also gave Gene Ely an envelope containing the personal belongings of Gene Kieras. Secured by Sergeant Jacob Koole after the crash, the envelope contained a strand of hair, a necklace, two pencils, and some pictures. He also gave Gene a sketch of the area indicating the crash site, the spot where Gene Kieras died, and the location of Gene and Ed's graves. Gene Ely took everything to America and presented it to the USAAF authorities and the Kieras family. Gene Kieras' dog tags were sent to the Foreign Office right after his death.

Piet mailed a letter to Gene Kieras' family that was published by Preston Grandon, Dave's father. It appeared in The Daily Post-Tribune on Thursday, January 3, 1946.

Piet wrote: *"You will perhaps be astonished to receive a package from unknown Dutch friends, but we want to express our sincere admiration for your beloved son and brother. As a member of the underground army I had the honor to play an active part in rescuing two members of the plane to which your son belonged. Under the nose of the Huns (I had a Hun officer billeted on me) I taught members of the underground army English. On the 18th of September 1944, I saw a burning four-engine bomber coming into my direction and a few moments later I heard a big bang and saw big clouds of smoke. The Huns who were at that moment in our village ran to the men who had bailed out. The following night I secretly got a message from the ARP to see the corpse of your son, in order to report if necessary. I saw him, as well as my friend the doctor, who gave a testimony of his death. A few days later we took Joseph Sulkowski and your son's friend Loyce Ely, to a fine hiding place where we often visited them. In March 1945, Eugene Ely, Loyce's brother, visited us and the local police to make an inquiry and a statement about your son. I translated that and gave it to Eugene hoping that he would be so kind as to give it to you personally. He left Europe in August, but since then we have not had any sign of life or letter, neither from him nor from you. Yet we hope that you now know all particulars. You may be sure that we shall never forget the heroism of your brave countrymen. You, your son and all other Americans can be sure of our love and gratitude. I hope Eugene Ely will have told you everything we did. If not ask him all particulars. He saw our friends and visited all the spots. We hope that he will inform the relatives of Edward Yensho about these particulars and drawings. In my letter to you I promised you that a friend of mine, a well-known painter[1], would make some original drawings of the scene. Enclosed I send you three paintings (water colors). The one with the two trees represents the scene where the plane crashed. The two trees on top of a dike near the farm of my uncle (who also played a prominent part in the rescue) were seriously burned by the flames of the burning machine. It is a sacred spot for us Dutchmen, and for our local group, full of recollections of the horrible five years of occupation. The second is the background of the meadow of which your son fell and died. It is about 100 yards from the summerhouse of the farm. The third represents the grave of your son and the other member of the crew, Edward Yensho. Very often the people and the children of the village place flowers and wreaths on their resting place. On the liberation of Holland, the end of the war in August, and the 18th of September 1945, wreaths were laid out and hundreds of people visited the place. Thanks to paper clippings I got from Eugene Ely I knew that you are Roman Catholics and I asked our local priest to bless the grave, which has also been done as well as high mass read for his eternal rest. It is a pity that Holland is in such a poor* state. We lack nearly everything, clothes, fuel, medical supplies etc. We were a happy peaceful country, well faring, but now everyone is poor, badly dressed, undernourished and lacking the most elementary things. The Hun prisoners of war even get more and better cigarettes and better food than we! You can imagine how glad we were to be liberated. For five years we had to endure on account of our own traitors, Gestapo and Siecherheits Polizei. Many relations of ours are still missing or dead. Some were shot. Some experienced concentration camps and now we begin anew to build up a new Holland but lack of everything hinders us most of all. Well, dear friends, we hope that you will never forget our admiration and gratitude and we can feel the grief you must have suffered. Be sure your son and brother rest among friends and his resting place will be cared for as long as we live and we have our children to honor the place where our friends lie. When I lived at Heinkenszand (I am now head master in a neighboring town called Goes) we often took the three children to the cemetery and showed them the place where Daddy's American friends rest. Dear American friends, write as soon as possible. We are all anxious to hear if you have received this letter. The painter had also the honor to play a part in the burial of your son. He doesn't want any fee; all has been done to show our gratitude towards your allies and your country."

On April 29, 1946 the same newspaper published a subsequent letter from Piet, dated February 28, 1946. In this letter, Piet requested supplies that were scarce in Zeeland. He also told about the graves of Gene and Ed. The reporter wrote: *"The Germans permitted the citizens of Holland to bury Kieras and Yensho and a Roman Catholic priest officiated at the burial services. In recognition of what the citizens of the United States did for Holland, the graves of the two boys have been made into a shrine. A propeller of the plane, a B-24, has been used as a monument for the graves, and the community has taken upon itself the task of perpetual care, with the children seeing that flowers are present whenever they are available."*

Piet wrote: *"… Your letter in which you expressed so deeply your gratitude for what we did, is our finest reward and frankly speaking, it was but our duty to show how much we appreciate the freedom that your brave countrymen brought us. With Kees Griep, who also lives in Goes now, we visited the whole group who contributed so much to the rescue of the two surviving pilots and the burial of the two other men. We would never have ventured to ask something, because we do not do that to get something. Just as your countrymen did everything they could, we have contributed a trifle for the common cause. In the name of all our underground friends and others who helped us we want to thank you for the good intention of helping us. But first of all, please don't think we Dutch are beggars. Frankly speaking:*

we feel rather ashamed to ask for things. We do it only because you asked us to do so. In return we shall do everything to embellish the grave of Eugene Kieras and Edward Yensho. We shall have a fine tombstone erected of stone with perennial plants and the bent propeller in front of it, and my cousins Ko van 't Westeinde, a horticulturist himself will take care that everything is done to have it adorned continually. In this way we hope to pay back for what you intend to do. As regards our question for cigarettes, we hope that you will excuse us. What we Dutch smoke is so bad and so little that you have no idea of our longing for a really good cigarette. Camel is only known by name! Follows is a list of articles that our friends want most. Some list may be long perhaps, but please don't think we wish to have all of this. We leave it to you to make a choice of them. Some people even asked to pay for it, if it comes to too much expense on your side. It would be better to not stand in need of so many things, but you in America have no idea in what lamentable a state we Dutch are."

Follows are the wishes of the families of the underground people and their helpers. This is a list made by Nico van Biezen: "*Ladies stockings size 9, children's stockings age 8 and 1½, socks size 10, shirt size collar 15½, ladies underwear and gent's underwear, frocks for girl of eight and suit of clothes for boy of 1½ years, piece of material for dress four yards, overall (denim) for blacksmith size 5 or 40 inches, underwear for children 8 and 1½ years, pepper, cinnamon, soap, shammy-leather, sponge, tie, boot polish (black), knitting wool, sewing cotton, cigarettes.*"

The first American packages arrived on April 29, 1946, the same day the above message appeared in the newspaper. The packages were gathered under the leadership of the families of Gene Kieras and Dave Grandon in La Salle.

My grandmother wrote a thank you letter to Preston Grandon, which he published in The Daily Post-Tribune of September 27, 1946: "*Dear friends. My husband asked me to write you because he has been so busy of late. I cannot write English as well as him, but I hope that you can understand me. When the Americans were with us they always said, 'mistakes are allowed' and so I hope you'll also do. A fortnight ago we received the first parcels numbered 3, 4. 5. 6, 7 and 8. Oh, I wanted that you could have been there. We went with all the parcels to the loft and there we unpacked them. When we had seen everything, we made 14 heaps and distributed it as fairly as possible. It seemed to us a feast of Santa Claus. The next day I went to Heinkenszand and gave it to the people. How glad they all were. Most unpacked it while I was there and the greatest reward was the gladness of the people. In one family everything was distributed immediately. This one is for the son, this for the daughter, this for the baby, etc. It was very, very wonderful. But two days ago it was a feast for the men when we received the parcel numbered 2 with the cigarettes. I think that all the women will say with me that their husbands were in high spirits, when they smoked their first American cigarettes. But the finest things for me were coffee, cinnamon, nutmeg and the chamois. So you see that all parcels were received in good order. All the things were in them. But now, how can I thank you and all of the people who have helped us? I said to my husband, 'I wanted to be rich and I could go to America and thank all the people who sent us something.' But now I hope you will do so. Everything was welcome and we thank you, very much. Mr. Grandon I must thank you especially for the trouble you have had and you still have with the parcels. I should like to know you in person and then I would shake hands with you. But be assured that we shall never forget what you and your good friends have done for us."*

During the war Preston Grandon organized a correspondence pool to inform all the families of the airmen involved. Whenever there was news of one of the crewmembers, he would inform the other families. This pool was maintained after the war, so other families could read the letters of Piet and Kartien.

After the war Piet maintained contact with Joe Sulkowski and Gene Ely for years. They both came to visit him several times.

In a post-war visit to Zeeland, at the request of his brother Loyce, Gene Ely and Piet searched behind the Boerendijk for Loyce's buried wallet. The search was not successful. Gene took pictures of the rectory for his brother and visited the families of the people who helped him.
During a trip in August 1966 to visit his sister in Canada, Joe invited Piet to America.

Joe's son, John Sulkowski, wrote to me: *"I have fond memories of your grandfather, the schoolmaster who I met in 1966. He came to Canada to visit his family. My parents and I picked him up and he accompanied us during a short tourist trip through the eastern United States and visited our family in Pennsylvania."*

Piet visited Canada and the U.S. in August 1966 the same month I was born. He brought back presents for his new grandson. At the end of Piet's visit with the Sulkowski family, Joe drove his Dutch guest to the airport. They were late because Piet spent so much time talking with Joe's family. Although Piet became quite nervous and told Joe that he really needed to hurry, Joe kept within the speed limit. Piet caught his plane just in time.

Later, Joe broke contact with Piet. Joe began experiencing nightmares about the war that dominated his life. Breaking contact was probably an attempt to leave the war behind him.

Joe was not alone in suffering emotional trauma after the war. Almost all American and Zeeland families involved in the war reported their fathers, brothers, uncles, or husbands experienced psychological symptoms in varying degrees. Some became very bitter. They often hated everything German. They were plagued by nightmares and flashbacks of life-threatening situations they endured. Sometimes, they would lose control for no reason. They could not help their families understand the problem because it was too painful. They thought it was better to say nothing about it and put the past behind them. Today, we recognize these symptoms as post-traumatic stress disorder (PTSD) [2], but this was unknown just after the war. Piet also suffered psychological trauma. The stress of participating in the local resistance, while a German officer was billeted in his house at the same time did not leave him. Piet had a nervous breakdown and was hospitalized for a few weeks. He recovered, but suffered from severe headaches for months afterwards.

One of the times I understood the impact of the war, I was a student, walking through downtown Goes with my grandfather. I had to buy something for school and started to enter a store, when my grandfather suddenly stopped me. He said, *"Mark, I do not care if we have to search the entire city for another shop or it's twice as expensive, you're not buying something in a shop of a NSB man."*

I also used to hear him talk with my father about his friendship with Kees Griep. They remained friends until their death. Kees Griep, the doctor's grandson, wrote to me: *"I have met your grandfather, Piet van den Dries, a few times when I was little. He came, when my grandfather physically started to deteriorate, regularly to the flat at the Valckeslotlaan in Goes and was a very loyal friend. My grandfather, who was always a bit grumpy when he got older, always flourished when your grandfather paid him a visit. Even as a child, I could feel that it was a very strong friendship, as one that never stops."*

A warm friendship developed between Piet and the Evelein family. André said about Piet: *"He was directly involved in the burial of the two crew members that were killed. Together with someone else he also brought us the two Americans to our rectory in 's-Heer Abtskerke. From this time on we had a lot of contact with him and his family. That remained a lasting friendship until the death of his first wife and then the death of his life companion, and finally his own death. This friendship was a valuable fruit from the war years!"*

Piet always maintained a close friendship with another member of the Group Griep, Cees Paauwe. Piet asked the accountant to act as the executor of his last will, a request that Cees complied with after Piet's death.

In 1945, all Zeelanders who helped Joe Sulkowski and Loyce Ely, received two certificates in recognition and gratitude. The first came from America, on behalf of President Harry Truman, signed by Dwight Eisenhower, the Supreme Commander of the Allied Forces. The second was a certificate from England to thank them for aiding Allied soldiers.

However, when America, which had a strong anti-colonial tradition, ensured the Independence of Indonesia, my grandfather sent the U.S. award back to America, protesting the role of President Sukarno.

In an interview for the weekly newspaper *The Bevelander* of February 15, 1989, Piet said: *"The Dutch army had in fact already lost the war in the Dutch East Indies, but refused to transfer to Sukarno's authority. I had no objection to the independence of Indonesia, but I did have objections to the person of Sukarno. He had collaborated with the Japs. Nevertheless Jessup (from the USA) insisted that the Netherlands had to leave Indonesia as soon as possible and that the country had to be surrendered to Sukarno. For me it was inconceivable that collaborators could get hold of our former colony. With returning my American award I wanted to get it off my chest. I felt deeply offended by the Americans. I wanted America to denounce the role of Sukarno. I could not bear that the Americans would cross us in the Security Council. The English were also against us in Malacca (in the so called rubber-argument). You cannot just swallow everything."*

In early 1949 Piet wrote to Philip C. Jessup, deputy delegate of the United States to the United Nations: *"Enclosed I send you my decoration given by your gallant President Roosevelt. I no longer want to possess this. It was given me for help towards several of your countrymen during the occupation of our country, for which we risked our lives to save theirs. Most people in Holland are shocked to the attitude of your Government towards our country, especially your attitude in the Security Council. We are shocked to see how your Government acts towards our small nation, which in your own words know nothing of restoring order and peace in the Dutch East Indies… I am so sorry about this change in your country's attitude towards us that I will not have this paper with which I was very glad, because it was a token of gratitude and I put it into your hands. I will love your country and your gallant soldiers who brought us the most beloved thing that man can have: freedom. Freedom that we also want to bring to the people in the East Indies, but not in the way you intend…"*

On February 3, 1949 Jessup replied, regretting Piet's decision. He tried to persuade Piet to take the decoration back, but Piet was a man of principle and refused. He caused quite a commotion, resulting in numerous articles in Dutch newspapers. The Dutch postal service had their hands full processing all the letters, cards and telegrams of support that Piet received. Many resistance men followed his example and returned their decorations to America.

Piet: *"The many responses encouraged me at that time. There were as many as 1400. They were nearly all in agreement with me. Only 4 letter writers had a different opinion."*

Later on, Dutch resistance fighters could apply for the *Verzetsherdenkingskruis* (Resistance Memorial Cross), an award that was established in 1980 on the 35th anniversary of the liberation. Inscribed on the silver award were the words *The Tyranny Expelled 1940-1945*. The cross was intended for participants in the resistance against occupiers of Dutch territory in World War II and was often awarded by Prince Bernhard himself. The resistance fighters, their families from Heinkenszand, Baarsdorp and 's-Heer Abtskerke wanted this memorial cross. However, its award was controversial. For many people, this recognition came much too late. Others spoke of arbitrariness in granting it. Some who presented themselves as pro-German during the war and who committed a single act of defiance in the last month, were awarded a resistance cross, while the families of true resistance men, like Nico van Biezen and Pier van 't Westeinde, had to go through much trouble to get the award. This caused hard feelings. My grandfather also disagreed with this state of affairs. He refused the medal when it was offered to him.

For his entire working life, Piet was the head of a primary school in Goes. On March 26, 1985, at the age of 78, my grandmother, Katrien Schipper, died in a nursing home in Goes. After her death, Piet lived with Rie van Veen for several years, until she died in 1989. On June 4, 1992, after a short illness, my grandfather, Piet van den Dries died in the Oosterschelde Hospital in Goes. He was 82. After the cremations of both Katrien and Piet in Middelburg, all the funeral flowers were laid at the monument, *The Causeway*, on the way to South Beveland, which commemorates the fallen soldiers at the Sloedam.

Soon after the war, **Kees Griep** and his family, like Piet's family**,** moved to Goes, where he took over a family practice. After the war, Kees also billeted Dutch soldiers of the Princess Irene Brigade in his home

Because of a Christmas card from Canada that Kees received in 1945, it is assumed he kept in touch with the commander of the liberator of Heinkenszand, Lieutenant Colonel Whitaker.

Kees became founder and chairman for North and South Beveland of the *Koninklijke Nederlandse Maatschappij tot Bevordering van de Ge-*

neeskunde (Royal Dutch Society for the Advancement of Medicine – *KNMG*) and the *Ziekenfonds Zuid- en Noord-Beveland* (Health Insurance Fund South and North Beveland). In 1964, his son, Pim, took over his practice while Kees stayed on as Controlling Physician. Before this, Kees was my grandparents' doctor. After he resigned, Pim became our family doctor.

Kees' great love was the Operetta Association of Goes, where he was director. On April 30, 1969, Kees was appointed Knight in the Order of Orange-Nassau as thanks for his broad community involvement. In 1970, at age 73 he stepped down from his directorships but remained as Controlling Physician for several more years. At the opening of the new health insurance office of the National Health Service Central Zeeland in Middelburg in 1975, a bronze plaque was unveiled, in the hallway, depicting Kees Griep, founder of the Health Insurance Fund South and North Beveland. The image was placed alongside that of Kees' substitute during the war, Doctor Staverman, who had long been chairman of the National Health Service in Walcheren. On December 29, 1981, Kees was awarded the Resistance Memorial Cross for his role in the resistance. His wife, Corry Duinker, died on December 30, 1979 at age 82. Kees died at the age of 87 on October 29, 1983, in the Ter Valcke nursing home in Goes.

After the war **Nico van Biezen** continued working as a blacksmith in Heinkenszand. Joe Sulkowski, along with some colleagues, traveled from Germany to Zeeland to visit him. After all, Nico was the man who disguised Joe as a blacksmith's helper and farmer, and led him to his hiding places. Joe and his American comrades drove up in an American Chevrolet and were received in the neat front room of the forge, which was only used on Sundays.

In the days after the war, there were five blacksmith shops in Heinkenszand. Nico and Suus faced a lot of competition. They sold their forgery to their assistant and Nico began teaching mechanics at the *Ambacht* (Crafts) School in Goes and Middelburg. He also gave lessons at home to students who wanted to learn horse-smithing. Suus wanted to leave Heinkenszand where they experienced so much hardship. They first planned to move to the village of Bant in the Noordoostpolder, an area in the new province Flevoland. But Nico learned of a blacksmith shop in Axel in Zeelandic Flanders, the city where Suus was born. They bought the blacksmith shop in 1953 and, through hard work they were successful. Nico also taught at the Agrarian School in Axel.

Suus died on September 9, 1966, at the age of 53. After her death, Nico sold the blacksmith shop and lived alone for a while. Because his health was deteriorating, he moved in with his daughter, Riet, in Terneuzen in Zeeland Flanders. The family built a larger home for themselves and Nico on property in nearby Zaamslag. Nico lived in this house until his death on January 11, 1982 after a long illness. His daughter Riet said, *"The 13 year period while father lived with us were very beautiful years for our family. Although father was quite ill, he never complained and showed much care for his grandchildren and us."*

Nico received both American and English decorations. Because he also helped airmen of the Commonwealth, Nico became an honorary member of the Royal Air Forces Escaping Society in 1946. Later in life, he wrote about his war experiences. These are included in this book. Before he could write about the crash of Feathered Injun, Nico died. When the Resistance Memorial Cross was awarded, the government forgot to give a posthumous cross to Nico. His son, Sjaak, protested and after some debate, received his father's award from Prince Bernhard.

Ko van't Westeinde and his brother, Pier, owned the Westhof tree nursery until 1969. Ko remained active as a nurseryman and fruit grower. For many years Ko visited his cousin, Piet van den Dries, every Tuesday. Afterward, he went to the *Korenbeurs* (Grain Fair) where all the farmers in the region gathered. Ko and Nele often traveled with Katrien and Piet van den Dries. In 1971, he and his wife moved to Heinkenszand. Ko held many management positions during his lifetime, both in the profession and in civil society. One of them was serving as a member of the Heinkenszand town council. In 1974, Ko's sons took over his nursery. The nursery is still in business and is now owned by two grandsons. Nele died on October 16, 1980. In the early eighties, Ko was awarded the Resistance Memorial Cross, pinned on by Prince Bernhard. Ko moved to nursing home De Kraayert in Lewedorp in 1990. He died that same year on December 22, at the age of 85.

After the war, **Pier van't Westeinde** married Anna Gorris from the province Limburg. They had a daughter, José. At his wife's request, Pier changed his name to Piet. Pier is the Zeelandic abbreviation of Peter, but, in other parts of the country, *pier* could also mean *worm*. He owned the tree nursery with Ko until 1969. After that he remained active as a fruit grower. He was an avid hunter and participated in hunting parties into old age. Pier was awarded the Resistance Memorial Cross. He died on his farm Westhof, on September 26, 1994. He was 86 years old.

After the war **Kees Franse** continued working in the town hall, in his father's shop, and as a rope maker. After his father died, Kees inherited the shop. In 1959 he married Lena Weijler from Sint-Annaland. When they met, she worked as a nurse in a retirement home in Koudekerke on Walcheren, where she cared for Kees' mother. In time, the shop was expanded to a larger building in the Dorpsstraat. Because he wanted to focus on the shop, Kees stopped working for the mayor and making ropes. From all over Zeeland and other provinces, people came to Kees' shop for repairations on their red coral necklaces and metal ornaments that were part of the traditional dress. He volunteered for the BB Bescherming Bevolking (Protection Population), a civilian organization that alerted the populace in event of an attack or disaster during the Cold War. After a long time of illness, Kees died in Goes on April 26, 1983, at the age of 62.

In 1946, **André and Cor Evelein** moved to Rozenburg, in the province South Holland, where they had two more children. André became minister of the Dutch Reformed Church *Immanuel*. He also spent a year as a pastoral employee in the city of Delft in South Holland, where he cared for elderly. He was active in Scouting. With his wife, he was an honorary member of the *Vereniging Oud Rozenburg* (Association of Old Rozenburg) and was an active member of Amnesty International and *Kerk and Israël* (Church and Israel). André sang in the church choir and worked in his garden until he was 91 years old. He was also an avid photographer. He photographed changes in Rozenburg, from a farming village to an industrial area, and presented slideshows and lectures. He also created slideshows about the church in countries like France and Israel. His primary interest was his ministry where he worked seven days a week. Throughout his life, he led 9094 church services, including funerals. His last formal service was in 1997, at age 86. For his work in the resistance, André received the Resistance Memorial Cross. He was also made a Knight in the Order of Orange-Nassau for his community involvement. During the war, André and Cor's home was a safe haven for many illegals and evacuees. Risking arrest, imprisonment, and execution, they had no bad memories and did not suffer from PTSD. They enjoyed the heartwarming and inspiring solidarity in those difficult years. However, they consciously avoided vacationing in Germany. There were other beautiful countries to visit. They kept in touch with several of the people they assisted during the war especially Joe Sulkowski, called Uncle Joseph by the children. André died on April 12, 2004, at age 93. Cor died on February 9, 2006 at the age of 87. The rectory in 's-Heer Abtskerke, a building dating from 1858, is now on the list of Dutch national monuments.

Like the others who aided U.S. soldiers, **Kees Bek** received American and English certificates. He was also awarded the Medal of Honor in Silver, attached to the Order of Orange-Nassau, and the Resistance Memorial Cross. After the war, the family moved to Zeelandic Flanders.

Adriana his wife died in 1981 at age 81. Kees died in Terneuzen on June 6, 1987, at age 88. Their daughter Natalie, died in 2009 at age 82.

Rienbouw van Iwaarden received American and English certificates for helping Joe Sulkowski. Joe was so grateful that, during a leave trip to Zeeland, he gave Rienbouw an expensive watch. On November 10, 1983, Rienbouw van Iwaarden received the Resistance Memorial Cross pinned on by Prince Bernhard in the Koorkerk (church) of Middelburg. People protested when he received the cross, because real resistance members like Nico van Biezen and Pier 't Westeinde were passed over. According to them, Rienbouw van Iwaarden was initially classified as pro-German, because his brother was an important member of the NSB and he was friendly with the billeted Germans. Not until September 1944, when the Germans were losing, did Rienbouw commit an act of resistance by informing the Group Griep about Joe, instead of the Germans. Even though their frustration was understandable, Rienbouw van Iwaarden risked his life and his family's lives to hide the American bombardier for several days. On May 13, 1985, Rienbouw van Iwaarden and Ploo celebrated their sixty-years of marriage at the Helenahoeve. After he had lived on the same farm for 85 years, Rienbouw and Ploo moved to an apartment in Goes. There, at the age of 88 years, Ploo died on April 3, 1986, Rienbouw van Iwaarden died at the age of 90 on July 22, 1990. His youngest daughter, Leny, still manages the Helenahoeve.

Lou Mes was reinstalled as mayor of Heinkenzand in November 1944. He held this position until June 1945. He was both a member of the Provincial Council of Zeeland and a member of the Executive Council of Zeeland (responsibilities included agriculture, utilities and ports) from 1946 until 1966. From October 1946 to July 1948, he was a member of the Dutch House of Representatives. After the death of A.F.Ch.de Casembroot, Lou spent six months as Acting Commissioner of the Queen in Zeeland. He also held positions with political parties *Rooms-katholieke Staatspartij* (Roman Catholic State Party - *RKSP*) and the *Katholieke Volkspartij* (Catholic People's Party - *KVP*). In April 1951, he was appointed a Knight of the Order of the Dutch Lion. He was also appointed by the Vatican to Knight of the Order of St. Gregory the Great and by the Kingdom of Belgium to Commander of the Order of Leopold II. In 1966, he received the Zeeland Culture Prize for his commitment to Dutch culture. Lou died in Middelburg on September 11, 1974, at the age of 75.

The Crew

On Thursday, March 7, 1946, the coffins containing the bodies of Gene Kieras and Ed Yensho were excavated at the General Cemetery in Heinkenszand. Many villagers were present to pay homage. According to the U.S. Army, the bodies were moved to the military cemetery in Margraten, Limburg to verify their identity. Then they were transported to temporary military cemeteries. Ed's remains were buried in Luxembourg and Gene's remains in Belgium, both in September or October 1946.

In 1947, the families of the deceased received a pamphlet called *Disposition of World War II Armed Forces Dead*. In this pamphlet the next of kin were informed of the options for permanent burial:

Option 1: The remains be interred in a permanent American military cemetery overseas.

Option 2: The remains be returned to the United States, or any possession or territory thereof, for interment by next of kin in a private cemetery.

Option 3: The remains be shipped within, or returned to a foreign country, the homeland of the deceased or next of kind, for interment by next of kin in a private cemetery.

Option 4: The remains be returned to the United States for final interment in a national cemetery.

Ed's father Andrew Yensho notified the Army that he wanted an overseas burial for his son. The remains of **Ed Yensho** were permanently interred at the Luxembourg American Cemetery in Hamm, Luxembourg in Plot I, Row 4, Grave 23. He was posthumously awarded the Air Medal with Oak Leaf Cluster and the Purple Heart, for those who were wounded or killed in battle. The text on the cross that marks his grave:

EDWARD YENSHO
PVT 2 AIR CARGO DET
OHIO SEPT 18 1944

The remains of **Gene Kieras** were permanently interred at the Ardennes American Cemetery in Neupré, Belgium in Plot D, Row 21, Grave 11. He was posthumously awarded the Air Medal with Oak Leaf Cluster. Because Gene's death was considered a parachute accident, he was not eligible for the Purple Heart. The text on the cross that marks his grave:

EUGENE J. KIERAS
T SGT 579 BOMB SQ 392 BOMB GP (H)
ILLINOIS SEPT 18 1944

Morton Baker was buried at the Cambridge American Cemetery in Cambridge, England. He was posthumously awarded the Air Medal with three Oak Leaf Clusters and the Purple Heart. Morton's body rests in Plot F, Row 2, Grave 142. The text on the Star of David that marks his grave:

MORTON BAKER
T SGT 392 BOMB GP
N.Y. MAR 22 1945

In 1946, **Jim Gerow** studied Mechanical Engineering at the University of Buffalo. To help pay for his education, he received the G. I. Bill, a government-paid scholarship for ex-servicemen. He graduated in 1949. He worked for the E. I. duPont Company, a world famous company specializing in the manufacture of plastics. DuPont has also manufactured flak vests, parachutes, and tires for the U.S. Army. Jim worked for DuPont in Buffalo, NY, and in Tennessee, New York, Chattanooga, Texas and Wilmington Delaware. Jim worked for DuPont for 32 years until his retirement. Jim and Delphine had three children, all born in Tennessee. They moved into an apartment in Palm Harbor, Florida in 1993.

When my book was published in Dutch, I sent copies to several families of the crew. In January 2013, Delphine wrote:

Dear Mark,

What a joy to receive your outstanding book in the mail yesterday. What a wonderful accomplishment and tribute to the men that were involved, both airmen and members of the underground army. Jim passed away on December 21, 2011 at age 90, after a relatively short illness. He would have been proud of your book. We are very grateful to you for sending us the copy of your book for our family.

Most sincerely,

Delphine Gerow.

Little is known about the family of **Fred Vallarelli**. Fred married Helen after the war and he died in July 1990, in New York, at the age of 71.

In 1980, he composed and owned the rights to two songs: *Suddenly* and *God Only Knows*.

Before the war **Dave Grandon** worked as an apprentice printer for his father's newspaper, The Daily Post-Tribune. His career was interrupted when he joined the army. In 1947, Dave moved to Sterling. His father sold The Daily Post-Tribune and now worked as editor of The Daily Gazette in Sterling. Dave held several jobs with the Gazette. When his father died in 1968, he became the editor. Dave married twice and had five children. After working 39 years for the Gazette, Dave died of a heart attack on March 16, 1986. Dave was 63 years old.

After the liberation, **Joe Sulkowski** was transferred home for Rest and Rehabilitation. He was still on leave when Germany surrendered. He expected to be sent to the Pacific area where the war against Japan was still raging, but Japan capitulated before he received his orders. Joe ended up at the air depot in Erding, Germany as part of the Allied occupation forces. His job was to investigate accidents caused by U.S. military personnel and handle civilian claims.

While stationed in Erding, Joe traveled freely throughout Europe while on leave. In Germany, he visited and photographed an abandoned concentration camp and witnessed a trial of Nazi leaders at the war crimes tribunal in Nuremberg. Joe visited Piet van den Dries in Goes and other resistance men several times. Joe drove to the Netherlands in a 1936 Adler Trumpf car, confiscated from the German army. He always claimed this was the best car he had ever driven. He once travelled to Zeeland on a military Harley Davidson, allthough Joe didn't have a driver's license. It appears that Joe did not enjoy this trip very much, because his son, John, told me that his father did not like motorcycles.

Joe often expressed his gratitude by giving gifts. For example, Piet van den Dries received two uniform emblems and later USAF Navigator Wings. The brothers Van 't Westeinde were gifted his Colt 45, a printed topographic map on silk, and a small compass that could be hidden in a button. As thanks for his commitment, André Evelein received an army radio with Joe's name stamped on it. There were still large shortages in Zeeland and Joe tried to help his Zeeland friends as much as possible. He wanted to give them money, but they would only accept items on the list of critical supplies. Like the packages from La Salle, everything was distributed in Heinkenszand.

In 1946, in the middle of his military service, Joe had to return home to care for his mother. Joe's brother, Vincent, came back from the Pacific carrying malaria without knowing it and infected his mother. After his mother recovered, Joe returned to Erding. On 18 September 1947, the United States Army Air Force (USAAF) converted to the United States Air Force (USAF). The USAF became an independent branch of the military, no longer under the command of the U.S. Army. Joe was still stationed in Germany and agreed to continue serving in the new Air Force.

Joe continued to travel throughout Europe and never seemed to get enough of it. He traveled to southern Germany and Switzerland and visited Czechoslovakia in February 1948, a few days before the Communists seized power. In the same year, when the Russians blocked the road, rail, and inland waterway connections to Berlin, the Americans and British created an airlift to supply Berlin. Joe was invited to help navigate a supply plane, a Gooney Bird C-47. The mission was to supply fuel and food to Berlin's Tempelhof Airport.

It is not certain when Joe left Germany, but in 1950 he was living in Denver, Colorado, and working on a large air base (Lowry Air Base) testing bombs. Around this time, the USAF, responding to the Korean War and the expansion of Russian influence in Europe, formed the Strategic Air Command (SAC), an organization involved in organizing and developing conventional and nuclear weapons capability. Because of his bombardier experience, Joe accepted an offer to move to SAC. After careful screening, he was sent to the Russian Language School in Fort Ord, California, where he received nine months of intensive training in the Russian language. The FBI questioned many of his neighbours about Joe's family and his reputation as part of his security clearance.

From 1954 to 1959 he flew as a Radar Navigator (the new term for bombardier) in the Convair B-36 Peacemaker. In May 1954, he married Martha Ann Marxen and moved to Limestone, Maine. In 1955, their son, John, was born. They moved to South Dakota in 1956. In 1959, Joe and his crew switched to the Boeing B-52 Stratofortress, a heavy, long-range nuclear or conventional weapons bomber, and transferred to Texas. Although the crew was not the first to fly this aircraft, they were probably one of the best. In 1959, they broke the world speed record and received special recognition. Joe was promoted to lieutenant colonel in 1961 and was transferred to the job of squadron intelligence officer. In 1964, after 22 years in the armed forces, he asked for a compassionate discharge in 1964. Joe's father-in-law died and his mother-in-law asked Joe to lead the family insurance business. Joe was honorably discharged and his family moved to Kansas City. After managing the insurance business for a short time, he convinced his mother-in-law to sell it, because company profits failed to provide for two families. Joe then worked for various companies, before he got a job with the U.S. Postal Service, where he worked until his retirement in 1984. The following year, Joe's wife, Martha, died.

His brother Ted wrote: *"After the funeral, Joe and I had several long conversations. This was the first time he told me that he frequently suffered from flashbacks and nightmares about events during the war. He was normally a moderate drinker, but alcohol took a significant toll. For this he received counseling for a time, and then he finally stopped drinking. During that time, we spoke on the phone every week. He said he still had nightmares. When he had a regularly recurring dream: he would wake up because he thought that German soldiers came in his bedroom."*

Like many of his comrades, Joe showed signs of PTSD. He lived alone until he suffered a stroke when his son John transferred him to South Carolina. Joe died on April 30, 2003, at age 85, and was buried beside his wife, two brothers and three sisters.

On November 2, 1944, **Loyce Ely** returned to the U.S. in a B-17. He brought two pairs of clogs home with him, the pair he wore while cycling to his hiding place and a pair for a child. On January 12, 1945, he was hospitalized at Santa Ana Air Base in California for observation and treatment. According to his wife Margaret, it was due to problems of psychological nature. After the traumatic crash, Ely only flew if necessary and he never flew a mission again. After his hospitalization, Ely trained as a gunner instructor at the AAF Central School for Flexible Gunnery at Laredo Army Air Field in Texas, as part of the 2126th Army Air Forces Base Unit. After successful training as a marksman, he was transferred to the 4th Air Force, 420th Army Air Force Base Unit, at March Field Air Force Base in California, to train gunner recruits. In the fall of 1945, Loyce met his future wife, Margaret. She served as a corporal in the Air Force. She drove a truck that brought crews to their aircraft. Ely was honorably discharged from the army on October 22, 1945. He and Margaret married on Christmas Day. At the end of 1946, Ely, Margaret and their firstborn daughter Toni moved to North Dakota, where Ely became a farmer. The couple eventually had twelve children. They moved to Greybull, Wyoming in 1971 because Ely liked to hunt in the Big Horn Mountains near Greybull. According to his daughter, Tina, her father, like his comrades, suffered from PTSD, manifested in nightmares and overreaction to loud noises. For many years after the war, especially around the Christmas season, Ely and Margaret corresponded with Nathalie, the daughter of Kees Bek, who brought him from the tree nursery to 's-Heer Abtskerke. After Ely died on March 26, 2005, at the age of 87, Margaret continued this contact until Nathalie passed away in 2009.

After the war, **Ben Brink** and his wife, Marge, moved to New York, where Ben earned a living as a bartender at a club and Marge worked as a saleswoman in a factory. They had one daughter, Penny. Ben later joined the Air Force again and worked as an instructor at Wright Patterson Air Force Base in Dayton, Ohio. They often returned to Pennsylvania to hunt with friends in the mountains around Irvona. After discharge from the Air Force, Ben worked for two years for Boeing Aircraft as an aircraft mechanic. While working for Boeing, he lived in an apartment in Philadelphia during the week and traveled home over the weekend to be with his wife and his daughter. Around this time Ben received an acre of land from his father, Samuel. Ben and his family moved to Irvona, built a house on his newly acquired land, and became the gamekeeper for Clearfield County. He loved fishing, hunting, and camping in the wild. He was an active member of the Association of Veterans of Foreign Wars (VFW) and the local Moose Club, a charitable organization. Ben loved motorcycling and was a member of the Motor Cycle Squad. Riding back from an event with his nephew, Russ, he rode an old refurbished BMW. They had an accident and both were seriously injured. Ben never rode a motorbike again. He died on November 20, 1998. He was 79 years old.

Having survived the Black March, **Normand (Frenchy) Hebert** returned home to his wife, Juanita, in America. They had a daughter named Floretta. Their marriage did not survive.

After his divorce from Juanita in the late 1950s, Normand married an Irish immigrant named Christine Byrne, in the early 60s. Normand and Christine had three children: Sean, who died in his second year, Michele, and Brian. Michele was born in Liberty, New York and she assumed her parents were married there, too. The family moved constantly, always remaining close to a military base. She can remember her father was called Frenchy. He walked with slight limp, a result of the broken ankle he sustained during his jump from the Feathered Injun which never healed properly. The family lived in Roswell, New Mexico, Phoenix, Arizona, and Colorado Springs, Colorado.

Christine told her daughter that two men came to the door asking for Normand. Michele was only four, and Christine was pregnant with Brian. Normand sent everyone to another room. Christine heard one of the men ask if *"they knew it too,"* to which Normand replied. *"No, and I want to keep it that way."*

The family never stayed in one place very long. They even lived out of their car and stayed in homeless shelters. When Michele was 7 or 8 years old, her father suddenly disappeared. Christine reported him to the police as missing. A few months later she was told the government had declared him officially dead and his file was labeled as secret.

In 2010, Michele discovered her father was dead. Four days before he would have been 85, he died of colon cancer in a Veteran Administration hospice and was buried in Casper, Wyoming. A friend of Normand's reported that someone, aged about 55 years, was present at the burial, who claimed he was a son of Normand. It is a sad story with strange twists. Due to his war experiences, Michele thought it likely that his behavior was partly caused by PTSD, a result of the horrors of the crash, his arrest, his imprisonment in Stalag IV and the Black March.

Bob Hebert, Normand's nephew, stated the last time the family saw his uncle was at the funeral of his grandfather, J. Arthur Hebert, in 1958. By the time his grandmother, Laura, died in 1977 no one knew where Normand was or even if he were alive.

However, one day in the early 1960s, Normand paid a surprise visit to his brother, Bertrand, Bob's father in Pittsfield, MA. Normand was working at Grossingers Resort near the Catskill Mountains in New York State. This was just before Normand planned to marry Christine. In the late 80s, Bob was stationed at Peterson AFB in Colorado Springs at Air Force Space Command. Prior to that assignment, he was also a member of the 8th Air Force like his uncle, only this time during the Vietnam War era. His father, Bertrand died in April 1992, just a few months before Bob planned to retire from the Air Force in August. He was attending a luncheon for a friend at the Citadel Mall in Colorado Springs. He looked up and saw a man limp by. The resemblance to his father was striking. One of his friends asked Bob if he were ill because he looked like he had seen a ghost. Bob told him he thought he saw his father walk by. Bob tried to find the man, but he had already disappeared into the crowd. It was a haunting incident. Later, Bob learned that Normand had been living in Colorado Springs.

After his retirement, Bob revived an interest in genealogy and began extensive research on his family. He focused on Normand, since he knew little about him. His research included the web pages of the 392nd Bomb Group Memorial Association. Annette Tison, the association's historian, put me in contact with Bob. He told me that in July 2009 he received an email from an unknown person who saw some of his research posted on Ancestry.com and suggested they may be related. It turned out to be his cousin, Michele, Normand's daughter who was trying to find family connections. Normand never told her that he had grown up with eight siblings. Bob wrote Michele that they should talk. If she were willing to give him her phone number, he would call her. You can imagine his surprise when he saw that the area code for her phone number was the same as his and they both lived in Colorado Springs. Neither of them knew the other existed, let alone lived in the same city. Michele has now met Bob's wife, Paula, and their three sons and wives. She has also met Bob's older brother Richard and his wife, Susan, and has made contact with Helen Carpenter, a cousin from Woonsocket, RI, where Normand grew up in.

Bob told me Michele has a strong resemblance to Normand's mother, their grandmother. Much of the above occurred when I was writing my Dutch version of the book. Since then Bob had put Michele in touch with me. Sometimes a sad story has a happy ending. Michele and Bob have established their family ties and have become friends.

After the war, **Elton Southwell** worked at the Cudahay meat processing company in Omaha. On May 14, 1946, he married, Darlene Ruzicka, and became a member of the First Presbyterian Church in Lyons, NE. Elton and Darlene had three children. He moved to Lyons to work at Holmquist, a grain elevator and feed supplier, where Elton's father was manager. Elton and his father worked together for many years. When his father retired, Elton succeeded him as manager of the company. Elton worked nearly 42 years for Holmquist until his retirement in 1987. He was a member of the volunteer fire department, a member of the local rescue team, and was one of the first ambulance drivers in their area. Elton spent 19 years as president of the Lyons School Board and was involved in numerous other local organizations. He was commander of the Veterans of Foreign Wars (VFW) and was a member of the organization of ex-prisoners in the POW-chapter of Omaha. In the last years of his life, Elton suffered from chronic lung disease, COPD, and was continuously administered oxygen. He died on Friday morning, July 26, 2002, in Oakland Memorial Hospital at the age of 79. According to his wife and children, he never wanted to talk about the war, but he decided to write his war story for them after he became ill. Elton's story is included in this book.

After the war, **Gene Ely**, brother of Loyce Ely, became the deputy-sheriff in Corcoran, California, until his retirement. He married Margaret and they had two children. Gene kept in contact with my grandfather for years and visited him in the 70s. He died on February 27, 1995, at the age of 74.

The **Crusaders** continued flying combat missions from Wendling Air Base through April 1945 and cargo missions until early May. After these missions the mechanics readied bombers to fly back to the US in June.

The unit was disbanded in September of that year. The Crusaders flew 285 combat missions during the war, with 1443 aviators lost through injury, captivity, or death. Seven-hundred and forty-seven airmen were killed in action and 184 aircraft were lost.

After the Americans left **USAAF station 118 at Wendling**, the base was transferred to the RAF. The RAF used it until November 22, 1961. From 1960 to 1964, USAF used it as a radio facility before it was closed and sold in 1964. After this, the runway of the airfield became a turkey farm. Most of the buildings and hardstands have been removed, but some are still there. A granite obelisk monument is located near the former airfield, to commemorate the fallen of the 392nd Bomb Group. The text on the memorial:

The 392nd Bomb Group
8th Air Force US Army Air Forces Station 118 Wendling
in honour of 747 airmen who gave their lives
and all who served with them at this base July 1943 to June 1945

During WWII the **8th Air Force** lost approximately 26,000 airmen. In 1946, it was merged with Strategic Air Command (SAC). The 8th Air Force is still in operation, flying the B-2A Spirit and the B-52 Stratofortress.

After the war, the **B-24 Liberator** was used as a cargo plane, but was eventually replaced with more modern aircraft. Of the 18,482 Liberators manufactured only about 17 complete planes still exist. At present, there are only two flying: the B-24J, named *Witchcraft*, in Massachusetts and the B-24A, named *Diamond Lil*, in Texas.

1: Wim Abeleven, a well-known artist, illustrator, author, theater director and designer of book covers.
2: A post-traumatic stress disorder (PTSD) is a mental disorder resulting from severe stressful situations in which there is a threat to life, serious injury, or a threat to the physical integrity. The symptoms include re-experiencing (nightmares and flashbacks), avoidance of reminders or switching them out emotionally, severe irritability and sleep disturbances, extreme stress due to certain stimuli, irritation and severe shock reactions.

An article in the Daily Post-Tribune from La Salle, Illinois, about Piet van den Dries. (173)

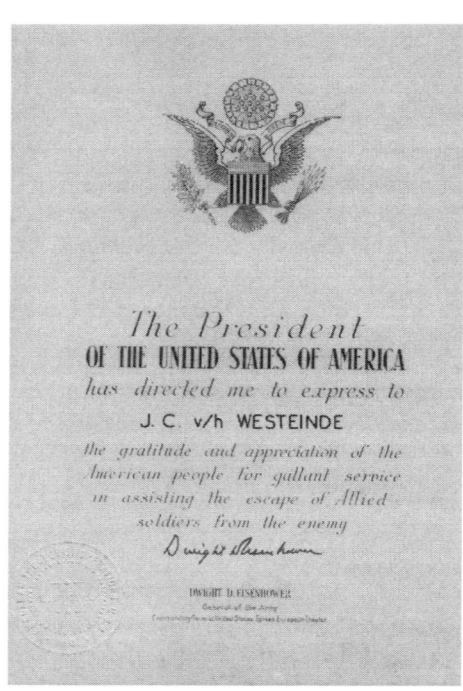

The American certificate Ko van 't Westeinde received. (175)

Joe Sulkowski while visiting Piet's family in Goes. On the grass is one of the propellers of the Feathered Injun. (174)

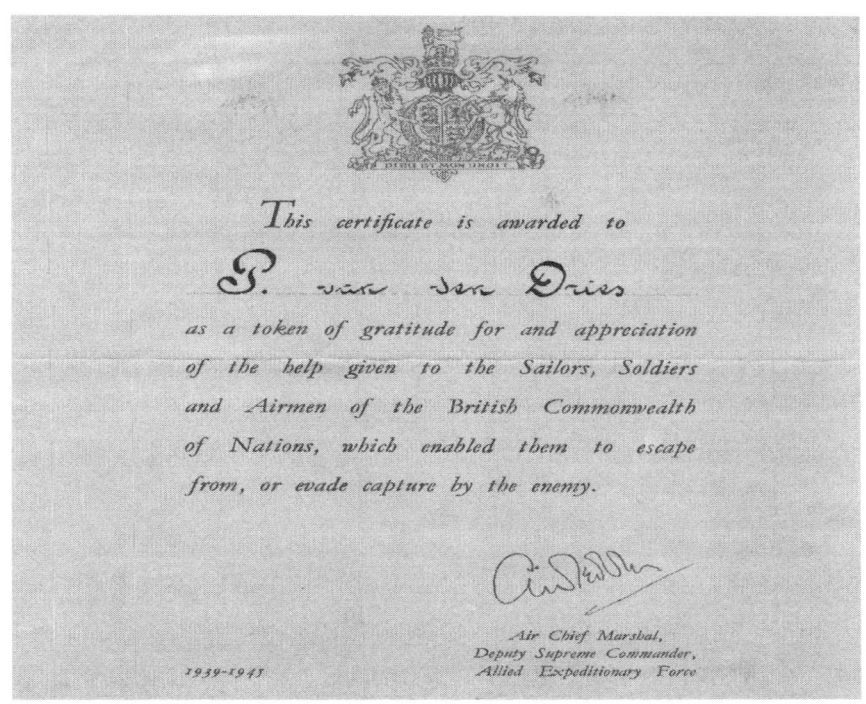

The British certificate that Piet van den Dries received. (176)

Me with my grandparents, Katrien and Piet, at their house in Goes. (177)

UNITED STATES MISSION TO THE UNITED NATIONS

2 PARK AVENUE
NEW YORK 16, N.Y.
MUrray Hill 3-6810

February 3, 1949

Dear Mr. van den Dries:

It is distressing to learn that you wish to return your well-earned decoration from our late President, since the action of my government on the Indonesian problem in no way lessens or denies our gratitude to you and your countrymen for your gallantry in the European war.

Rather than attempt to restate my government's position in a short letter, I am enclosing texts of two statements before the Security Council which go over the history of the Indonesian problem in the United Nations and outline the reasons for the position my government has taken in the Security Council.

The Resolution submitted jointly by the Representatives of China, Norway, Cuba and the U.S.A. specifically acknowledges the gestures made by the government of the Netherlands towards the establishment of a just peace in the Indonesian Republic but the Council, "conscious of its primary responsibility for the maintenance of international peace and security, and in order that the rights, claims and position of the parties may not be prejudiced by the use of force," agreed that it was essential to name the specific steps required to bring this about.

It is my hope and the hope of my colleagues that the conciliation Commission (created under the Resolution of January 28, 1949) will be able to achieve with the cooperation of the Dutch and Indonesian leaders, a satisfactory solution to the serious problem in Indonesia.

In view

Mr. P. J. Van den Dries
   Westsingel P.1
      Goes. (Z)
         Holland

A part of the letter from Philip C. Jessup to Piet van den Dries. (178)

Piet and Katrien celebrating their 45-year anniversary in 1981. (179)

The plaque of Kees Griep. (182)

Kees Griep smokes his pipe and reads the novel *The Door Between* by Ellery Queen. (180)

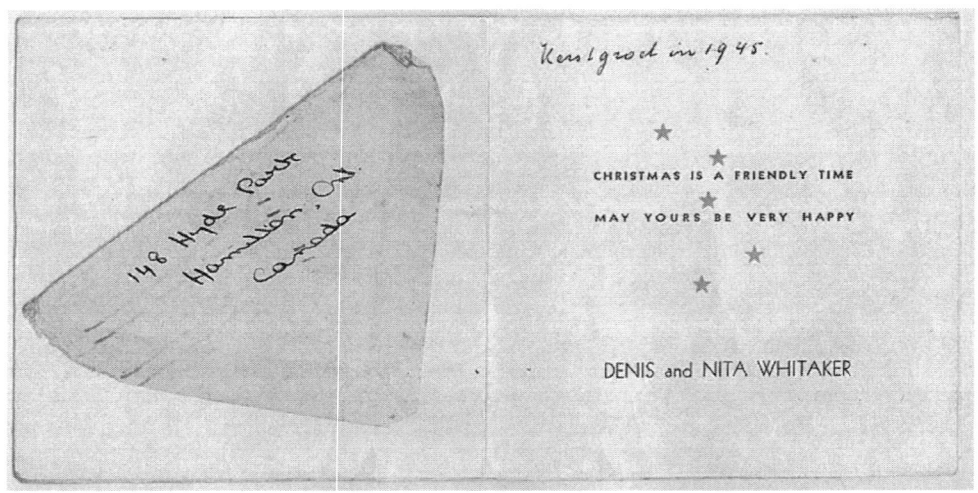

A Christmas card from Lt. Col. Whitaker to the Griep family, with his address in Canada. (181)

Kees Griep in 1969. (183)

Nico and Suus van Biezen with a granddaughter. (184)

Nico van Biezen at the marriage of his son Sjaak. (185)

Ko van 't Westeinde receives the Resistance Memorial Cross from Prince Bernhard in 1984. (186)

Pier van 't Westeinde and his cousin Piet van den Dries. (187)

André Evelein in 2000 with his decorations. Left: the knighthood. Right: the Resistance Memorial Cross. (188)

Cor and André in 2001. (189)

Rienbouw van Iwaarden receives the Resistance Memorial Cross from Prince Bernhard. (190)

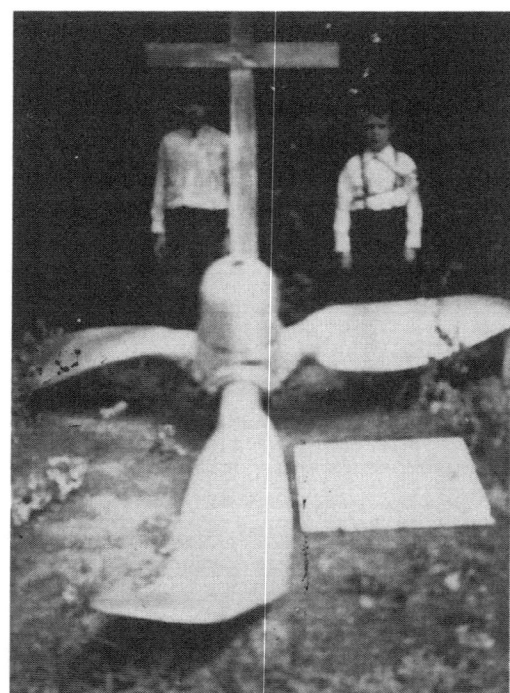

One of the propellers of the Feathered Injun placed on the grave of Ed and Gene in Heinkenszand. The two boys are Piet and Martien, both sons of Ko van 't Westeinde. (191)

The grave of Ed Yensho on the Luxembourg American Cemetery. (192)

The grave of Gene Kieras at the Ardennes American Cemetery. (193)

The grave of Morton Baker at the Cambridge American Cemetery. (194)

An article on Dave Grandon's death in his own newspaper The Daily Gazette. (195)

Joe Sulkowski visits the Evelein family. (196)

Joe visits Piet and his family in Goes. (197)

Peter van den Dries on Joe's 42WLA Harley Davidson. (198)

The radio that Joe gave to the Evelein family. (199)   The USAAF patch that Joe gave to Piet. (200)

Mayor Joe Sulkowski in a B-52 Stratofortress in 1962. (201)

Lieutenant Colonel Joseph Sulkowski when he retired from the military in June 1964. The second medal on the left is the Purple Heart, which he received for his broken ankle after bailing out of the Feathered Injun. (202)

Joe's wings and decorations. (203)

Ely's wife Margaret at the March Field Air Force Base in California. (204)

A collection of Ely's wings and decorations. (205)

Ely's Honorable Discharge from the Army. (204a)

Two brothers: Gene Ely and Loyce Ely in 1974. (206)

Ely at old age. (207)

Ely and his wife Margaret in November 2004 at a Support our Troops Rally. (208)

The grave of Ely at the Donald J. Ruhl Memorial cemetery in Greybull. (209)

The house that Ben Brink built in Irvona. (210)

Ben in later life. (211)

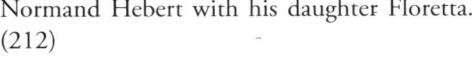

Normand Hebert with his daughter Floretta. (212)

Elton Southwell at Memorial Day in 1995, where he received a Community Americanism Award for WWII POWs, given by the Veterans of Foreign Wars and American Legion Post. (213)

Elton Southwell in 1994. (214)

The monument for the fallen of the 392nd BG. (214a)

Chapter 21

Traces of The Past

Most of the mangled Feathered Injun was taken to the local scrapheap but several fragments have been preserved.

On a photo in my grandfather's file, one can see two bent propellers, the rim of a wheel, three machine guns, and an ammunition belt in a garden on the Westhof farm. Later, one of these propellers was placed on the graves of Gene Kieras and Ed Yensho at Heinkenszand. After their reburial, this propeller was returned to the Westhof farm, where it was placed in the garden with the machine guns. One of the machine guns was later stolen. After that, Pier hung the other two guns in his barn. In September 2002, the propeller and machine guns were transferred to the *Bevrijdingsmuseum Zeeland* (Liberation Museum Zeeland) in Nieuwdorp in South Beveland for display in the forecourt of the museum. I designed the forecourt information board in both Dutch and English that informs the visitors about the Feathered Injun. It stands before these three relics. The fate of the ammo belt and the wheel rim is unknown.

In appreciation for his efforts, Piet van den Dries was given one of the two propellers in 1945, which he placed on his lawn at the Westsingel in Goes. In the early seventies, he sold the house, and moved with his wife to an apartment. After they moved, the house would be demolished. Because he could not store the propeller in the small apartment, Piet tried unsuccessfully to find another home for the prop. Nobody was interested. Unfortunately, the propeller ended up on the scrapheap.

In 1987, Jan van Huuksloot, member of the Wings to Victory[1] foundation, excavated a third propeller from the Feathered Injun. He found it at a depth of two meters in the orchard at the Brilletjes where the bomber crashed. Pier van 't Westeinde was present and helped with the digging. The propeller was restored by Willem Visser and is on exhibit at the Midden-Zeeland Airport.

Years later, residents unearthed a landing gear cylinder under a hedge in the orchard.

Jan Minnaard, son of the Heinkenszand baker, is still in possession of the parachute cloth from the Feathered Injun, found by his father.

On October 16, 2010, accompanied by Willem Visser, Marcel van Genderen, my wife Jacqueline, Piet van 't Westeinde, members of the foundation Wings to Victory, the foundation Aircraft Recovery Group 1940 - 1945, and others, I sought to locate other remnants of the Feathered Injun using metal detectors. Willem put up an old army tent where I talked with Piet van 't Westeinde and Sjaak van Biezen, both sons of the Group Griep resistance fighters. According to the current owner of the Brilletjes, the pond was previously dredged. The mud from the dredging was deposited next to the pond. Most of the artifacts were found in this dried layer. The most interesting artifacts were a rusted Browning 50 caliber machine gun, a mangled ammunition belt, and a metal plate with a serial number. In addition, we found many 50 caliber machine gun bullets, cylinder parts, other engine parts, and green and gray airframe fragments. On two subsequent searches, we found additional engine parts, a spark plug, shards of Plexiglas and Bakelite, and more bullets.

On Wednesday, July 13, 2011, I was pleased to guide Tina Ely, daughter of Loyce Ely, and her husband, Earl Miller, on a tour through South Beveland. Tina and Earl live in the state of Wyoming and were vacationing in the Netherlands and France. On the way from Amersfoort to Zeeland, I showed them the Vlake Bridge, bombed by Tina's father and his crew during their first mission. In the Midden-Zeeland Airport restaurant, they met the sons and daughters of the men who helped her father, Piet and Martien van 't Westeinde (Martien happened to be visiting from Australia), Sjaak van Biezen, Hanneke Evelein, Koos and Leny van Iwaarden, and my father, Peter van den Dries. We toured the Wings to Victory museum, where Tina saw the fragments we discovered the previous year. While admiring the propeller, she was presented two parts of the Feathered Injun, a piece of the cylinder cleaned and prepared by Willem Visser and a piece left in the state in which we found it.

After visiting the airport, we rode in a 1942 American radio truck, a Dodge WC *Beep* that had served in Africa. We drove via the Ankervere Polder (where two Flak guns once stood) to the Helenahoeve. The two daughters of Rienbouw and Ploo van Iwaarden gave us a warm welcome and lunch. Koos and Leny showed us where Joe landed and where he hid in the small hayloft in the barn. Leaving Helenahoeve, Tina had a surprise at the Bevrijdingsmuseum Zeeland. She was asked to unveil the information board, which had been placed there before the propeller and two machineguns that morning. After a tour of the museum and a visit to the local clog maker, we left to show Tina the hiding place on the Westhof farm and the bomber crash site. One of the highlights of the day was a visit to the rectory in 's-Heer Abtskerke to view the little room where her father and Joe were hidden and the cellar where the refugees sought protection during the shelling of 's-Heer Abtskerke. This day ended with a fine dinner in the An Fong Chinese restaurant, formerly the forge of Nico and Suus van Biezen.

Two days before Tina's arrival, I received an email from Joe's son, John Sulkowski. I was stunned. He was going to visit Liège, Belgium on business and asked if we could meet. On Wednesday July 20, one week after the tour with Tina, Willem and I organized the same tour for John. Again we met many descendants of the resistance fighters. This time, Jim Evelein was present. Instead of visiting the clog maker, we walked through Heinkenszand and showed John the various homes of resistance members, the home of Mayor Mes, the route of the bomber, and the local cemetery, the temporary burial place of Ed and Gene. John Sulkowski was especially impressed with the hayloft in the Helenahoeve barn where his father hid. He found that all was still as it used to be. The pillow on which his father rested and the bottles from which he drank were still there, covered with 67 years of dust. As before, we ended this special day with dinner at the former forge of Nico van Biezen.

These two days were very special. They were also instructive, because more information surfaced. For Tina, John, and the others, it was a moving experience. Although most of us had never met, we all felt connected by an event that began 67 years before with ten young Americans and a handful of courageous Zeelanders.

In December 2012, my book, *Noodsein boven Zeeland* (Distress call over Zeeland) was published. I gave the first copy to my father, who played a major role in the development of the book. During my presentation at the Bevrijdingsmuseum Zeeland, with family members of the resistance men and other eyewitnesses present, I presented a copy to a member of the Borsele city council, the Heinkenszand municipality.

In July 2013, my family and I flew to the U.S. for our summer holiday. We visited Wyoming for a week. Tina Ely and her husband, Earl, welcomed us at the Cody Airport and drove us to their home in Greybull. They showed us their beautiful state as we visited interesting places like Yellowstone Park and Cody. Tina and Earl also took us to the Big Horn Mountains where Tina's father, Ely, used to hunt. We met many family members, including sons and daughters, grandsons and granddaughters of Ely. Tina introduced me to her mother, Margaret, in Basin and showed me Ely's grave in Greybull.

The following week we flew to Denver, Colorado, where Bob Hebert, Normand's nephew, met us and drove us to Colorado Springs. There we met Michele Hebert, Normand's daughter, Bob's wife, Paula, and their family and friends. They showed us their amazing mountain state as we visited Denver, Garden of the Gods, Pikes Peak, Seven Falls and other places. Bob served as a Major in the U.S. Air Force. He took us to the Air Force Academy in Colorado Springs, where we saw an A-10 Thunderbolt on display, a fighter which Bob helped design and develop.

Bob organized two museum presentations for me. The first was at the Pueblo Weisbrod Aircraft Museum in Pueblo, Colorado. This museum is located on the former Pueblo Army Air Base, where Gerow's crew trained and where the group photo for the book cover was shot. After an introduction by the Dutch/American Air Force veteran, Fred Daams, the audience listened to my story of the Feathered Injun. After the presentation, I displayed some artifacts, pieces of the bomber, original photos, documents, and newspaper clippings. I presented a copy of my book to the museum's president, Don Blehm. Michele Hebert donated a shadow box containing her father's medals and Bob Hebert presented a framed photo of Gerow's crew. Fred Daams lead us on a tour through the museum, and a special display of the B-24 Liberator. He also took us on an incredible railway ride through the Royal Gorge near his hometown, Cañon City.

A few days later, I gave another presentation to the National Museum of World War II Aviation in Colorado Springs, courtesy of Colonel James Stewart, USAF (Retired). James, a former F-15 fighter pilot and now Co-chairman and a founding director of the museum, showed us around the museum and the workshops where WWII aircraft are restored.

I have given many presentations with photos and maps throughout the Netherlands. The two most memorable were the presentations in two retirement homes on November 30, 2013. The first was in Heinkenszand, the second in nearby Lewedorp. Many eyewitnesses of the crash were present. Several recognized the displayed photos. They told me what they had seen and experienced when the burning bomber flew over their village. Most of them knew the resistance members very well and some of them were even related. It was a day of reminiscing and heartwarming encounters.

In April 2014, my family and I visited the graves of Gene Kieras and Ed Yensho in Belgium and Luxembourg for the second time (the first time was in 2010). That same month we also visited the grave of Morton Baker at the Cambridge American Cemetery in the U.K. A few years earlier, I picked up a little rock from the streets of Jerusalem, as a souvenir. Because I knew Morton was Jewish, I put the rock on the Star of David on his grave, instead of flowers, according to the Jewish tradition.

During our holiday in England we admired the B-24 Liberator *Dugan* with the markings of the 392nd BG at the Imperial War Museum at Duxford. We could not make a trip to England without visiting the former Wendling Air Base. Annette Tison of the 392nd Bomb Group Memorial Association got me in contact with the British director of the association, John Gilbert. John was born in Norwich. When he was four years old, his house was destroyed during a bombing raid. During the rest of the war his family lived in temporary house near Wendling Air Base. As a boy he saw a lot of airmen and aircraft. When the USAAF left Wendling, many of the buildings on the air base were converted into housing. John and his family lived a couple of years in the Wendling Officer's Mess. He spent most of his childhood there. In addition to a career in the British Army, he has been the guide for countless American veterans and their families visiting the remains of Wendling Air Base. He also visits schools to tell the children about WWII and Wendling Air Base.

We were the guests at the home of John, his wife Doris and son Adrian. After a good English breakfast, John showed us around the old base, which is currently occupied by several civilian companies. We saw what is left of the perimeter, the runway, headquarters, a building where the bombardiers used to practice with the Norden Bombsight, several mural paintings at the site of the former officer's mess, the Nissen huts and washrooms of Site 8 (where Gerow's crew was quartered), a large Nissen hut at Site 4 and much more. At the Wendling Village Hall, we viewed a large mural painting created by the artist, Craig Banwell, and several local schoolchildren. The painting depicts a formation of 392nd BG Liberators flying over the village. We visited the memorial for the 392nd BG near Wendling and also the one for the 466th BG at Attlebridge, because the Feathered Injun was on loan from the 466th BG to the 392nd BG. John also took me to the 2nd Air Division Memorial Library in Norwich. This library, with books and videos about WWII and the U.S., commemorates the special bond between the people of Norfolk and the airmen of the 2nd Air Division.

1:     A foundation with the aim of mapping out all the information about the air war over Zeeland during World War II. The foundation also operates a small museum on Midden-Zeeland Airport at Arnemuiden.

Parts of the Feathered Injun just after the liberation are displayed in a garden of the Westhof. Left and right there are two propellers, three M2 Browning machine guns, an ammunition belt draped over the guns, and a wheel rim. The men and the boys in the background are (L-R) Ko van 't Westeinde, a son of Ko, Ko's father Piertje, a son of Ko, Joe Sulkowski, Pier van 't Westeinde and Piet van den Dries. (215)

Three M2 Browning machine guns in the garden of the Westhof. (216)

Pier's daughter, José, with a propeller of the Feathered Injun and an inner part of another propeller at the Westhof. (217)

The transport of the propeller from the Westhof to the Bevrijdingsmuseum Zeeland. (218)

The propeller and two M2 Browning machine guns of the Feathered Injun displayed at the museum. (219)

Peter van den Dries with the propeller that his father had placed in his garden in Goes. (220)

Jan Huuksloot with the propeller he has excavated in 1987. (221)

Peter de Meester and Willem Visser with the found propeller. (222)

Eyewitness, the late Cor Mallekote, unveils the restored propeller in 2008. (223)

John Sulkowski admires the propeller of his father's bomber at Midden-Zeeland Airport. (224)

Piet van 't Westeinde (son of Ko) and Wessel and Morris Visser (sons of Willem) are digging for parts of the Feathered Injun. (225)

The excavated M2 Browning .50 machine gun. (226)

Willem Visser, me and Marcel van Genderen with an ammunition belt. (227)

Tina Ely unveils the information panel for the propeller and guns of her father's bomber. (228)

Hanneke Evelein and Tina Ely in the small room in the rectory. (229)

The second generation: (L-R) Martien van 't Westeinde, Piet van 't Westeinde, Koos van Iwaarden, Tina Ely, Peter van den Dries, Hanneke Evelein and Leny van Iwaarden. (230)

Leny van Iwaarden tells John Sulkowski where his father landed. (231)

John Sulkowski in the hayloft of the Helenahoeve, where his father hid. (232)

Jim Evelein, John Sulkowski and Hanneke Evelein in the small room in the rectory. (233

At the Bevrijdingsmuseum: (L-R) Koos van Iwaarden, Jim Evelein, Hanneke Evelein, John Sulkowski, Leny van Iwaarden, me, Sjaak van Biezen, Peter van den Dries and Piet van 't Westeinde. (234)

The information panel with the story of the Feathered Injun at the Bevrijdingsmuseum in Nieuwdorp. (235)

The portrait of Ely that I painted for Tina and Earl, Ely's B-24 cap and the flag that was used at his funeral at 2005. (237)

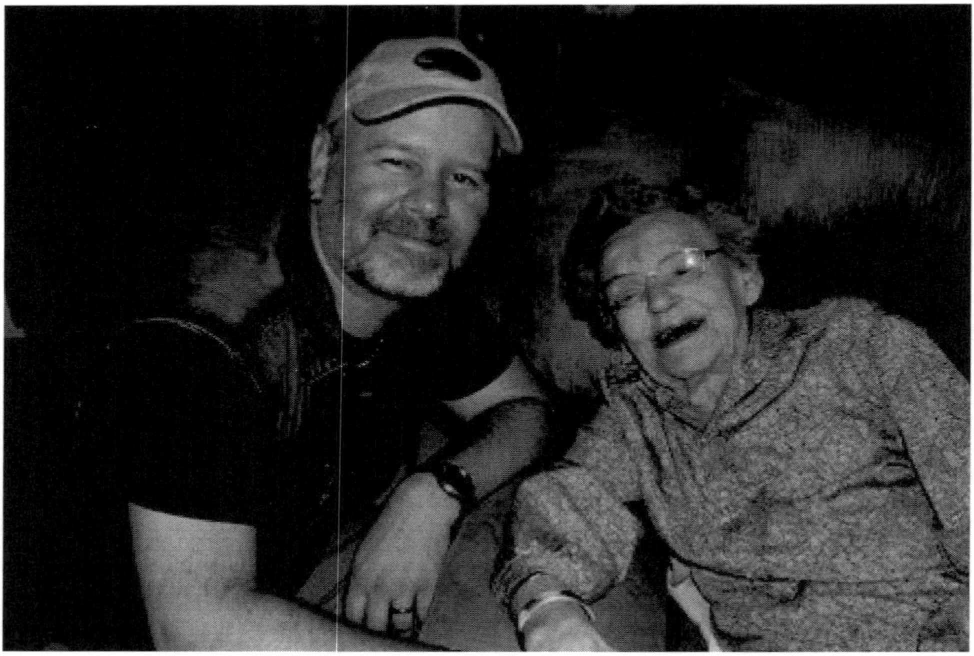

Visiting Margaret Ely at Basin, Wyoming. (239)

New book recounts plane crash over Netherlands

Greybull's Ely was on board

by marlys good

World War II: Sept. 18, 1944. An American B24 flying from England over the province of Zeeland in the Netherlands on its way to Germany was shot down and the 10 crewmen aboard the plane, that included Staff Sgt. L.E. Ely, a waist gunner, were forced to bail out. One of the crewman did not have a parachute so he jumped onto the back of his friend and they jumped together. However when the ripcord was pulled he could not hold on, and fell to his death. Another 19-year old was afraid to bail out. Sgt. Ely tried to persuade him but to no avail and Ely had jumped to save himself.

Of the eight survivors six were arrested by German soldiers, marched to Germany and placed in a prison camp (all six survived the camp).

Ely and 2nd Lt. Joe Sulkowski ended up with the Dutch Underground. The resistance group arranged for them to go to a safer place. (After teaching Ely to ride a bicycle) they disguised them as blacksmiths/farmers, got them through several roadblocks, and by a circuitous route took them to a "safe house" where they were hidden away until the province was liberated by the Canadian Army a month later.

Dutch author Mark van den Dries, grandson of a member of the resistance group, has recounted the story of the crash, the crew, his family and the connections in a book newly released in the Netherlands, "Noodsein Boven Zeeland," which translates as "Distress Call Over Zeeland."

Mark, his wife Jacqueline, and two of their three daughters were in Greybull this week visiting with Tina and Earl Miller and extended family of Ely.

Mark said, "As a kid I only knew my grandfather helped two Americans; I didn't know what happened. My oldest daughter asked me if I knew someone she could interview for a school paper about World War II. I gave her all of my grandfather's files; there were lots of documents and the police report about the crash. She got a good mark on the paper and that story was at our house so I read it. It was very interesting; I wanted to know

PHOTO BY NATHAN OSTER

Tina Ely of Greybull is shown here with Dutch author Mark van den Dries and his wife Jacqueline.

BOOK see page 2

Standard • 614 Greybull Ave., Greybull, WY 82426 • Contact us at: 765-4485

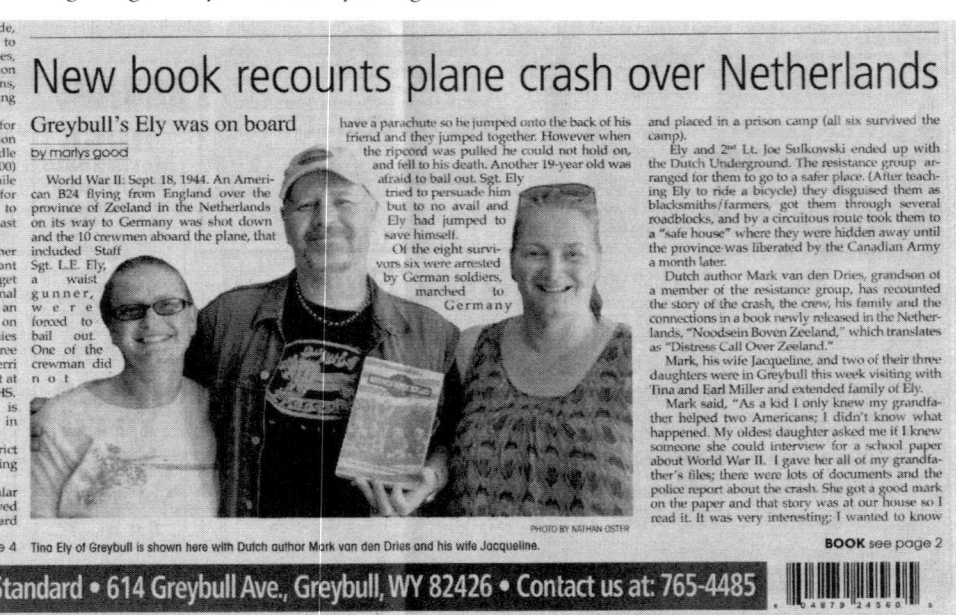

An article in the *Greybull Standard* about our visit to Wyoming. (240)

With Michele Hebert-Doyon and Bob Hebert at the Denver Museum of Nature and Science in Denver, Colorado. (241)

The Dutch/American Air Force veteran, Fred Daams introduces me before the presentation at the Pueblo Weisbrod Aircraft Museum in Pueblo, Colorado. (242)

The wings and medals that Normand's daughter Michele donated to the museum. The first medal on the left is the Purple Heart, received for his broken ankle after bailing out of the burning bomber. (243)

A flag of the 392nd Bomb Group at the museum in Pueblo. (244)

Bob Hebert giving a framed photo of Gerow's crew to retired fighter pilot Col. James Stewart of the National Museum of World War II Aviation in Colorado Springs, Colorado. (245)

The Pueblo Chieftain ▪ Pueblo, Colorado

PATRIOTISM

Story of WWII heroism told

Tale focuses on plane's crew that trained here

BY RYAN SEVERANCE
THE PUEBLO CHIEFTAIN

Mark van den Dries has a story to tell about his grandfather and a group of soldiers with whom he fought. And he wants everyone to remember their legacy.

Van den Dries was at the Pueblo Weisbrod Aircraft Museum on Thursday to give a presentation about his book, "Noodsein Boven Zeeland" ("Distress Call over Zeeland").

The book, written in Dutch, tells the story of a B-24 Liberator that crashed in the Dutch province of Zeeland while American were on a mission during World War II.

The crew aboard the plane did its training at the Pueblo Army Air Base during the early part of the 1940s.

About 40 people at the museum heard van den Dries talk about how a crew from Pueblo supported the war effort and he described the accounts of people they helped liberate.

On Sept. 18, 1944, a B-24 bomber carrying a platoon of airmen crashed during a mission over the Dutch town of Heinkenszand.

As van den Dries told it, civilians ran outside their homes to see the bomber flying toward their town and a number of parachutists bailing out.

The B-24 skimmed over buildings and crashed into a polder just outside the town.

Two airmen were killed and six others

> *The book is a tribute to my grandfather and the American boys who died fighting for their freedom.*
>
> MARK VAN DEN DRIES

were arrested by German soldiers.

Local resistance fighters, including van den Dries' grandfather, sprang into action by finding two displaced American airmen to help and managed to keep them out of the hands of occupying forces.

Van den Dries' book describes in great detail the team of American airmen who risked their lives on a foreign continent. It looks at their missions, the circumstances surrounding the fatal crash and their fate that followed there.

Van den Dries' grandfather died in 1992, but left an extensive file about the war.

"The book is a tribute to my grandfather and the American boys who died fighting for their freedom," van den Dries said.

Van den Dries gave a new copy of his book to the museum to keep and display.

"We are proud to have this here. What a tremendous story," Don Blehm, president of the museum, said.

ryans@chieftain.com

An article about my presentation in Pueblo in the *Pueblo Chieftain*. (246)

The mural painting at the Wendling Village Hall. (249)

John Gilbert and me in front of a Nissen hut at Site 8 on the former Wendling Air Base. (248)

The B-24 Liberator *Dugan* at the Imperial War Museum in Duxford, UK. (247)

Wendling Air Base in 2014. Just after takeoff the gunners of Wendling Air Base used to shoot a few rounds at this Butte, to warm up their guns. (247a)

Wendling Air Base in 2014. A Nissen hut on Site 8 and the farm that provided milk and eggs for the airmen. (247b)

Chapter 22

So, what's next?

I am writing this in May 2013. In September it will be seventy years since the Feathered Injun flew its last mission from Wendling Air Base. A stainless steel memorial plaque will be placed near the spot where Gene Kieras fell to his death. There are tentative plans to design a monument for Ed Yensho at the crash site and to commemorate the crash in Heinkenszand on September 20, 2014. Bob Hebert, his wife Paula, and John Sulkowski plan to be present. The remains of the barracks and camps in the Netherlands, Germany, and Poland, on the route Elton took are still there. I plan to visit them in the near future.

Photos of events like these are available on my Facebook page. There you will find additional information and photos concerning this period of WWII. When you *Like* the page you will get all the updates in English.

www.facebook.com/NoodseinBovenZeeland

Although I have done my best to ensure the historical accuracy of this event, I am aware it is neither complete nor flawless. If you have any additional information, relevant photos, corrections, or remarks concerning this history, please contact me by using my e-mail address: **featheredinjun@hotmail.com**, or by posting on my Facebook page.

During my research, writing, many trips and unforgettable encounters with people in Zeeland and the U.S., I often wondered what my grandfather would think of all these friendships that originated on that special September evening in 1944. I am certain he would love it.

Forever connected through history, friendship and gratitude,

Mark van den Dries, grandson of Piet van den Dries

A statue of an airman at the Cambridge American Cemetery by the American artist Wheeler Williams. (250

The crew and The helpers of Joe and Ely

The crew

Name: James (Jim) A. Gerow
Rank: 1/Lt
Army Serial Number: 0-817422
Position: Pilot
Year of birth: 1921
Residence 1944: Buffalo, New York
Marital status 1944: Married to Delphine
Profession after the war: Employed by E.I. du Pont Company
Year of death: 2011

Name: Frederick (Fred) J. Vallarelli
Rank: 2/Lt
Army Serial Number: 0-820858
Position: Co-pilot
Year of birth: 1919
Residence 1944: Rye, New York
Marital status 1944: Unmarried
Profession after the war: Unknown
Year of death: 1990

Name: David (Dave) P. Grandon
Rank: 2/Lt
Army Serial Number: 0-716421
Position: Navigator
Year of birth: 1923
Residence in 1944: La Salle, Illinois
Marital status 1944: Unmarried
Profession after the war: Publisher of *The Daily Gazette* from Sterling,

Illinois.
Year of death: 1986

Name: Joseph (Joe) T. Sulkowski
Rank: 2/Lt
Army Serial Number: O-717116
Position: Bombardier
Year of birth: 1918
Residence 1944: Everson, Pennsylvania
Marital status 1944: Unmarried
Profession after the war: Radio navigator and security officer at USAF, insurer, employed by US Postal Service.
Year of death: 2005

Name: Eugene (Gene) J. Kieras
Rank: T/Sgt
Army Serial Number: 36480578
Position: Engineer / top turret gunner
Year of birth:1924
Residence 1944: La Salle, Illinois
Marital status 1944: Unmarried
Profession after the war: -
Year of death: 1944

Name: Loyce (Ely) E. Ely
Rank: S/Sgt
Army Serial Number: 39685263
Position: Left waist gunner
Year of birth: 1918
Residence 1944: Corcoran, California
Marital status 1944: Unmarried
Profession after the war: Gunner instructor at USAAF, farmer in North Dakota and Wyoming
Year of death: 2005

Name: Morton Baker
Rank: T/Sgt
Army Serial Number: 32701560
Position: Radio operator
Year of birth: 1921

Residence 1944: Brooklyn, New York
Marital status 1944: Married to Mildred P. Hyman
Profession after the war: -
Year of death: 1945

Name: Elton E. Southwell
Rank: S/Sgt
Army Serial Number: 17077744
Position: Radio operator
Year of birth: 1922
Residence1944: Lyons, Nebraska
Marital status 1944: Unmarried
Profession after the war: Office employee at meat processor Cudahay's, manager of a grain elevator
Year of death: 2002

Name: Benjamin (Ben) E. Brink
Rank: S/Sgt
Army Serial Number: 6066148
Position: Right waist gunner
Year of birth: 1920
Residence1944: Clearfield, Pennsylvania
Marital status 1944: Unmarried
Profession after the war: Instructor at USAF, airplane mechanic at Boeing Aircraft, game warden at Clearfield County
Year of death: 1996

Name: Normand (Frenchy) B. Hebert
Rank: S/Sgt
Army Serial Number: 6905947
Position: Tail gunner
Year of birth: 1919
Residence 1944: Woonsocket, Rhode Island
Marital status 1944: Married to Juanita J. Dudley
Profession after the war: Initially employed with USAF
Year of death: 2004

Name: Edward (Ed) Yensho
Rank: S/Sgt
Army Serial Number: 35922650

Position: Transport technician
Year of birth: 1925
Residence 1944: Lakewood, Ohio
Marital status 1944: Unmarried
Profession after the war: -
Year of death: 1944

The helpers

Name: Cornelis (Kees) Griep
Profession: Family doctor, hospital director, controlling physician
Year of birth: 1896
Residence 1944: Heinkenszand
Marital status 1944: Married to Cornelia (Corrie) A. Duinker
Year of death: 1983

Name: Nicolaas (Nico) J. van Biezen
Profession: Blacksmith
Year of birth: 1912
Residence 1944: Heinkenszand
Marital status 1944: Married to Susanna (Suus) Geensen
Year of death: 1982

Name: Pieter (Piet) J. W. van den Dries
Profession: Head of a primary school
Year of birth: 1909
Residence 1944: Heinkenszand
Marital status 1944: Married to Katharina (Katrien) F. M. Schipper
Year of death: 1992

Name: Jacobus (Ko) C. van het Westeinde
Profession: Tree nurseryman
Year of birth: 1904
Residence 1944: 's-Heer Arendskerke
Marital status 1944: Married to Cornelia (Nele) G. Rijk
Year of death: 1990

Name: Pieter (Pier) C. van het Westeinde
Profession: Tree nurseryman
Year of birth: 1909
Residence 1944: 's-Heer Arendskerke
Marital status 1944: Unmarried
Year of death: 1994

Name: Casper (André) A. Evelein
Profession: Reverend at the Dutch Reformed Church.
Year of birth: 1911
Residence 1944: 's-Heer Abtskerke
Marital status 1944: Married to Adriana Cornelia (Cor) Westerveld
Year of death: 2004

Name: Cornelis I. Franse
Profession: Public Servant at the Town Hall/rope maker/juweler
Year of birth: 1920
Residence 1944: Heinkenszand
Marital status 1944: Unmarried
Year of death: 1983

Name: Marinus Bouwdewijn (Rienbouw) van Iwaarden
Profession: Farmer
Year of birth: 1900
Residence 1944: Heinkenszand
Marital status 1944: Married to Appolonia (Ploo) Lokerse
Year of death: 1990

Name: Cornelis (Kees) Bek
Profession: Farmer's hand
Year of birth: 1898
Residence 1944: Heinkenszand
Marital status 1944: Married to Adriana Mol
Year of death: 1987

A reconstruction of the nose art of the Feathered Injun. (251)

Acknowledgement

I want to thank everyone who has supported me on this historical journey. This book and its English translation could not have been published without the following contributors:

First of all I want to thank my True Liberator, Who was killed by the occupier during His own D-Day, but triumphed nonetheless so we can live in His liberty.

My grandfather, Piet van den Dries, who has preserved his memories for posterity in the form of photos, documents, newspaper clippings and stories. His memories form the basis for this book. I hope I have achieved what he planned to do himself.

I owe a lot of gratitude to my father, Peter van den Dries, who wrote down the memories of his father Piet for his granddaughter. After each visit to my parents, I came home with more pieces of the puzzle. I also thank my mother, Ineke, for the story of her parents and for renewing my father's memory. I also like to thank my father for editing my text and for his unstoppable enthusiasm.

Thanks to my dear wife, Jacqueline, for her patience and encouragement during this incredible journey. I thank her for joining me on my many trips, both in our country and abroad, for the necessary feedback and the editing of my text. I want to thank my daughters, Iona and Kyra, for their patience and encouragement and my daughter, Daphne, for the start of my project.

I am grateful to Willem Visser from Heinkenszand for his help, his enthusiasm, the interviews with the eyewitnesses in his hometown and for making the visits of both Tina and John unforgettable. I also thank him for helping me with the excavations and for reading my manuscript.

Without the work and enthusiasm of Bob Hebert and his wife, Paula, this translation would not been published. Thank you both for your effort and your hospitality during our visit in Colorado. Also, thank you, Bob, for your research on the lost files of Morton Baker and for helping me find more families of the crew.

Thanks to everyone at the 392nd Bomb Group Memorial Association for allowing me to use the many sources of information and photo's from their website (www.b24.net). I especially want to thank Annette Tison, secretary/treasurer and researcher of the 392nd BGMA, for introducing me to Bob Hebert, for her advice, for reviewing this translation, and for making this translation even more accurate and complete than the original. Annette's uncle, 2/Lt Douglas N. Franke, navigator from the 579th BS, 392nd BG, was killed in action during a mission to Berlin. I also want to thank the English director of the 392nd BGMA, John Gilbert, his wife Doris and son Adrian, for their warm hospitality at their home. Thank you for being our guide on and around Wendling Air Base.

Thanks to René Hoebeke, writer of the book *Slagveld Sloedam,* a fellow writer who wanted to read the first version of my Dutch manuscript and has given me a lot of comments and good advice. Thank you for sharing your archive files with me.

I want to thank the family members of the helpers who aided Ely and Joe. They include:

Piet van 't Westeinde and Martien van 't Westeinde, sons van Ko en Nele.

Sjaak van Biezen and Riet Meertens-van Biezen the son and daughter of Nico and Suus. I would like to thank Sjaak for sharing the impressive story of his father with me.

Also thanks to Lenny de Smit, granddaughter of Nico and Suus, for organizing the autograph session at the Bruna bookshop in Heinkenszand.

Hanneke Hilaul-Evelein, Jim Evelein and Nora Anninga, children of André and Cor.

Kees Griep, grandson of Kees and Corry.

Koos van der Weele-van Iwaarden and Lenie Klompe-van Iwaarden, daughters of Rienbouw and Ploo.

Elly Schipper-Franse en Chris Franse, daughter and son of Kees Franse.

Many thanks to all the other eyewitnesses who have told us their stories, and made an important contribution to this book:

Cor Mallekote from Heinkenszand †
Rinus Geschiere from Heinkenszand
Marien Mol from Heinkenszand
Jan Minnaard from Heinkenszand
Han Nijsse from Goes
Dies Hannewijk from Heinkenszand †

The late pilot, Jim Gerow, for his encouraging letter, in which he told me about himself, the crash and his imprisonment in Stalag Luft I.

I want to thank the following family members of the crew:

Again, Bob Hebert, nephew of Normand Hebert, and Paula for their work, hospitality and friendship.

Michele Doyon, daughter of Normand Hebert, Phil Palm, Jeremy and Lauren Hebert, Tami Vialpando, Josh Ulmer, Ric Rooney and everyone else who made our visit to Colorado unforgettable.

Theo Johnson, nephew of Dave Grandon.

Tina, daughter of Loyce Ely, her husband, Earl Miller, and Tina's sons, Kyle and Mackenzie for their hospitality and friendship.

The other sons and daughters of Ely we met: Pat, Steve, Toni, Denise, Cindy, and their kind families who made our visit unforgettable: Jerry, Stacy, Holly, Johnna, Jessie, Andie, Alex, McKenna and Erika.

Jerry and Denise, thanks for the hospitality and the WWII newspapers.

Kyle, thanks for helping Iona and Kyra with the horses.

Adam and Jason thanks for a fun time with the M4, AK 47, 44 Magnum... and the potato gun.

John and Ted Sulkowski, the son and brother of Joe Sulkowski

Darlene Southwell, Jackie Kohles and Katie Swiggart, the wife, a daughter and granddaughter of Elton Southwell. I owe my gratitude to them for sharing the impressive story of Elton with me.

John, Bob and Mary Kieras, nephews and niece of Gene Kieras.

Allen Senkovich and Becky Hornbeck, nephew and niece of Ed Yensho.

Delphine and Richard Gerow, wife and brother of Jim Gerow.

Debbie Savino, Jackie Rhoades and Brad Smith: nieces and nephew of Ben Brink. Richard and Karen Norman (Penny), grandson and daughter of Ben Brink.

Additionally:

Martien van Dijk, Peter de Meester, Hans Vergeer and Joop van Weele of Wings to Victory.

Kees Traas, Stef Traas and all volunteers at the Bevrijdingsmuseum Zeeland.

Hanny Louisse and everyone at the Heemkundige Kring de Bevelanden.

Jan de Ruiter, historian and writer of several books about the towns in the municipality Borsele.

Fred Daams, Don Blehm, and all other people at the Pueblo Weisbrod Aircraft Museum in Pueblo, Colorado for their great hospitality.

James Stewart and everyone else at the National Museum of World War II Aviation in Colorado Springs, Colorado for their hospitality.

Bob Livingstone, Tom Brittan en Alan Griffith of B24BestWeb for the use of the photos of the nose art.

Marcel van Genderen for his enthusiasm during the excavation, for his feedback and for joining me during our many trips to the Dutch museums.

Trudy Noordhoek, owner of the De Brilletjes.

Laura Caplan, daughter of Dr. Leslie Caplan and writer of *Domain of Heroes*.

Hans en Ellie Krijger, the current owners of the rectory at 's-Heer Abtskerke

Janneke Antheunisse-Schouten and everybody at *Poelpraat*, the town paper of 's-Heer Abtskerke.

Mevr. Leu van de Swaluw-Faes for the use of the postcards of Heinkenszand and the team of Heinkenszand.info for sending me digitized photos of these postcards.

The Borsele municipality archive for the use of photos from their website.

The Zeeuwse Bibliotheek database for the use of several photos.

Association Keep them Rolling for their interest and enthusiasm.

Hans van Breukelen for the use of the photo of Vliegbasis Soesterberg.

Rien Poleij for the use of the photo of Hotel Vlake.

Hans Sakkers, writer of *Enigma, de Strijd om de Westerschelde* and many more.

J.N. Houterman for the use of the German sketch.

John Rupp of Ben Burgess, for showing us around at the former HQ at Wendling Air Base.

The people of the 2nd Air Division Memorial Library in Norwich.

Sources

Memoirs and reports

Life of a German P.O.W., by Elton E. Southwell, early 90s.
Oorlog in een dorpje in Zeeland (*War in a small village in Zeeland*), by Peter van den Dries, 2006.
Without a title, by Nico van Biezen, 1981.
Recollections: a letter from Jim Gerow to me, 26 July 2010.

Interviews with eyewitnesses

Cor Mallekote from Heinkenszand, in 2008 invited by Willem Visser and Wings to Victory for unveiling the restored propeller. The statements in this book are from several talks he had with Willem.
Rinus Geschiere from Heinkenszand, interviewed by Willem Visser and Hans Vergeer on August 28, 2010.
Marien Mol from Heinkenszand, interviewed by Willem Visser on October 7, 2010.
Jan Minnaard from Heinkenszand, interviewed by Willem Visser on November 11, 2010.
Han Nijsse from Goes, interviewed by Willem Visser on November 17, 2010.
Dies Hannewijk from Heinkenszand, interviewed by Willem Visser on December 22, 2010.
Koos van der Weele-van Iwaarden en **Lenie Klompe-van Iwaarden**, interviewed by Willem Visser on April 27, 2011 and on May 5, 2011 by Willem Visser and Mark van den Dries.
Piet van 't Westeinde, interviewed by Mark van den Dries on October 28, 2010 and on May 4, 2011.

Documents
(Dutch titles are translated)

Bailing out of pilots from burning plane, a police rapport by sergeant Post-Commander Vermeulen, July 18, 1945, translated in English from Dutch by Piet van den Dries.

Missing Aircrew Report: # 10120 Aircraft: # 42-94886 "No Feathered Injun" "U-Bar.", USAAF, 1945.

Escape and Evasion Reports 2/Lt Joseph T. Sulkowski (E&E 2612) S/Sgt Loyce E. Ely (E&E 2613), USAAF, 1944.

Story of the crashed, 4-engined, American bomber at de Brilletjes in the former muncipal 's-Heer Arendskerke, by Ko van 't Westeinde. March 1984.

This is the story, how I have seen what happened with your son, a letter from Dr. Kees Griep to the family of Gene Kieras, 1945.

Correspondence of the National Socialist Movement in the Netherlands, by Group Leader C. Noom to Circle Leader P.I. Rosier, February 5, 1942.

Claim on wire, by the deputy-mayor of Heinkenszand G.P. Beaufort, April 18, 1944.

The trip of the children, by Mayor Chr. Koole to Piet van den Dries, May 1, 1944.

Crashed Allied Aviators (with several letters and en appendixes), by the deputy-mayor of Heinkenszand to the Military Commissioner of the provinces South Holland and Zeeland, October 19, 1945.

Identification of the killed French soldier (with several letters and appendixes), by the Province Commissioner of Zeeland, P. Dieleman to Mayor A. Mes of Heinkenszand, December 4, 1940.

Claim on church bells (with several letters and appendixes), by Province Commissioner of Zeeland P. Dieleman to Mayor A. Mes of Heinkenszand, December 3, 1942.

Sketch of shooting down a Liberator and **Battle Rapport**, Oberleutnant Bracke of Flaksscheinw. Abt. 369, September 1944.

Army Enlistment Records, individual rapports of the crew, NARA-AAD archives, 1944.

Records of World War II Prisoners of War, individual rapports of the crew who were POW, NARA-AAD archives, 1945.

Partly burned files concerning Morton Baker, National Personnel Records Center.

Letter concerning the returning of the American award, by Piet van den Dries to Philip C. Jessup, Deputy United States Representative to the United Nations, January 1949.

Letter concerning the returning of the American award, by Philip C. Jessup to Piet van den Dries, February 3, 1949.

Letters from Joe Sulkowski to his brother Ted, September 26, 1997 and February 10, 1999.

Letter with answers to questions by André Evelein to René Hoebeke for his book *Slagveld Sloedam*, October 1997.

Letter concerning the graves of Gene Kieras en Ed Yensho, of the Headquarters American Registration Command European Theater Area to Piet van den Dries, October 28, 1946.

Articles in newspapers and magazines
(Dutch titles are translated)

Lt. David Grandon is Prisoner of War, The Daily Post Tribune, 1944.

Sgt. Eugene Kieras Killed in Action, The Daily Post Tribune, 1944.

Lt. Grandon Writes Home-Bound Traffic Is a Bit Fouled Up, "The Daily Post Tribune", 1945.

Get Letter, Pictures of Kieras Grave in Holland, The Daily Post Tribune of January 3, 1946 with a letter by Piet van den Dries to the family of Gene Kieras, December 1, 1945.

Kieras memorial plan would honor friends in Holland, The Daily Post Tribune April 29, 1946, with a letter by Piet van den Dries to Preston Grandon, February 28, 1946.

Here are Hollanders Who Gave Aid to Our Airmen, The Daily Post-Tribune, Augustus 6, 1946, with a letter by Katrien van den Dries to Preston Grandon, spring 1946.

Bombardier On Kieras Plane Aids Hollanders, The Daily Post Tribune, July 2, 1946.
Holland Friends Express Thanks to Local Friends, "The Daily Post-Tribune", September 27, 1946.
Decoration returned!... , an interview with Piet van den Dries by C.A. Thomas of the R.C. Lady's Magazine, March 1949.
Headmaster upset about the attitude of the U.S. in the Security Council, Parool, early 1949.
Turning down the honor, Trouw, February 14, 1949.
Decoration went back! De Gelderlander, February 1949.
An upset Dutchman returns American decoration, Tubantia, February 1949.
You can keep the decoration, The Nieuwe Haagse Courant, February, 1949.
Dutchman sends American decoration back to the White House, The Bussemsche Courant, February 1949.
I don't want my decoration anymore, Het Dagblad, 14 February 1994.
'Master' van den Dries suddenly had national fame in 1949…, uit De Bevelander, February 15, 1989.
Headmaster has sent his American decoration back, De Gooien Eemlander, February 14, 1994.
A propeller as memorial and **Beyond all tensions** from an extra edition of **Poelpraat**, the town's paper of 's-Heer Abtskerke, remembering 50 years of liberation, with a story of Daan van 't Westeinde (grandson of Ko) and André Evelein, 1994.

Articles concerning my research, presentations and publication.

Not a pretty sight, (about the excavation at de Brilletjes), PZC, October 20, 2010.
Daughter American air gunner unveils propeller of in 1944 downed bomber, PZC, July 14, 2011.
Hiding place still intact after 66 years, De Bevelander, July 20, 2011.

Tribute to crew bomber Feathered Injun (Monument in front of Bevrijdingsmuseum Zeeland unveiled,) Bevelandse Bode, July 20, 2011.
The Passion of…, Rotsvast (publication of the Baptist Community Amersfoort,) October 2011.
Lecture about in 1944 crashed aircraft, PZC, October 19, 2011.
This small story from World War II is still alive, De Bevelander, July 2012.
Citizen of Leusden writes war book, Leusder Krant, December 12, 2012.
Presentation 'Noodsein boven Zeeland,' PZC, December 10, 2012.
Files of grandfather became war book and **'From the parachute fabric wedding dresses were made'**, PZC December 17, 2012.
'Otherwise this story would be lost,' De Bevelander, December 19, 2012.
A bomber crashed near Heinkenszand, De Bevelander December 19, 2012.
Book 'Noodsein boven Zeeland,' De Faam, December 2012.
News: Book: 'Noodsein boven Zeeland,' Air Mail (magazine of Wings to Victory), December 2012.
'I gave these men a face,' Leusder Krant, January 9, 2013.
Allies from: The Netherlands, The 392nd BGMA Newsletter, December 2012.
New book recounts plane crash over Netherlands (Greybull's Ely was on board) and **Story of downed plane a captivating one**, Greybull Standard, July 25, 2012
Story of WWII heroism told (tale focuses on plane's crew that trained here,) The Pueblo Chieftain, July 28, 2012.
Book impression: Noodsein boven Zeeland, de Spuije (magazine of historical union Heemkundige Kring de Bevelanden,) Summer 2013.

Articles written by the author.

B-24 Liberator downed over Heinkenszand, de Spuije, summer, 2011.
The Second Generation, Poelpraat (village paper of 's-Heer Abtskerke), September 2011.
The crash near Heinkenszand, de Spuije, Summer 2012.
Book Review: Noodsein boven Zeeland, KTR (magazine of WWII vehicle enthusiasts Keep Them Rolling,) autumn, 2013.

Books *(with italic translations)*

Slagveld Sloedam, (*Battlefield Sloedam*), René E. Hoebeke. Nieuw- en Sint Joosland, 2002.
Zeeland 1940/1945 part 1, L.W. de Bree. Den Boer Middelburg/ Uitgevers, 1979.
Zeeland 1940/1945 part 2, Gijs van der Ham. Waanders Uitgevers Zwolle, 1990.
De ontzetting van de Gans - *Goes en Zuid-Beveland in de oorlogsjaren '40-'44* (*The Liberation of the Geese – Goes and South Beveland in the years of war '40-'44*), A.J. Barth, F.H. de Klerk, L.J. Moerland and G. van der Wal. Heemkundige Kring De Bevelanden, 1985.
Bezet, verzet, ontzet - *Goes en omgeving in de bewogen jaren 1940-1944* (*Occupied, Defied and Liberated – Goes and surroundings in the tumultuous years 1940-1944*) Nic. J. Karhof, Algemene Boekhandel J. De Jonge, Goes.
De Slag om de Schelde, (*The battle for the Scheldt*), PZC en Vèrse Hoeven uitgeverij, 2009.
Huis aan huis in Heinkenszand - *een rondwandeling rond 1900*, (*From home to home in Heinkenszand – taking a walk around 1900*), M. Mallekoote, Archiefdienst, in cooperation with Heemkundige Kring de Bevelanden, 1993.
Heinkenszand in oude ansichtkaarten (*Heinkenszand in old postcards*), Jan de Ruiter, Europese Bibliotheek, 1974.

De schoonheid van de Zak (*The beauty of the Bag*) Jan de Ruiter, Engel Reinhoudt and Piet Grim. De Groote Roeibaerse-Kloetinge, 2011.

Kijk op Zeeland (*Perspective on Zeeland*), Tom Bouws, Elsevier-Amsterdam-Brussel, 1978.

Vlucht 648 - *Het relaas van een op 26 September 1944 boven het Westland neergeschoten Amerikaanse bommenwerper met haar elfkoppige bemanning* (*Flight 648 – The story of an American bomber and its crew of eleven men, shot down over the Westland on September 26, 1944*), door Harold E. Jansen, Elmar, 1985.

The Liberators from Wendling – *The combat story of the 392nd Bombardment Group (H) of the Eight Air Force during World War Two*, Colonel Robert E. Vickers Jr., Sunflower University Press, 1991.

The Army Air Forces of the United States – *Forword by General H.H. Arnold, Commanding General, Army Air Forces.* Rand McNally & Company - Chicago Infantry Journal, Inc., Washington, 1943

B-24 Liberator, Bert Kinzey. Squadron Signal Publications, 2000.

B-24 units of the Eighth Air force - ***Osprey Combat Aircraft 15***, Robert F. Dorr. Osprey Publishing Limited, 1999.

Pueblo Army Air Base – *A Chronological History 1942 – 1946*, dr. Ray L. Sisson, Pueblo Historical Aircraft Society.

USAAF Heavy Bomb Group markings & camouflage 1941-1945 consolidated B-24 Liberator - Aircam Aviation Series no. S13, E.A. Munday, with illustrations by Richard Ward. Osprey Publishing Limited

The 392nd Bomb Group in Norfolk - *A pictorial history of the USAAF's 392nd Bombardment Group at Wendling, during WWII,* Peter Bodle and John Gilbert

In Hostile Skies - *An American B-24 pilot in World War II*, James M. Davis. University of North Texas Press, 2006.

Domain of Heroes - *The Medical Journal, Writings, and Story of Dr. Leslie Caplan,* Laura Caplan. 2004.

Disposition of World War II Armed Forces Dead, War Department Office of the Quartermaster General, Washington 25, D.C. 1946

The Last Escape - *The untold story of Allied prisoners of war in Germany 1944-45*, John Nichols and Tony Rennell. Penguin Books, 2003.

Bombers of World Wars I and II, Francis Crosby. Southwater, Annes Publishing Ltd, 2005.

De luchtoorlog in Europa (*The air war in Europe*), Ronald H. Bailey, Time Life Books B.V., 1981.

Luchtbrug Market Garden - *De grootste luchtlandingsoperatie in de Tweede Wereldoorlog* (*Airlift Market Garden – The largest airborne operation of the Second World war*), Bart van der Klaauw and Bart M. Rijnhout, Violaero, 2011.

Gevangen in terreur (*Trapped in terror*) Christel Tijenk, a publication of Nationaal Monument Kamp Vught, 2007.

De Slag om de Ardennen (*Battle for the Ardennes*), C.W. Star Busman, Lecturama.

De Tweede Wereldoorlog (*The Second World War*), from the series *700 years of world history*, Lecturama, 1977.

Related websites

www.b24.net of the 392nd Bomb Group Memorial Association. My first and most important source of information.

www.wingstovictory.nl of "Wings to Victory", with a database with information on the crash of the Feathered Injun, partly written by me.

aad.archives.gov/aad/ American military database of the U.S. National Archives & Records Administration.

www.merkki.com about Stalag Luft I and other Stalag Luft camps

www.pegasusarchive.org about the British Airborne units.

www.stalagluft4.org about Stalag Luft VI.

www.b24bestweb.com about B-24 Liberators.

www.abmc.gov/home.php about American Military Cemeteries.

www.fallingbostelmilitarymuseum.de about the museum of Camp Fallingbostel.

www.beeldbank.zeeuwsebibliotheek.nl with a lot of photos of WWII in Zeeland.

www.walnoten.nl, the website of the walnut nursery of the family Van 't Westeinde.
www.axpow.org about American POW.
www.strijdbewijs.nl about WWII.
www.people.zeelandnet.nl/cgriep/cornelis_griep about dr. Kees Griep.
www.hkdebevelanden.nl of the Heemkundige Kring de Bevelanden.
www.wartimememoriesproject.com with personal stories from both world wars.
www.answest-oost.nl/HO/S1/ho-s1-092.htm about the attack on the Vlakebrug.
www.vliegbasis-soesterberg.nl about the history of the Dutch air base.
www.AGDJ.nl the website of Bram de Jong, the Dutch artist who made the cover painting.

Inspiring movies, television series en documentaries

Memphis Belle, Warner Brothers, 1990. This movie gives a good view on the crew of a B-17 (comparable with crews of a B-24). It is about their life on the air base in England and their last mission.
The Great Escape, MGM, 1963. A movie about the escape from German POW camp Stalag Luft III.
Stalag 17, Paramount Pictures, 1953. A movie about the POWs of a barrack in the Austrian camp that in real life was called, Stalag Luft 17B.
Bombardier, RKO Pictures, 1943. A movie made to interest men to become a bombardier. It is about the training and a mission against Japan in B-17's.
Fortress, about a B-17 bomber crew flying over Italy.
Follow the Boys, Universal Pictures, 1944. A movie with a lot of famous performers especially made to encourage the military personnel abroad.
Colditz, Bridge Pictures, 2005. A movie about the escape attempt from the heavily guarded POW camp Oflag IV C.

A Bridge Too Far, MGM, 1977. The famous movie about Operation Market Garden.
Battleground, MGM, 1949. A movie about the Battle of the Bulge.
The Longest Day, Twentieth Century Fox, 1962. A movie about D-Day.
Saving Private Ryan, Paramount, 1998. A movie about a group of soldiers during D-Day and their mission through the north of France.
Band of Brothers, Warner Brothers, 2001. A television series about the Easy Company of the 101st Airborne Division. We see the training of these *Screaming Eagles*, their parachuting into Normandy, the battle in France, the Netherlands, the Ardennes, Germany and the liberation.
Der Untergang, Constantin Film, 2004. A movie about the last days of Adolf Hitler.
Operation Valkyrie, The Weinstein Company, 2004. A movie about the assassination attempt on Adolf Hitler.
Stille getuigen van de Slag om de Schelde (*Silent witnesses of the Battle for the Scheldt*), Studio Haak &Visser, 2009. A documentary with personal stories about the Battle for the Scheldt in 1944.
De Oorlog (*The War*), NPS, 2009. A documentary series about the Netherlands during WWII.
The Occult History of the Third Reich, Bridge Pictures, 2004. A documentary that gives a good view on the neo-pagan influences on National Socialism.

Visited museums and their websites

www.wingstovictory.nl of Wings To Victory in Arnemuiden, NL
www.slagomdeschelde.info of the Bevijdingsmuseum Zeeland in Nieuwdorp, NL
www.nmkampvught.nl of Nationaal Museum Kamp Vught, NL
www.kampamersfoort.nl of Kamp Amersfoort, NL
www.airbornemuseum.nl of the Airborne Museum 'Hartenstein' in Oosterbeek, NL

www.oorlogsmuseum.nl of the Liberty Park in Overloon, NL

www.arnhemsoorlogsmuseum.com of the Arnhems Oorlogsmuseum, NL

www.bevrijdingsmuseum.nl of the Nationaal Bevrijdingsmuseum 1940-1945 in Groesbeek, NL

www.historischmuseumdebevelanden.nl of the Historisch Museum de Bevelanden in Goes, NL

www.betuwsoorlogsmuseum.nl of the Betuws Oorlogsmuseum in Heteren, NL

www.wingsofliberation.nl of the Museum Bevrijdende Vleugels in Best, NL

www.forfreedommuseum.be of the For Freedom Museum in Knokke-Heist, BE.

www.nmm.nl of the Nationaal Militair Museum in Soesterberg, NL

www.pwam.org of the Pueblo Weisbrod Aircraft Museum in Pueblo, CO.

www.worldwariiaviation.org of the National Museum of World War II Aviation in Colorado Springs, CO.

www.baugnez44.be of the Baugnez 44 Historical Centre near Malmedy, BE.

No website. Bastogne Barracks (Koninklijk Legermuseum) in Bastogne, BE.

www.iwm.org.uk/visits/iwm-duxford of the Imperial War Museum in Duxford, UK.

www.2ndair.org.uk of the 2nd Division Memorial Library at Norwich, UK.

Photos, documents and artwork

Archive Mark van den Dries: 002, 002a, 005, 006, 019, 024, 040, 045, 046, 047, 048, 049, 050, 051, 052, 053, 058, 082a, 088, 089, 108, 112, 113, 114a, 114b, 117, 122a, 122b, 122c, 124, 125, 126, 128a, 128b, 128c, 129, 130, 135, 136, 142, 142a, 142b, 143, 150, 151, 155, 156, 157, 159, 165, 169, 170, 173, 174, 176, 177, 178, 179, 187, 191, 192, 193, 194, 197, 198, 200, 205, 209, 215, 219, 220, 224, 227, 228, 230, 231, 233, 236, 239, 241, 242, 243, 244, 245, 247, 247a, 247b, 248, 249, 250
Artwork by Mark van den Dries: Front cover, 001, 003, 004, 013, 022a, 026, 027, 028, 033, 039, 065, 077, 084a, 085, 094, 097, 101, 102, 107, 109, 138, 158, 163, 168, 172 , 251, 252
Sjaak van Biezen: 007, 008, 009, 010, 017, 194, 185
Archive J. de Ruiter: 011
Mrs. Leu van de Swaluw-Faes/Heinkenszand.info: 012, 105, 015, 016,
Katholiek Documentatie Centrum: 014
Zeeuwse Bibliotheek / Beeldbank Zeeland: 015, 071, 166
Kees Griep: 016, 018, 081, 049, 119, 180, 181, 182, 183
Piet van 't Westeinde: 020, 021, 023, 175, 186, 216, 217
Riet de Beukert: 022
Family van Iwaarden: 106, 110, 111, 127, 128, 190
Family Evelein: 134, 146, 147, 148, 188, 189, 196, 199, 231, 232, 233, 237, 238
Photo archive Borsele: 025
www. b24.net: 029, 034, 038a, 038b, 041, 042, 043, 044, 056, 061, 062, 063, 064, 069, 070, 074, 075, 076, 080, 082, 086, 087, 103, 104, 139, 140, 144, 145, 161, 162, 164, 167 (Many of these photos are from the archives of John Gilbert)
U.S. Air Force Photo: 030, 031, 032, 035, 037, 038, 054, 055, 057, 066, 067, 073, 074a, 074b, 079, 083, 084, 099, 100, 123
Family Ely: 036, 051, 060, 082b, 152, 204, 206, 207, 208
Family Sulkowski: 048, 132, 133, 160, 201, 202, 204,

Family Brink: 052, 082c, 171, 210, 211
Family Hebert: 053, 082c, 153, 154, 212
Family Southwell: 090, 092, 093, 101a, 121a, 122, 164a, 213, 214
Theo Johnson: 059, 195
Becky Hornbeck: 091, 101b
Beeldbank Rijkswaterstaat: 068
www.answest-oost.nl: 072
www.b24bestweb.com: 095 and 096
U.S. Army: 098, 118
Collectie J.N. Houterman: (original) 107
National Archives and Record Administration: 083a, 084b, 097a, 097b, 114
Willem Visser: 119, 223
www.vliegbasis-soesterberg.nl: 121
Kees Traas: 218
Wings to Victory: 221, 222
The Pueblo Chieftain: 246
Christella Dahlkamp: 225
Jaap Geensen: 226
Family Franse: 025a, 025b, 120a, 120b
Jan Minnaard: 120c
National Jewish Welfare Board: 167a

The cover of the Dutch version of this book. (252)

Names Register

(Acknowledgement, Sources not included)

Abeleven, Wim: 300, 319
Aken, van: 25
Alexander, A.B.: 138
Andrew Sisters: 109
Baker, Jeanette: 74
Baker-Hyman, Mildred P.: 74, 367
Baker, Morton: 74, *79*, *82*, 88, *79*, *82*, 88, 91, 92, 94, 120, 135, 136, 247, 274, *279*, *280*, 299, 312, *329*, 344, 366
Baker, Rose: 74
Banwell, Craig: 345
Barnes, L.J.: 274
Bartnowski, Matthew A.: 122, 261
Beaufort, G.P.: 38, 39
Bek, Kees: 47, *166*, 191, 192, 209, 259, 309, 310, 315, 369
Bek-Mol, Adriana: 191, 209, 310, 369
Bek, Natalie: 191, 209, 315
Bell, J.W.: 135
Benson, R.J.: 247
Berger, Gottlob: 275
Beukert-Rijk, Riet: 47
Beuns, Leendert: 8, 9
Beuns-Westdorp, Mina: 8,9
Beyerly, Jean R.: 236, 293
Biezen, Nico van: 12, 24 - 27, 29 - *34*, 39 - 43, 48, *50*, *53*, 110, 111, 112, *115*, 206 - 209, 211, 212, 225, 226, 234, 240, 302, 306, 307, 308, 310, *325*, 343, 368
Biezen-Meertens, Riet van: 24 -27, 41, 206, 226, 234, 308
Biezen-Geensen, Suus van: 24 - 27, *32*, *33*, *34*, 41, 206, 211, 226, 234, 307, 308, *325*, 343, 368
Biezen, Sjaak van: 12, 226, 234, 308, *325*, 342, *354*
Blaskowitz, Johannes: 295

Blehm, Don: 344
Bliek, Frans: 157, 158, 162, *166*
Boidin: 243
Bombach, Aribert O.: 236, 261
Boonman: 225
Bouyeri, Mohammed: 199
Braam, P.: 224, 240
Braamse, Adriaan: 173
Bracke: 141, 152, *165*
Braun, Eva: 293
Brink, Ben: 75, *79*, *82*, 88, 90, 92, 139, *146*, 151, 152, 157, 158, *163*, 177, 184, 185, 186, 212, 237, 264, 271, 275, 292, 295, 296, *297*, 316, *338*, 367
Brink, Edith: 75
Brink, Evelyn: 75
Brink, Grace: 75
Brink-Kashtok, Marge: 316
Brink, Norma: 75, 292, 296, *297*
Brink, Penny: 316
Brink, Robert: 75
Brink, Samuel: 75, 316
Caplan, Leslie: 272, 273
Carpenter, Helen: 318
Carson, Jack: 109
Casembroot, A.F.Ch. de: 310
Chapman, Richard M.: 237
Cheshire, W.T.: 136
Churchill, Winston: 261, 295
Clarke Victor. R.: 237
Daams, Fred: 344, *357*
Daniëlse: 224, 225
Darling: 223, 224
Daser, Wilhelm: 44, 246, 247
Davidoski, Stan: 76, 77, *79*, *82*
Deans, Jimmy (Dixie): 281, 292
Dekker, Jan: 29, 119
Deurloo: 239

Dieleman, Petrus: 28, 36, 37, 38
Dietrich, Marlene: 109
Dijke, Geert van: *53*, 110
Dönitz, Karl: 294
Doolittle, Jimmie H.: 58
Dormic, Jean Marie: 36
Dries, Adam van den: 19
Dries, Adriaan van den: 19, 20
Dries-Beuns, Ineke van den: 8, 9, *54*
Dries, Corrie van den: 42
Dries, Daphne van den: 7, 9, 10,
Dries, Jacobus van den: 19, *22*, 46, *54*
Dries, Jacobus II van den: 46, *54*
Dries, Mark van den: 7 - 14, *15*, 17, *54*, 161, 303, 304, *321*, 342 - 345, *351*, *354*, *356*, *357*, *360*, *361*, 363
Dries, Paula van den: 42, *253*
Dries, Peter van den: 7, 9 - 11, 14, 19, 42, 45, 46, *54*, 241, *253*, *331*, 342, 343, *348*, *352*, *354*
Dries, Piet van den: 7 - 12, 19, 42 - 47, *50*, *53*, *54*, *55*, *56*, 110, 134, *166*, *170*, 183, 196, 208 - 211, *219*, *220*, 241, 243, 245, 246, 248, *253*, *257*, *258*, 274, *278*, 299, 300 - 306, 308, 313, *320 - 323*, *326*, *331*, *332*, 341, *346*, *348*, 363, 368
Dries, Pieter van den: 19, 42, 46
Dries-Remijn, Tannetje van den: *22*, *54*
Dries-Schipper, Katrien van den: 9, 10, 42, 43, 44, 46, *54*, 208, 245, 302, 303, 306, 308, *321*, *323*, 368
Dries-van der Schilden: Jacqueline: 342, *356*
Dries-van 't Westeinde, Cornelia van den: 46
Dries -Verachterd, Maria van den: 19
Duke, J.A.: 138
Durbin, Deanna: 106
Eaker, Ira C.: 58
Eisenhower, Dwight D.: 87, 305
Ely, Gene: 75, *252*, 273, 274, *278*, 299, 300, 303, 318, *336*
Ely, Loyce: *68*, 75, *79*, *82*, *85*, 88, 90, 92, 93, *118*, 124, *127*, *128*, 139, *146*, 151, 156, 157, *163*, 173, 177, 184, 191, 209, 210, 215, *217*, 222, 227, 228, 229, 233, 239, 243, 244, 249, *251*, *252*, 259, 273, 274, *278*, 292, 299, 300, 303, 305, 315, 318, *334 - 337*, 342, 343, *351*, 355, 366
Ely, Margaret (wife of Loyce): 315,
334, *337*, 343, *356*
Ely, Margaret (wife of Gene): 318
Ely, Ruth: 249, *254*
Ely, Tina: 315, 342, 343, *351*, *352*, *355*, *356*
Engelse, Piet: 183
Evelein, André: 208, 210, 215, 216, *217*, 224, 227 - 230, 239, 240, 246, 247, *251*, 274, 304, 309, 313, *326*, *327*, *330*, *332*, 369
Evelein, Freddy: 208, 215, 227
Evelein, Hanneke: 208, 215, 227, 342, *352*, *354*
Evelein, Jim: 343, *354*
Evelein-Westerveld, Cor: 208, 210, 215, 227, 228, 309, *327*, 369
Fahnert, Reinhard: 230, 236
Fassaert, Rudolf: 134, 141
Fields, W.C.: 109
Filkel, Owen: 106
Flair, Louie: 292
Foulkes, Charles: 295
Frank, Anne: 202, 216, 274
Frank, Margot: 202, 274
Franse-Schipper, Elly: 48
Franse, Kees: 48, *56*, 176, *182*, 183, 186, 212, 300, 308, 309, 369
Franse-Weijler, Lena: 309
Freeman, Roger 77
Friedeburg, Hans-Georg von: 294
Frost, John D.: 131
Gavin, James M.: 131
Geelhoed, Gilles: 174
Genderen, Marcel van: 342, *351*
Gerow, Delphine: 72, 295, *297*, 312, 365
Gerow, Jim: 71, 72, 75, 76, *79*, *82*, 88, 91, 92, 96, 121, 122, 129, 136, 139, 140, *146*, 152, 155, 156, 157, *163*, 173, 177, 184, 235, 260, 293, 294, 295, *297*, 312, 365
Geschiere, Gilles: 48, 121, 153
Geschiere, Rinus: 121, 153, 161, *166*, 176, 192
Gilbert, Adrian: 345
Gilbert, Doris: 345
Gilbert, Lawrence G.: 58
Gilbert, John: 345, *361*
Goebels, Joseph: 293
Gogh, Theo van: 199
Goldstein, Sidney: 193, 195, 197, 214, 212
Good, R.E.: 274

Grandon, Dave: 72, 73, 74, *79*, *82*, *85*, *86*, 88, 91, 139, 140, *146*, 152, 156, 157, *163*, 177, 184, 235, 244, 245, *256*, 260, 293, 295, 296, 299, 302, 313, *330*, 365, 366
Grandon, Preston: 72, 244, 245, *255*, *256*, 296, 299, 302, 303, 313
Grettum, R.B.: 274
Gremore, Lavern:
Griep, Attie: 41, *53*
Griep-Duinker, Corry: 41, 42, *53*, 307, 368
Griep, Iet: 41, *53*
Griep, Kees: 41, 42, 43, *50*, *52*, *53*, 94, 96, 110, *117*, 120, *166*, *181*, 183, 194, 196, 198, 209, *220*, 226, 227, 243, 300, 301, 304, 306, 307, *323*, *324*, 368
Griep, Kees jr.: 304
Griep, Nannie: 41, *53*
Griep, Pim: 41, *53*, 307
Gruber: 237
Hannewijk, Dies: 154, 155, *166*, 173, 174,
Harris, Arthur: 57
Harthoorn, Willem: 8, 9
Hebert, Arthur J.: 76, 317
Hebert, Bertrand: 317
Hebert, Brian: 14, 316
Hebert-Byrne, Christine: 316, 317
Hebert, Edgar: 76
Hebert, Floretta: 316, *339*
Hebert-Dudley, Juanita: 76, 212, 316, 367
Hebert-Duval, Laura: 76, 317
Hebert-Doyon, Michele: 14, 316, 317, 318, 344, *357*, *358*
Hebert, Normand (Frenchy): 13, 76, *79*, *82*, 88, 92, *118*, 124, *127*, *128*, 140, *146*, 151, 155, 158, *163*, 177, 184, 185, 186, 212, 237, *254*, 264, 271, 275, 292, 295, 316, 317, 318, *339*, 343, 344, *358*, 367
Hebert, Paul: 76
Hebert, Paula: 14, 344, 363
Hebert, Richard: 318
Hebert, Robert (Bob): 13, 14, *15*, 317, 318, 343, 344, *357*, *359*, 363
Hebert, Sean: 316
Hebert, Susan: 318
Heineken, Freddy: 199
Hildebrand, family: 211
Himmler, Heinrich: 129, 228, 261, 293
Hitler, Adolf: 24, 30, 49, 87, 109, 129, 197, 222, 247, 261, 274, 275, 293, 294
Hoebeke, René: 216, 230
Holiday, Billie: 177
Holleder, Willem: 199
Horrocks, Brian G.: 131
Hübner, Hans: 141
Hulsman, Aleida: 194, 195
Huuksloot, Jan van: 341, *349*
IJzerman, Jaap: 196, 197
Iwaarden, Cor: 175
Iwaarden, Kaat van: 153, 158, *167*, 175
Iwaarden, Koos van: 153, 158, 159, 161, *166*, *167*, 175, 176, 186, 197, 207, 242, 243, 342, *352*, *354*
Iwaarden, Leny van: 156, 158, 159, 161, *166*, *167*, 175, 176, 186, 196, 197, 207, 242, 243, 310, 342, *352*, *353*, *354*
Iwaarden-Lokerse, Ploo van: 158, *164*, *167*, 175, 196, 203, 242, 243, 310, 342, 369
Iwaarden, Rienbouw van: 153, 158, 159, *167*, 175, 186, 187, 196, 197, 202, 207, 242, 243, 310, *327*, 342, 369
Jackson: 275
Jessup, Philip C.: 305, 306, *322*
Jodl, Alfred: 295
Johnson, L.B.: 138
Johnson, Lorin L.: 58
Johnson, Nevin: 171
Johnston: 247
Kelley, John: 266
Kersten, family: 95
Keilman, Myron H.: 77
Keitel, Wilhelm: 295
Kieras, Ernest: 74
Kieras, Gene: 14, 74, 75, *79*, *82*, 88, 90, 91, 96, 108, *118*, 139, 140, *146*, 151, 152, 157, 158, *163*, *164*, 173, 176, 177, 183, 193, 194, 208, 209, 246, *256*, 273, 299, 300, 301, 302, 311, 312, *329*, 341, 343, 344, 363, 366
Kieras, John: 74
Kieras, Raymond: 74
Kieras, Stanley: 74
Klap, Kees: 37, 110, 111, 112, *115*, 119

Kloosterman, Piet: 40, 45, 47
Koch, Ilse: 249
Kole, Christiaan: 38, 45, 111, 119, 192, 198
Koole, Jacob: 158, 162, 176, 183, 299
Kramer, Josef: 290, 296
Lammers, Arie: 174
Lawrence, J.S.: 122
Liere, Family van: 156
Linde, Willem van der: 157, *166*
Lippe-Biesterfeld, Bernhard van: 248, 295, 306, 308, *326, 327*
Lokerse, Cornelis: 158, *164*, 183
Lord, John: 281
Magee, John Gillespie: 16
Mallekote, Cor: 157, 162, *166, 349*
Markusse, Bastiaan: 243
Martin, Russ: 229, 238, 263, 264, 272, 276, 277, 282 - 287, 289
Massee, Ko: 41
Mazurkiewicz, Jerzy: 224, 225
Meester, Peter de: *349*
Merry Macs: 112
Mes, Aloys (Lou): 36, 37, 38, 41, 48, 49, *50, 52*, 110, 120, 177, 194, 198, 245, 310, 343
Mes, Caroline: 38
Meyers, J.P.: 106
Miller, Earl: 342, 343, *355*
Miller, Glenn: 109, 113, *115*
Miller, Willard C.: 237
Minnaard, Adriaan: 153, 173, 174, 175, 341
Minnaard, Jan: 153, 154, 155, 161, *166*, 175, *180*, 341
Mol, Maaike: 41
Mol, Marien: 154, 161, *166*, 240, 241
Mol (mother of Maaike): 41
Montgomery, Bernhard L.: 87, 130, 216, 294
Moon, Don P.: 76
Münzer, Willi: 28,
Mussert, Anton: 37
Mussolini, Benito: 281
Naayer, Jan: 173
Naayer, Kees: 175
Nijsse, Han: 154, 161, *166*, 173, 174, 175
Norden, Carl: 91
Oranje-Nassau, Wilhelmina van: 26, 274, *279*, 294
Paauwe, Cees: 48, 111, 305
Patton, George S.: 87, 291

Paules, Francis: 237
Pickardt, Walther: 236
Pierrepoint, Albert: 296
Pollack, Robert: 239, 272, 273
Pruisen, Wilhelm II von: 23
Raft, George: 109
Rauter, Hanns: 30, 37
Reed, Vincent L.: 141
Remijnse, Quinten: 227
Rendle, Irvine A.: 58
Renting, J.H.: 27
Rhoades, Jackie: 292
Rijk, Ille: 225
Rijk, Ko: 174, 175,
Rommel, Erwin: 49
Roo, A. de: 47
Roosevelt, Franklin D.: 75, 261, 283, 288, 305
Ruyter, Michiel de: 113
Scheffers: 41
Schipper, Cor: 174,
Schipper, Johan: 134, 135, *143*
Schipper, Johannes: 134, *143*
Schipper, Pauwtje: 134, *143*
Schmidt, Hans (Big Stoop): 229, 230, 238, 261, 272, 291, 292
Seiberling, Mike: 283, 284, 285, 286, 287
Seyss-Inquart, Arthur: 28
Shore, Dinah: 109, 112, 277
Snagge, John: 87
Sommers: 236, 273
Sosabowski, Stanisław: 193
Southwell, Dale: *150*
Southwell, Elton: 12, 13, 135, 136, 138, 139, 141, *144, 146, 150*, 152, 160 - *163*, 172, 173, 176, 177, *182*, 184, 185, 186, 187, *189*, 191, 192 - 195, 197, 198, 205, 206, 212 - 215, 221 - 224, 228, 229, 231, 237, 238, 239, 260 - 266, *269 - 277, 280 - 292*, 295, *297*, 318, *339, 340*, 367
Southwell-Ruzicka, Darlene: 12, 13, 318
Southwell, Vera: *150*
Spaatz, Carl A.: 57
Stalin, Jozef: 248, 260, 261, 293, 296
Stauffenberg, Claus von: 87
Staverman, Piet: 42, 226, 307
Stewart, James: 344, *359*
Sukarno: 305
Sulkowski, Cecilia: 73, 244, *267*,
Sulkowski, Joe: 73, 74, *79, 82, 85*,

88, 91, 105, 124, 125, *146*, 152, 155, 158, 159, 160, *163*, *168*, 173, 177, 184, 186, 187, *190*, 191, 196, *201*, 206, 207 - 210, 212, 215 - *218*, *220*, 222, 227, 228, 229, 239, 243, 244, 245, 249, *251*, *252*, 259, *267*, 274, 292, 300, 303, 304, 305, 307, 309, 310, 313, 314, 315, *320*, *330 - 334*, 343, *346*, *350*, *353*, 366
Sulkowski, John: 125, 208, 243, 303, 304, 314, 315, 343, *350*, *353*, *354*, 363
Sulkwoski-Marxen, Martha Ann: 314, 315
Sulkowski, Ted: 212, 216, 244, 245, 315
Sulkowski, Tom: 244
Sulkowski, Vincent: 73, 314
Sulkowski, Walt: 73, 244
Tasman, Abel: 18
Taylor, Maxwell D.: 131
Tienpont: 154
Tison, Annette: 13, 14, 317
Tromp, Maarten: 113
Troy, Francis: 237
Truman, Harry: 305
Tyson, Ralph: 214
Urquhart, Roy: 13
Vallarelli, Fred: 72, *79*, *82*, 88, 91, 92, 96, *146*, 152, 155, 160, 161, *163*, 172, 173, 176, 177, 184, 235, 260, 293, 312, 313, 365
Vallarelli, Helen: 312
Veen, Rie van: 306
Vergeer, Hans: 125, 161
Vermaire, A.: 192
Vermeulen: 152, 157, 158, *166*, 299
Vermue, family: 225
Vickers, Robert E.: 58
Visser, Morris: *350*
Visser, Wessel: *350*
Visser, Willem: 12, 125, 161, 162, 341, 342, 343, *347*, *350*, *351*
Vroombout: 40
Warnstadt : 293
Weinert: 237
Welles, Orson: 109
Werkum-Cohen, Clarisse van: 37
Werkum, Dirk van: 37
West, Mae: 90
Westeinde, Bas van 't: 47, *55*
Westeinde, Cornelis van 't: *54*
Westeinde, Jan van 't: 47

Westeinde, José van 't: 308, *347*
Westeinde, Kee van 't: 47, 48, *54*, 259
Westeinde, Kees van 't: 47, *55*
Westeinde, Ko van 't: 40, 41, 43, 45, 46, 47, 48, *50*, *54*, *55*, 155, 162, *166*, 173, 174, 176, *181*, 208, 209, 210, 245, 246, 259, 302, 308, 313, *320*, *326*, *328*, *346*, 368
Westeinde, Marietje van 't: 47
Westeinde, Martien van 't: 47, *55*, *328*, 342, *352*
Westeinde, Pier (Piet) van 't: 11, 46, 47, 48, *50*, *54*, 155, 162, *166*, 176, 209, 210, 245, 259, 306, 310, 313, *326*, 341, *346*, *347*, 368, 369
Westeinde, Piertje van 't: 46, 47, *54*, 191, 207, 208, 300, 308, *346*
Westeinde, Piet van 't: 47, 48, *55*, *328*, 342, *350*, *352*, *354*
Westeinde-Rijk, Nele van 't: 47, *55*, *181*, 308, 368
Westeinde, Wim van 't: 47, *55*
Westeinde-Gorris, Anna van 't: 308
Westeinde-van den Dries, Maria van 't: 46, *54*
Whitaker, William D.: 241, 245, 249, *252*, *257*, 306, *324*
Williams, Wheeler: *364*
Winkelman, Henri: 23, 24
Wisse, W.: 155, *166*
Wolf: 237
Woodnough, John H.: 141
Wyman, Jane: 109
Wynsen, Henry: 239
Yensho, Andrew: 137, 311
Yensho, Ed: 14, 137, 139, *144*, *146*, *150*, 151, 155, 156, *163*, 176, 177, 183, 194, 208, 213, *220*, 246, 274, 299, 300, 301, 302, 311, *328*, 341, 343, 344, 367, 368
Yensho, Jay: 137, *150*
Yensho, Nick: 137
Zallman: 237
Zemke, Hubert (Hub): 293, 294, 295
Zhukov, Georgi: 295,
Zorina, Vera: 109